CW00503043

Understanding Procrastination at Work

Understanding Procrastination at Work focuses primarily on procrastination in the workplace, and offers a synthetic and comprehensive review of major theoretical concepts and empirical findings on general procrastination and its specific manifestations, causes, and consequences in the workplace. Building on theoretical insights and empirical research, the monograph proposes and empirically verifies an expanded conceptual framework that integrates individual and work-related factors that contribute to work procrastination and mechanisms explaining this phenomenon. It sits at the intersection of two disciplines, integrating psychological and management knowledge so that a wider audience may benefit from its content. It thus sheds more light on sources and explanatory mechanisms underlying procrastination as a universal behavior in the work setting, with meaningful implications for individuals and organizations alike. Overall, the monograph can serve as a contemporary compendium of knowledge that enables the scientific community and organizational practitioners to better understand procrastination behavior and its implications in professional settings. From the theoretical and empirical perspectives, the monograph provides practical cues to develop prevention and intervention strategies to effectively address and manage procrastination and enhance employee productivity in the organization.

Beata Bajcar is Assistant Professor at Wroclaw University of Science and Technology, Poland, and works at the Faculty of Management, Department of Management Systems and Organizational Development in the Psychology and Ergonomics Team. Her research interests include the causes and consequences of leadership styles, dysfunctional work and organizational behavior, and cyberdeviance, such as cyberloafing and cyberchondria. She has also researched time perspective and temporal aspects of human thought, mood, and performance. In addition, she specializes in the development and validation of standardized questionnaires to measure leadership styles, strategic thinking, professional interests, work values, cyberloafing, cyberchondria, and temporal orientation.

Routledge Advances in Management and Business Studies

For more information about this series, please visit: www.routledge.com/ Routledge-Advances-in-Management-and-Business-Studies/book-series/ SE0305

Understanding Procrastination at Work

Individual and Workplace Perspectives

Beata Bajcar

Routledge
Taylor & Francis Group

NEW YORK AND LONDON

First published 2025
by Routledge
605 Third Avenue, New York, NY 10158

and by Routledge
4 Park Square, Milton Park, Abingdon, Oxon, OX14 4RN

Routledge is an imprint of the Taylor & Francis Group, an informa business

© 2025 Beata Bajcar

The right of Beata Bajcar to be identified as author of this work has been asserted in accordance with sections 77 and 78 of the Copyright, Designs and Patents Act 1988.

All rights reserved. No part of this book may be reprinted or reproduced or utilised in any form or by any electronic, mechanical, or other means, now known or hereafter invented, including photocopying and recording, or in any information storage or retrieval system, without permission in writing from the publishers.

Trademark notice: Product or corporate names may be trademarks or registered trademarks, and are used only for identification and explanation without intent to infringe.

Library of Congress Cataloging-in-Publication Data
Names: Bajcar, Beata, author.
Title: Understanding procrastination at work: individual and workplace perspectives / Beata Bajcar.
Description: New York, NY : Routledge, 2025. | Series: Routledge advances in management and business studies | Includes bibliographical references and index.
Identifiers: LCCN 2024027243 | ISBN 9781032728223 (hardback) | ISBN 9781032728605 (paperback) | ISBN 9781003422860 (ebook)
Subjects: LCSH: Procrastination. | Work environment--Psychological aspects.
Classification: LCC BF637.P76 B35 2025 | DDC 155.2/32--dc23/eng/20240719
LC record available at https://lccn.loc.gov/2024027243

ISBN: 978-1-032-72822-3 (hbk)
ISBN: 978-1-032-72860-5 (pbk)
ISBN: 978-1-003-42286-0 (ebk)

DOI: 10.4324/9781003422860

Typeset in Times New Roman
by Deanta Global Publishing Services, Chennai, India

Contents

List of Figures

List of Tables

Introduction

Today's competitive and rapidly changing world requires organizations to demonstrate unprecedented competencies, high flexibility, and the ability to adapt to new conditions. This presents modern management with numerous organizational problems and challenges. The ongoing changes also pose a significant challenge for employees, who are the organization's most valuable resources. Human resources are a crucial component of any organization and play a fundamental role in achieving an organization's goals. Although organizations may have the best technology and facilities, they cannot thrive without specialized and efficient employees. Therefore, people, with their diverse knowledge, attitudes, qualifications, competencies, and motivations, form the foundation of an organization, despite being susceptible to threats and problematic organizational behaviors. Individuals in a stable and familiar environment exhibit various behaviors that enable them to adapt to work conditions and achieve positive work outcomes. However, these behaviors may not be adequate to adapt to changes and may not be beneficial to the organization. As a result, they increase the psychological costs of work for employees. These costs include reduced motivation, productivity, physical and mental health, the need for new skills and qualifications, increased stress, frustration, exhaustion, and burnout. In the face of incessant uncertainty, employees try to reduce the feeling of discomfort and look for a safe space. If the organization does not provide mechanisms to address tensions, employees may resort to specific behaviors to cope with unfavorable working conditions and protect or restore their emotional and energy resources. While these behaviors can be constructive ways to cope with stress at work, they are often dysfunctional. Employees sometimes prioritize their personal goals over the organization's objectives, leading to a decrease in work productivity. This behavior can be challenging to identify and evaluate within the company. It is crucial to recognize and address these issues to ensure the success of the company. Therefore, investigating dysfunctional organizational behavior and its sources, mechanisms, and consequences is crucial in management science. Procrastination at work is a prevalent organizational behavior with predominantly negative consequences for both the individual and the organization, despite some potential benefits. It refers to the tendency to irrationally delay tasks and engage in non-work-related activities, both offline and

DOI: 10.4324/9781003422860-1

online, during work hours. Delaying work may provide an immediate boost in mood for the employee, but they are aware of the negative consequences in the long term. Therefore, this monograph addresses the issue of procrastination at work through the lens of organizational behavior. Procrastination is an extremely common behavior in modern times. It is considered a dispositional tendency to irrational delay, manifested in various life domains or situationally induced behavior by external factors. It is predominantly construed as a maladaptive behavior that can lead to negative consequences for the individual. The prevalence and severity of procrastination in modern times appear to be linked to the rapidly increasing levels of contextual demands and personal aspirations. Individuals often pursue multiple objectives and long-term plans to fulfill various needs, including higher-order ones, such as academic or professional success, improving performance, and attaining higher socioeconomic status. When faced with increasing responsibilities, obligations, deadlines, and challenging or aversive tasks, people can experience pressure, stress, and anxiety about achieving their goals. As a result, they are more likely to procrastinate in dealing with emotional discomfort and exhaustion.

Procrastination in Contemporary Work Setting

Procrastination is a growing concern in work environments where employees are expected to complete tasks within specified time frames. The work environment and specific tasks can create an enabling environment for procrastination behaviors, especially when the timeliness of tasks is emphasized. Employers must address this issue and provide support for employees in managing their time effectively. Procrastination behaviors pose a high risk, particularly in self-organized and controlled work conditions where time cannot simply quantify work outcomes. However, in jobs where meeting deadlines is less critical, procrastination can be triggered by various factors. Delays in starting or completing tasks, a trait known as procrastination, can manifest itself across various types of professional activities. It is important to note that procrastination can have negative effects on productivity and should be avoided. Procrastination at work often involves delaying assigned tasks or prioritizing enjoyable non-work-related activities, which is commonly referred to as 'soldiering'. This may include taking excessive coffee breaks, browsing social networks, making personal phone calls, or running errands or personal errands during work hours. In some cases, employees may spend a significant portion of their workday doing these activities. Additionally, the rapid evolution of technology brings about significant transformations in organizational operations, employee requirements, and available labor resources. Technological advancements have fundamentally reshaped the modern organizational and work environment, altering the demands placed on employees and the resources available for their tasks. Contemporary workplaces are increasingly transitioning to virtual, borderless, and flexible settings, which requires individuals to adapt in new ways. This shift has led to the emergence of new forms of procrastination, particularly related to online activities. The Internet provides numerous entertainment options that divert attention from work-related responsibilities. Consequently, cyberslacking has become the primary form of procrastination in the workplace. It is characterized by employees excessively engaging in non-work-related online activities such as browsing news websites, online shopping, visiting social media platforms, downloading music, playing games, planning vacations, or searching for jobs. At the organizational level, procrastination involves postponing critical managerial and organizational decisions, such as expanding activities, planning investments, implementing innovations, or restructuring human resources. This undoubtedly incurs costs at the individual, social, and organizational levels. In general, procrastination has been found to lead to unfavorable consequences for individuals, and it can significantly impact an organization's productivity and overall effectiveness.

In the work environment, numerous factors can distract employees, making their tasks more challenging and leading to a reduction in working hours in favor of non-work-related activities. However, it is important to note that employee procrastination does not necessarily signify insubordination or laziness, although it does result in wasted working time, often perceived as work abuse within organizational contexts. Employees often delay their responsibilities as a way to manage discomfort rather than neglect them. Procrastination in the workplace can take various forms, such as taking frequent coffee breaks, quickly scanning the press, checking social media updates, making personal phone calls, handling personal errands, or engaging in other non-work-related tasks. However, some employees may spend a considerable amount of time on these activities. Delaying or avoiding tasks or projects by employees or managers can result in missed deadlines, reduced work quality, and increased stress levels for individuals and teams. Procrastination can also cause a chain reaction, leading to delays in other projects or tasks that depend on the completion of the procrastinated work. Disrupting workflow, hindering collaboration, and ultimately affecting the organization's ability to meet its goals and objectives on time are all potential consequences of procrastination.

Procrastination has often negative implications for both organizations and employees, including reduced performance and increased labor expenses. Therefore, it is important to recognize and better understand procrastination in the context of organizational behavior to mitigate its negative consequences and associated costs at the individual and management levels. The topic of procrastination at work is important for scholars and organizational practitioners for various reasons. First, it affects organizations that employ people who procrastinate frequently. Second, it is important from the employee's perspective as procrastination is often a way of coping with stressful working conditions. Third, procrastination can be considered a risk factor in human resource management, particularly in recruitment, selection, career development, and competency development. These reasons appear to justify the need to accurately diagnose procrastination behavior at work and explore its sources, mechanisms, and outcomes.

Although the general tendency to procrastinate is well documented in psychology, knowledge about procrastination behavior at work appears to be fragmentary and highly dispersed. Moreover, the same organizational behaviors take on new meanings and present challenges for theoreticians and practitioners in various situations and realities of social, technological, or economic development. The increasing automation, innovation, and digitalization of life and work bring about significant changes in the structural and social aspects of the workplace. Forms of work have evolved from traditional workplace settings with designated hours at the organization's headquarters to more flexible mobile working conditions. These new work environments as well as business transformation pose challenges and risks for maximizing individual and organizational productivity and exhibiting specific employee behavior and well-being. This sheds new light on procrastination behaviors, which take the form of cyberbehaviors, online, and become a challenge in a remote work setting. Therefore, it requires continuous investigations to recognize the nature, potential sources, and mechanisms that trigger employee procrastination offline and online. In response to this need, the monograph offers a theoretical and empirical study of procrastination in work settings focusing on individual and work-related causes, positive and detrimental consequences, as well as potential explanatory mechanisms.

Procrastination at Work from the Perspective of Management Science

According to the Organization for Economic Co-operation and Development (OECD) classification of science divisions (2007), this monograph proposes a broader view of procrastination behavior at work. It can be viewed from two perspectives of social sciences subdisciplines, that is psychology and management. Psychological studies enable the investigation of procrastination at work at the individual level, often providing valuable and unique information on employee responses. The research presented in this monograph extends the empirical findings on procrastination at work by identifying potential sources and mechanisms of procrastination induction among employees in terms of emotional and motivational processes. From the second perspective, these results have also significant managerial and organizational implications. Therefore, the study of procrastination at work presented in this monograph contributes to the development of management science both in the theoretical and practical spheres, classified by Bełz et al. (2019).

The findings presented here enrich the achievements of organization and management theory by identifying procrastination behavior as a source of potential hindrances and stimulators of efficient and effective management and organization functioning. The monograph aims to systematize existing knowledge in this field and extend it through further empirical exploration of the individual and work-related factors that determine procrastination behaviors at the workplace. It provides a systematic overview of theoretical conceptions and the research findings on a general tendency to procrastinate and procrastination behavior in the workplace with a focus on individual and work-related sources, consequences, and explaining processes. Thereby, it ensures access to the most current information for a comprehensive understanding of procrastination as a specific phenomenon in the workplace, including its offline and online manifestations. This overview serves as a theoretical background for research design. Based on this, a conceptual framework of procrastination at work was designed and empirically verified to enrich knowledge about its individual and work-related sources and the underlying mechanisms. The research results support the usability of applied research methods in the area of management and organizational behavior, such as the validation of measurement instruments and modeling the relationships between predictors and procrastination behavior at within- and between-person levels. Furthermore, this provides a methodological background for future research on work procrastination in different theoretical frameworks and organizational contexts.

The knowledge of the nature, sources, and consequences of procrastination behavior at work can be useful for business and organizational practices. From the practical perspective of management science, the monograph contributes to management science in subdisciplines of management at the operational level (1) organizational behavior, (2) supporting managerial decisions, and at the functional level (3) human resources management.

The issue of procrastination in the workplace fits into the paradigm of research on organizational behavior from the perspectives of individual differences and contextual determinants. Therefore, this monograph sheds light on the personal and work-related factors that impact procrastination behavior at work. It provides valuable insight into understanding the nature and underlying mechanisms of this prevalent phenomenon in professional settings. This systematic and comprehensive knowledge of procrastination behavior may help in identifying its risk and protective factors, as well as proposing strategies for coping with employee procrastination behavior. This can help businesses maximize their efficiency in achieving their objectives and managing their human resources. It provides management staff with insight into when employees procrastinate, whether it has negative consequences, and on how to motivate and guide them to change their behavior at work. Thus, organizations can foster employee engagement, creativity, and performance while reducing employee procrastination behaviors. Furthermore, the research findings provided or amplified potential premises for developing interventions at both individual and organizational levels to mitigate the negative effects of work procrastination. By integrating previous findings with the results of current research, the monograph adds value in terms of the fresh view and discoveries that enhance the understanding of procrastination as a type of organizational behavior. This suggests that procrastination behaviors can be a challenge for management to address, rather than an insurmountable problem in the workplace.

Thus, the monograph presents a theoretical and empirical study of the sources, consequences, and potential explanatory mechanisms of procrastination behavior at work. Chapter 1 presents a systematic review of the literature on the main themes related to general procrastination. This includes its definition, characteristics, multidimensionality, typology, stability, and universality, as well as its detrimental and proactive nature that manifests itself in different domains of everyday life. Furthermore, the main psychological mechanisms of procrastination are discussed, including self-regulation, the intention–action gap, self-handicapping, and the temporal motivation approach. It also covers sociodemographic, personality, affective, and motivational factors, as well as task characteristics associated with general procrastination. This chapter discusses the consequences of the tendency to procrastinate for performance, well-being, and health. Chapter 2 focuses on a definition and conceptualization of procrastination at work, including soldiering (offline procrastination) and cyber-loafing (online procrastination), as well as their relationships with counterproductive work behaviors, which share similarities and differences. Furthermore, the prevalence and consequences of offline and online procrastination in the work environment for employee performance and well-being were also reported. This chapter also investigates individual antecedents of procrastination, including sociodemographic factors, personality traits, and emotional and motivational factors. Additionally, the various job characteristics and organizational and employment-related factors associated with offline and online procrastination were reviewed. Chapter 3 presents a broad range of research findings that verify a conceptual framework that integrates individual and work-related sources of procrastination at work, along with energetic and motivational processes as underlying potential mechanisms. Section 3.1 begins by presenting empirical verification of the two-dimensional construct of procrastination at work, manifested in offline procrastination (soldiering) and online procrastination (cyberloafing). This chapter first presents methods and tools to measure procrastination at work. It then reports the validation of the Procrastination at Work Scale, including the results of the confirmatory factor analysis, its scale-level reliability (internal consistency, temporal stability), and item-level reliability indices (item-total, interclass, and intraclass correlations). The chapter then discusses the theoretical validity of the Procrastination at Work Scale in relation to general tendencies to procrastinate and counterproductive work behaviors. Subsequently, Section 3.2 presents the empirical verification of a conceptual framework that considers individual and work-related predictors and mediational effects of work stress and motivation at work to explain procrastination at work, using the job demands and resources model (Bakker & Demerouti, 2014). Five studies conducted on a total sample of 3,000 employees revealed systematic effects of individual and work-related characteristics in the regulation of procrastination at work. The results of these studies are discussed in light of theoretical concepts and previous findings. Based on this, theoretical contributions and managerial and organizational implications have been developed.

References

Bakker, A. B., & Demerouti, E. (2014). Job Demands–Resources theory. In P. Y. Chen & C. L. Cooper (Eds.), *Wellbeing: A complete reference guide* (pp. 1–28). John Wiley & Sons Inc. https://doi.org/10.1002/9781118539415.wbwell019

Bełz, G., Cyfert, S., Czakon, W., Dyduch, W., Latusek-Jurczak, D., Niemczyk J., Sopińska A., Szpitter, A., Urbaniak, M., & Wiktor, J. (2019). *Subdyscypliny w naukach o zarządzaniu i jakości 2.0.* [Subdisciplines in management and quality sciences 2.0]. Komitet Nauk Organizacji i Zarządzania Polskiej Akademii Nauk [Committee on Organizational and Management Sciences of the Polish Academy of Sciences]. Retrieved from www.knoiz.pan.pl/images/stories/pliki/pdf/Subdyscypliny _nauk_o_zarzdzaniu_i_jakoci.pdf (access: 3.03.2024).

OECD (2007). *Revised Field of Science and Technology (FOS) classification in the Frascati manual*, February 26, 2007.

1 General Procrastination

1.1 The Nature of General Procrastination

Procrastination is typically viewed as a dispositional trait of individuals, although researchers also recognize that situational factors can contribute to procrastination. This chapter offers an overview of general procrastination, focusing on its definition, characteristics, and explanatory conceptions and approaches.

1.1.1 Definition of Procrastination

The word 'procrastination' is derived from the Latin word *procrastinatio*, which means 'postponement' or 'delay'. Before the Industrial Revolution, this term had a neutral connotation and referred to the rational act of putting off matters, tasks, or goals. However, with time and industrial and technological developments, procrastination has acquired a negative meaning. Currently, procrastination is defined as the 'voluntary delay of an intended course of action despite expecting to be worse off for the delay' (Steel, 2007, p. 66). During their research, scholars aimed to provide a comprehensive understanding of procrastination by highlighting various key definitional aspects of the phenomenon, including irrational delay, feelings of discomfort, and negative consequences. However, upon further review of the concept, it became evident that procrastination encompasses additional components such as delay, chronicity, voluntariness, unintentionality, irrationality, dysfunctionality, self-destructiveness, and instrumental behavior in self-regulation.

Delay: The essence of procrastination is the behavioral tendency to delay the start or completion of necessary tasks, activities, or decisions required to achieve a goal or accomplish a task (Ferrari, 2010; Lay, 1986; Steel, 2007). While procrastination involves delaying the start or completion of tasks, activities, or decisions, it is important to note that not every delay constitutes procrastination (Chowdhury & Pychyl, 2018). However, the delay is not always irrational and may be necessary to accomplish a goal or perform a task. To distinguish delay from procrastination, scholars proposed terms such as strategic or purposeful delay, which are devoid of irrationality, negative emotions, and negative consequences. Procrastination is typically defined as an irrational delay, which

DOI: 10.4324/9781003422860-2

is unnecessary and undesired for task performance, and is often accompanied by emotional discomfort due to the delay (Blunt & Pychyl, 2005; Klingsieck, 2013b; Steel & Ferrari, 2013). Behavioral delay in procrastination can refer to engaging in alternative and more enjoyable activities, which indirectly delay task completion. The study by Huang and Golman (2019) showed that procrastination was not determined by the length of the delay.

Chronicity: Scholars suggest that procrastination may be a chronic behavior (e.g. Ferrari et al., 2007) that stems from a general dispositional tendency to delay tasks. However, according to Milgram and Tenne (2000), procrastination refers rather to a series of actions than to a single behavioral act of postponing. In this sense, procrastination should be understood as the repeated and habitual postponement of starting and/or completing intended tasks. This behavior is likely driven by perceiving situations as threatening and avoiding them by postponing action. Repetition of delaying behavior is based on negative reinforcement (Bennett & Bacon, 2019; Ferrari & Emmons, 1995). If procrastination allows individuals to reduce stress, they may continue to exhibit this behavior in similar situations despite their efforts to stop. Awareness of missed opportunities to complete a task in time can trigger negative emotions that may lead to further inaction and procrastination. This can result in a cycle of procrastination where individuals fail to learn from past experiences and continue to procrastinate.

Voluntariness: Procrastination is often considered a voluntary behavior, where individuals choose between competing activities and opt for one over another (Grund & Fries, 2018). While delaying a task may result in immediate positive emotions, in the long run, it can hinder individuals from achieving their goals and lead to emotional discomfort. Therefore, individuals must consciously choose between completing tasks and procrastinating. This decision is often motivated by the need for instant gratification or to avoid unpleasant circumstances.

Unintentionality: Scholars suggest that individuals prone to procrastination do not intentionally postpone their responsibilities, but rather act contrary to their original intentions. Failure to act following one's intentions is a defining characteristic of poor self-regulation. Therefore, procrastination can be seen as an unintentional action that results from an inability to effectively regulate one's behavior (van Hooft et al., 2005). However, recent research suggests that distinguishing between unintentional and intentional procrastination alludes to positive and negative metacognitive beliefs about procrastination (Fernie et al., 2017). When an individual with positive beliefs about procrastination intentionally delays an assigned task, this could induce negative beliefs about procrastination, emotional discomfort, and cognitive processes that reduce personal resources. According to Fernie et al. (2017, 2018), in response to delay, an individual may unintentionally perpetuate procrastination behavior.

Irrationality: Procrastination is the irrational tendency to delay tasks and actions, as demonstrated by numerous studies (Akerlof, 1991; Lay, 1986; Simpson & Pychyl, 2009; Steel, 2007). This means that there is no justified reason for delaying. Therefore, individuals who postpone act inconsistently with their rational judgments regarding the evaluation of benefits and costs. Individuals may recognize the importance of completing a task, but also may experience difficulty in initiating and completing activities within the desired time frame (Ferrari, 2010). Ellis and Knaus (1977) suggested that irrational beliefs are a significant factor contributing to illogical procrastination behavior. Individuals who procrastinate often doubt their ability to complete a task and fear the negative social consequences of task failure, even when these concerns are not justified. Procrastination involves engaging in maladaptive behavior despite having sufficient resources to perform the task. However, individuals continue to delay decision-making or taking action (Klingsieck, 2013a; Steel, 2007) despite the psychological discomfort of negative consequences.

Instrumentality: Procrastination can be a way to regulate mood in difficult and stressful situations, such as aversive tasks, highly engaging activities, or social exposure. It may be a strategy to avoid unfavorable situations or tasks or to enhance the current negative mood associated with performance pressure. According to Pychyl and Flett (2012), individuals who tend to procrastinate often engage in alternative activities that provide momentary pleasure and alleviate negative emotions to avoid crucial but unpleasant tasks. These activities may include socializing, hobbies, browsing the Internet, using social media, and playing online games. Furthermore, individuals may procrastinate to protect their self-esteem or ego when threatened (Ferrari, 1991b, 1994).

Dysfunctionality: Procrastination is a dysfunctional phenomenon that can have negative impacts on an individual's life and environment. Procrastination is known to have detrimental consequences on one's well-being, mental and physical health (Sirois & Pychyl, 2013; Pychyl & Sirois, 2016), social relationships, education, employment (Klingsieck, 2013a), as well as performance and outcomes (Steel, 2007). The dysfunctionality of procrastination can lead to the stigmatization of individuals who procrastinate. Individuals who procrastinate are often perceived as causing harm to themselves and others, even by fellow procrastinators (Ferrari & Pychyl, 2012). Several studies have confirmed that procrastination is a significant issue in the lives of procrastinators (Ferrari & Patel, 2004; Klingsieck, 2013a; McCown et al., 1989). Most of them (95%) perceive procrastination as a problematic behavior and declare a desire to reduce it (Steel, 2007). According to Ferrari and Tice (2000), procrastination is a maladaptive behavior associated with engaging in self-handicapping activities and being aware of the costs involved.

Self-destructiveness: Procrastination has detrimental effects on the behavior of those who procrastinate. It concerns awareness of the negative outcomes to which individuals voluntarily expose themselves to by procrastinating. Procrastinators recognize that delaying tasks can lead to negative outcomes and is an ineffective and ethically questionable behavior (Steel, 2007). This assertion implies that they understand that they are avoiding the assignment and that this is a wrong behavior. Procrastinators continue to delay even after realizing that their inability to complete a task and achieve their goals will disadvantage them. Hen and Goroshit (2018) found that 14% of individuals who procrastinate recognized the detrimental effects of delay on their health, 12% on their careers and education, and 11% on their relationships and families.

Following Klingsieck's (2013b) integrative view, procrastination is 'the voluntary delay of an intended and necessary and/or personally important action, despite expected potential negative consequences that outweigh the positive effects of the delay' (p. 26). In summary, procrastination can be conceptualized as a trait or behavioral tendency expressed through maladaptive forms of self-regulation, which involve intentionally delaying planned tasks. The behavior of procrastination is a common and irrational phenomenon that is often linked to dysfunctional self-regulation (Ferrari, 2010; Steel, 2007).

1.1.2 Characteristics of Procrastination

Procrastination combines emotional, cognitive, motivational, and behavioral aspects (Pychyl & Flett, 2012), as well as includes a temporal dimension (Steel, 2007; Steel & König, 2006).

The *emotional* aspect of procrastination involves negative affective reactions associated with delaying scheduled tasks. Procrastinating individuals often experience stress due to task overload or time constraints, fear of failure or public judgment, dissatisfaction with personal performance, frustration in achieving goals, aversion to tasks, and feelings of guilt and shame (Feyzi Behnagh & Ferrari, 2022). At the same time, procrastination can elicit positive emotions such as satisfaction, pleasure, or relief from delaying annoying tasks or duties, as well as engaging in more attractive activities. However, despite these positive emotions, procrastination is generally accompanied by ambiguous feelings, with a predominance of negative affect (Sirois & Pychyl, 2013).

The *cognitive* aspect of procrastination is represented by subjective expectations, beliefs, and judgments about the value of acting on specific tasks and situations. Procrastinators tend to postpone tasks that they consider uninteresting, unpleasant, or challenging (Steel, 2007; van Eerde, 2000). Ellis and Knaus (1977) have highlighted the significant role of irrational beliefs in the onset of procrastination behavior. Procrastination is often amplified by negative and illogical thoughts, such as unfounded doubt about one's abilities, fear of failure, unrealistic task evaluations, and disregarding the positive effects of procrastination.

Researchers suggest that the cognitive component of procrastination is expressed in a specific pattern of automatic negative thoughts about oneself, the task, or procrastination itself (Duru et al., 2023; Flett et al., 2012). These thoughts can take the form of specific ruminations, for instance, 'Everything is due to my procrastination', 'I should have started earlier', or 'I always procrastinate', and occur not only during and after procrastination but also before beginning a task. Over time, these thoughts become an essential component of the procrastination self-schema, referred to as automatic procrastination cognitions (Flett et al., 2012). Recent research has also emphasized the role of metacognitive processes in inducing or undermining procrastination (Fernie et al., 2017; Fernie et al., 2018), as discussed in Section 1.1.1.

The *behavioral* dimension of procrastination refers to the tendency to delay or avoid tasks, as described by Ferrari et al. (2007), Steel (2007), and Svartdal et al. (2018). This can manifest as putting off starting or completing tasks, missing deadlines, engaging in unproductive activities instead of working, task switching, or rushing to finish tasks. The behavioral aspect of procrastination refers to observable characteristics, such as the frequency and duration of delay, which can be measured in various ways. To quantify procrastination behaviors, researchers have recorded the actual time spent on the task between its assignment and submission, breaks taken during task performance, rating of task completion within a given time frame, and duration of delayed tasks. The behavioral nature of procrastination may indicate that it can be externally induced and, therefore, potentially susceptible to reinforcement.

The *temporal* component is essential to express the significance of time-related attributes of delay. The timing of tasks and meeting deadlines are crucial aspects of delay behavior. Procrastinators often underestimate the time required to complete tasks and start them at the last minute (Blunt & Pychyl, 2005). Furthermore, individuals who procrastinate tend to allocate less time to prepare tasks that have a higher likelihood of success and more time for those that are likely to fail (Lay, 1990). Additionally, they spend less time searching for the information required to complete a task (Ferrari & Dovidio, 2000). Procrastination is motivated by the desire to avoid negative emotions and is focused on the present. In the short term, procrastinators tend to prioritize behaviors that improve their current mood, reduce arousal, and provide immediate gratification over pursuing long-term goals (Sirois & Pychyl, 2013). In summary, procrastination is a multidimensional construct that combines emotional, cognitive, behavioral, and temporal components. It is a complex phenomenon that manifests in different domains of life.

1.1.2.1 Theoretical Perspectives – Procrastination as a Trait or State

Various definitions and theoretical approaches have been developed to understand procrastination, including differential, motivational/volitional, clinical, and situational perspectives (Klingsieck, 2013b). The differential perspective emphasizes the importance of individual differences in comprehending and addressing procrastination. By recognizing how personality traits, motivation, goal orientation, and cognitive factors can impact one's approach to procrastination, individuals can develop strategies to overcome procrastination and improve their productivity and well-being. From a motivational and volitional perspective, procrastination can be viewed as the result of low motivation and self-regulation failure. It focuses on exploring motivational factors related to our goals, values, and self-regulation that may influence procrastination. The clinical perspective investigates conditions and negative consequences in explaining dysfunctional procrastination through the prism of psychoanalysis, cognitive behaviorism, and neuropsychology. From a situational perspective, procrastination is viewed as a response to specific contextual factors, such as task characteristics, time pressures, or distractions, and not as a stable personality trait.

However, two approaches to understanding procrastination appear to be dominant, either as a personality trait or as a state (Ferrari & Tibbett, 2020; Feyzi Behnagh & Ferrari, 2022). The first approach defines procrastination as a generalized dispositional tendency toward habitual and chronic delay behavior. General procrastination is relatively stable over time and in various situations. Numerous studies have revealed a high degree of short-term stability of trait procrastination measured twice 42 days apart and long-term stability assessed at an interval of 10 years. Twin studies supported the dispositional nature of procrastination, which explained 22% of the variance attributed to genetic factors (Steel, 2007). However, this stability may be limited by within-person fluctuations in procrastination (Claessens et al., 2007; Kühnel et al., 2018). The situational approach views procrastination as a phenomenon that arises in particular circumstances. This suggests that procrastination occurs in some life domains but not in others. Consequently, procrastination depends on the nature of the activity and other external circumstances. Tasks that are perceived as unpleasant, difficult, frustrating, or lacking structure or meaning are often avoided or postponed (Steel, 2007). It is important to note that task aversiveness is highly subjective. Additionally, tasks that are perceived as short, unimportant, or subjectively uninteresting may also contribute to the reluctance to start them. Other factors that can affect the level of procrastination include the time interval between task completion and receipt of rewards or penalties, time constraints related to the task (Ariely & Wertenbroch, 2002; Ferrari et al., 2006; Steel, 2007), and the anticipation of potential failure (Senécal et al., 1997). Therefore, activities that people tend to put off can be different, for example, buying gifts, replying to messages, and paying bills. Academic procrastination, work procrastination (Steel & Klingsieck, 2015), and bedtime procrastination (Kroese et al., 2016; Sirois et al., 2019) are examples of situational procrastination that need to be addressed more comprehensively. In search of empirical evidence for situation-based procrastination, Klingsieck (2013a) revealed that among students procrastination is prevalent in six life domains: academic and work activities (studying for an exam, returning work-related phone calls), everyday duties and obligations (e.g. tax returns, administrative tasks, household chores), health (making an appointment with a doctor, purchasing a prescription, or engaging in health behaviors (e.g. dieting), leisure (e.g. getting tickets to a cultural event, practicing a hobby regularly), family and partnerships (e.g. visiting parents, buying a Valentine's Day gift for a partner), and social contacts (e.g. returning calls, writing e-mails, meeting friends). The study revealed that procrastination is prevalent in all six life domains, albeit with varying frequency. Students tended to procrastinate more frequently when it came to studying and working, daily responsibilities, and health, and slightly less so when it came to leisure activities, family and relationships, and social interactions. Compared to students, adults procrastinate in slightly different areas. The study by Hen and Goroshit (2018) revealed that adults tend to procrastinate in 11 different areas of life such as health, career, education, family, friends, self, leisure, community, finances, and parenting. The results showed that the participants reported a high level of procrastination in health behaviors (41%), leisure behaviors (28%), and about 20% in matters related to self, social, friends, and career. Approximately 25% of the respondents reported a high tendency to procrastinate in at least four areas of life, which may indicate chronic procrastination. Furthermore, the general tendency to procrastinate was moderately related to procrastination in achievement-oriented matters (such as education, career, and finances) and somewhat less related to procrastination in other areas of life.

In summary, the nature of procrastination remains a topic of ongoing academic debate. Although there is an increasing amount of research indicating that procrastination has dispositional sources, it is also influenced by situational or life-domain factors. However, research suggests that the impact of dispositional procrastination on adult behavior is low to moderate, and contextual factors are recognized as increasingly important (Beutel et al., 2016; Feyzi Behnagh & Ferrari, 2022; Klingsieck, 2013a). Therefore, procrastination appears to be a developmental and situational phenomenon. Thus, it can be inferred that stability represents its universal component, and variations in procrastination can be attributed to specific characteristics of procrastination in different life domains (Hen & Goroshit, 2018; Klingsieck, 2013a). Therefore, researchers employ an interactional approach in investigating both dispositional and contextual predictors of procrastination (Senécal et al., 1997; van Eerde, 2000).

1.1.2.2 Types of Procrastination

Several types of trait procrastination have been distinguished in the literature, including avoidant, arousal, decisional, behavioral, and active procrastination. Additionally, scholars have mentioned irrational procrastination (Steel, 2010) and unintentional procrastination (Fernie et al., 2017), which are specific components of trait procrastination (see Section 1.1.1). Ferrari (1992) proposed a threefold classification of procrastination known as arousal, avoidant, and decisional procrastination, which have been extensively studied.

Arousal Procrastination: This refers to an intentional delay of tasks until the last moment to experience a pleasant thrill caused by increasing time pressure. This behavior is often motivated by the belief that the pressure of a pending deadline helps in completing tasks. Therefore, people often perform tasks under time pressure and high arousal (Ferrari et al., 2005b, 2009a; Steel, 2010).

Avoidant Procrastination: This involves avoiding tasks that cause negative emotions such as fear of failure, fear of success, or task aversiveness. Fear of failure arises from the belief that one lacks the necessary skills, while task aversiveness stems from a genuine dislike for the task. Additionally, some individuals fear success because of the increased responsibilities and expectations it may bring (Ferrari et al., 2005b, 2009a; Hammer & Ferrari, 2002).

Decisional Procrastination: Also known as indecision, this type of procrastination refers to the difficulty individuals face in making timely decisions about tasks or actions. Decisional procrastination can occur when a person perceives a task as complex, anticipates conflicts arising from the decision, or wants to protect their self-esteem (Janis & Mann, 1977). However, an analysis by Steel (2010) did not confirm the trichotomy of arousal, avoidant, and decisional procrastination, particularly the distinction between arousal and avoidant procrastination. Nevertheless, numerous studies found significant differences among the three types of procrastination in relation to sociodemographic and psychological factors (Ferrari, 1992; Ferrari et al., 2005a, 2005b, 2009a, 2009b).

Bedtime Procrastination: Bedtime procrastination is a psychological phenomenon that involves the voluntary and unnecessary delay of going to bed, without any external circumstances causing the delay (Kroese et al., 2014). Bedtime procrastination has been identified as a common and serious problem that negatively affects sleep quality, physical efficiency, and intellectual efficiency in the short and long term (Kroese et al., 2016; Kroese et al., 2014; Kühnel et al., 2016). A meta-analysis of 11 studies (Hill et al., 2022) revealed a significant association between bedtime procrastination and low self-control ($\bar{r} = -0.37$), as well as a high evening chronotype ($\bar{r} = 0.41$). Additionally, it revealed a significant correlation between bedtime procrastination and low sleep duration ($\bar{r} = -0.30$; $K = 17$), poor sleep quality ($\bar{r} = -0.33$; $K = 12$), and daytime fatigue ($\bar{r} = 0.30$; $K = 9$).

Active Procrastination: This is an emerging trend in research that suggests that procrastination can be constructive (Chauhan et al., 2020; Choi & Moran, 2009; Chu & Choi, 2005; Fernie et al., 2017; Fernie et al., 2018; Ferrari et al.,

1995). This perspective challenges the traditional notion of procrastination as harmful and may reflect adaptive behavior promoting effectiveness and performance. Some researchers have thus proposed distinguishing functional vs. dysfunctional (Ferrari et al., 1995), active vs. passive (Chu & Choi, 2005), and intentional vs. unintentional procrastination (Fernie et al., 2017). Functional procrastination involves an occasional delay to optimize performance. On the other hand, dysfunctional procrastination is a chronic delay in starting or finishing tasks, resulting in negative outcomes (Ferrari, 1994). Passive procrastination is a type of dysfunctional behavior that leads to detrimental outcomes, while active procrastination can potentially lead to positive outcomes for performance and well-being. It is similar to purposeful delay, where an individual intentionally delays taking action to gain some advantages (Choi & Moran, 2009; Chu & Choi, 2005; Kim et al., 2017). Intentional procrastination occurs when individuals intentionally and consciously delay completing a task, whereas unintentional procrastination refers to an unintentional and involuntary postponement of tasks (Fernie et al., 2017).

Some researchers have raised doubts about whether these behaviors can be regarded as procrastination. They argued that every instance of procrastination constitutes a delay, while not every instance of delay qualifies as procrastination. Previous studies revealed that these constructs differ in their etiology, emotional correlates, and consequences. Dysfunctional procrastination arises from an internal need to maintain well-being, is associated with low conscientiousness, neuroticism, and low self-control, and can lead to negative emotional, health, social, and economic outcomes. Functional procrastination is typically initiated by situational demands, driven by the desire to maximize achievements. It is correlated with a proactive personality pattern, including high self-control, conscientiousness, and emotional stability. However, Pixten et al. (2019) did not support the beneficial effect of purposeful delay on achievement in the academic domain. Furthermore, it offers long-term advantages (Haghbin & Pychyl, 2016). Therefore, active procrastination appears to be rather strategic or active delay than procrastination *per se* (Chowdhury & Pychyl, 2018; Corkin et al., 2011). It seems that functional and dysfunctional procrastination has distinct theoretical and empirical foundations. For this reason, many researchers view active procrastination as a myth and oxymoron (e.g. Chowdhury & Pychyl, 2018; Sirois, 2022). Additionally, the situation-based approach distinguished types of procrastination in the dependence of life domain. Procrastination in the academic, financial, work, health, and sleep domains was particularly well documented.

Academic Domain: Academic procrastination (or student procrastination) is considered a specific type of behavioral procrastination and refers to delaying tasks and activities related to studying. The phenomenon of academic procrastination has been relatively well researched. Previous research showed that procrastination largely occurs among young adults during their academic education.

This is evidenced by statistics showing that 80–95% of students procrastinate to some extent and approximately 70% of students procrastinate regularly (Steel & Klingsieck, 2016). Procrastination is equally common among undergraduate and graduate students (Klassen et al., 2008, 2010). Procrastination in education refers to failure to meet assignment deadlines, postponing deadlines, and delaying task completion. Students tend to procrastinate in writing term papers, studying for exams, and completing homework assignments.

A meta-analysis of studies (Kim & Seo, 2015) demonstrated its negative relationships with achievement and individual academic outcomes, such as assignment grades, test scores, course grades, and semester grade point averages, were negatively associated with student procrastination at low, moderate, and high levels depending on the outcome measure.

Work Domain: Procrastination at work is sometimes compared to academic procrastination due to the similarity in postponing assigned tasks and the connection with achievements or outcomes (Klingsieck, 2013a). However, numerous findings indicate differences between procrastination in academic and work settings. The work is performed as part of an exchange understood differently from academic education. Employees receive different gratifications for completing tasks than students. Procrastination at work has been investigated in the context of related phenomena such as time management at work (van Eerde, 2003b, 2015), cyberslacking (O'Neill et al., 2014; Tandon et al., 2022; Yan & Yang, 2014), presenteeism (D'Abate & Eddy, 2007), or empty work (Paulsen, 2015). Chapter 2 presents a review of the findings on procrastination at work, which has garnered significant scientific interest and contributed to a substantial increase in knowledge about this phenomenon.

Economic and Financial Domain: People procrastinate in various economic domains such as setting or achieving financial goals (Topa et al., 2017), planning personal finances (Gamst-Klaussen et al., 2019), investing (O'Donoghue & Rabin, 2001), saving (Börsch-Supan et al., 2023), repaying or overusing credit cards (Barboza, 2018; Keys & Wang, 2019), paying bills, taxes (Martinez et al., 2023), or saving for retirement (Ferrari et al., 2009a; Gamst-Klaussen et al., 2019; Topa et al., 2017). For example, procrastination as a moderator decreased the mediational effect of financial knowledge, savings goals, and actual retirement savings behavior. This relationship was significant only in conditions of low trait procrastination (Topa et al., 2017).

Individuals often procrastinate when it comes to paying taxes, which can lead to higher costs due to mistakes related to tax overpayment (Martinez et al., 2023; Steel, 2007). According to Gamst-Klaussen et al. (2019), procrastination is a predictor of unfavorable financial behavior, specifically financial impulsivity and a low propensity to save. The study also found that the relationship between procrastination and financial problems was mediated by financial self-efficacy. Additionally, procrastinators may face other financial costs, such as penalties for missing deadlines, not paying bills on time, or shopping at the last minute, as a result of their financial decisions. Procrastination has a harmful impact on consumer behavior. For instance, individuals who chronically procrastinate may postpone their Christmas shopping, leading to missed opportunities to receive gift vouchers. Such financially detrimental behaviors among procrastinators are linked to the risk of financial losses, missed gains, and ultimately reduced material status and financial well-being (Akerlof, 1991; Gamst-Klaussen et al., 2019; Steel, 2007). Specifically, Mc Cown et al. (1989) found that nearly 40% of respondents reported experiencing personal financial losses due to procrastination in the past year.

Health Domain: Numerous studies have shown that procrastination extends to behaviors related to healthcare and prevention. Procrastinators are more likely to delay diagnostic and follow-up medical visits for physical and mental health care (Sirois et al., 2003; Sirois, 2007), postpone decisions about starting treatment (Sirois et al., 2003; Steel, 2007), and delay medical procedures (Stead et al., 2010). Procrastination typically involves delaying health-promoting behaviors such as rational eating, healthy sleep, physical activity, and noncompliance with medical recommendations (Kroese & Ridder, 2016; Sirois, 2007; Sirois et al., 2023). Such practices may indirectly contribute to poor health or the development of disease in the long term, particularly for individuals who are more susceptible to developing diseases. Research has confirmed that procrastination is correlated with diseases, acute health problems, and serious diseases, as well as delayed treatment, medical checks, dental check-ups, and taking care of one's physical condition (Sirois, 2007, 2016).

After analyzing the research on conceptualizing procrastination, two main points emerge. First, extensive research has enhanced our understanding of procrastination's specifics and nature. However, it has also resulted in significant conceptual diversity. Procrastination, viewed as a behavioral tendency that is stable over time and situations, and influenced by contextual factors, has driven two main research streams. The trait approach considered procrastination to be the general tendency to delay tasks and decision-making in different facets of life, accentuating its universality. The situational approach posits that procrastination is determined by contextual factors. Scholars concur that procrastination is a multifaceted issue that integrates cognitive, emotional, and behavioral factors, including a temporal element that signifies the cut-off date for accomplishing the assignment (Ferrari, 2010; Ferrari et al., 1995).

A review of the procrastination theories suggests that procrastination is a dysfunctional behavior that negatively affects both individuals and the environment. Furthermore, it is regarded as a maladaptive and self-destructive pattern with dispositional and situational sources, which may provide short-term advantages but have long-term ramifications. Although there are conceptual inconsistencies, most scholars agree that procrastination is a common problem that impairs functioning. Therefore, interventions of varying formality are necessary, depending on the type and specificity of procrastination (i.e. trait vs. state).

1.1.3 Conceptions and Mechanisms Explaining Procrastination

Many theories and models of self-regulation, mood control, self-handicapping, motivational processes, temporal motivation, and the intention-action gap are used to explain procrastination. Each conceptualization of procrastination emphasizes slightly different aspects of this phenomenon.

1.1.3.1 A Self-Regulation Failure

Procrastination is often defined as a failure in self-regulation, either as underregulation or misregulation (Ferrari, 2001; Rebetez et al., 2018; Sirois & Pychyl, 2013; Steel, 2007). Self-regulation processes are crucial in understanding procrastination (Baumeister et al., 2018; Ferrari, 2001; Steel, 2007; van Eerde, 2000). Self-regulation refers to the ability to control one's behavior, feelings, and thoughts, and plays a significant role in human behavior. It encompasses cognitive and emotional processes, as well as thoughts and behaviors. Self-regulation allows individuals to focus on goals, effectively implement plans, inhibit impulses and temptations, and regulate behavior (Baumeister et al., 2018). Therefore, individuals who struggle with procrastination appear to have limited self-regulation skills such as self-control, emotion regulation, motivation regulation, or time management.

Procrastination as a Form of Underregulation: Baumeister and Heatherton (1996) suggested that procrastination can be attributed to poor self-regulation, which results in failure to take action. This underregulation is associated with inappropriate performance standards, disorganization, inadequate performance monitoring, high internal motivation, and reorienting efforts to cope with emotions. The findings support the notion that academic procrastination is positively associated with disorganization and low achievement motivation, which are attributes of failed self-regulation. Students who procrastinate exhibited a high-performance avoidance orientation and a low mastery orientation (Howell & Watson, 2007). Procrastinators also struggle with assessing, structuring, and managing their time. In other studies, it was found that students who lacked intrinsic motivation to learn and did not put in sufficient effort to regulate their behavior were more prone to procrastination. Similarly, studies revealed that planning, organizational, self-monitoring, and task-monitoring skills were related to low procrastination (Rabin et al., 2011; Zhao et al., 2021). A meta-analysis of studies

(Steel, 2007) confirmed the negative relationship between procrastination and internal motivation ($\bar{r}$ = −0.35; K = 34), organization ($\bar{r}$ = −0.36; K = 25), and self-control ($\bar{r}$ = −0.58; K = 21). In summary, the available evidence suggests that poor self-regulation is a determining factor in procrastination.

Procrastination as a Form of Misregulation: Misregulation refers to the ineffective initiation, change, or inhibition of behavior (Baumeister & Heatherton, 1996). It is an attempt to control an inappropriate aspect of a process or something that is essentially uncontrollable. The most common form of misregulation is the regulation of current task-induced negative affect rather than task performance. Focusing on regulating emotions can undermine self-control in other areas of activity. Therefore, when faced with challenging tasks that induce anxiety, individuals may be inclined to delay or abandon task initiation. This is because they desire to avoid negative emotions in the given situation (Sirois & Pychyl, 2013).

Procrastination is a strategy for emotional regulation aimed at improving one's current mood. However, it can also have negative effects. In the short term, it can provide immediate relief from negative emotions such as frustration, stress, anxiety, and boredom. Although Baumeister et al. (2018) suggest that procrastination can have positive consequences, such as improved current mood and higher levels of well-being and health, it is important to note that these benefits are not long-lasting and can be outweighed by the negative effects; in the long run, it can lead to increased stress and negative emotions, as well as a lower level of well-being and impaired health (Pychyl & Sirois, 2016). Numerous studies showed negative correlations between general or academic procrastination and self-regulation (Balkis & Duru, 2016; Sirois & Pychyl, 2013; Steel, 2007; van Eerde, 2000). Misregulation appears to be a mechanism that can better explain procrastination.

1.1.3.2 Intention–Action Gap

The theory of planned action (Ajzen, 1991) suggests that there is often a gap between behavioral intention and implementation. This gap is crucial in explaining procrastination (Steel, 2007). Gollwitzer (1999) introduced the concept of intention implementation, which appears to mediate the relationship between goals, intentions, and behavior. Intention implementation involves translating an individual's intentions into actions. However, during the time between intention and action, various circumstances and events may arise that distract an individual from taking action (Ajzen, 1991). Procrastination may contribute to the intention–action gap. Studies have shown that individuals who heavily procrastinate exhibit a greater discrepancy between their intentions and actions than nonprocrastinators (Steel et al., 2001). Procrastination can create a gap between intention and action, as noted by Steel (2007). However, it is not the delay time itself that influences the implementation of intentions. This may be caused by problems related to self-control. According to scholars, procrastinators do not differ from non-procrastinators in terms of their intentions, but rather in their ability to follow through with them (Steel, 2007; van Hooft et al., 2005). Individuals who procrastinate often struggle to initiate and maintain progress toward their goals. To accomplish their goals, people frequently use maladaptive techniques, such as avoiding or delaying unpleasant, challenging, or monotonous tasks, and instead opting for more enjoyable or interesting ones. However, this distraction can hinder the achievement of the intended goals and prevent their implementation. Procrastinators may struggle to implement their intentions due to the encountered obstacles (Ferrari, 2010; Ferrari & Pychyl, 2000). The reasons for procrastination may include problems with self-control when initiating and persevering in the pursuit of goals. Thus, dispositional procrastination seems to be —a confounding factor in the relationship between intentions and actions. However, it is not related to intentions but only to the difficulty of implementing them.

1.1.3.3 Self-Handicapping Strategy

Self-handicapping is an attributional strategy in which individuals intentionally set barriers and obstacles to achieving their goals (Snyder, 1990). This strategy is employed in situations where failure is anticipated, and the individuals seek to justify their poor performance by creating an external obstacle, such as a lack of time, rather than acknowledging a personal skill deficit. On the other hand, if a person achieves success despite an impairment, they may receive additional recognition for overcoming a personal or situational obstacle. Procrastination is often conceptualized as a self-handicapping behavior (Barutçu Yıldırım & Demir, 2020; Ferrari, 1991b; Ferrari & Tice, 2000). It can be a form of self-handicapping to delay the start or completion of a task and not make any effort that could increase the chances of success. According to Ferrari et al. (2007), chronic procrastinators may actively seek excuses or substitute activities to justify their lack of time and failure to complete tasks. A meta-analysis of 16 studies (Steel, 2007) demonstrates an average positive correlation between procrastination and self-handicapping ($\bar{r} = 0.46$). Experimental studies have also supported this relationship, showing that procrastinators more frequently choose conditions that make task completion challenging, such as distracting noise, compared to nonprocrastinators (Ferrari, 1991b). Similarly, individuals who procrastinate are more likely to participate in activities that negatively impact their performance on diagnostic tasks (Ferrari, 1991b; Ferrari & Tice, 2000). Procrastinators may also delay their efforts by using other forms of self-handicapping, such as avoiding practicing for tests (Steel, 2007). Research suggests that procrastination may be linked to impression management and self-esteem protection, since individuals fear failure, evaluation, or incompetence (Barutçu

Yıldırım & Demir, 2020; Ferrari, 1991a, 1991b). Those who procrastinate are often preoccupied with their self-image and tend to avoid situations that may reflect negatively on themselves. For some individuals, it is better to refrain from taking action than to risk exposing their incompetence, embarrassment, and failure. Procrastinators intentionally delay tasks by strategically managing their image as resourceful, competent, and capable of completing tasks. They may have false beliefs about their high efficacy and competence, leading them to believe that they are more capable than they are.

Individuals may use the self-handicapping strategy to protect their private and public self-esteem while carrying out tasks. This involves searching for external hindrances that impede their ability to accomplish tasks, which may include delaying the initiation or completion of tasks and attributing any resulting failure to outside causes (Ferrari, 1991b; Ferrari & Tice, 2000). Individuals may attempt to rationalize their failures regardless of the circumstances to obtain validation and empathy from others. This can lead to the use of self-handicapping techniques, such as delaying task completion and attributing any shortcomings to insufficient effort rather than lack of competence (Ferrari & Tice, 2000). Procrastinators may also delay or avoid completing tasks due to their low self-esteem regarding their ability to complete a particular task. Thus, procrastination as a self-handicapping strategy seems to have a protective function in the short term for the subject in the face of possible failure. However, procrastination undoubtedly exhibits self-destructive behavior. Despite its short-term benefits, it causes more harm than good, such as reduced productivity, wasted time, and increased stress.

1.1.3.4 Economic Approach

In the context of economic theory, human behavior is deemed rational since individuals carefully weigh profits and costs when making choices. This leads to consistent preferences over time, resulting in the demonstration of a constant preference for a task by each individual. However, individuals tend to show time inconsistency in estimating utility components based on hyperbolic discounting principles (Ainslie & Haslam, 1992). This results in prioritizing tasks with higher utility based on the assessment of benefits and costs at a given moment. Economic models attempt to explain procrastination through preference inconsistency over time and intertemporal discounting (Ainslie & Haslam, 1992; Akerlof, 1991). Procrastination is defined as the tendency to discount the value of delayed rewards and the preference for immediate benefits over long-term rewards. According to this, the individual considers the timing of completing a single task. However, people have various tasks to choose from, each with direct costs during task performance and delayed benefits after task completion. As a result, they must decide not only when to perform a task but also which task to prioritize (O'Donoghue & Rabin, 2001). When presented with multiple tasks, individuals tend to prioritize those that offer immediate rewards, rather than those whose benefits will be realized in the future. Procrastination occurs when an individual perceives the present costs of an action to be higher than future costs, while future benefits remain at their full value. Consequently, despite the future benefits being unchanged, deferring the task appears to yield a higher net benefit. Furthermore, individuals tend to overestimate future benefits in comparison to future costs (O'Donoghue & Rabin, 2001). Discounting future costs of a task may involve the need to finish other ongoing tasks. Focusing on these immediate responsibilities at the expense of neglecting future tasks probably results from the illusory belief that there will be more time in the future than there will be.

Therefore, procrastination will only occur when activities have low short-term utility and high long-term utility. This would support the thesis that procrastination is indeed an irrational postponement associated with the awareness of its negative consequences (Steel, 2007, 2010; Steel & König, 2006). However, the subjective utility of an action may be greater in the present than in the future. Then delay will be a rational strategy. Procrastination occurs in both aversive and pleasant activities due to higher cost discounting, but lower benefit discounting (Shu & Gneezy, 2010). Economic models accurately describe the phenomenon of procrastination using hyperbolic discounting but do not explain it. It seems that although they illustrate the dynamics of procrastination well, they lack reference to the relevant psychological processes/mechanisms. To better understand procrastination, it would be worth recognizing how the elements of the formal model are represented by psychological constructs. A proposal for such an integration of the economic approach with psychological concepts is temporal motivation theory (Steel & König, 2006).

1.1.3.5 Temporal Motivation Theory

Among the concepts explaining procrastination, temporal motivation theory (TMT; Steel & König, 2006) is of particular importance. This is a meta-theory that integrates various approaches to the motivation of human behavior, such as hyperbolic discounting theory (Ainslie & Haslam, 1992), expectancy theory (Vroom et al., 2015), prospect theory (Tversky & Kahneman, 1992), and needs theory (Dollard & Miller, 1950).

According to the TMT, people prefer activities with maximum utility at a specific time, which is expressed in the equation:

$$\text{Utility} = \frac{\text{Expectations} \times \text{Value}}{\text{Sensitivity to Delay} \times \text{Delay}}$$

In this equation, motivation to action depends on the subjective evaluation of utility, which is a function of four variables: expectation (efforts lead to reward), value V of a specific action (sensibility or attractiveness vs. aversiveness of the task), delay (time to delay task completion/amount of time available to complete the task), and sensitivity to delay (inability to delay). Thus, the motivation to action is directly proportional to the expectations and value of the action and inversely proportional to delay and the sensitivity to delay (Steel, 2007; Steel & König, 2006). All utility components may have subjective and situational sources. Thus, expectations may result from self-efficacy or task difficulty, value – from the need for achievement or task aversiveness, and sensitivity to delay – from impulsivity, distractibility, or time distance (Steel, 2012). According to the TMT, task procrastination depends on the perceived low utility of these tasks. In other words, individuals delay completing a task when at least one of the following conditions is true: (1) they perceive a low probability of success in the task (low expectancy); (2) they perceive no value or pleasure in performing the task (low value); or (3) there is a long delay between completing a task and experiencing any significant benefits or costs (high delay and high sensitivity to delay). Therefore, it can be assumed that procrastination occurs when motivation to act is low. Therefore, people are more likely to procrastinate when: (1) they have low self-esteem and self-efficacy, which results in a low level of expectancy; (2) tasks are of low importance or aversive; (3) the delay in completing the task is high; and (4) impulsivity and distractibility in performing the task are high, which is an indicator of the sensitivity to delay (Steel, 2012).

The TMT is a highly universal meta-theory, useful in explaining procrastination as a multidimensional construct related to self-regulation failure, including cognitive, emotional, behavioral, and temporal components. Expectancy, valence, sensitivity, and delay seem to simplify understanding factors related to procrastination as the tendency to delay or avoid activities with higher long-term utility due to the existence of more pleasuring activities (higher short-term utility). For example, the TMT facilitates an understanding of why procrastinators plan to work but change their minds, and fail to act on their plans. However, there are several weaknesses of the theory. Individual differences in preferences and subjective evaluation of the TMT components seem problematic because they may confound the results of the equation. What is boring, difficult, or valuable to one person may be attractive, feasible, or worthless to another. The theory ignores the role of cognitive and neurological processes in explaining procrastination (Fernie et al., 2017). Despite weaknesses, there is some empirical support for procrastination in terms of the TMT (Steel et al., 2018, 2021; Zhang et al., 2019).

In summary, the above overview includes the most important theoretical models and approaches that explain the phenomenon of procrastination. These models emphasize different emotional, cognitive, and temporal aspects. It is important to note that these models do not exhaust all potential positions and hypotheses that attempt to understand the mechanisms underlying procrastination behavior.

1.2 Consequences of General Procrastination

Procrastination can have numerous negative consequences, such as reduced work efficiency or academic performance, deterioration of mental and physical health, disorganized social life, or financial problems. Procrastination may provide short-term benefits, such as improving an individual's current mood by delaying task completion and engaging in more appealing activities instead (Tice & Baumeister, 2018). However, the negative consequences that procrastinators experience in the long term, including reduced performance and negative emotions, typically outweigh these benefits. Procrastination has thus been recognized as a dysfunctional and irrational behavior associated with impairment in functioning in various domains of life (Klingsieck, 2013a).

1.2.1 Performance

Procrastination, whether it involves deliberate inactivity or engages in alternative activities, can have a detrimental effect on an individual's ability to perform tasks, whether academic or professional. Previous studies have shown that procrastination can have negative effects on both objective and subjective performance (Steel et al., 2001; Tice & Baumeister, 2018). However there are views that procrastination improves performance by marshaling one's resources to cope with an oncoming deadline (Steel et al., 2001; Tice & Baumeister, 2018). In this chapter, research results on the relationship between general or academic procrastination and academic performance are presented, while results on these relationships in work settings are presented in Section 2.2.2.

Meta-analyses (Kim & Seo, 2015; Steel, 2007; van Eerde, 2003a) have confirmed a low to moderate negative association between procrastination and performance, particularly in terms of task completion and the ability to achieve academic and career goals. Individuals who procrastinate are more likely to participate in activities that negatively impact their performance on diagnostic tasks or assignments and thereby delay or avoid their completion (Ferrari, 1991b; Ferrari & Tice, 2000; Steel, 2007). As research has indicated, people who procrastinate tend to experience a larger-than-average discrepancy between intentions and actions in task completion, especially at the beginning of the course. As the deadline approaches, the intention–action gap reduces, and motivation for task completion increases (Steel et al., 2001). In research by Cormack et al. (2020), a task submission closer to the deadline was associated with obtaining a lower grade. However, submission time is an extremely weak predictor of a grade for a student on an assignment.

In the academic domain, the relationship between procrastination and performance depends on indicators of performance, such as general point average (GPA), examination grades, assignment grades, quiz scores, course grades, and college test scores (Kim & Seo, 2015; Steel et al., 2001). The correlations between procrastination and academic performance ranged from −0.26 to −0.66

(Jackson et al., 2003; Tice & Roy, 1998). It is worth noting that this relationship was substantially larger in the case of coursework performance grades rather than examination grades. Moreover, previous studies have shown the negative effects of procrastination on both *objective-* and *subjective-rated* performance (Steel et al., 2001; Tice & Baumeister, 2018). However, higher correlations were observed when performance or grades were externally observed than when not self-reported (Kim & Seo, 2015). This may suggest that the use of self-reported grades may be underestimated or overestimated, and thereby the results of investigations into the association between procrastination and academic performance may be biased.

The relationship between procrastination and performance may also be a result of using *self-reported measures* of procrastination (e.g. Steel et al., 2001). The correlation between self-reported procrastination and course grade was moderate (0.36), while observed procrastination was strongly correlated with grades (0.87) (Steel et al., 2001). To conclude, the strongest relationship was between externally rated procrastination and externally rated performance (Kim & Seo, 2015). Furthermore, the level of academic performance may also be different for various types of procrastination. As was mentioned earlier, (passive) procrastination is detrimental to students' GPAs (Kim & Seo, 2015; Steel et al., 2001). However, the link between active procrastination and performance is inconclusive (Choi & Moran, 2009; Chu & Choi, 2005). This is probably due to self-reported measures of the variables. Nevertheless, active procrastination predicted GPA, which was measured objectively (Kim et al., 2017). Thus, active and deliberate procrastination can potentially lead to positive outcomes for performance, particularly among students who under time pressure are motivated to achieve their objectives.

The effect of procrastination on task performance is often not direct, but mediated by various factors. Previous studies have shown that procrastination among students can lead to decreased self-esteem, both directly and through other mechanisms such as poor academic performance (Duru & Balkis, 2017). Specifically, procrastination leads to poorer outcomes, which negatively affects self-esteem. Furthermore, self-esteem mediates the relationship between procrastination and well-being, moderated by academic achievements. Balkis (2013) identified that the negative relationship between procrastination and performance is mediated by rational beliefs about studying and academic life satisfaction. Thus, decreasing procrastination enhanced rational beliefs about studying, which led to high life satisfaction and then academic achievement. The relationship between procrastination and performance may vary depending on other factors related to the student, assignment, course, and discipline. Additionally, people who procrastinate achieve various levels of task performance, particularly in tasks that are boring, difficult, pointless, or require personal sacrifices. These issues have been described in detail in Sections 1.3.3 and 1.3.4.

1.2.2 Emotions

Numerous studies have found that procrastination has a significant impact on elevating stress levels in cross-sectional studies (Beutel et al., 2016; Reinecke et al., 2018; Sirois, 2023) and longitudinal studies (Rahimi et al., 2023; Rice et al., 2012; Sirois, 2013). This may be due to individuals negatively evaluating their procrastination, which contributes to feeling distressed (Flett et al., 2012; Sirois & Tosti, 2012; Sirois, 2013). Delaying one task may lead to delaying subsequent ones, which may cause anxiety and stress due to the potential loss of control and the sense of helplessness. This can occur both directly (Sirois, 2007; Tice et al., 2001) and indirectly through self-compassion (Sirois, 2013) or low mindfulness (Sirois & Tosti, 2012). Furthermore, maladaptive coping strategies were found to play a mediating role in the relationship between procrastination and elevated stress levels (Sirois & Kitner, 2015). Chronically elevated stress can, in turn, lead to poorer health outcomes (Sirois, 2007). Past procrastination behaviors can contribute to anxiety, worry, and self-depreciation during current procrastination. Irrational delay in completing a task at the last minute can cause stress. Procrastination can increase stress and anxiety about expectations and the consequences of delaying tasks. Procrastination may cause stress due to its association with self-regulation failure. This can lead to feelings of stress and mental discomfort. Individuals who procrastinate may struggle to effectively manage aversive stimuli due to poor self-control, which in turn leads to higher levels of stress (Sirois, 2007, 2016; Tice & Baumeister, 2018). The direction of the relationships is unclear because research suggests that negative affect can also predict procrastination.

Guilt and Shame: Procrastination is associated with shame and guilt (Blunt & Pychyl, 2005; Feyzi Behnagh & Ferrari, 2022; Rahimi et al., 2023). These emotions serve as motivations for both dispositional and situational procrastination, as well as the consequences of procrastination. Guilt is a natural reaction when realizing that one has committed a legally or morally wrong act. Thus, guilt arises in individuals when they evaluate their behavior negatively and experience remorse with the desire to make amends. Procrastinators feel guilty due to the unnecessary delay in completing a task or the potential negative consequences of procrastination for the individual and the environment. Although procrastination may provide temporary mood improvement by engaging in pleasant activities, the resulting feelings of pleasure are often overshadowed by feelings of guilt (Fee & Tangney, 2000). Chronic procrastinators may feel shame in response to failures and incomplete tasks due to their procrastination behavior. According to a recent review of research (Feyzi Behnagh & Ferrari, 2022), there is a positive correlation between guilt and situationally induced procrastination. Chronic procrastinators may experience shame in response to failures and exceeding norms related to task completion, due to their guilt about their procrastination behavior. They are more likely to react to failures and exceed norms with a sense of shame, regardless of the cause of the failure or transgression. Shame is linked to a negative self-evaluation as the perpetrator of a behavior or omission that triggers a desire to hide, escape, or deny responsibility for the actions committed. Individuals who procrastinate may experience shame due to avoiding task performance. Dispositional procrastination, however, is associated with susceptibility to feelings of shame (shame proneness) rather than guilt (Fee & Tangney, 2000). In summary, chronic procrastinators tend to respond to failure with feelings of shame, as supported by longitudinal studies that demonstrate the negative impact of procrastination on increased shame (Rahimi et al., 2023). Therefore, it can be concluded that feelings of shame may play a significant role in explaining procrastination behavior as a strategy to protect self-presentation.

Anger and Regret: Longitudinal studies supported that procrastination can lead to feelings of regret or anger over missed opportunities or incomplete tasks (Rahimi et al., 2023). Regret is often experienced when reflecting on past decisions and actions, realizing that they could have been done differently for a better outcome. In general, people tend to regret their inactions or failures to act more often than they regret their actions. Regret typically refers to a missed opportunity or task that could have been successful or beneficial. Research has shown that arousal and avoidant procrastination are weakly associated with a sense of regret in various life domains, such as education, family, finances, friends, and health (Ferrari et al., 2009a; Goroshit et al., 2020). According to Ferrari et al. (2009a), chronic procrastinators experience more regret in community service and leisure time activities compared to nonprocrastinators, while chronic avoidant procrastinators report significantly less regret than arousal procrastinators in parenting interactions. Another study (Goroshit et al., 2020) found that the level of regret increases with the severity of procrastination, with education and work being the most regrettable areas. Tibbett and Ferrari (2019) revealed that decisional procrastination is linked to regret in education, finance, and career, which can reinforce an individual's tendency to procrastinate. Procrastination behavior can induce negative emotions, particularly anger, especially when used as a strategy for revenge due to perceived harm or unfair treatment by others. Previous research has shown that individuals frequently experience anger when procrastinating (Ferrari, 1994; Ferrari & Emmons, 1995; Laybourn et al., 2019; Rahimi et al., 2023). This feeling of anger can be directed toward oneself for procrastinating or toward the task or situation. Individuals who procrastinate may subsequently experience self-directed anger due to delaying task completion in favor of more enjoyable activities and their inability to persistently pursue their goals.

Life Satisfaction: Research has consistently shown that procrastination is associated with low life satisfaction. Specifically, academic procrastination reduces overall satisfaction with life (Balkıs & Duru, 2017; Grunschel et al., 2016; Yang, 2021) and academic life (Balkis & Duru, 2016; Uzun et al., 2022). In the adult population, procrastination was related to low satisfaction with life or work (Beutel et al., 2016; Steel, 2007; Tudose & Pavalache-Ilie, 2021). These relationships ranged from weak to moderate. Probably, individuals who procrastinate engage in more pleasurable activities. Thus, their obligations pile up, and the task anxiety compounds, resulting in a decrease in overall life satisfaction. Yang (2021) revealed that the negative relationship between procrastination and life satisfaction occurred among Chinese students with low self-regulation, but not among British students. In summary, emotional states are the effect, not the cause, of procrastination.

1.2.3 Health

Procrastination behavior is a risk factor for compromised physical health, reduced physical well-being, and the development of somatic illnesses (e.g. Sirois et al., 2003; Sirois, 2007, 2016; Stead et al., 2010; Tice & Baumeister, 2018). Chronic procrastination can result in the accumulation of health-related problems or chronic diseases in the long-term perspective, while situation-induced procrastination can lead to immediate health-related conditions, such as infections, headaches, or insomnia. Furthermore, procrastination can lead to deterioration of one's health due to frequent activation of the stress response and related changes in psychophysiology (*direct pathway*; Sirois, 2007, 2016; Sirois et al., 2023). The stress response can potentially worsen physical health, leading to various health conditions such as cold, infections, digestive problems, headaches, insomnia, and eating disorders. In the long term, these issues can result in chronic ailments associated with long-term stress, such as decreased vitality and immunity; metabolic disorders; symptoms of coronary syndrome; as well as severe health problems (Sirois, 2016). Procrastination can also worsen health by delaying important behaviors related to treatment, such as scheduling a doctor's check-up, undergoing preventive examinations, or starting treatment. It can also delay health prevention behaviors, such as following a healthy diet, engaging in physical activity, or quitting smoking (*indirect pathway*; Sirois, 2016; 2023).

In summary, procrastination can lead to physical health deterioration, particularly when individuals habitually delay or postpone healthcare behaviors related to prevention and treatment. While procrastination may have short-term benefits for performance and mood repair, it is generally a detrimental behavior.

1.3 Antecedents of General Procrastination

Dispositional procrastination is influenced by various proximal (individual) and distal (contextual) factors. While individual factors that contribute to procrastination have been well documented, less attention has been given to its contextual determinants. This chapter presents findings on sociodemographic, personality, emotional, and motivational factors that contribute to an individual's tendency to procrastinate.

1.3.1 Sociodemographic Factors

Large epidemiological studies (Steel & Ferrari, 2013) conducted in English-speaking countries have provided evidence that procrastination is influenced by gender, age, marital status, education, and nationality of the subjects. According to this research, the typical profile of a procrastinator is a young, single man with lower levels of education residing in countries with lower levels of self-discipline.

Gender: Both earlier meta-analytic studies (Steel, 2007; van Eerde, 2003a) and a recent one (Lu et al., 2021) have shown that there is a significant difference in the tendency to procrastinate between men and women. The findings indicate that women are less prone to procrastination than men, which may be due to a significant difference in self-control between the genders. This suggests that women have a greater ability to self-control their efforts compared to men (Steel, 2007). According to the meta-analysis of Lu et al. (2021), gender differences were lower for general procrastination than academic procrastination ($z = 5.14$).

Age: Steel's meta-analysis (2007) found a relatively high negative correlation between procrastination and age among adults ($\bar{r} = -0.48$, $K = 16$), indicating that procrastination decreases with age. However, many subsequent studies revealed a weak-to-moderate correlation (Beutel et al., 2016; Díaz-Morales et al., 2008; Steel & Ferrari, 2013). Studies in the USA, Australia, Canada, India, Ireland, New Zealand, the Philippines, and Great Britain (Steel & Ferrari, 2013), as well as in European countries (i.e. Sweden, Finland, Norway, Germany, Italy, and Poland) (Svartdal et al., 2016) have confirmed these findings. The significant relationship between age and procrastination may be due to the development of higher cognitive functions during adolescence that are necessary for self-regulation and goal-setting. The decline in procrastination with age is attributed to greater conscientiousness, self-control, and reduced impulsivity resulting from the development of the prefrontal cortex (Steel & Ferrari, 2013). As scholars suggested, adults procrastinate less not only due to greater self-control but also because they have developed patterns to overcome procrastination. Individuals can learn to avoid procrastination, so with experience, they become less inclined to procrastinate (Ainslie & Haslam, 1992; Baumeister & Heatherton, 1996; O'Donoghue & Rabin, 2001).

Education: Individuals with higher education reported lower levels of procrastination compared to those with less education (Steel & Ferrari, 2013). Interestingly, Hen and Goroshit (2018) found that individuals with higher education tend to procrastinate more, but in different areas than those with lower education. Educated individuals tend to procrastinate more in regard to health-care and leisure activities, and to a slightly lesser extent in personal, social, and career-related matters. Additionally, research suggests that the relationship between education and procrastination is influenced by gender. Research conducted in Germany and Scandinavian countries revealed that individuals with secondary education exhibited greater procrastination compared to individuals with higher education (Svartdal et al., 2016). The effect of education in explaining procrastination may be related to age, as being a student is associated with greater procrastination and a lower level of characteristics that determine higher levels of education (e.g. self-control and self-regulation) (Steel, 2007). From the perspective of the individual's development, procrastination increases significantly during undergraduate education, peaks in the mid-twenties, and then declines gradually with age (Steel & Ferrari, 2013). However, a meta-analysis of 42 studies (Lu et al., 2021) revealed a nonsignificant association between education level and procrastination.

Marital and Family Status: The level of procrastination is affected by one's marital and family status. Empirical studies have established that individuals who are not in a relationship are predisposed to more procrastination than those who are in one. This trend has been observed to be consistent in various countries, except Finland (Svartdal et al., 2016), and is reasonably weak ($r = 0.06$, $p < 0.001$; Steel & Ferrari, 2013). Procrastinators (24%) also tend to postpone beginning or ending a relationship. They have a lower likelihood of being in a committed relationship, including separation and divorce ($r = 0.07$), and are also less likely to form such relationships (Steel & Ferrari, 2013). Additionally, procrastination may be related to deferring parenthood and delaying birth control methods due to poor conscientiousness and impulsivity (Steel & Ferrari, 2013). A meta-analysis of 61 studies (Lu et al., 2021) revealed a nonsignificant effect of family size on the tendency to procrastinate.

1.3.2 Personality Traits

Personality traits are defined as relatively stable dispositions that are determined by biological factors and interactions with the environment. They are responsible for individual adaptation patterns, including behaviors, attitudes, habits, motives, adapting, and coping strategies (McCrae & Costa, 2003). Personality traits are universal and relatively stable across situations and time. From the individual differences perspective (Klingsieck, 2013b; Steel & Klingsieck, 2016), procrastination is defined as a personality trait related to other personality traits and trait-like variables, such as self-control, impulsivity, perfectionism, self-esteem, self-efficacy, and locus of control. Meta-analyses (Kim et al., 2017; Meng et al., 2024; Steel, 2007; van Eerde, 2004) indicated that dispositional procrastination is strongly associated with the Big Five personality traits, such as conscientiousness, neuroticism, and extraversion, as well as dark personality traits (Meng et al., 2024). Currently, there is no empirical evidence to confirm the relationship between procrastination and openness to experience and agreeableness.

Conscientiousness: Conscientiousness is a personality trait that encompasses an individual's tendency to regulate their behavior in a socially acceptable manner. Those with high conscientiousness are typically self-disciplined, organized, purposeful, reflective, goal-oriented, and adhere to socially accepted norms (McCrae & Costa, 2003). Some meta-analyses (Kim et al., 2017; Meng et al., 2024; Steel, 2007; van Eerde, 2004) have demonstrated a strong association between the trait of procrastination and low conscientiousness ($\bar{r} = -0.62$), a trait related to good organization, thoroughness, and persistence. These characteristics activate the inhibitory function necessary for timely task completion and likely reduce the tendency to procrastinate (Gao et al., 2021; Steel, 2007). Individuals with low levels of conscientiousness may exhibit disorganized, undisciplined, and inconsistent behavior, which can contribute to increased procrastination. The strong negative correlation between conscientiousness and procrastination suggests that those who struggle with chronic procrastination may have deficient levels of this trait, making it difficult to effectively regulate their work tasks. Conscientiousness indirectly affects procrastination through self-efficacy (Singh & Bala, 2020; Sparfeldt & Schwabe, 2024), and motivational regulation (Bäulke et al., 2021) in academic settings. Additionally, self-control and motivation mediate conscientiousness' impact on procrastination through parallel pathways (Gao et al., 2021).

Research has shown that lower-order traits of conscientiousness, such as competence, order, dutifulness, achievement striving, self-discipline, and deliberation, are moderately to highly correlated (0.34 to 0.75) with lower levels of procrastination (Steel & Klingsieck, 2016; van Eerde, 2004; Watson, 2001). Additionally, high levels of competence and achievement striving were found to be negatively correlated with rebellion against control as a dimension of academic procrastination (Watson, 2001). Another study found that procrastination was more strongly influenced by orderliness, a time-related facet of conscientiousness, than by goal striving and dependability, which are motivation-related facets.

Neuroticism: The meta-analyses indicate a consistent positive relationship between neuroticism and procrastination (Kim et al., 2017; Meng et al., 2024; Steel, 2007; van Eerde, 2004). Neuroticism (named also emotional instability) is a tendency to experience negative emotions, such as emotional instability, anger, anxiety, depression, irritability, and self-consciousness. Individuals with high levels of neuroticism may experience elevated levels of anxiety, low self-confidence, and a lack of self-competence when it comes to accomplishing tasks. This can result in avoiding or delaying task completion. Additionally, they tend to make mistakes, experience feelings of hopelessness and low self-esteem, lack self-control, act impulsively, and struggle to handle pressure or panic during emergencies (McCrae & Costa, 2003). Studies have revealed a curvilinear relationship between neuroticism and procrastination. This implies that individuals with a high tendency to procrastinate may have either high or low levels of neuroticism. Therefore, the neuroticism trait may foster procrastination in some individuals while inhibiting it in others (Johnson & Bloom, 1995; McCown et al., 1989). The relationship between neuroticism and task-avoidant procrastination may be weaker due to the disruptive effects of neuroticism facets, such as anxiety, depression, impulsivity, and self-consciousness. Research results showed that procrastination was associated weakly to moderately with angry hostility, anxiety, depressiveness, impulsivity, hypersensitivity, and self-criticism (Schouwenburg & Lay, 1995; van Eerde, 2004; Watson, 2001). Neuroticism was also indirectly related to procrastination through self-efficacy (Wang et al., 2018), low motivation and persistence, or low time management (Markiewicz, 2017). Some studies have also shown a nonsignificant relationship between neuroticism and procrastination (Lay, 1986; Steel et al., 2001).

Extraversion: Extraversion refers to the degree to which individuals experience sociability, positive emotions, and high activity (McCrae & Costa, 2003). Previous research has shown ambiguous relationships between extraversion, energy level, positive affect, and procrastination. Meta-analyses have shown positive (Steel et al., 2001) and negative relationships between extraversion and procrastination (Kim et al., 2017; Meng et al., 2024; van Eerde, 2004). These inconclusive findings may be due to differences in the conceptualization of extraversion. Eysenck's definition of extraversion includes impulsivity, which has been strongly linked to high levels of procrastination. In the Big Five model, impulsivity is a component of neuroticism (Johnson & Bloom, 1995). Other research has found no significant relationship between extraversion and self-reported procrastination (Lay, 1986; Steel et al., 2001; Steel & Klingsieck, 2016; van Eerde, 2004). At the level of lower-order traits, all facets of extraversion were associated with procrastination. A meta-analytical review conducted by van Eerde (2004) revealed negative correlations between procrastination and warmth, assertiveness, gregariousness, positive emotions, and activity, while a positive correlation was found with excitement-seeking. As revealed by meta-analyses (Kim et al., 2017; Meng et al., 2024; Steel, 2007; Steel & Klingsieck, 2016; van Eerde, 2004), two other traits, namely openness to experience and agreeableness, are usually weakly or nonsignificantly correlated with procrastination. Among the facets of openness, only fantasy was positively correlated with procrastination (Schouwenburg & Lay, 1995).

Perfectionism: Perfectionism is a personality trait characterized by striving for flawlessness and setting overly high standards for performance, coupled with excessively critical self-evaluation (Hewitt & Flett, 1991). Research has provided ample empirical evidence for the robust relationship between procrastination and perfectionism. However, the strength and direction of this relationship vary between studies. Conceptualizations of perfectionism can be understood as either one-dimensional and dysfunctional or multidimensional, including adaptive and nonadaptive or negative and positive components (Frost et al., 1990; Hewitt & Flett, 1991). Perfectionistic strivings reflect the tendency to set excessively high standards for oneself, whereas perfectionistic concerns reflect the tendency to be overly preoccupied with making mistakes and receiving negative evaluations. The first one expresses a maladaptive form of perfectionism, while the second one represents an adaptive form. A meta-analysis of research by Steel (2007) revealed weak relationships ($\bar{r} = 0.18$; $K = 24$) between procrastination and one-dimensional perfectionism. However, the low effect size may result from the opposite relationships of perfectionism dimensions (i.e. perfectionistic concerns and perfectionistic strivings) with procrastination, which produces an attenuated or nonsignificant effect of the unidimensional construct. According to the latest meta-analysis of studies (Sirois et al., 2017), there are weak-to-moderate correlations between procrastination and perfectionistic concerns ($\bar{r} = 0.23$) and perfectionistic strivings ($\bar{r} = -0.22$). Procrastination is often associated with higher-order perfectionism, particularly with maladaptive dimensions of perfectionistic concerns and weakly with adaptive dimensions of perfectionistic strivings (Sirois et al., 2017). This suggests that individuals who are excessively concerned about making mistakes, are full of self-doubt, and are preoccupied with the judgments of others are more likely to engage in procrastination. However, individuals who strive for perfection and demand it from themselves are less likely to exhibit procrastination. Sirois et al. (2017) found that nonadaptive perfectionistic concerns and procrastination are linked to self-regulation failure. Both phenomena involve negative self-evaluation, which hinders effective self-regulation and goal achievement. Consequently, individuals with high standards may struggle to control their behavior because they believe their goals are unattainable. At first, a person with perfectionistic tendencies may become aware of the difference between their current status and their ideal condition. They may then conclude that bridging this gap is unattainable, leading them to abandon or postpone the task. On the other hand, adaptive perfectionistic striving can result in timely task completion. Perfectionistic concerns may be linked to avoidance behavior driven by fear of failure, while perfectionistic strivings may be associated with approach behavior motivated by the pursuit of success. Therefore, the tendency to set unrealistic standards and the fear of making mistakes can trigger unpleasant emotions, which perfectionists try to reduce by delaying or avoiding starting and completing tasks.

Self-esteem: Self-esteem is a generalized and relatively stable attitude toward oneself, especially toward one's capabilities and other socially desirable attributes (Rosenberg, 1965). Many studies have found that procrastination is associated with low self-esteem in academic or adult samples (Ferrari, 1994; Klassen et al., 2008; Steel, 2007; van Eerde, 2003a). This relationship ranges from low to moderate. Harrington (2005) observed that self-esteem correlates moderately negatively with two aspects of procrastination, i.e. its frequency (−0.40) and problematic nature (−0.44). Low self-esteem can contribute to procrastination because individuals may doubt their ability to complete a task or achieve academic success. This self-doubt can lead to lack of motivation, increased anxiety, and a tendency to delay tasks, as individuals may think that they are not good enough to meet the demands of the task. In the study by Chen et al. (2016), the effect of low self-esteem on procrastination was mediated by weak resistance to peer influence. Furthermore, self-esteem was associated with procrastination through self-efficacy (Batool, 2020), self-efficacy for self-regulation, and fear of failure (Zhang et al., 2018).

However, the direction of the relationship between self-esteem and procrastination remains unclear. While some studies have found that self-esteem predicts procrastination (e.g. Batool, 2020; Burka & Yuen, 2008; Ferrari, 2000; Steel, 2010), others have observed the opposite relationship (Duru & Balkis, 2017; Flett et al., 2012). Research suggests that individuals may use procrastination as a strategy to protect their self-esteem in the face of possible failure (Balkis & Duru, 2016; Burka & Yuen, 2008; Chen et al., 2016; Klassen et al., 2008). Section 1.1.3.3 provides further insight into the impact of procrastination on self-esteem. Studies have shown that procrastination among students can lead to decreased self-esteem, both directly and through other mechanisms such as poor academic performance (Duru & Balkis, 2017). Specifically, procrastination leads to poorer outcomes, which negatively impacts self-esteem. In addition, self-esteem mediates the relationship between procrastination and well-being, moderated by academic achievements.

Self-efficacy: According to Bandura (1997), self-efficacy is the belief in one's ability to successfully implement behaviors that lead to positive outcomes. It is defined as a positive image or belief in one's competence to implement behaviors that will lead to successful outcomes. Social learning theory suggests that individuals are more likely to attempt tasks that they believe they can accomplish and avoid those they perceive as unattainable. This adaptive feature enables the individual to cope with changes in the environment by taking adaptive actions. Two meta-analyses (Steel, 2007; van Eerde, 2003a) suggested a moderate negative relationship between procrastination and self-efficacy ($\bar{r} = -0.38$ to -0.44). It should be noted that self-efficacy turned out to be one of the strongest predictors of academic procrastination (Batool, 2020; Howell et al., 2006). Individuals with low self-efficacy lack confidence in their ability to perform tasks, which can lead to procrastination or task avoidance. Additionally, individuals may attempt to present themselves as self-sufficient and efficient while rationalizing failures in task implementation. Later research, particularly numerous in an academic setting, supported earlier findings (Hall et al., 2019; Hen & Goroshit, 2014; Klassen et al., 2010; Klassen et al., 2008). Limited evidence suggests an indirect relationship between self-efficacy and academic procrastination through self-esteem (Hajloo, 2014). This indicates that low self-efficacy leads to decreased self-esteem, resulting in a greater tendency to procrastinate. In this way, students protect their image by justifying low performance and poor academic achievement. Furthermore, self-efficacy can affect procrastination by reducing self-control (Liu et al., 2020). Self-efficacy and procrastination mutually reinforce each other, creating a vicious cycle (Wäschle et al., 2014). Students who heavily procrastinate tend to rate their goal achievement poorly, which in turn reinforces their tendency to delay goal pursuit. Additionally, self-efficacy mediates the impact of perceived goal achievement on academic procrastination. Therefore, students with low self-efficacy may find themselves in a cycle of procrastination.

Locus of Control: Locus of control is a personality trait that describes a person's tendency to attribute responsibility for events either to themselves – individuals with an internal locus of control, or external forces – individuals with an external locus of control (Rotter, 1966). Individuals with an internal locus of control (internals), also known as intra-directed, believe that the outcomes of their actions lie within their control, and are based on their effort or abilities. Individuals with an external locus of control (also known as externals) maintain the belief that external factors, such as luck, fate, and other people, ultimately determine the course of events. Internals usually initiate tasks more quickly and finish in less time as opposed to externals. Numerous studies have demonstrated a moderate association between external locus of control and academic procrastination (Choy & Cheung, 2018; Hen & Goroshit, 2014; Siah et al., 2021). Externals exhibit a greater tendency to procrastinate than internals. Thus, the tendency to attribute success to external and unstable factors, which align with the external locus of control pattern, can trigger high procrastination. There are studies indicating a nonsignificant relationship between locus of control and procrastination (e.g. Boysan & Kiral, 2017; Hen & Goroshit, 2014; Pearlman-Avnion & Harduf, 2019). Students with a higher tendency to delay were less likely to perceive internal sources of control and less satisfied with their academic task performance (Brownlow & Reasinger, 2000). Moreover, Lonergan and Maher (2000) found that the locus of control moderated the association between task autonomy and procrastination in work-related assignments.

Impulsiveness: Impulsiveness is conceptualized as a trait and a behavioral or cognitive tendency to rapid, unplanned responses to external and internal stimuli without considering the potential negative consequences of these actions.

It is also characterized by a propensity for risk-taking, unplanned actions, and quick decision-making (Evenden, 1999). Behavioral impulsiveness refers to a tendency to automatically react to stimuli and an inability to inhibit responses. This includes a wide range of immature, dangerous, and situationally inappropriate behaviors that are executed without forethought, often leading to negative consequences. In addition, impulsive individuals lack self-control and the ability to delay gratification. A meta-analysis (Steel, 2007) found a strong correlation between impulsiveness and procrastination ($\bar{r} = 0.41$, $K = 22$). According to Ferrari's (1993) research, procrastination is linked to dysfunctional impulsivity, characterized by high speed and many errors, but not to functional impulsivity, which is characterized by high speed and few errors. Procrastinators tend to delay task completion until the last minute but then act impulsively and hastily, resulting in decreased performance and increased errors. In this scenario, procrastinators may attribute their task failures to external circumstances (e.g. limited time) rather than their abilities.

Whiteside and Lynam (2001) identified different aspects of impulsivity, including persistence, which is the ability to start and concentrate on a task until it is finished; premeditation, which is the ability to anticipate the consequences of one's actions in advance; sensation seeking, which refers to the willingness to engage in new activities; and urgency, which is the tendency to act quickly when experiencing negative emotions. According to Rebetez et al. (2018) and Wypych et al. (2018), the persistence component has a negative correlation with the general tendency to procrastinate, while urgency has a positive correlation with procrastination. This suggests a potential correlation between persistence and the ability to stop irrelevant thoughts and avoid procrastination. Procrastination is positively associated with dimensions of behavioral impulsivity, such as inhibition deficits (Gustavson et al., 2014; Rebetez et al., 2016), less accurate error processing (Michałowski et al., 2017), and lack of persistence (Wypych et al., 2018). There is evidence for a high genetic correlation between impulsiveness and procrastination (Gustavson et al., 2014), indicating that these constructs overlap and share neurobiological mechanisms. This may suggest that procrastination is an evolutionary by-product of impulsivity (Liu & Feng, 2017). Procrastination and impulsivity may be viewed as two interrelated aspects of the same construct (Ainslie, 2010; Ferrari, 1993). It extends our understanding of procrastination as the tendency to make impulsive decisions to delay personal costs when action is postponed, prioritizing immediate consequences over delayed rewards. This results in the task being postponed until the last minute.

Self-control: Self-control is defined as the ability to manage one's thoughts, emotions, and behaviors by delaying immediate gratification for a better outcome in the future (Mischel et al., 1996), and it is closely related to impulsivity. High self-control enables individuals to delay immediate gratification in favor of achieving long-term rewards, which has many positive consequences, such as improved performance outcomes and more effective achievement of long-term goals. Individuals with low self-control tend to be highly impulsive, react immediately to stimuli, and prefer simple tasks that offer immediate pleasure. Furthermore, they exhibit less perseverance, lower diligence, and a greater inclination toward adventures and hazardous situations. Lower self-control is associated with lower achievement and problematic and dysfunctional behavior, including task procrastination (Ferrari & Emmons, 1995; Zhao et al., 2021). Meta-analyses of predictors of procrastination (Ferrari, 2010; Steel, 2007; van Eerde, 2003a) indicate that self-control is relatively strongly associated with low procrastination ($\bar{r} = -0.58$). The latest research confirmed these relationships (Ariely & Wertenbroch, 2002; Ferrari & Emmons, 1995; Ferrari, 1993; Sümer & Büttner, 2022; Zhao et al., 2021). Furthermore, low self-control was an important factor in predicting academic procrastination (e.g. Gao et al., 2021; Kim et al., 2017; Zhao et al., 2021). There is increasing evidence that self-control plays a mediating role between various subjective (proximal) characteristics and procrastination. For instance, research has shown that individuals with higher trait anxiety tend to procrastinate more due to low self-control (Zhang et al., 2020). Similarly, higher impulsiveness has been found to be associated with procrastination through low self-control (Zhang & Feng, 2018). Self-control is a key factor in understanding procrastination, as it requires choosing between immediate and long-term tasks or actions. Individuals with low self-control tend to prioritize specific and current tasks while postponing the execution of more abstract and distant tasks (Ferrari et al., 1995). This could stem from a lack of motivation and low expectations of success, which can lead to increased procrastination. Research confirmed that individuals who engage in procrastination tend to favor immediate rewards over delayed gratification (Steel et al., 2021; Wu et al., 2016). In addition, these individuals are easily influenced by pleasant impulses and distractions, which make task completion difficult and promotes procrastination.

Dark Triad: Dark triad is a composition of three negative personality traits, such as narcissism, psychopathy, and Machiavellianism. A meta-analysis by Meng et al. (2024) found that negative personality traits were positively related to procrastination. Machiavellianism is characterized by cynical, pragmatic, misanthropic, and immoral beliefs, emotional detachment, self-centered motives, strategic planning, manipulation, and deception. Narcissism involves an inflated self-view, fantasies of control and admiration, and a desire for validation from others. Psychopathy is characterized by charming behavior, shallow emotions, and parasitic lifestyles and may involve criminal activities. These traits may determine the tendency to procrastinate, probably to fulfill personal needs, achieve benefits, or protect their own positive self-image at the expense of other people and their well-being.

1.3.3 Emotional Factors

Procrastination has a negative influence on overall well-being and can cause negative emotions such as anxiety, stress, fatigue, and depression. However, there is also evidence of a positive relationship between procrastination and these emotions.

Stress: Procrastination is generally viewed as a dysfunctional response to negative emotions that arise in specific situations. Under stress, people may be inclined to delay completing tasks and fulfilling obligations that they perceive could cause additional stress. Tasks are usually evaluated according to personal benefits *versus* costs. Perceiving reality negatively and interpreting situations as stressful or unpleasant are often linked to negative emotions (Lazarus & Folkman, 1986). Procrastination is commonly viewed as the avoidance of arduous tasks that are aversive, frustrating, or anxiety-inducing, boring, difficult, require high effort, and lack structure or meaning (Ferrari & Tice, 2000; Milgram et al., 1988; Senécal et al., 1997). Individuals who experience negative moods may spend more time procrastinating. To reduce negative mood, they often postpone unpleasant tasks by engaging in more enjoyable, diverting, and appealing activities. This supports the hypothesis that procrastination is a form of short-term mood regulation that comes at the expense of long-term goals (Sirois, 2023). Procrastination may initially provide a temporary mood improvement, but in the long run, it can lead to a decline in mood. Emotional sources of procrastination may be based on a negative feedback loop that reinforces the reciprocal relationship between negative mood and procrastination (Pychyl & Sirois, 2016). According to Lindsley et al. (1995), this mechanism is associated with a downward spiral of depression. Low mood can enhance procrastination, which can then potentially induce negative emotions. Therefore, a negative mood may not only be a result but may also contribute to procrastination. The above considerations suggest that the relationship between negative mood and procrastination is driven by positive feedback, creating a cyclical connection in which the two factors reinforce each other. Discomfort, stress, or worry related to tasks can cause procrastination, which in turn can temporarily improve mood. However, the resulting time loss and failure to complete tasks can lead to increased stress and guilt, which are likely to be stronger than before the task delay. This mechanism seems to be more applicable to situational procrastination than a generalized and stable disposition to procrastinate. Sirois (2023) proposed a conceptual framework that suggests that stressful contexts increase vulnerability to procrastination by depleting coping resources and decreasing tolerance to stress and negative emotions. Individuals often cope with task-related stress by procrastinating as an avoidance-based strategy. This, in turn, induces intrapersonal appraisal processes such as ruminative thoughts, maladaptive coping, low self-compassion, and low mindfulness, thereby further increasing stress. This relationship between stress and procrastination can create a vicious cycle, amplifying further stress and procrastination.

Anxiety: The relationship between anxiety and procrastination has been widely studied. Research has consistently shown that trait anxiety characterized by maintaining a long-lasting anxious experience in the absence of stressors predicted procrastination (Ferrari et al., 1995; Feyzi Behnagh & Ferrari, 2022; Flett et al., 1995; Rahimi et al., 2023; Steel, 2007). Individuals who experience higher levels of anxiety are more likely to engage in procrastination behaviors. This relationship may be underpinned by the negative episodic perspective as a mental simulation of negative future events. Procrastination could be caused by negative episodic prospection as a cognitive bias characteristic of trait anxiety. Anxious individuals expecting negative future events were likely to experience excessive task aversiveness and then exhibit more procrastination behaviors (Zhang et al., 2020). One potential explanation for the relationship between anxiety and procrastination is the use of avoidance coping mechanisms. When individuals feel anxious, they may become overwhelmed by their tasks and worry that they will not meet expectations or that their work will not be satisfactory. As a result, they may be more inclined to avoid starting or finishing tasks. Tice and Baumeister (2018) observed that individuals who experience anxiety tend to procrastinate more due to the negative emotions associated with the task, which further intensifies their anxiety. Procrastination is often used as a maladaptive coping mechanism to deal with anxiety. Individuals may postpone tasks in an attempt to temporarily alleviate their anxiety, but this can ultimately result in increased stress and anxiety, perpetuating the cycle of procrastination (Pychyl & Sirois, 2016). This mechanism is based on the anticipation of negative consequences associated with delayed tasks, which, in turn, increases anxiety and leads to further procrastination. Moreover, the effect of anxiety on the tendency to procrastinate is moderated by other variables. For instance, Barel et al. (2023) found that a low testosterone level amplified the effect of state anxiety on procrastination, while at a high level, this association was nonsignificant. However, an experimental study (Xu et al., 2016) showed the effect of a high-anxiety state on reduced actual procrastination. Probably, individuals do not procrastinate to alleviate their anxiety. As researchers suggested, anxiety motivates people to increase efforts to carry out actions that reduce a threat and advance a task, thus reducing procrastination. These findings are in line with self-regulation theory (Carver & Scheier, 2008; Tice et al., 2001), which assumes that negative emotions motivate people to increase their effort toward reaching a goal and take proactive behaviors for the most important task, thus reducing procrastination.

Fears of Failure, Incompetence, or Negative Evaluation: There is ample evidence that specific fears, such as fear of failure, negative evaluation, or incompetence during task performance, can act as emotional antecedents of procrastination. Relationships between these fears and academic procrastination are well explained by research. Fear of failure refers to the inclination to feel anxious when faced with situations where failure is a possibility (Baumeister

& Heatherton, 1996). This fear often leads individuals to perceive threats and develop irrational beliefs about the consequences of not achieving their goals. For example, they might worry about being viewed as incompetent or receiving criticism from others. Consequently, they may feel pressured to attain exceptionally high levels of ability and success to validate their self-worth. It's widely acknowledged that anxiety, stemming from the fear of failure, is a common emotional trigger for procrastination. According to research by Solomon and Rothblum (1984), fear of failure accounted for 49.4% of the variance in academic procrastination. Other studies have also found moderate positive relationships between fear of failure and procrastination (Ferrari et al., 1995; Haghbin et al., 2012; Rebetez et al., 2018; Steel, 2007; van Eerde, 2003a). Individuals who are afraid of failure often seek a logical explanation for their expected failure and, as a result, avoid or procrastinate on tasks. As a consequence, they hold onto the belief that they can complete the task successfully and have not failed. Procrastination can also arise when individuals are afraid of receiving negative feedback from others (cf. Ferrari et al., 1995), or when they feel incompetent while performing the task (Haghbin et al., 2012). Consequently, individuals with a significant fear of failure or negative evaluation are more prone to procrastinate. Thus, procrastination may become a maladaptive strategy for managing anxiety and protecting self-esteem.

However, other research found a nonsignificant relationship between fear of failure and procrastination (Fee & Tangney, 2000; Ferrari, 2001; Schouwenburg, 1992). This suggests that the relationship may be more complex and involve other variables that strengthen or weaken the effect. For example, Haghbin et al. (2012) found that the relationship between fear of failure and procrastination was mediated by autonomy and moderated by perceived competence. The impact of fear of failure on procrastination is also mediated by the need for autonomy, particularly when individuals perceive a high sense of competence. Those who perceive themselves as highly competent experience less procrastination when they have a strong fear of failure, which motivates them to achieve optimal results. Procrastination can also arise from a fear of success, as procrastinators may paradoxically fear both failure and success (Burka & Yuen, 2008). After attaining success, these individuals may struggle to enjoy it due to a mismatch between their self-image and their competencies or because they do not recognize it as success. Nevertheless, this relationship deserves further exploration.

Boredom: An important factor that triggers procrastination behavior is boredom, which an individual experiences as a result of insufficient stimulation from the environment, attention deficits, or low importance of undertaken activities (Elpidorou, 2018). Boredom is conceptualized as a state and as a trait. Individuals who are more susceptible to boredom tend to experience it more frequently, with greater intensity and perceive their lives as more monotonous. Chronic experiences of boredom have been linked to various problematic behaviors and mental health issues. Boredom proneness is related to avoidant procrastination (Blunt & Pychyl, 2000, 2005; Ferrari, 1992, 2000), decisional, and arousal procrastination (Blunt & Pychyl, 2000, 2005). The longitudinal study supported that boredom is a determining factor in procrastination (Rahimi et al., 2023). Individuals who are more prone to boredom perceive even the most mundane tasks as requiring effort and tend to procrastinate more. They also incorrectly estimate the time required to complete a task. However, individuals may experience boredom proneness in certain situations, such as monotonous or uninteresting tasks, which can lead to procrastination (Feyzi Behnagh & Ferrari, 2022).

Recent research displayed more inconsistent findings on the relationship between procrastination and multidimensional boredom, including internal and external factors (Vodanovich & Rupp, 1999). Internal stimulation is crucial to maintaining motivation, while external stimulation satisfies the ongoing need for change and variety in life. Therefore, procrastination may be related to each of these variables. High external stimulation was related to arousal procrastination (Ferrari, 2000; Sederlund et al., 2020). Procrastinators intentionally delay tasks in search of stimulating experiences, putting them off until the last minute, hoping to achieve a rush or high upon completion (Ferrari et al., 1995; Ferrari & Pychyl, 2000). This tendency seems to be a motivator for procrastination to avoid boredom. It is a means of escaping a mundane task by introducing an exciting or challenging element. Furthermore, avoidant procrastination was negatively associated with internal stimulation, while positively associated with external stimulation. Arousal-based procrastination and the desire for external stimulation have similarities. Individuals with both tendencies struggle with self-control and exhibit impulsive behavior. Moreover, both traits are related to tedious surroundings and require various stimuli or challenges to motivate engagement in a particular task (Sederlund et al., 2020).

Frustration: Few studies have examined the relationship between frustration and procrastination. Frustration is defined as the unpleasant feeling that arises from the failure to achieve a goal or satisfy a need. It is a combination of disappointment, irritation, and stress caused by the collision of expectations with an uncompromising reality (Jeronimus & Laceulle, 2020). Low frustration tolerance frequently occurs in situations of stress, fatigue, or novelty when individuals are unwilling or unable to endure current discomfort for future benefits. This can result in anger, annoyance, depression, or self-destructive actions. According to Ellis and Knaus (1977), low frustration tolerance is associated with procrastination. Low frustration tolerance due to the inability or unwillingness to endure present pain for future gains may promote self-destructive behavior. In the face of boredom and frustration, task completion is difficult and requires a degree of self-control and emotion regulation. Therefore, frustration is often regulated by engaging in distracting activities such as watching task-irrelevant videos and playing video games (Blunt & Pychyl, 2000). Harrington (2005) investigated the correlation between procrastination and subdimensions of frustration intolerance, namely discomfort intolerance, emotional intolerance, achievement frustration, and entitlement. The findings indicate that discomfort intolerance serves as a substantial predictor of frequent and problematic procrastination behaviors, while emotional intolerance serves as a distinctive predictor of low procrastination frequency among students. A different study revealed positive links between four dimensions of frustration intolerance and academic procrastination (Sudler, 2014). Furthermore, frustration intolerance served as a mediator in the correlation between perfectionism and academic procrastination. These findings suggest that the impact of frustration on procrastination is not yet fully understood and requires further examination. In summary, negative emotions are an important source of procrastination, as they seem to provide a way of improving negative mood. Procrastination can therefore be viewed as a maladaptive strategy to regulate negative emotions aimed at avoiding or reducing negative mood or stress. Empirical evidence suggests that there are reciprocal relationships between emotional sources and the consequences of procrastination, perpetuating a vicious cycle of procrastination through negative affect (Pychyl & Sirois, 2016).

1.3.4 Task Characteristics

The situational approach to procrastination focuses on external factors that can contribute to procrastination. As researchers have suggested, procrastination depends not only on dispositional characteristics but also on the specific nature of the activity or task. Therefore, much attention has been paid to the characteristics of tasks and activities as potential predictors of procrastination. The most frequently cited external factor contributing to procrastination is task aversiveness, which reflects how unpleasant or pleasant the task is to perform.

Aversiveness: Task aversiveness, which is the reluctance to complete a task, has been identified as a major factor that triggers procrastination behavior (e.g. Blunt & Pychyl, 2000; Huang & Golman, 2019; Milgram et al., 1995; van Eerde, 2000). Aversiveness is a reaction to task features rather than an inherent task attribute. Aversion to a task can result not only from the task itself but also from the individual's perception of its aversiveness. Expanding the definition of task aversiveness from a sole dimension of pleasant vs. unpleasant to a multidimensional construct that encompasses uncertainty and boredom as variables for assessing task performance is justified.

In general, individuals tend to delay doing tasks that evoke unpleasant feelings. This is because they have a preference for avoiding unpleasant experiences and a disposition toward flexibility, which can lead to an increased tendency to procrastinate when faced with unpleasant tasks. Early research by Milgram et al. (1988) revealed that aversion to academic tasks was strongly correlated with procrastination ($r = 0.58$), explaining 33% of the variance in procrastination. In another study, students rated their level of procrastination on pleasant, unpleasant, or neutral academic tasks. Of the three types of tasks, participants reported greater procrastination in unpleasant tasks compared to neutral or pleasant tasks (Milgram et al., 1995). A meta-analysis of research conducted by Steel (2007) showed that the relationship between task aversiveness and procrastination is strong. This finding was supported by experimental research with a more rigorous methodology, although the effect of task aversiveness on procrastination was weak (Huang & Golman, 2019). Tasks are perceived as aversive when they are unstimulating, boring, unpleasant, difficult, frustrating, unimportant, lack sense or structure, or are imposed (Blunt & Pychyl, 2000; Lay, 1992; McCown et al., 1989; Milgram et al., 1995; Steel, 2007). Blunt and Pychyl (2000) revealed that boredom, frustration, and anger represent relatively stable components of task aversion, as well as a significant correlation between task aversion and procrastination during the action phase. Task aversiveness is thus probably a predictor of task avoidance rather than task delay. Consequently, procrastination can be influenced by the aversiveness toward tasks, but also the value of outcomes. Individuals decide to procrastinate when expecting a higher outcome value, but perceive the task as less unpleasant to do later than immediately (Zhang & Feng, 2020; Zhang et al., 2021). These results suggest that both factors should be taken into account when addressing procrastination. Pychyl et al. (2000) showed in a qualitative study that students tended to procrastinate on tasks and activities that they believed were more difficult, confusing, stressful, or important than the ones currently being performed. Three separate studies conducted by Lay (1992) demonstrated that procrastination is associated with person-task factors, such as task aversiveness, perceived incompetence, and lack of autonomy in their implementation. Individuals tend to delay completing tasks that are deemed more challenging, unpleasant, or assigned by others. Procrastinators frequently anticipate having insufficient time to prepare for exams, possess less confidence in their abilities, and perceive themselves as having less autonomy than nonprocrastinators. Consequently, monotonous and repetitive tasks, coupled with a lack of challenge and variety, can trigger procrastination (Ferrari et al., 1995).

Task Ambiguity: Task ambiguity can be a significant factor in task avoidance or procrastination. Task ambiguity arises from a lack of information about the task and can result in uncertainty. Three common sources of task ambiguity include uncertainty around how to complete a task, the temporal sequencing of activities, and performance standards (Breaugh & Colihan, 1994). However, task ambiguity has been associated with various negative outcomes, including increased stress, anxiety, decreased job performance, and procrastination. A study conducted among faculty members and students (Ackerman & Gross, 2005, 2007) has found that procrastination was related to the perception of task ambiguity in terms of what was required to perform and how to proceed. Both cross-sectional and experimental studies indicated that state procrastination is a consequence of ambiguous tasks, particularly when there is missing information about how to complete a task and in what sequence to complete it (Hoppe et al., 2018).

Deadlines and Time Pressure: Procrastination could be determined by deadlines and time pressure during task performance (Schraw et al., 2007). Setting a deadline for completing a task may affect the likelihood of completing it on time. When a task deadline is far-off, individuals perceive it as less pressing, and consequently delay its completion (Steel, 2007). However, procrastination decreases as the deadline for task completion is shorter (Knowles et al., 2022). When the deadline for task completion is close, the probability of procrastinating is low. Research results indicated that students spent more time on an assignment when the deadline was close, and the number of submissions increased violently just before the deadline, resembling a hyperbolic curve (Dewitte & Schouwenburg, 2002; Howell et al., 2006).

Task completion under time pressure promotes appraising this task as more challenging (Prem et al., 2018) and facilitates the initiation of action. Short deadlines are associated with time pressure, which signals a discrepancy between the task-related goal and the current performance. Time pressure increases focus and aids in its completion. It may prompt people to initiate action or invest extra effort (Carver & Scheier, 2008). It suggests that procrastinators tend to work more intensively at the last minute before a deadline, whereas task completion without set deadlines may be delayed indefinitely (Steel et al., 2021). Research suggests that procrastination is positively associated with aversion to tasks with short or no deadlines and negatively associated with tasks under time pressure (Kühnel et al., 2022). Researchers emphasized the impact of deadlines on procrastination within the context of the intention–action gap. The farther the time between the initiation or delegation of a task and the due date for its completion, the higher the probability that unforeseen events hinder the link between intention and execution. However, as the deadline draws near, this discrepancy between intention and action diminishes (Steel et al., 2001; Van Hooft et al., 2005). This was confirmed by a meta-analysis of six studies, indicating a moderate correlation between intentions and performance that reflects short periods of procrastination in task completion (Steel, 2007).

Regulating task efficiency and reducing procrastination can be achieved by imposing deadlines on oneself or others. According to research by Ariely and Wertenbroch (2002), self-imposed deadlines can actually impede performance and increase the tendency to procrastinate, more so than externally imposed deadlines. Procrastination in submitting three academic assignments was less prevalent when deadlines were externally imposed and evenly spaced, followed by self-imposed deadlines, with the poorest performance seen with a single deadline. Individuals with self-control issues set deadlines for themselves to manage procrastination, but this is not as effective as externally imposed deadlines. These findings suggest that implementing evenly distributed deadlines can weaken procrastination behavior. Individuals who procrastinate tend to delay completing tasks that they find aversive, such as those that are dull, arduous, unimportant, frustrating, stressful, or mandated by others. Procrastination can be influenced by task characteristics, circumstances, and subjective factors. When developing strategies to address problematic procrastination behaviors, it is important to focus on more than just improving an individual's self-regulatory abilities. It is also crucial to reduce the emphasis on aversive task attributes and ensure that assigned tasks are perceived as less burdensome. This can be achieved by making tasks more engaging or less challenging and setting appropriate deadlines.

The characteristics of tasks and external circumstances, together with subjective factors, can augment or diminish procrastination behavior. Therefore, when devising effective prevention and intervention strategies for problematic procrastination behaviors, it is essential to de-emphasize aversive task attributes and not solely concentrate on enhancing the self-regulatory abilities of the individual. The assigned tasks should be perceived as less burdensome, either as more engaging or less challenging and should have appropriately timed deadlines.

References

Ackerman, D. S., & Gross, B. L. (2005). My instructor made me do it: Task characteristics of procrastination. *Journal of Marketing Education, 27*(1), 5–13. https://doi.org/10.1177/0273475304273842

Ackerman, D. S., & Gross, B. L. (2007). I can start that JME manuscript next week, can't I? The task characteristics behind why faculty procrastinate. *Journal of Marketing Education, 29*(2), 97–110. https://doi.org/10.1177/0273475307302012

Ainslie, G. (2010). Procrastination, the basic impulse. In C. Andreou & M. White (Eds.), *The thief of time: Philosophical essays on procrastination* (pp. 11–27). Oxford University Press.

Ainslie, G., & Haslam, N. (1992). Hyperbolic discounting. In G. Loewenstein & J. Elster (Eds.), *Choice over time* (pp. 57–92). Russell Sage Foundation.

Ajzen, I. (1991). The theory of planned behavior. *Organizational Behavior and Human Decision Processes, 50*(2), 179–211. https://doi.org/10.1016/0749-5978(91)90020-T

Akerlof, G. A. (1991). Procrastination and obedience. *The American Economic Review, 81*, 1–19.

Ariely, D., & Wertenbroch, K. (2002). Procrastination, deadlines, and performance: Self-control by precommitment. *Psychological Science, 13*(3), 219–224. https://doi.org/10.1111/1467-9280.00441

Balkis, M. (2013). Academic procrastination, academic life satisfaction and academic achievement: the mediation role of rational beliefs about studying. *Journal of Cognitive and Behavioral Psychotherapies, 13*(1), 57–74.

Balkis, M., & Duru, E. (2016). Procrastination, self-regulation failure, academic life satisfaction, and affective well-being: Underregulation or misregulation form. *European Journal of Psychology of Education, 31*(3), 439–459. https://doi.org/10.1007/s10212-015-0266-5

Balkıs, M., & Duru, E. (2017). Gender differences in the relationship between academic procrastination, satifaction with academic life and academic performance. *Electronic Journal of Research in Educational Psychology, 15*(1), 105–125. https://doi.org/10.14204/ejrep.41.16042

Bandura, A. (1997). *Self-efficacy: The exercise of control.* Freeman.

Barboza, G. (2018). I will pay tomorrow, or maybe the day after. Credit card repayment, present biased and procrastination. *Economic Notes, 47*(2–3), 455–494. https://doi.org/10.1111/ecno.12106

Barel, E., Shahrabani, S., Mahagna, L., Massalha, R., Colodner, R., & Tzischinsky, O. (2023). State anxiety and procrastination: The moderating role of neuroendocrine factors. *Behavioral Sciences, 13*(3), 204. https://doi.org/10.3390/bs13030204

Barutçu Yıldırım, F., & Demir, A. (2020). Self-handicapping among university students: The role of procrastination, test anxiety, self-esteem, and self-compassion. *Psychological Reports, 123*(3), 825–843. https://doi.org/10.1177/0033294118825099

Batool, S. S. (2020). Academic achievement: Interplay of positive parenting, self-esteem, and academic procrastination. *Australian Journal of Psychology, 72*(2), 174–187. https://doi.org/10.1111/ajpy.12280

Bäulke, L., Daumiller, M., & Dresel, M. (2021). The role of state and trait motivational regulation for procrastinatory behavior in academic contexts: Insights from two diary studies. *Contemporary Educational Psychology, 65*, 101951. https://doi.org/10.1016/j.cedpsych.2021.101951

Baumeister, R. F., & Heatherton, T. (1996). Self-regulation failure: An overview. *Psychological Inquiry, 7*(1), 1–15. https://doi.org/10.1207/s15327965pli0701_1

Baumeister, R. F., Tice, D. M., & Vohs, K. D. (2018). The strength model of self-regulation: Conclusions from the second decade of willpower research. *Perspectives on Psychological Science, 13*(2), 141–145. https://doi.org/10.1177/1745691617716946

Bennett, C., & Bacon, A. M. (2019). At long last – A reinforcement sensitivity theory explanation of procrastination. *Journal of Individual Differences, 40*(4), 234–241. https://doi.org/10.1027/1614-0001/a000296

Beutel, M. E., Klein, E. M., Aufenanger, S., Brähler, E., Dreier, M., Müller, K. W., Quiring, O., Reinecke, L., Schmutzer, G., Stark, B., & Wölfling, K. (2016). Procrastination, distress and life satisfaction across the age range - A German representative community study. *PLoS One, 11*(2), e0148054. https://doi.org/10.1371/journal.pone.0148054

Blunt, A. K., & Pychyl, T. A. (2000). Task aversiveness and procrastination: A multi-dimensional approach to task aversiveness across stages of personal projects. *Personality and Individual Differences, 28*(1), 153–167. https://doi.org/10.1016/S0191-8869(99)00091-4

Blunt, A. K., & Pychyl, T. A. (2005). Project systems of procrastinators: A personal project-analytic and action control perspective. *Personality and Individual Differences, 38*(8), 1771–1780. https://doi.org/10.1016/j.paid.2004.11.019

Börsch-Supan, A., Bucher-Koenen, T., Hurd, M. D., & Rohwedder, S. (2023). Saving regret and procrastination. *Journal of Economic Psychology, 94*, 102577. https://doi.org/10.1016/j.joep.2022.102577

Boysan, M., & Kiral, E. (2017). Associations between procrastination, personality, perfectionism, self-esteem and locus of control. *British Journal of Guidance & Counselling, 45*(3), 284–296. https://doi.org/10.1080/03069885.2016.1213374

Breaugh, J. A., & Colihan, J. P. (1994). Measuring facets of job ambiguity: Construct validity evidence. *Journal of Applied Psychology, 79*(2), 191–202. https://doi.org/10.1037/0021-9010.79.2.191

Brownlow, S., & Reasinger, R. D. (2000). Putting off until tomorrow what is better done today: Academic procrastination as a function of motivation toward college work. *Journal of Social Behavior & Personality, 15*(5), 15–34.

Burka, J. B., & Yuen, L. M. (2008). *Procrastination: Why you do it, what to do about it now.* Hachette Books.

Carver, C. S., & Scheier, M. F. (2008). *On the self-regulation of behavior* (Transferred to digital pr). Cambridge University Press. https://doi.org/10.1017/CBO9781139174794

Chauhan, R. S., MacDougall, A. E., Buckley, M. R., Howe, D. C., Crisostomo, M. E., & Zeni, T. (2020). Better late than early? Reviewing procrastination in organizations. *Management Research Review, 43*(10), 1289–1308. https://doi.org/10.1108/mrr-09-2019-0413

Chen, B.-B., Shi, Z., & Wang, Y. (2016). Do peers matter? Resistance to peer influence as a mediator between self-esteem and procrastination among undergraduates. *Frontiers in Psychology, 7*, 1529. https://doi.org/10.3389/fpsyg.2016.01529

Choi, J. N., & Moran, S. V. (2009). Why not procrastinate? Development and validation of a new active procrastination scale. *The Journal of Social Psychology, 149*(2), 195–211. https://doi.org/10.3200/SOCP.149.2.195-212

Chowdhury, S. F., & Pychyl, T. A. (2018). A critique of the construct validity of active procrastination. *Personality and Individual Differences, 120*, 7–12. https://doi.org/10.1016/j.paid.2017.08.016

Choy, E. E. H., & Cheung, H. (2018). Time perspective, control, and affect mediate the relation between regulatory mode and procrastination. *PLoS One, 13*(12), e0207912. https://doi.org/10.1371/journal.pone.0207912

Chu, A. H. C., & Choi, J. N. (2005). Rethinking procrastination: Positive effects of "active" procrastination behavior on attitudes and performance. *The Journal of Social Psychology, 145*(3), 245–264. https://doi.org/10.3200/SOCP.145.3.245-264

Claessens, B. J., van Eerde, W., Rutte, C. G., & Roe, R. A. (2007). A review of the time management literature. *Personnel Review, 36*(2), 255–276. https://doi.org/10.1108/00483480710726136

Corkin, D. M., Yu, S. L., & Lindt, S. F. (2011). Comparing active delay and procrastination from a self-regulated learning perspective. *Learning and Individual Differences, 21*(5), 602–606. https://doi.org/10.1016/j.lindif.2011.07.005

Cormack, S. H., Eagle, L. A., & Davies, M. S. (2020). A large-scale test of the relationship between procrastination and performance using learning analytics. *Assessment & Evaluation in Higher Education, 45*(7), 1–14. https://doi.org/10.1080/02602938.2019.1705244

D'Abate, C. P., & Eddy, E. R. (2007). Engaging in personal business on the job: Extending the presenteeism construct. *Human Resource Development Quarterly, 18*(3), 361–383. https://doi.org/10.1002/hrdq.1209

Dewitte, S., & Schouwenburg, H. C. (2002). Procrastination, temptations, and incentives: The struggle between the present and the future in procrastinators and the punctual. *European Journal of Personality, 16*(6), 469–489. https://doi.org/10.1002/per.461

Díaz-Morales, J. F., Ferrari, J. R., & Cohen, J. R. (2008). Indecision and avoidant procrastination: The role of morningness-eveningness and time perspective in chronic delay lifestyles. *The Journal of General Psychology, 135*(3), 228–240. https://doi.org/10.3200/GENP.135.3.228-240

Dollard, J., & Miller, N. E. (1950). *Personality and psychotherapy; An analysis in terms of learning, thinking, and culture.* McGraw-Hill.

Duru, E., & Balkis, M. (2017). Procrastination, self-esteem, academic performance, and well-being: A moderated mediation model. *International Journal of Educational Psychology, 6*(2), 97. https://doi.org/10.17583/ijep.2017.2584

Duru, E., Balkis, M., & Duru, S. (2023). Procrastination among adults: The role of self-doubt, fear of the negative evaluation, and irrational/rational beliefs. *Journal of Evidence-Based Psychotherapies, 23*(2), 79–97. https://doi.org/10.24193/jebp.2023.2.11

Ellis, A., & Knaus, W. (1977). *Overcoming procrastination: Or how to think and act rationally in spite of life's inevitable hassles.* Institute for Rational Living.

Elpidorou, A. (2018). The bored mind is a guiding mind: Toward a regulatory theory of boredom. *Phenomenology and the Cognitive Sciences, 17*(3), 455–484. https://doi.org/10.1007/s11097-017-9515-1

Evenden, J. L. (1999). Varieties of impulsivity. *Psychopharmacology, 146*(4), 348–361. https://doi.org/10.1007/PL00005481

Fee, R. L., & Tangney, J. P. (2000). Procrastination: A means of avoiding shame or guilt? *Journal of Social Behavior & Personality, 15*(5), 167–184.

Fernie, B. A., Bharucha, Z., Nikčević, A. V., Marino, C., & Spada, M. M. (2017). A metacognitive model of procrastination. *Journal of Affective Disorders, 210*, 196–203. https://doi.org/10.1016/j.jad.2016.12.042

Fernie, B. A., Kopar, U. Y., Fisher, P. L., & Spada, M. M. (2018). Further development and testing of the metacognitive model of procrastination: Self-reported academic performance. *Journal of Affective Disorders, 240*, 1–5. https://doi.org/10.1016/j.jad.2018.07.018

Ferrari, J. R. (1991a). A second look at behavioral self-handicapping among women. *Journal of Social Behavior & Personality, 6*(2), 195–206.

Ferrari, J. R. (1991b). Self-handicapping by procrastinators: Protecting self-esteem, social-esteem, or both? *Journal of Research in Personality, 25*(3), 245–261. https://doi.org/10.1016/0092-6566(91)90018-L

Ferrari, J. R. (1992). Psychometric validation of two Procrastination inventories for adults: Arousal and avoidance measures. *Journal of Psychopathology and Behavioral Assessment, 14*(2), 97–110. https://doi.org/10.1007/BF00965170

Ferrari, J. R. (1993). Procrastination and impulsiveness: Two sides of a coin? In W. G. MacCown (Ed.), *The impulsive client: Theory, research, and treatment* (1st ed., pp. 265–276). American Psychological Association. https://doi.org/10.1037/10500-014

Ferrari, J. R. (1994). Dysfunctional procrastination and its relationship with self-esteem, interpersonal dependency, and self-defeating behaviors. *Personality and Individual Differences, 17*(5), 673–679. https://doi.org/10.1016/0191-8869(94)90140-6

Ferrari, J. R. (2000). Procrastination and attention: Factor analysis of attention deficit, boredomness, intelligence, self-esteem, and task delay frequencies. *Journal of Social Behavior & Personality, 15*(5), 185–196.

Ferrari, J. R. (2001). Procrastination as self-regulation failure of performance: Effects of cognitive load, self-awareness, and time limits on 'working best under pressure'. *European Journal of Personality, 15*(5), 391–406. https://doi.org/10.1002/per.413

Ferrari, J. R. (2010). *Still procrastinating? The no-regrets guide to getting it done.* Wiley.

Ferrari, J. R., Barnes, K. L., & Steel, P. (2009a). Life regrets by avoidant and arousal procrastinators. *Journal of Individual Differences, 30*(3), 163–168. https://doi.org/10.1027/1614-0001.30.3.163

Ferrari, J. R., Díaz-Morales, J. F., O'Callaghan, J., Díaz, K., & Argumedo, D. (2007). Frequent behavioral delay tendencies by adults. *Journal of Cross-Cultural Psychology, 38*(4), 458–464. https://doi.org/10.1177/0022022107302314

Ferrari, J. R., Doroszko, E., & Joseph, N. (2005a). Exploring procrastination in corporate settings: Sex, status, and settings for arousal and avoidance types. *Individual Differences Research, 3*(2), 140–149.

Ferrari, J. R., & Dovidio, J. F. (2000). Examining behavioral processes in indecision: Decisional procrastination and decision-making style. *Journal of Research in Personality, 34*(1), 127–137. https://doi.org/10.1006/jrpe.1999.2247

Ferrari, J. R., & Emmons, R. A. (1995). Methods of procrastination and their relation to self-control and self-reinforcement: An exploratory study. *Journal of Social Behavior and Personality, 10*(1), 135–142.

Ferrari, J. R., Johnson, J. L., & McCown, W. G. (1995). *Procrastination and task avoidance: Theory, research, and treatment.* Springer Science & Business Media.

Ferrari, J. R., Mason, C. P., & Hammer, C. (2006). Procrastination as a predictor of task perceptions: Examining delayed and non-delayed tasks across varied deadlines. *Individual Differences Research, 4*(1), 28–36.

Ferrari, J. R., O'Callaghan, J., & Newbegin, I. (2005b). Prevalence of procrastination in the United States, United Kingdom, and Australia: Arousal and avoidance delays among adults. *North American Journal of Psychology, 7*(1), 1–6. https://psycnet.apa.org/record/2005-03779-001

Ferrari, J. R., Ozer, B. U., & Demir, A. (2009b). Chronic procrastination among Turkish adults: Exploring decisional, avoidant, and arousal styles. *The Journal of Social Psychology, 149*(3), 402–408. https://doi.org/10.3200/SOCP.149.3.402-408

Ferrari, J. R., & Patel, T. (2004). Social comparisons by procrastinators: Rating peers with similar or dissimilar delay tendencies. *Personality and Individual Differences, 37*(7), 1493–1501. https://doi.org/10.1016/j.paid.2004.02.006

Ferrari, J. R., & Pychyl, T. A. (2000). The scientific study of procrastination: Where have we been and where are we going? Foreword. *Journal of Social Behavior and Personality, 15*(5), 7–8.

Ferrari, J. R., & Pychyl, T. A. (2012). "If I wait, my partner will do it:" The role of conscientiousness as a mediator in the relation of academic procrastination and perceived social loafing. *North American Journal of Psychology, 14*(1), 13–24.

Ferrari, J. R., & Tibbett, T. P. (2020). Procrastination. In V. Zeigler-Hill & T. K. Shackelford (Eds.), *Encyclopedia of personality and individual differences* (1st ed., pp. 4046–4053). Springer. https://doi.org/10.1007/978-3-319-24612-3_2272

Ferrari, J. R., & Tice, D. M. (2000). Procrastination as a self-handicap for men and women: A task-avoidance strategy in a laboratory setting. *Journal of Research in Personality, 34*(1), 73–83. https://doi.org/10.1006/jrpe.1999.2261

Feyzi Behnagh, R., & Ferrari, J. R. (2022). Exploring 40 years on affective correlates to procrastination: A literature review of situational and dispositional types. *Current Psychology, 41*(2), 1097–1111. https://doi.org/10.1007/s12144-021-02653-z

Flett, G. L., Blankstein, K. R., & Martin, T. R. (1995). Procrastination, negative self-evaluation, and stress in depression and anxiety. In J. R. Ferrari, J. L. Johnson, & W. G. McCown (Eds.), *Procrastination and task avoidance* (pp. 137–167). Springer US. https://doi.org/10.1007/978-1-4899-0227-6_7

Flett, G. L., Stainton, M., Hewitt, P. L., Sherry, S. B., & Lay, C. (2012). Procrastination automatic thoughts as a personality construct: An analysis of the procrastinatory cognitions inventory. *Journal of Rational-Emotive & Cognitive-Behavior Therapy*, *30*(4), 223–236. https://doi.org/10.1007/s10942-012-0150-z

Frost, R. O., Marten, P., Lahart, C., & Rosenblate, R. (1990). The dimensions of perfectionism. *Cognitive Therapy and Research*, *14*(5), 449–468. https://doi.org/10.1007/BF01172967

Gamst-Klaussen, T., Steel, P., & Svartdal, F. (2019). Procrastination and personal finances: Exploring the roles of planning and financial self-efficacy. *Frontiers in Psychology*, *10*, 775. https://doi.org/10.3389/fpsyg.2019.00775

Gao, K., Zhang, R., Xu, T., Zhou, F., & Feng, T. (2021). The effect of conscientiousness on procrastination: The interaction between the self-control and motivation neural pathways. *Human Brain Mapping*, *42*(6), 1829–1844. https://doi.org/10.1002/hbm.25333

Gollwitzer, P. M. (1999). Implementation intentions: Strong effects of simple plans. *American Psychologist*, *54*(7), 493–503. https://doi.org/10.1037/0003-066X.54.7.493

Goroshit, M., Hen, M., & Ferrari, J. R. (2020). Life-Domain Regret Regarding Procrastination (LDR-P): Scale validation in the United States and Israel. *Current Psychology*, *39*(3), 900–912. https://doi.org/10.1007/s12144-018-9801-2

Grund, A., & Fries, S. (2018). Understanding procrastination: A motivational approach. *Personality and Individual Differences*, *121*, 120–130. https://doi.org/10.1016/j.paid.2017.09.035

Grunschel, C., Schwinger, M., Steinmayr, R., & Fries, S. (2016). Effects of using motivational regulation strategies on students' academic procrastination, academic performance, and well-being. *Learning and Individual Differences*, *49*, 162–170. https://doi.org/10.1016/j.lindif.2016.06.008

Gustavson, D. E., Miyake, A., Hewitt, J. K., & Friedman, N. P. (2014). Genetic relations among procrastination, impulsivity, and goal-management ability: Implications for the evolutionary origin of procrastination. *Psychological Science*, *25*(6), 1178–1188. https://doi.org/10.1177/0956797614526260

Haghbin, M., McCaffrey, A., & Pychyl, T. A. (2012). The complexity of the relation between fear of failure and procrastination. *Journal of Rational-Emotive & Cognitive-Behavior Therapy*, *30*(4), 249–263. https://doi.org/10.1007/s10942-012-0153-9

Haghbin, M., & Pychyl, T. A. (2016). Measurement of health-related procrastination: Development and validation of the exercise and healthy diet procrastination scales. In F. M. Sirois & T. A. Pychyl (Eds.), *Procrastination, health, and well-being* (pp. 121–142). Academic Press. https://doi.org/10.1016/B978-0-12-802862-9.00006-2

Hajloo, N. (2014). Relationships between self-efficacy, self-esteem and procrastination in undergraduate psychology students. *Iranian Journal of Psychiatry and Behavioral Sciences*, *8*(3), 42–49. https://pubmed.ncbi.nlm.nih.gov/25780374/

Hall, N. C., Lee, S. Y., & Rahimi, S. (2019). Self-efficacy, procrastination, and burnout in post-secondary faculty: An international longitudinal analysis. *PLoS One*, *14*(12), e0226716. https://doi.org/10.1371/journal.pone.0226716

Hammer, C. A., & Ferrari, J. R. (2002). Differential incidence of procrastination between blue and white-collar workers. *Current Psychology, 21*(4), 333–338. https://doi.org /10.1007/s12144-002-1022-y

Harrington, N. (2005). It's too difficult! Frustration intolerance beliefs and procrastination. *Personality and Individual Differences, 39*(5), 873–883. https://doi.org/10.1016/j .paid.2004.12.018

Hen, M., & Goroshit, M. (2014). Academic procrastination, emotional intelligence, academic self-efficacy, and GPA: A comparison between students with and without learning disabilities. *Journal of Learning Disabilities, 47*(2), 116–124. https://doi.org /10.1177/0022219412439325

Hen, M., & Goroshit, M. (2018). General and life-domain procrastination in highly educated adults in Israel. *Frontiers in Psychology, 9*, 1173. https://doi.org/10.3389/ fpsyg.2018.01173

Hewitt, P. L., & Flett, G. L. (1991). Perfectionism in the self and social contexts: Conceptualization, assessment, and association with psychopathology. *Journal of Personality and Social Psychology, 60*(3), 456–470. https://doi.org/10.1037//0022 -3514.60.3.456

Hill, V. M., Rebar, A. L., Ferguson, S. A., Shriane, A. E., & Vincent, G. E. (2022). Go to bed! A systematic review and meta-analysis of bedtime procrastination correlates and sleep outcomes. *Sleep Medicine Reviews, 66*, 101697. https://doi.org/10.1016/j .smrv.2022.101697

Hoppe, J., Preissler, B. I., & & Forster, K. (2018). A cross-lagged panel design on the causal relationship of task ambiguity and state procrastination: A preliminary investigation. *North American Journal of Psychology, 20*(2), 383–396.

Howell, A. J., & Watson, D. C. (2007). Procrastination: Associations with achievement goal orientation and learning strategies. *Personality and Individual Differences, 43*(1), 167–178. https://doi.org/10.1016/j.paid.2006.11.017

Howell, A. J., Watson, D. C., Powell, R. A., & Buro, K. (2006). Academic procrastination: The pattern and correlates of behavioural postponement. *Personality and Individual Differences, 40*(8), 1519–1530. https://doi.org/10.1016/j.paid.2005.11.023

Huang, J., & Golman, R. (2019). The influence of length of delay and task aversiveness on procrastination behaviors. *International Journal of Psychological Studies, 11*(4), 73. https://doi.org/10.5539/ijps.v11n4p73

Jackson, T., Weiss, K. E., Lundquist, J. J., & Hooper, D. (2003). The impact of hope, procrastination, and social activity on academic performance of midwestern college students. *Education, 124*, 310–321.

Janis, I. L., & Mann, L. (1977). *Decision making: A psychological analysis of conflict, choice, and commitment*. Free Press.

Jeronimus, B. F., & Laceulle, O. M. (2020). Frustration. In V. Zeigler-Hill & T. K. Shackelford (Eds.), *Encyclopedia of personality and individual differences* (pp. 1–5). Springer International Publishing. https://doi.org/10.1007/978-3-319-28099-8_815-1

Johnson, J. L., & Bloom, A. (1995). An analysis of the contribution of the five factors of personality to variance in academic procrastination. *Personality and Individual Differences, 18*(1), 127–133. https://doi.org/10.1016/0191-8869(94)00109-6

Keys, B. J., & Wang, J. (2019). Minimum payments and debt paydown in consumer credit cards. *Journal of Financial Economics, 131*(3), 528–548. https://doi.org/10 .1016/j.jfineco.2018.09.009

Kim, K. R., & Seo, E. H. (2015). The relationship between procrastination and academic performance: A meta-analysis. *Personality and Individual Differences, 82,* 26–33. https://doi.org/10.1016/j.paid.2015.02.038

Kim, S., Fernandez, S., & Terrier, L. (2017). Procrastination, personality traits, and academic performance: When active and passive procrastination tell a different story. *Personality and Individual Differences, 108,* 154–157. https://doi.org/10.1016/j.paid.2016.12.021

Klassen, R. M., Ang, R. P., Chong, W. H., Krawchuk, L. L., Huan, V. S., Wong, I. Y., & Yeo, L. S. (2010). Academic procrastination in two settings: Motivation correlates, behavioral patterns, and negative impact of procrastination in Canada and Singapore. *Applied Psychology, 59*(3), 361–379. https://doi.org/10.1111/j.1464-0597.2009.00394.x

Klassen, R. M., Krawchuk, L. L., & Rajani, S. (2008). Academic procrastination of undergraduates: Low self-efficacy to self-regulate predicts higher levels of procrastination. *Contemporary Educational Psychology, 33*(4), 915–931. https://doi.org/10.1016/j.cedpsych.2007.07.001

Klingsieck, K. B. (2013a). Procrastination in different life-domains: Is procrastination domain specific? *Current Psychology, 32*(2), 175–185. https://doi.org/10.1007/s12144-013-9171-8

Klingsieck, K. B. (2013b). Procrastination: When good things don't come to those who wait. *European Psychologist, 18*(1), 24–34. https://doi.org/10.1027/1016-9040/a000138

Knowles, S., Servátka, M., Sullivan, T., & Genç, M. (2022). Procrastination and the non-monotonic effect of deadlines on task completion. *Economic Inquiry, 60*(2), 706–720. https://doi.org/10.1111/ecin.13042

Kroese, F. M., Evers, C., Adriaanse, M. A., & de Ridder, D. T. D. (2016). Bedtime procrastination: A self-regulation perspective on sleep insufficiency in the general population. *Journal of Health Psychology, 21*(5), 853–862. https://doi.org/10.1177/1359105314540014

Kroese, F. M., & de Ridder, D. T. D. (2016). Health behaviour procrastination: A novel reasoned route towards self-regulatory failure. *Health Psychology Review, 10*(3), 313–325. https://doi.org/10.1080/17437199.2015.1116019

Kroese, F. M., de Ridder, D. T. D., Evers, C., & Adriaanse, M. A. (2014). Bedtime procrastination: Introducing a new area of procrastination. *Frontiers in Psychology, 5,* 611. https://doi.org/10.3389/fpsyg.2014.00611

Kühnel, J., Bledow, R., & Feuerhahn, N. (2016). When do you procrastinate? Sleep quality and social sleep lag jointly predict self-regulatory failure at work. *Journal of Organizational Behavior, 37*(7), 983–1002. https://doi.org/10.1002/job.2084

Kühnel, J., Bledow, R., & Kuonath, A. (2022). Overcoming procrastination: Time pressure and positive affect as compensatory routes to action. *Journal of Business and Psychology,* 1–17. https://doi.org/10.1007/s10869-022-09817-z

Kühnel, J., Sonnentag, S., Bledow, R., & Melchers, K. G. (2018). The relevance of sleep and circadian misalignment for procrastination among shift workers. *Journal of Occupational and Organizational Psychology, 91*(1), 110–133. https://doi.org/10.1111/joop.12191

Lay, C. H. (1986). At last, my research article on procrastination. *Journal of Research in Personality, 20*(4), 474–495. https://doi.org/10.1016/0092-6566(86)90127-3

Lay, C. H. (1990). Working to schedule on personal projects: An assessment of person-project characteristics and trait procrastination. *Journal of Social Behavior & Personality*, *5*(3), 91–103.

Lay, C. H. (1992). Trait procrastination and the perception of person-task characteristics. *Journal of Social Behavior & Personality*, *7*(3), 483–494.

Laybourn, S., Frenzel, A. C., & Fenzl, T. (2019). Teacher procrastination, emotions, and stress: A qualitative study. *Frontiers in Psychology*, *10*, 2325. https://doi.org/10.3389 /fpsyg.2019.02325

Lazarus, R. S., & Folkman, S. (1986). Cognitive theories of stress and the issue of circularity. In M. H. Appley & R. Trumbull (Eds.), *The Plenum series on stress and coping. Dynamics of stress: Physiological, psychological and social perspectives* (pp. 63–80). Springer US. https://doi.org/10.1007/978-1-4684-5122-1_4

Lindsley, D. H., Brass, D. J., & Thomas, J. B. (1995). Efficacy-performance spirals: A multilevel perspective. *The Academy of Management Review*, *20*(3), 645. https://doi .org/10.2307/258790

Liu, G., Cheng, G., Hu, J., Pan, Y., & Zhao, S. (2020). Academic self-efficacy and postgraduate procrastination: A moderated mediation model. *Frontiers in Psychology*, *11*, 1752. https://doi.org/10.3389/fpsyg.2020.01752

Liu, P., & Feng, T. (2017). The overlapping brain region accounting for the relationship between procrastination and impulsivity: A voxel-based morphometry study. *Neuroscience*, *360*, 9–17. https://doi.org/10.1016/j.neuroscience.2017.07.042

Lonergan, J. M., & Maher, K. J. (2000). The relationship between job characteristics and workplace procrastination as moderated by locus of control. *Journal of Social Behavior & Personality*, *15*(5), 213–224.

Lu, D., He, Y., & Tan, Y. (2021). Gender, socioeconomic status, cultural differences, education, family size, and procrastination: A sociodemographic meta-analysis. *Frontiers in Psychology*, *12*, 719425. https://doi.org/10.3389/fpsyg.2021.719425

Markiewicz, K. (2017). Zewnętrzna lokalizacja kontroli jako mediator związku neurotyczności i zachowań prokrastynacyjnych studentów. *Annales Universitatis Mariae Curie – Skłodowska Lublin – Polonia*, *30*(3), 161–178. https://doi.org/10 .17951/j.2017.30.3.161

Martinez, S.-K., Meier, S., & Sprenger, C. (2023). Procrastination in the field: Evidence from tax filing. *Journal of the European Economic Association*, *21*(3), 1119–1153. https://doi.org/10.1093/jeea/jvac067

McCown, W., Johnson, J., & Petzel, T. (1989). Procrastination, a principal components analysis. *Personality and Individual Differences*, *10*(2), 197–202. https://doi.org/10 .1016/0191-8869(89)90204-3

McCrae, R. R., & Costa, P. T. (2003). *Personality in adulthood: A five-factor theory perspective* (2nd ed.). Guilford Press. https://doi.org/10.4324/9780203428412

Meng, X., Pan, Y., & Li, C. (2024). Portraits of procrastinators: A meta-analysis of personality and procrastination. *Personality and Individual Differences*, *218*, 112490. https://doi.org/10.1016/j.paid.2023.112490

Michałowski, J. M., Koziejowski, W., Droździel, D., Harciarek, M., & Wypych, M. (2017). Error processing deficits in academic procrastinators anticipating monetary punishment in a go/no-go study. *Personality and Individual Differences*, *117*, 198–204. https://doi.org/10.1016/j.paid.2017.06.010

Milgram, N. A., Marshevsky, S., & Sadeh, C. (1995). Correlates of academic procrastination: Discomfort, task aversiveness, and task capability. *The Journal of Psychology*, *129*(2), 145–155. https://doi.org/10.1080/00223980.1995.9914954

Milgram, N. A., Sroloff, B., & Rosenbaum, M. (1988). The procrastination of everyday life. *Journal of Research in Personality, 22*(2), 197–212.

Milgram, N. A., & Tenne, R. (2000). Personality correlates of decisional and task avoidant procrastination. *European Journal of Personality, 14*(2), 141–156. https://doi.org/10.1002/(SICI)1099-0984(200003/04)14:2<141::AID-PER369>3.0.CO;2-V

Mischel, W., Cantor, N., & Feldman, S. (1996). Principles of self-regulation: The nature of willpower and self-control. In E. T. Higgins & A. W. Kruglanski (Eds.), *Social psychology: Handbook of basic principles* (pp. 329–360). The Guilford Press.

O'Neill, T. A., Hambley, L. A., & Chatellier, G. S. (2014). Cyberslacking, engagement, and personality in distributed work environments. *Computers in Human Behavior, 40*, 152–160. https://doi.org/10.1016/j.chb.2014.08.005

O'Donoghue, T., & Rabin, M. (2001). Choice and procrastination. *The Quarterly Journal of Economics, 116*(1), 121–160. https://doi.org/10.1162/003355301556365

Paulsen, R. (2015). Non-work at work: Resistance or what? *Organization, 22*(3), 351–367. https://doi.org/10.1177/1350508413515541

Pearlman-Avnion, S., & Harduf, R. (2019). Procrastination, perfectionism, and locus-of-control in academic settings. *Special School, LXXX*(2), 108–124. https://doi.org/10.5604/01.3001.0013.1973

Pinxten, M., De Laet, T., Van Soom, C., Peeters, C., & Langie, G. (2019). Purposeful delay and academic achievement. A critical review of the active procrastination scale. *Learning and Individual Differences, 73*, 42–51. https://doi.org/10.1016/j.lindif.2019.04.010

Prem, R., Scheel, T. E., Weigelt, O., Hoffmann, K., & Korunka, C. (2018). Procrastination in daily working life: A diary study on within-person processes that link work characteristics to workplace procrastination. *Frontiers in Psychology, 9*, 1087. https://doi.org/10.3389/fpsyg.2018.01087

Pychyl, T. A., & Flett, G. L. (2012). Procrastination and self-regulatory failure: An introduction to the special issue. *Journal of Rational-Emotive & Cognitive-Behavior Therapy, 30*(4), 203–212. https://doi.org/10.1007/s10942-012-0149-5

Pychyl, T. A., Lee, J. M., Thibodeau, R., & & Blunt, A. (2000). Five days of emotion: An experience sampling study of undergraduate student procrastination. *Journal of Social Behavior & Personality, 15*(5), 239–254.

Pychyl, T. A., & Sirois, F. M. (2016). Procrastination, emotion regulation, and well-being. In F. M. Sirois & T. A. Pychyl (Eds.), *Procrastination, health, and well-being* (pp. 163–188). Academic Press. https://doi.org/10.1016/B978-0-12-802862-9.00008-6

Rabin, L. A., Fogel, J., & Nutter-Upham, K. E. (2011). Academic procrastination in college students: The role of self-reported executive function. *Journal of Clinical and Experimental Neuropsychology, 33*(3), 344–357. https://doi.org/10.1080/13803395.2010.518597

Rahimi, S., Hall, N. C., & Sticca, F. (2023). Understanding academic procrastination: A Longitudinal analysis of procrastination and emotions in undergraduate and graduate students. *Motivation and Emotion, 47*(4), 554–574. https://doi.org/10.1007/s11031-023-10010-9

Rebetez, M. M. L., Rochat, L., Barsics, C., & van der Linden, M. (2016). Procrastination as a self-regulation failure: The role of inhibition, negative affect, and gender. *Personality and Individual Differences, 101*, 435–439. https://doi.org/10.1016/j.paid.2016.06.049

Rebetez, M. M. L., Rochat, L., Barsics, C., & van der Linden, M. (2018). Procrastination as a self-regulation failure: The role of impulsivity and intrusive thoughts. *Psychological Reports, 121*(1), 26–41. https://doi.org/10.1177/0033294117720695

Reinecke, L., Meier, A., Beutel, M. E., Schemer, C., Stark, B., Wölfling, K., & Müller, K. W. (2018). The relationship between trait procrastination, Internet use, and psychological functioning: Results from a community sample of German adolescents. *Frontiers in Psychology, 9,* 913. https://doi.org/10.3389/fpsyg.2018.00913

Rice, K. G., Richardson, C. M. E., & Clark, D. (2012). Perfectionism, procrastination, and psychological distress. *Journal of Counseling Psychology, 59*(2), 288–302. https://doi .org/10.1037/a0026643

Rosenberg, M. (1965). *Rosenberg Self-Esteem Scale (RSES).* APA PsycTests. https://doi .org/10.1037/t01038-000

Rotter, J. B. (1966). Generalized expectancies for internal versus external control of reinforcement. *Psychological Monographs: General and Applied, 80*(1), 1–28. https://doi.org/10.1037/h0092976

Schouwenburg, H. C. (1992). Procrastinators and fear of failure: an exploration of reasons for procrastination. *European Journal of Personality, 6*(3), 225–236. https://doi.org /10.1002/per.2410060305

Schouwenburg, H. C., & Lay, C. H. (1995). Trait procrastination and the big-five factors of personality. *Personality and Individual Differences, 18*(4), 481–490. https://doi.org /10.1016/0191-8869(94)00176-S

Schraw, G., Wadkins, T., & Olafson, L. (2007). Doing the things we do: A grounded theory of academic procrastination. *Journal of Educational Psychology, 99*(1), 12–25. https://doi.org/10.1037/0022-0663.99.1.12

Sederlund, A. P., Burns, L. R., & Rogers, W. (2020). Multidimensional models of perfectionism and procrastination: Seeking determinants of both. *International Journal of Environmental Research and Public Health, 17*(14). https://doi.org/10 .3390/ijerph17145099

Senécal, C., Lavoie, K., & Koestner, R. (1997). Trait and situational factors in procrastination: An interactional model. *Journal of Social Behavior and Personality, 12*(4), 889–903.

Shu, S. B., & Gneezy, A. (2010). Procrastination of enjoyable experiences. *Journal of Marketing Research, 47*(5), 933–944. https://doi.org/10.1509/jmkr.47.5.933

Siah, P. C., Ang, H. Q., Chan, S. M., & Wong, E. L. (2021). The effects of locus of control on procrastination among undergraduates: the coping strategy as a mediator. *Journal of Educational Sciences & Psychology, 11*(73), 91–103. https://doi.org/10.51865/jesp .2021.1.09

Simpson, W. K., & Pychyl, T. A. (2009). In search of the arousal procrastinator: Investigating the relation between procrastination, arousal-based personality traits and beliefs about procrastination motivations. *Personality and Individual Differences, 47*(8), 906–911. https://doi.org/10.1016/j.paid.2009.07.013

Singh, S., & Bala, R. (2020). Mediating role of self-efficacy on the relationship between conscientiousness and procrastination. *International Journal of Work Organisation and Emotion, 11*(1), Article 109422, 41. https://doi.org/10.1504/IJWOE.2020.109422

Sirois, F. M. (2007). "I'll look after my health, later": A replication and extension of the procrastination–health model with community-dwelling adults. *Personality and Individual Differences, 43*(1), 15–26. https://doi.org/10.1016/j.paid.2006.11.003

Sirois, F. M. (2013). Procrastination and stress: Exploring the role of self-compassion. *Self and Identity*, *13*(2), 128–145. https://doi.org/10.1080/15298868.2013.763404

Sirois, F. M. (2016). Procrastination, stress, and chronic health conditions: A temporal perspective. In F. M. Sirois & T. A. Pychyl (Eds.), *Procrastination, health, and well-being* (pp. 67–92). Academic Press. https://doi.org/10.1016/B978-0-12-802862-9.00004-9

Sirois, F. M. (2022). *Procrastination: What it is, why it's a problem, and what you can do about it.* American Psychological Association.

Sirois, F. M. (2023). Procrastination and stress: A conceptual review of why context matters. *International Journal of Environmental Research and Public Health*, *20*(6), 5031. https://doi.org/10.3390/ijerph20065031

Sirois, F. M., & Kitner, R. (2015). Less adaptive or more maladaptive? A meta–analytic investigation of procrastination and coping. *European Journal of Personality*, *29*(4), 433–444. https://doi.org/10.1002/per.1985

Sirois, F. M., Melia-Gordon, M. L., & Pychyl, T. A. (2003). "I'll look after my health, later": An investigation of procrastination and health. *Personality and Individual Differences*, *35*(5), 1167–1184. https://doi.org/10.1016/s0191-8869(02)00326-4

Sirois, F. M., Molnar, D. S., & Hirsch, J. K. (2017). A meta–analytic and conceptual update on the associations between procrastination and multidimensional perfectionism. *European Journal of Personality*, *31*(2), 137–159. https://doi.org/10.1002/per.2098

Sirois, F. M., Nauts, S., & Molnar, D. S. (2019). Self-compassion and bedtime procrastination: An emotion regulation perspective. *Mindfulness*, *10*(3), 434–445. https://doi.org/10.1007/s12671-018-0983-3

Sirois, F., & Pychyl, T. (2013). Procrastination and the priority of short-term mood regulation: Consequences for future self. *Social and Personality Psychology Compass*, *7*(2), 115–127. https://doi.org/10.1111/spc3.12011

Sirois, F. M., Stride, C. B., & Pychyl, T. A. (2023). Procrastination and health: A longitudinal test of the roles of stress and health behaviours. *British Journal of Health Psychology*, *28*(3), 860–875. https://doi.org/10.1111/bjhp.12658

Sirois, F. M., & Tosti, N. (2012). Lost in the moment? An investigation of procrastination, mindfulness, and well-being. *Journal of Rational-Emotive & Cognitive-Behavior Therapy*, *30*(4), 237–248. https://doi.org/10.1007/s10942-012-0151-y

Snyder, C. R. (1990). Self-Handicapping processes and sequelae. In R. L. Higgins, C. R. Snyder, & S. Berglas (Eds.), *The Springer series in social / clinical psychology. Self-handicapping: The paradox that isn't* (pp. 107–150). Springer. https://doi.org/10.1007/978-1-4899-0861-2_4

Solomon, L. J., & Rothblum, E. D. (1984). Academic procrastination: Frequency and cognitive-behavioral correlates. *Journal of Counseling Psychology*, *31*(4), 503–509.

Sparfeldt, J. R., & Schwabe, S. (2024). Academic procrastination mediates the relation between conscientiousness and academic achievement. *Personality and Individual Differences*, *218*, 112466. https://doi.org/10.1016/j.paid.2023.112466

Stead, R., Shanahan, M. J., & Neufeld, R. W. (2010). "I'll go to therapy, eventually": Procrastination, stress and mental health. *Personality and Individual Differences*, *49*(3), 175–180. https://doi.org/10.1016/j.paid.2010.03.028

Steel, P. (2007). The nature of procrastination: A meta-analytic and theoretical review of quintessential self-regulatory failure. *Psychological Bulletin*, *133*(1), 65–94.

Steel, P. (2010). Arousal, avoidant and decisional procrastinators: Do they exist? *Personality and Individual Differences, 48*(8), 926–934.

Steel, P. (2012). *The procrastination equation: How to stop putting things off and start getting things done.* Harper.

Steel, P., Brothen, T., & Wambach, C. (2001). Procrastination and personality, performance, and mood. *Personality and Individual Differences, 30*(1), 95–106. https://doi.org/10.1016/S0191-8869(00)00013-1

Steel, P., & Ferrari, J. (2013). Sex, education and procrastination: An epidemiological study of procrastinators' characteristics from a global sample. *European Journal of Personality, 27*(1), 51–58. https://doi.org/10.1002/per.1851

Steel, P., & Klingsieck, K. (2015). Procrastination. In J. D. Wright (Ed.), *The international encyclopedia of the social & behavioral sciences* (2nd ed., Vol. 19, pp. 73–78). Oxford: Elsevier.

Steel, P., & Klingsieck, K. B. (2016). Academic procrastination: Psychological antecedents revisited. *Australian Psychologist, 51*(1), 36–46. https://doi.org/10.1111/ap.12173

Steel, P., & König, C. J. (2006). Integrating theories of motivation. *Academy of Management Review, 31*(4), 889–913. https://doi.org/10.5465/amr.2006.22527462

Steel, P., Svartdal, F., Thundiyil, T., & Brothen, T. (2018). Examining procrastination across multiple goal stages: A longitudinal study of temporal motivation theory. *Frontiers in Psychology, 9*, 327. https://doi.org/10.3389/fpsyg.2018.00327

Steel, P., Taras, D., Ponak, A., & Kammeyer-Mueller, J. (2021). Self-regulation of slippery deadlines: The role of procrastination in work performance. *Frontiers in Psychology, 12*, 783789. https://doi.org/10.3389/fpsyg.2021.783789

Sudler, E. L. (2014). *Academic procrastination as mediated by executive functioning, perfectionism, and frustration intolerance in college students* [Doctoral dissertation]. St. John's University.

Sümer, C., & Büttner, O. B. (2022). I'll do it - after one more scroll: The effects of boredom proneness, self-control, and impulsivity on online procrastination. *Frontiers in Psychology, 13*, 918306. https://doi.org/10.3389/fpsyg.2022.918306

Svartdal, F., Granmo, S., & Færevaag, F. S. (2018). On the behavioral side of procrastination: Exploring behavioral delay in real-life settings. *Frontiers in Psychology, 9*, 746. https://doi.org/10.3389/fpsyg.2018.00746

Svartdal, F., Pfuhl, G., Nordby, K., Foschi, G., Klingsieck, K. B., Rozental, A., Carlbring, P., Lindblom-Ylänne, S., & Rębkowska, K. (2016). On the measurement of procrastination: Comparing two scales in six European countries. *Frontiers in Psychology, 7*, 1307. https://doi.org/10.3389/fpsyg.2016.01307

Tandon, A., Kaur, P., Ruparel, N., Islam, J. U., & Dhir, A. (2022). Cyberloafing and cyberslacking in the workplace: Systematic literature review of past achievements and future promises. *Internet Research, 32*(1), 55–89. https://doi.org/10.1108/INTR-06-2020-0332

Tibbett, T. P., & Ferrari, J. R. (2019). Return to the origin: what creates a procrastination identity? *Current Issues in Personality Psychology, 7*(1), 1–7. https://doi.org/10.5114/cipp.2018.75648

Tice, D. M., & Baumeister, R. F. (2018). Longitudinal study of procrastination, performance, stress, and health: The costs and benefits of dawdling. In R. F. Baumeister (Ed.), *Self-regulation and self-control* (pp. 299–309). Routledge. https://doi.org/10.4324/9781315175775-9

Tice, D. M., Bratslavsky, E., & Baumeister, R. F. (2001). Emotional distress regulation takes precedence over impulse control: If you feel bad, do it! *Journal of Personality and Social Psychology, 80*(1), 53–67. https://doi.org/10.1037/0022-3514.80.1.53

Tice, D. M., & Roy, F. B. (1998). Longitudinal study of procrastination, performance, stress, and health: The costs and benefits of dawdling. *Psychological Science, 8*, 454–458. http://dx.doi.org/10.1111/j.1467-9280.1997.tb00460.x

Topa, G., Lunceford, G., & Boyatzis, R. E. (2017). Financial planning for retirement: A psychosocial perspective. *Frontiers in Psychology, 8*, 2338. https://doi.org/10.3389/fpsyg.2017.02338

Tudose, C.-M., & Pavalache-Ilie, M. (2021). Procrastination and work satisfaction. *Social Science and Law, 14*(63), 37–46. https://doi.org/10.31926/but.ssl.2021.14.63.1.4

Tversky, A., & Kahneman, D. (1992). Advances in prospect theory: Cumulative representation of uncertainty. *Journal of Risk and Uncertainty, 5*(4), 297–323. https://doi.org/10.1007/BF00122574

Uzun, B., LeBlanc, S., Guclu, I. O., Ferrari, J. R., & Aydemir, A. (2022). Mediation effect of family environment on academic procrastination and life satisfaction: Assessing emerging adults. *Current Psychology, 41*(2), 1124–1130. https://doi.org/10.1007/s12144-021-02652-0

van Eerde, W. (2000). Procrastination: Self-regulation in initiating aversive goals. *Applied Psychology, 49*(3), 372–389. https://doi.org/10.1111/1464-0597.00021

van Eerde, W. (2003a). A meta-analytically derived nomological network of procrastination. *Personality and Individual Differences, 35*(6), 1401–1418. https://doi.org/10.1016/S0191-8869(02)00358-6

van Eerde, W. (2003b). Procrastination at work and time management training. *The Journal of Psychology, 137*(5), 421–434. https://doi.org/10.1080/00223980309600625

van Eerde, W. (2004). Procrastination in academic settings and the big five model of personality: A meta-analysis. In H. C. Schouwenburg, C. H. Lay, T. A. Pychyl, & J. R. Ferrari (Eds.), *Counseling the procrastinator in academic settings* (pp. 29–40). American Psychological Association. https://doi.org/10.1037/10808-003

van Eerde, W. (2015). Time management and procrastination. In M. D. Mumford & M. Frese (Eds.), *The psychology of planning in organizations: Research and applications* (pp. 312–333). Routledge/Taylor & Francis Group.

van Hooft, E. A., Born, M. P., Taris, T. W., van der Flier, H., & Blonk, R. W. (2005). Bridging the gap between intentions and behavior: Implementation intentions, action control, and procrastination. *Journal of Vocational Behavior, 66*(2), 238–256. https://doi.org/10.1016/j.jvb.2004.10.003

Vodanovich, S. J., & Rupp, D. E. (1999). Are procrastinators prone to boredom? *Social Behavior and Personality: An International Journal, 27*(1), 11–16. https://doi.org/10.2224/sbp.1999.27.1.11

Vroom, V., Porter, L., & Lawler, E. (2015). Expectancy theories. In *Organizational behavior 1* (pp. 94–113). Routledge. https://doi.org/10.4324/9781315702018-9

Wang, W., Han, R., Luo, Y., Wu, Z., Jin, Y., Li, Q., & Li, B. (2018). The mediating role of self-efficacy between neuroticism and procrastination among undergraduates. In *IEEE International Conference on Mechatronics and Automation (ICMA), Changchun, China* (pp. 67–71). https://doi.org/10.1109/ICMA.2018.8484534

Wäschle, K., Allgaier, A., Lachner, A., Fink, S., & Nückles, M. (2014). Procrastination and self-efficacy: Tracing vicious and virtuous circles in self-regulated learning. *Learning and Instruction, 29*, 103–114. https://doi.org/10.1016/j.learninstruc.2013.09.005

Watson, D. C. (2001). Procrastination and the five-factor model: A facet level analysis. *Personality and Individual Differences*, *30*(1), 149–158. https://doi.org/10.1016/S0191-8869(00)00019-2

Whiteside, S. P., & Lynam, D. R. (2001). The five factor model and impulsivity: Using a structural model of personality to understand impulsivity. *Personality and Individual Differences*, *30*(4), 669–689. https://doi.org/10.1016/s0191-8869(00)00064-7

Wu, H., Gui, D., Lin, W., Gu, R., Zhu, X., & Liu, X. (2016). The procrastinators want it now: Behavioral and event-related potential evidence of the procrastination of intertemporal choices. *Brain and Cognition*, *107*, 16–23. https://doi.org/10.1016/j.bandc.2016.06.005

Wypych, M., Matuszewski, J., & Dragan, W. Ł. (2018). Roles of impulsivity, motivation, and emotion regulation in procrastination - Path analysis and comparison between students and non-students. *Frontiers in Psychology*, *9*, 891. https://doi.org/10.3389/fpsyg.2018.00891

Xu, P., González-Vallejo, C., & Xiong, Z. H. (2016). State anxiety reduces procrastinating behavior. *Motivation and Emotion*, *40*(4), 625–637. https://doi.org/10.1007/s11031-016-9554-x

Yan, J., & Yang, J. (2014). Trait procrastination and compulsive Internet use as predictors of cyberloafing. In *Proceedings of ICSSSM '14: June 25–27, 2014, Beijing, China* (pp. 1–4). IEEE. https://doi.org/10.1109/ICSSSM.2014.6874119

Yang, Z. (2021). Does procrastination always predict lower life satisfaction? A study on the moderation effect of self-regulation in China and the United Kingdom. *Frontiers in Psychology*, *12*, 690838. https://doi.org/10.3389/fpsyg.2021.690838

Zhang, R., Chen, Z., Xu, T., Zhang, L., & Feng, T. (2020). The overlapping region in right hippocampus accounting for the link between trait anxiety and procrastination. *Neuropsychologia*, *146*, 107571. https://doi.org/10.1016/j.neuropsychologia.2020.107571

Zhang, S., & Feng, T. (2018). How impulsiveness influences procrastination: Mediating roles of self-control. *Advances in Psychology*, *8*(2), 272–282. https://doi.org/10.12677/ap.2018.82034

Zhang, S., & Feng, T. (2020). Modeling procrastination: Asymmetric decisions to act between the present and the future. *Journal of Experimental Psychology. General*, *149*(2), 311–322. https://doi.org/10.1037/xge0000643

Zhang, S., Liu, P., & Feng, T. (2019). To do it now or later: The cognitive mechanisms and neural substrates underlying procrastination. *Wiley Interdisciplinary Reviews: Cognitive Science*, *10*(4), e1492. https://doi.org/10.1002/wcs.1492

Zhang, S., Verguts, T., Zhang, C., Feng, P., Chen, Q., & Feng, T. (2021). Outcome value and task aversiveness impact task procrastination through separate neural pathways. *Cerebral Cortex*, *31*(8), 3846–3855. https://doi.org/10.1093/cercor/bhab053

Zhang, Y., Dong, S., Fang, W., Chai, X., Mei, J., & Fan, X. (2018). Self-efficacy for self-regulation and fear of failure as mediators between self-esteem and academic procrastination among undergraduates in health professions. *Advances in Health Sciences Education*, *23*(4), 817–830. https://doi.org/10.1007/s10459-018-9832-3

Zhao, J., Meng, G., Sun, Y., Xu, Y., Geng, J., & Han, L. (2021). The relationship between self-control and procrastination based on the self-regulation theory perspective: The moderated mediation model. *Current Psychology*, *40*(10), 5076–5086. https://doi.org/10.1007/s12144-019-00442-3

2 Procrastination at Work

2.1 Conceptualization of Procrastination at Work

Initially, procrastination at work was considered a manifestation of a general tendency to delay of the work. It was assumed that studying general procrastination would provide a comprehensive understanding and explanation of procrastination in work settings. As a result, procrastination at work has been underrepresented in research. Additionally, the measurement of work-related procrastination was often conducted using general procrastination assessment tools, which may result in a lower level of reliability and validity of the measure when applied to the specific work environment. For some time, there have been claims in the literature that work-related procrastination may have unique attributes and therefore must be approached as a distinct phenomenon from general procrastination. Consequently, it requires different conceptualization and measurement techniques to capture procrastination behaviors typical of the work context (Klingsieck, 2013; Metin et al., 2016), such as taking extended breaks or browsing for personal purposes during work hours. A tool for measuring procrastination at work has recently been developed, which has led to an increase in research on this phenomenon in the workplace. Despite the growing body of research in this area, knowledge remains limited. This chapter provides an overview of theoretical assumptions and research findings on the two-dimensional structure of procrastination.

2.1.1 Definition and Nature of Procrastination at Work

Procrastination at work was considered a form of situation-based behavior (Harris & Sutton, 1983; Klingsieck, 2013). Initially, Harris and Sutton (1983) defined work/task procrastination as a persistent and/or cyclical pattern of behavior, in which an individual avoids starting and completing tasks or activities that should be performed within a specific time frame, and causing dysfunctional consequences of inaction. This approach emphasizes the need to focus on the situational aspects of the work environment, which can lead employees to delay task completion. Metin et al. (2016) define procrastination at work as the postponement of work-related activities by engaging in non-work-related

DOI: 10.4324/9781003422860-3

activities, either cognitively or behaviorally, without the intention of causing harm to the employer, coworkers, workplace, or clients. This definition includes components, such as work tasks and responsibilities, procrastination of tasks over time, engaging in non-work-related activities, and lack of intent to harm others. Procrastination at work can be viewed as a type of dysfunctional self-regulation that results in not performing an intended work (Nguyen et al., 2013). According to this view, procrastination at work is a maladaptive and unproductive work style that reflects different forms of inactivity at work. Thereby, it distracts employees from the actual work and engages them in other activities not related to work (Metin et al., 2016). Thus, definitions of procrastination at work emphasize two components: avoiding work and engaging in non-work activities.

2.1.2 Two-Dimensional Conceptualization of Procrastination at Work

Relatively recently, procrastination at work has been conceptualized as a two-dimensional construct containing two types of work delaying behaviors of soldiering and cyberslacking, which allow one to avoid completion of boring, unpleasant, or too challenging work tasks. This conception resulted in the development of the two-dimensional Procrastination At Work Scale (PAWS) (Metin et al., 2016, 2020) to measure both dimensions of procrastination in the workplace.

Soldiering: Soldering is defined as the act of postponing work by engaging in various non-work-related activities that are more appealing at the time, either cognitively or behaviorally (Metin et al., 2016, 2020). This phenomenon is also known as *offline procrastination* and can take many different forms, such as taking long and frequent breaks for meals or coffee, smoking, gossiping, chatting with coworkers, tidying up the workspace, avoiding planning and daydreaming, or simply mentally checking out. This conceptualization views procrastination as a diversion of attention from work-related activities. Even in cases where an employee is not involved in extracurricular activities, procrastination at work might involve postponing the completion of tasks. Giving less important or simple work-related activities less priority than more important assignments is another example of this kind of procrastination. Delays in starting or finishing professional tasks may represent offline procrastination, therefore researchers often refer to studies on general procrastination.

Cyberslacking: Cyberslacking refers to delaying work by engaging the Internet for personal purposes on digital devices during work hours (Metin et al., 2016). This can include non-work-related activities such as browsing social media, instant messaging, online shopping, or gaming. Therefore, this behavior is commonly referred to as *online procrastination* (Lavoie & Pychyl, 2001; Tandon et al., 2022), Internet procrastination (Sümer & Büttner, 2022; Thatcher et al., 2008), computer procrastination (Breems & Basden, 2014), cyberslacking (Lavoie & Pychyl, 2001) or cyberloafing (Lim & Teo, 2024), or Facebocrastination as using Facebook to procrastinate (Meier et al., 2016). Cyberslacking has become prevalent due to the widespread availability of the Internet, which is a necessity for modern work. Unrestricted access to online resources can lead to excessive use during work hours, resulting in procrastination on work tasks. Advancements in information technology have brought significant changes to the way employees work. They are no longer restricted to working at company locations solely to access organizational resources such as hardware, software, and Internet connectivity; these resources are now available to them from remote locations. Researchers are increasingly emphasizing that the Internet can lead to procrastination. It is easily accessible through electronic devices such as computers, smartphones, and tablets. Employees regularly engage in non-work activities via the Internet, such as watching movies, browsing the news, following social media sites, shopping, communicating privately, playing computer games, and other online activities, all of which negatively impact their performance. There is ample evidence in the literature to classify cyberslacking as a form of technological procrastination at work, which refers to the practice of engaging in non-work-related Internet activities during work hours, resulting in a waste of organizational resources (Garrett & Danziger, 2008a; Lavoie & Pychyl, 2001; Vitak et al., 2011).

Few studies have supported moderate correlations (0.28) between cyberslacking and dispositional procrastination (O'Neill et al., 2014b; Yan & Yang, 2014), as well as with soldiering from 0.25 to 0.56 (Metin et al., 2016, 2020; van den Berg & Roosen, 2018). This relationship is additionally supported by well-established empirical connections between procrastination and a general tendency to problematic Internet use (Lavoie & Pychyl, 2001; Thatcher et al., 2008; Yan & Yang, 2014), which is considered dysfunctional behavior in work conditions and has negative consequences for individual work efficiency and organizational effectiveness (Lim, 2002; Lim & Teo, 2024). Empirical evidence highlights the significance of self-regulation and self-control problems as the predictors of both procrastination behavior and cyberslacking. Internet-related distractions, such as private e-mails, web browsing, and other online activities for personal purposes, likely activate procrastination, potentially diverting attention from work (O'Neill et al., 2014b). Researchers have investigated workplace procrastination in various cultural contexts using the PAWS as a research instrument. These contexts include the Netherlands, Turkey (Metin et al., 2016, 2018, 2020; van den Berg & Roosen, 2018), Israel (IIen et al., 2021), Romania (Tudose & Pavalache-Ilie, 2021), Ukraine, Slovenia, Czech Republic, Croatia, Finland, and Great Britain (Metin et al., 2020).

In summary, soldering and cyberslacking are often regarded as maladaptive behaviors. They are characterized by impaired self-regulation and entails evading or delaying task completion by engaging in non-work activities. However, procrastination is more frequently irrational and is not self-regulated. Engaging in non-work-related online activities during work hours can also be voluntary and controllable based on mental evaluation of effort in relation to reward (Lim, 2002) or expectation of desired outcome (Garrett & Danziger, 2008a).

2.1.3 Cyberslacking – A New Manifestation of Procrastination at Work

Cyberslacking has become highly prevalent in the workplace. More and more jobs are digital and require the use of computers and access to the Internet. With free access to mobile devices and the Internet, many forms of work can now be performed remotely, leading to a shift away from the conventional understanding of working time and location to a more adaptable work structure. Cyberslacking is not as visible as other Internet overuse behaviors at work, and therefore employees spend a significant amount of time engaged in personal activities in the office during work hours. Initially, cyberslacking was construed as dysfunctional behavior related to wasting time or being unproductive while using computers or the Internet. Employees spend a lot of work time reading and writing e-mails, browsing social networking sites, auctions, Internet communication, and other online activities (Cheng et al., 2014; Kim & Byrne, 2011; Moody & Siponen, 2013; Ugrin & Pearson, 2013). Cyberslacking may occur due to the immediate gratification provided by the Internet, which allows individuals to engage in pleasurable short-term distractions and postpone tasks, thereby providing immediate relief from stress (Lavoie & Pychyl, 2001).

A review of studies (Lim & Teo, 2024) indicate that cyberslacking may have a dualistic nature of cyberloafing; it can be both counterproductive and restorative. Cyberloafing viewed as counterproductive work behavior (Akbulut et al., 2017; Lim, 2002; Lim & Teo, 2005) relates to the concepts of moral disengagement, organizational justice, and escapism. When employees are dissatisfied with their work or the organization, they engage in non-work-related activities on the Internet to avoid job responsibilities or to retaliate against organizational injustices. Cyberloafing can therefore have negative consequences on work performance, work attitudes, risk of behavioral addiction, Internet-related abuse, and even illegal practices (Lim & Teo, 2005). On the contrary, cyberslacking can have a restorative function (Lim & Teo, 2024), when employees are working long hours or coping with a heavy workload. It can serve as a break or respite from work and help to replenish depleted resources (Ivarsson & Larsson, 2011) due to work and family demands (Koay et al., 2017a). Following the conservation of resources (COR) (Hobfoll, 2012) theory, browsing the Internet serves as a respite from work to help in recovering resources. Thus, cyberloafing can be a way for employees to conserve resources.

Research on cyberslacking has revealed various types and forms of Internet misuse at work. One of the first categorizations was proposed by Lim (2002), distinguishing the activities of browsing the Internet and e-mailing. In other classifications, researchers identify such forms of cyberslacking as (1) purchasing and personal business, (2) seeking and viewing information, (3) interpersonal communication, (4) interactive entertainment and passing time, and (5) personal downloading (Mahatanankoon et al., 2004). Similarly, Ramayah (2010) classified behaviors into four categories: personal *communication*, personal *information research*, personal downloading, and personal e-commerce. Empirically validated, cyberloafing has also been classified into *sharing, shopping, real-time updating, accessing online content,* and *gambling* (Akbulut et al., 2017; Koay, 2018a; Şahin, 2021). Based on Robinson and Bennett's (1995) typology of deviant work behavior, Blanchard and Henle (2008) distinguished between *minor* and *serious* cyberloafing. *Minor* activities include sending/receiving private e-mails or checking news portals during work; visiting news or sports sites, visiting financial sites, and shopping online. *Serious* cyberloafing activities included visiting adult websites, gambling sites, and virtual communities, participating in chat rooms, reading blogs, maintaining personal web pages, checking personals, and downloading music. In turn, Li and Chung (2006) categorized goal-based cyberslacking activities into four types: *social* (communication with people), *informational* (searching for information), *recreational* (meeting needs), and *virtual* activities (searching for and satisfying the needs of the virtual self). Blau et al. (2006) distinguished between *passive* cyberloafing (including browsing and non-work-related e-mail) and *interactive* cyberloafing (containing downloading information, playing games, or using a chat room), which requires more effort and energy and is perceived as more serious than simply browsing the Web. The first two behaviors correspond to production deviance in the typology of deviant behaviors (Robinson & Bennett, 1995). Interactive cyberloafing can be seen as a form of property deviance. Anandarajan and Simmers (2004) categorized behaviors related to Internet abuse at work for private purposes as *destructive* (such as visiting adult websites and online gaming), *recreational* (such as online shopping), and *personal learning* (active online participation in websites and professional groups). In subsequent research, they detected four types of behaviors related to the personal use of the Internet at work: hedonistic, self-development, civic, and related to the work–family relationship (Anandarajan et al., 2011).

With the development of information technologies, the number of online activities for personal purposes has increased. Mastrangelo et al. (2006) divided personal use of work computers into unproductive and counterproductive. *Unproductive computer use* occurs when an employee uses a computer during work hours for activities that are unproductive but not potentially disruptive to the organization, such as shopping, chatting, or playing games. *Counterproductive computer use* occurs when an employee engages in behavior that may interfere with company goals, such as uploading or downloading pornography, creating computer viruses, or even drug dealing. Another classification distinguishes cyberloafing into online behavior types, such as *deviant* (with negative consequences for the organization), *developmental* (to increase employee knowledge and skills), *recovery* (oriented to reduce work-related stress and anxiety and relax the employee), and addictive behaviors (resulting from Internet addiction) (Aghaz & Sheikh, 2016; van Doorn, 2011). Deviant and addictive behaviors usually have negative consequences for the organization and the employee's performance and mental health. Developmental and regenerative behaviors usually have a positive impact on employees' mental health and work performance. Aghaz and Sheikh (2016) distinguished the above cyber behaviors from activities focused on achieving different goals (i.e. social, informational, leisure, and virtual).

Kim and Byrne (2011) proposed a conceptual framework for various forms of personal Internet use in the work context as *aimless*, *strategic*, and *problematic* forms. *Aimless* forms of using the Internet at work include cyberslacking and cyberslacking as careless, dysfunctional, and purposeless behaviors associated with low self-control. *Strategic* use of the Internet at work is goal-oriented, even if it is not directly related to work (e.g. visiting a bank's website to pay a bill). *Problematic* Internet use includes forms of pathological Internet abuse and Internet addiction, which may be dysfunctional at an individual or societal level. All typologies focus on distinguishing behaviors or forms of cyberloafing that center on content or non-work-related Internet use. Compared to traditional non-work activities in the workplace, such as long lunch breaks and socializing with coworkers, cyberloafing does not relate to leaving the workplace, making it less noticeable to others. Despite the differences in vocabulary and definitions used, scholars agree that cyberslacking pertains to employee behavior that (1) concerns the unproductive use of the Internet at work; (2) results in loss of work time; (3) is voluntary; (4) occurs during work hours or designated work time; (5) uses stationary or organizational or mobile devices; and (6) is for non-work-related purposes. Jiang et al. (2021) synthesized the aspects of all phenomena related to non-work-related Internet use during work under the umbrella term of personal use of technology at work. This term encompasses Internet use in a broad sense and includes working conditions using organizational and personal devices, such as tablets and smartphones.

2.1.4 Procrastination at Work in Relation to Counterproductive Work Behavior

The literature is divided on whether procrastination and cyberprocrastination are counterproductive. Counterproductive work behavior is defined as voluntary acts that are intended to harm the organization or its members (Fox & Spector, 2005). It can lead to counterproductive outcomes that are contrary to the expectations of either the employee or the employer. An essential aspect of deviant behavior is its intentionality and voluntariness to harm the organization or people associated with it. In this context, numerous deviant, aggressive, retaliatory, or sabotaging behaviors can occur within an organization. Robinson and Bennett (1995) divided counterproductive work behavior into organizational vs. interpersonal and serious vs. minor subtypes. Organizational counterproductive work behavior aims to harm the organization as a whole (e.g. wasting time at work by taking excessively long breaks), whereas interpersonal counterproductive work behavior targets individuals associated with the organization (e.g. aggression toward coworkers or clients). In addition, serious and minor counterproductive work behaviors differ in the degree of harm they cause. Fox and Spector (2005) identified five types of counterproductive work behavior including *interpersonal abuse*, which causes mental or physical harm to coworkers through negative comments, threats, or ignoring them; *production deviance* as an intentional failure to perform tasks properly; *sabotage*, which refers to the intentional damage or manipulation of work equipment, destruction of organizational property, *theft* of both organizational and coworker property; and *withdrawal* behaviors limiting working time below the required standard (e.g. through unjustified absences, tardiness, early departure from work, or taking longer breaks than allowed). Additionally, researchers classified active and passive counterproductive work behaviors (Bauer & Spector, 2015). Active behavior (i.e. abuse, sabotage) is triggered by negative emotions and is oriented toward retaliating against mistreatment by the organization (usually by the supervisor, coworkers, or subordinates). Passive counterproductive work behavior (e.g. withdrawal) involves shirking responsibilities, avoiding unpleasant stressors, and intentionally decreasing the time and effort committed to work (e.g. arriving late, leaving early, or failing to appear altogether), resulting in reduced performance. These behaviors are driven by a desire to gain personal advantage, manage stress, or protect or retain resources.

Given their detrimental effects on both the person and the organization, procrastination, can be included in the broad category of counterproductive work behavior (Ferrari, 1992; Metin et al., 2016; Skowronski & Mirowska, 2013) and cyberslacking at work (Henle & Blanchard, 2008; Liberman et al., 2011; Lim, 2002). Counterproductive work behavior, procrastination, and cyberslacking entail a decrease in employee productivity and thus in the effectiveness of the organization. Moreover, they can be similarly motivated by the desire to achieve short-term pleasures, avoid aversive tasks, or protect or recover depleted resources. Both types of behavior result in lower employee work performance and diminished organizational outcomes. According to Skowronski and Mirowska (2013), procrastination is particularly problematic in work environments where timely performance is required. Employers face significant financial consequences when employees waste time on non-work-related activities, leading to reduced productivity. It can be assumed that the counterproductive nature of procrastination refers mainly to the 'theft' of work time as the most important and scarce resource in the organization. This assumption is supported by research (Metin et al., 2016; Mosquera et al., 2022). Results showed a moderate correlation between procrastination and low work engagement and job performance (Metin et al., 2018, 2020; van den Berg & Roosen, 2018; Wang et al., 2021). This provides further evidence of the detrimental effects of procrastinating at work. Furthermore, research revealed that both behaviors are also influenced by underload at work (Bruursema et al., 2011) or high workload (Metin et al., 2016) mediated through boredom.

Procrastination and counterproductive work behavior share similar sources. Low conscientiousness and high neuroticism are the main personality predictors of procrastination (Huang et al., 2023), cyberslacking (Tandon et al., 2022), and counterproductive work behavior (Zhou et al., 2014). Self-efficacy was related to counterproductive work behavior (Fida et al., 2015), procrastination (Singh & Bala, 2020), and cyberslacking (Mercado et al., 2017b). Furthermore, decreased self-control has been found to be a significant factor in counterproductive work behavior (Spector, 2010), as well as work procrastination (van Eerde & Venus, 2018), and cyberslacking (Mercado et al., 2017b). Individuals who struggle with delaying immediate rewards in favor of future accomplishments are more likely to delay tasks and misuse the Internet (Kim et al., 2017; Pychyl & Sirois, 2016). Procrastination differs from counterproductive work behavior in that it lacks the intention to harm others or the entire organization. Counterproductive work behavior harms the organization, whereas procrastination is primarily detrimental to employees, although it extends beyond one's personal life and unintentionally leads to an increase in organizational costs. In this sense, procrastination can be considered a self-destructive behavior rather than a form of counterproductive work behavior (van Eerde, 2016). However, in certain situations, procrastination behavior may intentionally reduce performance by decreasing work hours, reducing effort expended on tasks, extending breaks, increasing delay at work, arriving late, intentionally wasting work time, unexcused absences, or unproductive presence at work or non-work-related Internet use at work (van Eerde, 2016). However, the motives of procrastinators may be more instrumental and egocentric, aimed at avoiding uncomfortable situations or regaining control, rather than directed against the organization. Procrastination at work seems to be most similar to employee *withdrawal*, but there are some differences. However, it is unintentional and therefore distinct from counterproductive work behavior. Carpenter and Berry (2017) noted in their meta-analysis that withdrawal, which differs from other types of counterproductive work behavior, does not necessarily have to be intentional.

Researchers often treat cyberslacking as deviant computer use or cyberdeviance at work (Mastrangelo et al., 2006; Weatherbee, 2010), defined as voluntary behavior using information and communication technology that threatens or causes harm to an organization, its members, or stakeholders (Weatherbee, 2010). From this perspective, cyberslacking, as voluntary non-work-related Internet use during work time for personal purposes and other online activities (Lim, 2002), corresponds to the definitional criteria of counterproductive work behavior (Askew et al., 2014; Mercado et al., 2017a; O'Neill et al., 2014a). In addition, cyberslacking can be considered a counterproductive work behavior due to its associations with reduced work performance (Andreassen et al., 2014b; Askew & Buckner, 2017; Mercado et al., 2017a; Ramayah, 2010; Tandon et al., 2022) and increased organizational costs (Lim, 2002; Tandon et al., 2022). From this perspective, the time spent in cyberslacking could otherwise have been allocated toward productive work activities. This may suggest that non-work-related online activities may prove advantageous for employees but harmful to their organization. Furthermore, the use of computers for non-work-related activities has a more harmful effect on work performance compared to traditional offline non-work-related activities (Bock & Ho, 2009). Therefore, cyberslacking seems to extend the taxonomy of counterproductive work behavior (O'Neill et al., 2014). According to Spector and Fox's typology (2005), cyberslacking is more similar to *production deviance*, which results in mishandled or subpar work tardiness and prolonged breaks (Lim, 2002); and *withdrawal* as employee's behavior related to reducing work time and task performance in comparison to the expectations of the organization (Askew et al., 2014; Askew & Buckner, 2017; Pindek et al., 2018; Ugrin & Pearson, 2013). Similarly to purposely decrease performance, employees who engage in cyberslacking do so intending to avoid work. As a result, they put in less effort, which negatively affects their output (Lim & Teo, 2024; Ng et al., 2016; Paulsen, 2015). A meta-analysis of nine studies (Mercado et al., 2017b) confirmed a moderate positive correlation of cyberslacking with overall counterproductive work behavior ($\bar{r} = 0.32$), and with time theft/loafing ($\bar{r} = 0.39$). Cyberslacking thus seems to be a modern form of counterproductive work behavior.

Some researchers argue that only serious forms of cyberslacking can be counterproductive (Mastrangelo et al., 2006). Counterproductive computer use includes behaviors that may expose an organization to risk or liability through misuse of company Internet access (e.g. illegally downloading software, exposing company systems to viruses, or 'malware' while surfing). Minor cyberslacking was seen as an unproductive computer use behavior. Although they pose substantially little risk of negative consequences for the organization, they result in lost productive work time (Mastrangelo et al., 2006). Despite the much-debated counterproductive nature of cyberslacking at work, several researchers suggest the potentially favorable consequences of Internet use for personal purposes for both employees (e.g. Lim & Teo, 2024; Tandon et al., 2022), described in Section 2.2.2. Taking brief breaks and engaging in minor recreational activities on the Internet can serve as a coping mechanism when employees experience excessive stress or fatigue (Andel et al., 2019; Tandon et al., 2022; Varghese & Barber, 2017), and provide employees with opportunities to relax, regenerate resources, and return to their tasks with renewed energy and motivation (Lim & Chen, 2012; Oravec, 2018; Tandon et al., 2022). However, this approach does not undermine the hypothesis of counterproductive aspects of cyberslacking.

Even if cyberloafing is an effective method for employees to recover resources, it can still harm the organization (Koay & Soh, 2018; Mercado et al., 2017). From the perspective of employers, cyberloafing appears to be a counterproductive phenomenon, since it hinders employee performance (Pindek et al., 2018). Therefore, some researchers refer to cyberloafing as unproductive behavior, rather than counterproductive behavior (Mastrangelo et al., 2006; van Eerde, 2016).

Summarizing, theoretical considerations and empirical evidence suggests that procrastination behavior in work settings partially meets the criteria of counterproductivity. The counterproductive nature of procrastination at work, both offline and online, is mainly related to the 'stealing' of working time or abuse of resources, as identified by Gruys and Sackett (2003) in their research on counterproductive work behavior.

2.2 Prevalence and Consequences of Procrastination at Work

2.2.1 Prevalence and Costs

Procrastination among employees is a common and problematic issue that can have serious implications for both the individual and the organization. It is often viewed in terms of lost productivity and financial costs to the organization. Given that most industries rely on timely task completion, addressing procrastination is crucial to mitigate its negative effects. Statistics show that employee procrastination can have severe and frequent negative effects on firms, resulting in significant expenses. The modern work environment often enables prolonged and increased participation in online activities during work hours. Although the Internet's abundance of resources encourages users to partake in activities unrelated to their jobs, its accessibility and presence at work also promote continuous online connectivity. Consequently, the potency of the Internet triggers excessive use of network resources for activities that are not related to work. Internet misuse during work hours is common in office and corporate settings (Ferrari et al., 2005; Sirois, 2022), where computers are the primary work tool. Employees use personal and work devices, such as laptops, smartphones, and tablets, for both professional and personal activities while working. The advancement in mobile technology and personal phone Internet connectivity has blurred the boundaries between cyberslacking in the workplace and non-work-related activities on digital devices. Thus, the Internet is a growing distraction for employees in organizations.

According to salary.com survey data (2013), approximately 69% of people reported having wasted time at work every day. Of the 1,000 workers surveyed, 34% estimated that they waste 30 minutes or less a day; 24% – from 30 to 60 minutes; and 11% – at least 2 hours a day. Of those who don't waste time every day, 21% said they slack off 1–2 times a week, while only 10% said they never waste time at work. Additionally, 37% of respondents reported that browsing news on the Internet consumed most of their time at work. Other online activities were also indicated, including social networking (14%), online shopping (12%), entertainment (8%), sports (3%), and travel (2%). Just 20% of employees stated that they did not visit any non-work-related websites. In another study by the salary.com portal (2014), it was observed that the number of people who waste time at work every day increased by 20% compared to 2013. The proportion of individuals who spend most time at work has also risen. In that study, 31% of employees reported wasting about 30 minutes a day, another 31% of individuals – about 1 hour, 16% – about 2 hours, 6% – about 3 hours, and 4% wasted four or more working hours, i.e. at least half of the average working day. An upward trend was also observed in the number of employees who use the Internet for personal reasons during work hours. Specifically, 24% reported using it for Internet searches, 23% for social networking, and to a slightly lesser extent, other online activities. The 2015 annual Internet productivity survey (CareerBuilder, 2015) found that out of 5,000 workers, 68% of them reported being distracted by non-work-related online activities at work, such as checking e-mails, browsing websites, and social media. The results showed that during work, respondents made private phone calls and sent text messages (49%), talked to coworkers (42%), surfed the Internet (38%), used social media (37%), extended or took more breaks for a cigarette, coffee, or snack (27%).

A research study conducted by Darius Foroux (2019) revealed that approximately 88% of working Americans delay work for at least 1 hour each day, with 30.4% postponing work between 1 and 2 hours, 31.9% between 2 and 3 hours, and 26% of employees wasting more than 3 hours a day. So, for a person earning $40,000 a year, this loss is approximately $15,000. When comparing the frequency of intense procrastination at work based on professional status, the study revealed that entrepreneurs (76%) procrastinate slightly less (1–4 hours per day) than employees (80%). A 2019 investigation conducted by the Statista Research Department on a sample of 1,002 respondents revealed that 24% of French individuals admit to procrastinating on work tasks. This result does not appear excessively elevated compared to procrastination behavior in sports activities (60%), household responsibilities (51%), or scheduling appointments or medical examinations (46%) (Statista, 2019). According to OfficeTeam (2017), a recruitment agency that conducts workplace research worldwide, office workers dedicate an average of 8 hours per week to non-work-related activities (OfficeTeam, 2017). Respondents reported that they use their mobile devices for most of this non-work-related time. Specifically, employees spend around 56 minutes each day browsing the Web for personal purposes, equating to roughly 5 hours during a typical workweek. Employees who during work use social media (28%), personal e-mail accounts (30%), browse sports websites (9%), shop online (5%), and play online games (6%). However, 58% of surveyed participants affirm that such activities are taking place more frequently through personal smartphones due to some limitations on employer-provided electronic devices.

A survey conducted by the LiveCareer portal (2021) in a group of 653 Polish employees showed that they spend on average about 1 hour 18 minutes of working time on non-work-related activities, such as meals, conversations with coworkers, using the restroom, smoking cigarettes, moving around the office, standing in lines, and waiting for the meeting to start. Furthermore, 48% of employees take 3 to 5 cigarette breaks at work, 8% take cigarette breaks 6 to 10 times a day, and almost 9% take cigarette breaks more than 10 times a day. More than 58% of Polish respondents use the Internet during working hours for private purposes, and the group of the youngest employees (from 18 up to 25 years old) use a private phone (over 65%) and a business laptop (40% of respondents) for this purpose. Instead of working, employees often respond to private e-mails (41%), shop (32%), or search for other job opportunities (30%). Additionally, Facebook is the platform used most frequently by employees during work, as indicated by more than 43% of respondents. Second is YouTube (31%), followed by Instagram (20%), Snapchat, and TikTok (14% each). In particular, the use of TikTok consumes most of the younger employees' time. One-fifth of the users surveyed confessed to spending 1–2 work hours per day on TikTok. In particular, nearly 70% of employees under 25 years of age use TikTok at work. Approximately 5% of them use the app for 2–3 hours, and almost 6% spend more than 4 hours a day. Conversely, Facebook and Instagram users usually spend less than an hour a day on their respective platforms. The extent of procrastination at work offline and online is challenging to estimate and compare due to the various research methodologies employed in studies, such as distinct modes and time frames of computer use, as well as access to online resources during work hours. Nevertheless, the findings provide insights into the procrastination behavior specific among workers in different employment categories. As researchers reported (e.g. Sirois, 2022), the loss of work productivity due to procrastination results in an average cost of $8,000 to $10,000 for one employee per year. This shows the serious financial costs of procrastination at work.

In summary, the presented findings indicate that procrastination is prevalent and intense in work and organizational settings. Excessive time spent on non-work-related activities significantly hinders actual work performance, which is problematic for both the employee and the organization. Employers face significant challenges in identifying the causes of procrastination at work, developing ways to address it, and creating working conditions that discourage or reduce non-work-related activities by employees.

2.2.2 Work Outcomes

Job performance refers to an employee's behavior that is aligned with organizational goals and regarded as the primary work outcome in occupational research. Procrastination of work tasks can result in reduced work performance, decreased work quality, and various counterproductive employee behaviors. Previous research has shown that general procrastination can negatively impact both the speed and quality of task performance (Steel, 2007). Similarly, employee procrastination has been linked to reduced work outcomes and performance (Beheshtifar et al., 2011; Skowronski & Mirowska, 2013). Also, soldiering and cyberslacking at work is significantly associated with low job performance (Metin et al., 2018, 2020). Employees with a high tendency to procrastinate allocate more time to non-work-related activities than to work-related ones, which can lead to decreased performance (Beheshtifar et al., 2011).

In the workplace, employees frequently face time-sensitive assignments. However, individuals with a high tendency to procrastinate delay task completion, which can lead to longer working hours and a significant decrease in performance. Consequently, they are forced to work hastily under pressure of meeting deadline and are more prone to making errors in their work (Ferrari, 2001). Furthermore, individuals who procrastinate are more likely to miss deadlines in comparison to their non-procrastinating counterparts (Skowronski & Mirowska, 2013). Consequently, procrastination has been found to decrease the efficiency and quality of work among various employees and management staff (Ahmad et al., 2021) and service employees (Singh & Singh, 2018), particularly in the public sector (Ahmad et al., 2021). Ferrari et al. (2005) have found that procrastination is a stronger predictor of decreased job performance among white-collar employees than among blue-collar ones. When employees regularly and frequently procrastinate completing work tasks, it not only lowers their work performance, but also decreases team motivation, hinders collaboration, and as a result, declines overall organizational productivity. Research in this area is relatively sparse. Researchers often indirectly assess the impact of procrastination on work performance by examining the effects of personal predictors such as conscientiousness, internal motivation, and self-efficacy (Steel, 2007; van Eerde, 2004). Employees who are ineffective at work experience negative emotions and reduced self-efficacy that can result in postponing tasks and a further decline in outcomes. Steel (2007) posited that poor job performance encourages procrastination, which represents a negative cycle of failures in action. This process could clarify the loop between procrastination and job performance. Procrastination at work that results in low job performance can lead to other serious negative outcomes. Research has shown that employees who procrastinate face lower remuneration, shorter periods of employment, and a greater likelihood of remaining unemployed or underemployed (Nguyen et al., 2013). Moreover, delaying work and specific career development activities can result in diminished professional accomplishments, decreased probability of attaining professional success or career advancement (Steel, 2007), less financial accomplishment, a desire to switch jobs, or a missed opportunity to attain a lucrative position (Senécal & Guay, 2000). Based on the theoretical postulates and research results, procrastination at work appears to be counterproductive or unproductive work behavior (Nguyen et al., 2013), which can manifest itself in different forms of non-work-related activities. Although few studies confirmed these claims, the adverse effect of procrastinating on employee performance seems undeniable.

Cyberslacking has also been found to have negative consequences for employees and organizations (Garrett & Danziger, 2008b; Lim & Chen, 2012), including decreased performance (Andreassen et al., 2014b; Tandon et al., 2022). Moreover, Jiang et al. (2021) revealed that job performance is a function of four behavioral aspects of personal use of technology at work, such as cognitive load, arousal level, timing, and frequency or duration. Employees who use the Internet at work for personal purposes are wasting time that could be spent performing their job duties. These employees may perceive cyberslacking as an escape from the effort and persistence required to complete tasks (O'Neill et al., 2014). The impairing effect of cyberslacking on work performance is often amplified by heightened stress and depletion of cognitive resources needed to perform tasks (Elrehail et al., 2021; Lim & Chen, 2012). Excessive use of the Internet at work indirectly leads to lower wages through reduced performance (König & La Caner de Guardia, 2014; Liberman et al., 2011; Ugrin & Pearson, 2013). Deterioration of individual performance can lead to loss of overall organizational productivity (Garrett & Danziger, 2008b; Lim & Chen, 2012), employee layoffs, loss of time, breach of confidentiality, malware on computers and mobile phones, customer dissatisfaction (Zoghbi-Manrique-de-Lara, 2012), loss of intellectual property, data theft (Bock & Ho, 2009; Lim, 2002), loss of time (Anandarajan & Simmers, 2004; Bock & Ho, 2009), and procrastination at work (Lavoie & Pychyl, 2001). Reduced work performance is more likely when employees engage in *serious* forms of cyberslacking, while *minor* forms may have no effect on performance or may even have a positive effect on performance (Blanchard & Henle, 2008; Lim, 2002). Online shopping and e-commerce activity at work are moderately correlated with low performance (-0.41) (Mahatanankoon et al., 2004). Internet abuse at work has a stronger effect on performance in small organizations, while in large organizations it sometimes is not recognized as a problem (Huma et al., 2017; Moody & Siponen, 2013). Recent studies have shown that the relationship between cyberslacking and work performance is curvilinear (She & Li, 2023). Low and high levels of non-work online activity are associated with lower performance, while moderate cyberslacking is associated with higher employee performance.

Procrastination at work may also promote better work performance, particularly in work tasks that require creative thinking (Harris & Sutton, 1983; van Eerde, 2016), although it may also increase creativity (Adeel et al., 2023; Anderson, 2016) Research has shown that there is a curvilinear relationship between procrastination and creativity. Specifically, under conditions of moderate procrastination, employees tend to generate more creative ideas than under conditions of low or high procrastination, especially when intrinsic motivation and/or high task engagement are high (Adeel et al., 2023; Shin & Grant,

2021). Although employees may delay completing a difficult task, they continue to consciously or unconsciously process it. Thus, procrastination can provide additional time for problem incubation, leading to new insights and solutions. Additionally, delaying the task can increase psychological distance and activate abstract thinking, allowing for a reframing of the problem and the development of new knowledge and approaches. It is important to note that moderate procrastination is necessary for these benefits and should not be confused with chronic procrastination, which can lead to negative consequences. Procrastination can also have beneficial effects in performing simple tasks with a low risk of failure when it creates the stimulating time pressure that makes the task more challenging and consequently can increase employee performance (van Eerde, 2003).

Procrastination may also free up time for the performance of other tasks and search for additional information (Brinthaupt and Shin, 2001). Furthermore, procrastinators working under time pressure can achieve higher work performance. Scholars suggest that an active type of procrastination may increase productivity at work (Chauhan et al., 2020). Employees who procrastinate actively work just ahead of schedule but get the job done effectively. When working in a hurry, they may overlook important information or inefficiently use resources that may be less costly when they are prepared in advance. However, it may be confused with functional delay (Chowdhury & Pychyl, 2018), only seems to be procrastination.

Cyberslacking has a slightly broader array of positive consequences for employees (Lim & Teo, 2024; Oravec, 2018; Spector, 2024). Scholars pointed out that non-work-related Internet use at work can increase work performance (Coker, 2011; Mohammad et al., 2019; Oravec, 2018), specifically information search on the Internet was strongly correlated (0.63) with high performance (Mahatanankoon et al., 2004). This effect is stronger when employees browse the Web with the permission of their supervisors (Lim & Chen, 2012). Coker (2011) found that allowing employees to engage in personal Internet use at work can foster perceived autonomy, and thereby higher performance. However, this effect occurred when cyberslacking did not exceed 12% of the work time. This positive effect is consistent with the assumptions of the conservation resources theory (Hobfoll, 2012) and suggest that cyberslacking replenishes employees' depleted resources at work. Browsing the Internet can make employees happier, less stressed, and, therefore, more productive at work. Also, the use of the Internet for non-work purposes promotes learning new skills that can be useful at work (Anandarajan & Simmers, 2004; Baskaran et al., 2019), acquisition of competencies valued in the organization, including digital competencies (Anandarajan & Simmers, 2004; Belanger & van Slyke, 2002), recover attentional resources (Coker, 2011), and stimulate creative thinking (Derin & Gökçe, 2016; Sawitri & Mayasari, 2017; Tsai, 2023). The relationship between online procrastination and creativity depends on the type of cyberbehavior (Lim & Teo, 2024). Engaging in minor forms of cyberslacking reduces work-related mental fatigue (e.g. in the afternoon) and can increase creativity, whereas serious forms of cyberslacking may diminish creativity at work (Sawitri & Mayasari, 2017). There are also studies suggesting a nonsignificant or weak relationship between cyberslacking and work performance. A meta-analysis of 14 studies (Mercado et al., 2017b) showed that cyberslacking is not significantly associated with job performance ($\bar{r} = -0.05$). Other studies show relatively weak associations between Internet misuse at work and organizational or employee performance (Tandon et al., 2022). Additionally, the relationship between cyberslacking and performance was moderated by the timing, frequency, or type of cyberslacking, with only certain forms or levels being problematic. Baskaran et al.'s study (2019) showed that developmental and recovery cyberslacking is associated with increased work performance (0.25 and 0.15, respectively).

2.2.3 Emotions

Engaging in non-work-related activities offline and online during work hours can lead to negative emotions, stress, emotional exhaustion, burnout, job dissatisfaction, and ultimately deterioration of physical and mental health. Numerous research showed that general procrastination has a detrimental impact on one's well-being and can result in negative emotional states, such as guilt, shame, anxiety, stress, and depression (see Section 1.2.2). However, the effects of procrastination at work have not been thoroughly investigated. Although there is empirical evidence that emotional consequences of procrastination at work and cyberslacking include lower self-efficacy, fatigue, mental detachment, stress, and boredom at work (as well as reduced job satisfaction) and are described in more detail in this chapter.

Stress at Work: Work stress is an individual's reaction to working conditions that are perceived as emotionally or physically threatening. Procrastination behavior at work can increase stress levels (Mohsin & Ayub, 2014; Mosquera et al., 2022). Engaging in non-work-related activities can contribute to stress and emotional discomfort among employees due to delayed task completion. This may be because people may equate procrastination with the accumulation of work tasks and the waste of time to complete them (Mosquera et al., 2022). Procrastination behavior in the workplace might result in the depletion of vital work resources, such as time and energy, and subsequently lead to emotional distress.

Similar findings were revealed in studies on cyberslacking. This form of dysfunctional behavior at work is likely to result in negative emotional consequences, including stress from being caught and sanctioned for the behavior, stress from not completing work tasks, and feelings of guilt toward the employer for using work time for private activities. The negative consequences of cyberslacking confirm its dysfunctional nature at both individual and organizational levels. The use of the Internet for personal purposes during work hours can distract employees from completing their tasks, resulting in longer working hours, cumulative work, and even taking work home (Lim & Teo, 2024). In such situations, employees may find their resources consumed by non-work-related activities, leading to feelings of stress, anxiety, or guilt for not completing their duties. Increasingly, studies suggest that cyberslacking may reduce stress at work (Koay et al., 2017a; Lim & Chen, 2012; Lim & Teo, 2024). The Internet is viewed by employees as a source of positive stimulation and entertainment, which can alleviate stress, improve mental well-being, or relax the mind (Oravec, 2018). Engaging in various enjoyable online activities can alleviate two types of stress: technostress associated with the use of modern technology (Güğerçin, 2020) and job stress (Koay et al., 2017). Cyberslacking allows an employee to detach from stressful work conditions, excessive workload, fatigue, or boredom (Lim & Teo, 2024). A study conducted among workers in the United States, India, and other Asian countries found that excessive job demands have led to an increase in their non-work-related Internet use at work (Ugrin et al., 2007). Similarly, employees in Singapore engaged in personal Internet use due to excessive or inconsistent expectations placed on them at work (Lim, 2002). Respondents often reported feeling less stressed after using the Internet for non-work-related purposes, viewing it as a stress-relieving tool. Additionally, using the Internet for personal purposes at work can mitigate the negative effects of work–family conflict (Gözü et al., 2015), and improve employees' mental health (Ivarsson & Larsson, 2011).

Emotional Exhaustion and Burnout: Chronic procrastination at work leads to high levels of emotional exhaustion caused by workplace stressors, resulting in feelings of dullness, boredom, depression, weakness, and fatigue (Janssen et al., 2010). It is also associated with negative emotional responses such as anger and depression, decreased performance, and dissatisfaction. According to Michielsen et al. (2007), the two main causes of emotional exhaustion include an unfavorable work environment and a perceived 'weak' employee's personality. Among personality traits that cause emotional exhaustion are neuroticism, anxiety, introversion, low self-esteem, low self-efficacy, conscientiousness, agreeableness, and low resilience. Various job demands, such as qualitative and quantitative demands, work pressure, work–family conflict, conflict or role ambiguity, injustice, poor social support, low work autonomy, and negative leadership contribute to emotional exhaustion among employees (van Daalen et al., 2009). Studies of US office workers (Roster & Ferrari, 2020), nurses in China (Ma et al., 2021), and university employees from 69 countries (Hall et al., 2019) have demonstrated a significant moderate relationship between procrastination and emotional exhaustion. This suggests that procrastination in the workplace can heighten stress levels, build-up of pressure, and negative emotions ultimately causing a sense of fatigue and exhaustion in employees (Abbas & Al

Hasnawi, 2020). According to recent research, employees may also experience increased frustration when observing their supervisors' procrastination behavior. Furthermore, a high level of procrastination significantly moderated the indirect effect of job demands on emotional exhaustion mediated by perceived time control (Roster & Ferrari, 2020). Specifically, among chronic procrastinators, control of time played a weaker role in reducing emotional exhaustion than among individuals with a high tendency to procrastinate.

Cyberslacking can also promote fatigue and resource exhaustion (van Doorn, 2011). Excessive Internet use at work can deplete personal resources needed for work, such as energy, time, and concentration (Lim & Chen, 2012; Wong et al., 2023). Engaging in non-work activities, particularly those that require more resources, can also leave employees feeling exhausted. According to the conservation of resources theory (Hobfoll, 2012), procrastination and cyberslacking can lead to negative emotions that individuals must cope with when faced with heavy workloads. This can result in the depletion of resources and ultimately result in emotional and physical exhaustion. However, a relatively large number of studies have shown that non-work-related online employee activities during working hours can have positive emotional effects, such as reducing stress, tension, or exhaustion (Aghaz & Sheikh, 2016; Koay & Soh, 2018; Oravec, 2018; Wu et al., 2020). In situations of excessive exploitation at work, employees may experience fatigue and resource exhaustion, leading them to avoid work or take breaks to regain mental and physical energy. Wong et al. (2023) conducted a study on the effects of cyberloafing on work-related and non-work-related exhaustion, as well as its interaction with cyber-life interruption. The study found that while cyberloafing may increase work exhaustion, it may also diminish non-work exhaustion. Furthermore, cyberloafing may alleviate non-work exhaustion caused by interruptions in online activities, while cyber-life interruptions may reduce work exhaustion caused by cyberloafing.

Job Satisfaction: According to some definitions, job satisfaction is an attitude that comprises an individual's beliefs and opinions about their work, including the emotional aspect of their job and their responses to work-related situations. If an individual believes that their work provides an opportunity to realize essential ideals or is a calming experience, they are likely to be satisfied with their job, as long as these values align with their needs (Locke, 1978). Mosquera et al. (2022) supported the negative effect of soldiering on job satisfaction. Employees who procrastinate with work tasks often experience discomfort and dissatisfaction due to incomplete assignments or reduced performance. By delaying unpleasant work tasks, they only prolong, rather than resolve the problem with perceived frustration and aversion to the task, which only increases their discomfort when returning to complete it. This mechanism is consistent with the assumptions of self-determination theory (Deci & Ryan, 2008), which posits that the satisfaction of basic psychological needs is associated with higher levels of job satisfaction.

Relatively large numbers of studies have found that cyberslacking is directly associated with increased job satisfaction (Andel et al., 2019; Lim & Chen, 2012; Mohammad et al., 2019). This effect was particularly significant for the use of social networks (Farivar & Richardson, 2021). Given the diversity of cyberslacking behaviors, their links to job satisfaction are inconclusive. Stanton (2002) has found that frequent Internet users at work reported higher levels of satisfaction with their jobs, pay, and opportunities for advancement than other employees. Furthermore, the work-Internet leisure dimension was moderately associated with high employee satisfaction (0.41) among Malaysian banking sector employees (Mohammad et al., 2019). On the other hand, browsing activities were significantly related to positive affect but nonsignificantly to e-mailing activities (Lim & Chen, 2012). In another study, only personal e-commerce significantly predicted job satisfaction, while personal online communication and information search were insignificant in explaining job satisfaction (Mahatanankoon et al., 2004). Studies have found the moderating effect of cyberslacking on the impact of negative aspects of work on reduced job satisfaction, buffering the stressful effect of exposure to verbal and physical aggression (Andel et al., 2019). This suggests that cyberloafing is an emotion-focused coping strategy, alleviating the adverse effects of workplace aggression exposures. Cyberslacking likely increased employee satisfaction with work, providing them with a respite to cope with workplace stress. However, some researchers suggest that excessive Internet use at work is an outcome rather than an antecedent of job satisfaction (Galletta & Polak, 2003). These relationships are presented in Section 2.3.2.

Restorative Consequences: Cyberslacking can have both negative and positive emotional consequences. Cyberslacking can promote well-being (Gözü et al., 2015), positive affect (Lim & Chen, 2012), or higher job satisfaction (Farivar & Richardson, 2021; Mohammad et al., 2019; Stanton, 2002). Employees engage in non-work-related online activities that they enjoy (e.g. reading entertaining articles, and exploring personal interests) (Coker, 2011). This may be indicative of the restorative nature of cyberslacking that leads to improved mood. As studies' reviews have reported, the use of technology to take care of personal matters during work hours can help maintain work–life balance, ensuring the integrity of family life while meeting extensive professional demands (Lim & Teo, 2024; Tandon et al., 2022). Wu et al. (2020) found that employees' social cyberloafing at work contributes to psychological detachment as an effective mechanism for employees' recovery of personal resources and their well-being. The study by Liu et al. (2021), which integrated the positive and negative nature of Internet use, revealed that evening cyberleisure affected psychological vitality and performance the next day in two ways: (1) undermined by bedtime procrastination and low-quality and quantity of sleep, and (2) improved through psychological detachment and high quality and quantity of sleep. Restorative effects are obtained from cyber-entertainment that facilitates psychological detachment, but if it leads to bedtime procrastination, the regenerative benefits are diminished. In this way, the employee does not lose the resources needed for work to find a convenient opportunity to deal with important matters.

To summarize, procrastination and cyberslacking at work can potentially result in employees' negative and positive emotional states. This may suggest its restorative function. These relationships seem to create a vicious or virtuous cycle, in which emotions may trigger or alleviate non-work-related activities offline and online, which subsequently induce an emotional response. For more information on the role of stress in inducing procrastination at work (see Section 2.3.2).

2.3 Individual Antecedents of Procrastination at Work

To fully understand the phenomenon of procrastination at work, it is necessary to investigate its potential causes. Thus, this chapter examines three categories of antecedents of procrastination offline and online, such as (1) personality traits such as neuroticism, conscientiousness, extraversion, openness to experience,agreeableness, self-control, self-efficacy, self-esteem, locus of control,narcissism, Machiavellianism, psychopathy: (2) sociodemographic factors such as gender, age, and education; (3) and emotional and motivational factors including stress, exhaustion, burnout, boredom, satisfaction, work engagement, and organizational commitment.

2.3.1 Personality Traits

Personality traits play an important role in regulating cognitive, emotional, and motivational processes and determining behavioral patterns in the workplace. According to Judge et al. (2021), personality traits determine both positive and negative work behavior. However, only a few studies have examined the relationship between personality traits and work procrastination. There are slightly more findings on the personality determinants of cyberslacking.

Neuroticism: Meta-analyses of research on general procrastination have shown an association with neuroticism (Meng et al., 2024; Steel, 2007). A similar effect was found for procrastination at work (Huang et al., 2023; Pearlman-Avnion & Zibenberg, 2018). Neurotic individuals tend to pessimistically interpret situations and events, which can lead to stress and negative emotions. Employees with high neuroticism exhibit a relatively weak ability to cope with environmental job demands, perceiving challenges and hindrance demands as threats. They are also more prone to losing control of their emotions and engaging in impulsive behavior. Additionally, they often utilize avoidant coping strategies, such as procrastination behaviors and cyberslacking at work. Numerous studies consistently indicated that neuroticism is moderately associated with cyberslacking. Employees with higher levels of neuroticism are more prone to browsing the Internet during work hours and engaging in other non-work-related cyber behaviors as a means of coping with stressful work situations (Tandon et al., 2022). A meta-analysis of eight studies (Mercado et al., 2017b), and further studies (Sheikh et al., 2019; Varghese & Barber, 2017) found a weak correlation between emotional stability and cyberslacking ($\bar{r} = -0.13$). Thus, neuroticism can be regarded as a risk factor for inducing procrastination at work.

Conscientiousness: Conscientiousness as a personality trait is represented by components of accuracy, carefulness, responsibility, organization, and persistence in achieving goals (McCrae & Costa, 2003). It is most strongly associated with work procrastination. Employees with high conscientiousness tend to have great responsibility for completing tasks at work and thereby a lower tendency to procrastinate. The findings supported a moderate to high relationship between conscientiousness and procrastination at work (-0.31 to -0.61) in Israeli employees (Pearlman-Avnion & Zibenberg, 2018), Chinese public service workers (Huang et al., 2023), and Indian managers in the textile industry (Singh & Bala, 2020). Conscientiousness was related to low workplace procrastination directly and indirectly through high self-efficacy (Singh & Bala, 2020). In the Pearlman-Avnion and Zibenberg (2018) study, this effect was stronger among people with high anxiety dysregulation than those with low anxiety dysregulation. Huang et al. (2023) found that the association between challenge stressors and procrastination at work was moderated by conscientiousness. Specifically, among employees with high conscientiousness, challenge stressors strengthened procrastination. These findings supported previous empirical evidence on the role of conscientiousness in predicting dispositional procrastination (Steel, 2007; Wright, 2015). Conscientiousness effectively predicted low cyberslacking in the workplace (Jia et al., 2013; Tandon et al., 2022; Varghese & Barber, 2017). A meta-analysis of 11 studies consistently revealed a negative correlation ($\bar{r} = -0.09$) between conscientiousness and cyberslacking (Mercado et al., 2017b). As researchers suggest, individuals with high conscientiousness tend to use self-management strategies that help them regulate cyberslacking behavior.

Extraversion: Among the Big Five personality traits (McCrae & Costa, 2003), extraversion was found to be negatively correlated (-0.30) with work procrastination (O'Neill et al., 2014b). This relationship is consistent with research findings on general procrastination (Steel, 2007). Other studies suggest a positive (Meng et al., 2024) or nonsignificant association of extraversion with general procrastination (Steel & Klingsieck, 2016; van Eerde, 2004). Furthermore, extraversion has shown a weak positive correlation with cyberloafing (Andreassen et al., 2014a; Jia et al., 2013; Sheikh et al., 2019; Varghese & Barber, 2017). Employees with high extraversion tend to seek social stimulation in the work environment, therefore they may be more susceptible to engaging in interpersonal interaction in real and virtual situations and delay work tasks, such as visiting social media or other entertainment websites. Extraverts derive social benefits from the Internet, therefore they feel encouraged to seek out social networking sites or other sources of entertainment through cyberloafing. However, the meta-analysis of seven studies indicated a nonsignificant relationship between extraversion and cyberslacking ($\bar{r} = 0.01$; Mercado et al., 2017b).

Openness to Experience: Empirical evidence was not found for a significant relationship between openness to experience and procrastination at work. There are few studies examining openness in predicting cyberloafing, which indicated a positive correlation (Sheikh et al., 2019) or a nonsignificant relation between them (Jia et al., 2013). Individuals with high openness are more likely to engage in non-work-related online activities to explore virtual reality for private purposes. However, the meta-analysis of seven studies did not support a significant relationship between openness and cyberslacking ($\bar{r} = 0.01$; Mercado et al., 2017b).

Agreeableness: Agreeable individuals are naturally tolerant, altruistic, gentle, humble, cheerful, caring, compliant, and trusting of others (McCrae & Costa, 2003). It was predicted that employees with such traits would emphasize trust and respect for others and minimize procrastination and cyberslacking as detrimental behaviors to the organization. Studies revealed a moderate effect of agreeableness on procrastination at work (−0.29 to −0.39) (O'Neill et al., 2014a; Pearlman-Avnion & Zibenberg, 2018). In Pearlman-Avnion & Zibenberg study (2018) , this relationship is moderated by anxiety dysregulation. Therefore, individuals with low anxiety dysregulation showed a positive relationship between agreeableness and procrastination whereas individuals with high anxiety dysregulation showed a negative relationship between agreeableness and procrastination.

Some studies supported the negative relationship between agreeableness and cyberslacking. A meta-analysis of seven studies revealed weak correlations between these variables ($\bar{r} = -0.09$; Mercado et al., 2017b). There were also findings showing no relationship between agreeableness and cyberloafing (Jia et al., 2013). The characteristic of agreeableness, a positive attitude toward others, can decrease instances of violating organizational regulations and engaging in dysfunctional work behavior, such as soldiering and cyberslacking. Highly agreeable individuals assess procrastination and cyberslacking as inappropriate behavior in the workplace. Therefore, they refrain from engaging in procrastination or non-work-related activities in the workplace.

Self-control: Low self-control has been found to relate to undesirable and deviant behaviors in various domains, including work settings (Restubog et al., 2010). Associations between self-control and general procrastination were well documented (see Section 1.3.2). There was also empirical evidence for a negative association of self-control with procrastination at work and cyberslacking. Individuals low in self-control have limited resources, which decreases their ability to impulse regulation at any given time in the workplace. A meta-analysis of studies (Mercado et al., 2017b) indicated that self-control was moderately and positively related to cyberloafing ($\bar{r} = -0.32$). Thus, individuals high in self-control are less likely to engage in non-work-related Internet use during work time. This relationship is significant in both other-reported and self-reported cyberloafing (Restubog et al., 2011). Self-control was often a moderator or mediator of the effects of various individual and work-related characteristics on procrastination or cyberloafing. For example, van Eerde and Venus (van Eerde & Venus, 2018) found that low sleep quality affected employees' work procrastination, who exhibited low self-control. Furthermore, self-control reinforces a negative relationship between perceived organizational justice and cyberloafing (Restubog et al., 2011). Zhang et al. (2015) revealed that high future orientation led to reduced cyberloafing behaviors through self-control. In summary, low self-control may be viewed as a vulnerability factor for procrastination and cyberloafing at work.

Self-efficacy: Research showed that self-efficacy significantly predicted general and work-related procrastination (see Section 1.3.2). According to the available knowledge, one study revealed a negative effect of self-efficacy on lower employee procrastination. Additionally, self-efficacy mediated the relationship between conscientiousness and procrastination at work (Singh & Bala, 2020). Configuration of conscientiousness with self-efficacy creates an important pattern in predicting high employee performance and reduced dysfunctional work behavior. This finding is part of a large stream of research showing a strong negative relationship between self-efficacy and dispositional procrastination (Steel, 2007). There is also limited research on the relationship between self-efficacy and cyberslacking. A meta-analysis of six studies showed a moderate relationship between self-efficacy and cyberslacking ($\bar{r} = 0.17$; Mercado et al., 2017b). Effect of self-efficacy on cyberslacking was also mediated through job satisfaction (Korzynski & Protsiuk, 2022). On the one hand, high self-efficacy makes employees believe in the effective completion of difficult work tasks, which can lead to higher performance (Stajkovic & Luthans, 1998), lower procrastination at work, and avoidance of non-work-related activities. On the other hand, individuals with low self-efficacy are prone to misuse the Internet for non-work purposes in the workplace. According to Prasad and colleagues (2010), the relationship between self-efficacy and cyberslacking depends on self-regulation. Individuals with low self-efficacy perceive themselves as incapable of attaining their goals and therefore may allocate more time to more attractive online activities than work. Individuals with high self-efficacy and low self-regulation are enticed to browse the Internet during work, erroneously believing that they require fewer resources to complete a task than is actually necessary. In contrast, individuals with elevated self-efficacy and self-regulation possess the ability to maintain concentration on tasks. These associations expose a specific paradox regarding the impact of self-efficacy in the workplace, which enhances task performance and the risk of cyberslacking.

Self-esteem: Global self-esteem was not examined as a correlate of procrastination at work, while relatively a lot of studies indicated that self-esteem is a strong predictor of cyberslacking in the workplace. Vitak et al. (2011) found a correlation between using the Internet at work and low self-esteem and self-control problems. Individuals with low self-esteem use the Internet as an escape from their problems, such as a sense of isolation or rejection from others. These findings are in the line of research on associations between global self-esteem and general procrastination (see Section 1.3.2).

Locus of Control: Procrastination in work settings is significantly associated with locus of control (Khoshouei, 2017; Lonergan & Maher, 2000; Munjal & Mishra, 2019). As research results suggest, people who procrastinate have a stronger external locus of control than people who do not procrastinate. In work settings, procrastination has also been associated with an external locus of control in a group of nurses (Khoshouei, 2017), healthcare workers (Lonergan & Maher, 2000), and managers of private and public companies (Aziz & Tariq, 2013). Externals tend to have high work procrastination, whereas internals showed a decreased tendency to procrastinate as work autonomy increased. The above results supported previous findings on the relationship between the locus of control and dispositional procrastination (Spyridaki & Galanakis, 2022) and point to the predictive role of an external locus of control. Aziz and Tariq (2013) found that less experienced managers with a lower internal locus of control reported higher decisional procrastination, while more experienced managers exhibited an internal locus of control and lower decisional procrastination. Apparently, individuals with an external locus of control tend to procrastinate more because of their inability to perceive a connection between their actions and the resulting consequences.

The internal locus of control also predicted cyberloafing in the workplace. However, the findings are inconsistent. On the one hand, internals tend to use the Internet for personal reasons because they are responsible for their actions and aware of their consequences, while externals believe that their actions are influenced by external factors (Jamaluddin et al., 2015; Vitak et al., 2011). Furthermore, those who are externally driven showed reduced self-control in their use of the Internet, which in turn contributes to their cyberslacking within the workplace (Vitak et al., 2011). However, several studies suggest the opposite (Blanchard & Henle, 2008; Blau et al., 2006; Chen et al., 2008), indicating that externals tend to non-work-related Internet use without guilt, whereas the discovery of this behavior by supervisors attributed to chance, bad luck, or other individuals' actions.

Dark Triad: No research has examined the relationship between the 'dark triad' traits including narcissism, Machiavellianism, and psychopathy (Paulhus & Williams, 2002) and procrastination at work, but some studies have found their significant associations with cyberslacking (Cohen & Özsoy, 2024; Lowe-Calverley & Grieve, 2017; Rahman & Muldoon, 2020). Employees with negative personality traits are more likely to misuse the Internet despite the fact that this practice reduces their work efficiency and increases organizational costs. Machiavellianism and psychopathy are particularly associated with non-work-related browsing and emailing activities (Cohen & Özsoy, 2024). Due to their cunning and selfish nature, individuals with a high negative traits cyberloaf with more negative intentions. Employees with high levels of Machiavellianism and psychopathy tend to engage in manipulative, dishonest, and unethical behaviors, such as cyber-aggression and cyber-bullying. In addition, psychopathy includes a component of impulsivity that accounts for emotional deficits, a preference for risk and short-term gain. In the workplace, these activities can limit the time and quality of work performed. Previous research has shown that individuals high in narcissism engage in non-work-related activities on the Internet (Rahman & Muldoon, 2020). Moreover, they have more extensive social networks and tend to engage in antisocial, violent, and unethical behaviors on social media (e.g. the Facebook platform) (Moor & Anderson, 2019). However, recent findings (Cohen & Özsoy, 2024) revealed a nonsignificant associations between narcissism and non-work-related browsing and emailing. Lowe-Calverley and Grieve (2017) also found a positive indirect effect of dark traits on high cyberslacking through perceived ability to deceive.

Summarizing, the review of empirical findings presented above suggests that personality traits are an important source of explained variance in procrastination and cyberslacking at work. However, the body of research in this area is limited, especially in the prediction of procrastination at work. Although the results are inconsistent, they suggest the location of personality characteristics in the nomological network of procrastination or cyberslacking.

2.3.2 Emotional and Motivational Factors

2.3.2.1 Emotional Factors

Extensive research showed that components of well-being determine general procrastination (e.g. Pychyl & Sirois, 2016). There seems to be an analogous significant relationship between well-being and procrastination in the work setting. However, its specific emotional and motivational antecedents may also appear. Some studies have established emotional predictors of procrastination at work, such as work stress, boredom, emotional exhaustion, and job dissatisfaction.

Work Stress: Stress at work refers to physical, psychological, and behavioral responses when employees are unable to fully coordinate individual needs and environmental demands (Le Blanc et al., 2000). Unfavorable working conditions induce work-related stress and deplete employees' cognitive and emotional resources, which has negative consequences for employees' functioning and the organization. While the relationship between stress and trait procrastination is well-documented (Sirois, 2023), there is little research that illustrates the association of stress with procrastination in the workplace. Results of the existing studies showed that stress is positively correlated with procrastination behavior at work (Wan et al., 2014). A study by Verešová (2013) found that cognitive, emotional, and social symptoms of stress were associated with work-related procrastination. It also revealed a tendency to use avoidant strategies in stress coping among teachers with high and proactive strategies among those with low procrastination. Procrastination among teachers was determined by stress experienced in emotionally difficult situations while performing aversive tasks (Laybourn et al., 2019). Probably, employees may engage in non-work activities to escape from work accumulation and find relief from negative emotions (D'Abate & Eddy, 2007).

In today's world, it seems obvious that employees may engage in non-work-related online activities because of troubles or stress they are experiencing at work. Research showed that workplace stress is related to non-work-related Internet misuse in the workplace (Henle & Blanchard, 2008; Mishra & Tageja, 2022). Under stressful work conditions, employees are more likely to engage in non-work-related online activities, such as sending e-mails and browsing news sites (Lim, 2002), which are perceived by employees as acceptable forms of stress relief and work breaks. This behavior may help reduce stress by allowing employees to temporarily ignore problems or avoid stressful work environments (Sampat & Basu, 2017; Tandon et al., 2022; Varghese & Barber, 2017; Wu et al., 2020). In this way, cyberslacking can promote the recovery of lost resources. Engaging in non-work-related Internet use at work may help employees detach from the stressful work, as well as have some respite and relaxation (Lim et al., 2021). However, the link between stress and cyberslacking is entangled in more complex patterns of relationships. For example, a study by Elrehail et al. (2021) found that the relationship between work stress and cyberslacking was negative when considered in the context of high work motivation. Employee motivation may reduce the impact of work stress on cyberslacking behavior. Additionally, mindfulness was found to moderate the direct positive relationship between stress and cyberslacking behavior. Individuals with high mindfulness were less likely to engage in non-work-related online activities when experiencing high levels of stress (Mishra & Tageja, 2022). In addition, stress often mediates the relationship between high job demands and non-work-Internet use among university employees (Elrehail et al., 2021) and IT workers (Bajcar & Babiak, 2020). In a study by Koay et al. (2017b), stress was found to be a significant mediator in the positive relationship between private demands and cyberslacking.

In summary, stress may play a significant role in predicting high procrastination and cyberslacking behavior in the workplace. Under stressful work conditions, employees procrastinate by engaging in non-work activities offline and online to reduce stress and avoid or procrastinate work. Nevertheless, procrastination may be considered a strategy for coping with work-related stress (Lavoie & Pychyl, 2001; Wan et al., 2014). According to Sirois (2023) considerations, stress in the workplace can be both a predictor and an effect of procrastination in complex work environments, creating a vicious cycle that can mutually either strengthen or weaken this phenomenon in work conditions.

Emotional Exhaustion and Burnout: Emotional exhaustion is defined as a chronic state of psychological distress resulting from repeated exposure to work-related stress (Janssen et al., 2010). It affects motivation, attitudes, and behavior. Exhaustion can manifest itself in various ways, such as dullness, boredom, depression, fatigue, and distress, and is the actual or potential loss of resources (Hobfoll, 2012; Hobfoll et al., 2018). Thus, exhaustion is an emotional response to adverse work conditions that can trigger dysfunctional emotion regulation. In a resource-depletion situation, employees can postpone work and engage in activities that regenerate depleted resources. It seems that procrastination is a response to overwhelming fatigue and exhaustion after a long and fulfilling work. According to the theory of conservation of resources (Hobfoll, 2012), the actual or potential loss of resources makes the employee feel stressed. Therefore, when an employee lacks resources, she will most likely procrastinate due to depleted resources, and engage in activities she considers regenerative for lost resources thus relieving negative emotions. Employees generally avoid or delay work when they are tired or physically or mentally exhausted (DeArmond et al., 2014; Roster & Ferrari, 2020). The relationship between exhaustion, fatigue, and procrastination at work was supported by findings from Korean hotel workers (Jung & Yoon, 2022) and academic staff in various countries (Hall et al., 2019). The findings indicate that demanding work can deplete resources, leading to reduced self-control and increased procrastination in the future. DeArmond et al. (2014) confirmed that excessive workload leads to physical and mental fatigue, which in turn causes procrastination of work tasks. The study also found that psychological detachment (parallelly to fatigue) mediates the relationship between workload and procrastination. Probably, employees engage in non-work-related activities to recover their exhausted resources. In remote work settings, emotional exhaustion was moderately correlated with decisional and behavioral procrastination (Ferrari et al., 2021).

Recent studies supported the important role of emotional exhaustion in predicting cyberslacking (Koay, 2018b; Lim et al., 2021; Zhou et al., 2021). Exhaustion was directly related to Internet misuse at work (0.20 to 0.39), but it also mediated the relationship between work-related characteristics and cyberslacking in all studies. For example, exhaustion mediated effect of workplace ostracism (Koay, 2018b), authoritarian leadership (Zhang et al., 2022), and abusive supervision on employee cyberslacking, but only under conditions of low organizational commitment (Lim et al., 2021). Another study found that emotional exhaustion mediated the impact of both challenge and hindrance demands on increased cyberslacking (Zhou et al., 2021). In situations of fatigue or stress, employee's resources can become depleted, leading to increased tension and a greater tendency to procrastinate. According to the conservation of resources theory (COR) (Hobfoll, 2012), individuals are driven to protect or regenerate the physical and mental energy needed for work. Therefore, engaging in enjoyable, non-work-related online activities seems to meet the conditions for recovering lost resources (Tandon et al., 2022; Wu et al., 2020). Taking breaks from work to non-work-related Internet browsing appears to be an effective way to regenerate mental and physical energy (Reinecke, 2009). For example, recreational browsing of the Web and playing computer games during work hours leads to psychological detachment from work, builds internal resources (e.g. knowledge and new skills), and improves mental well-being. Furthermore, research findings confirmed that short-term recreational cyberslacking allows employees to recover, resulting in reduced stress levels, improved mood, and satisfaction, as well as increased creativity and performance (Oravec, 2018). This seems particularly important in the context of excessive work hours and potential negative emotional effects (such as stress and burnout). To date, one study (Aghaz & Sheikh, 2016) showed that burnout is associated with both *cyberloafing behaviors* (recreational, learning, deviant, addictive) and *cyberloafing activities* (such as social, informational, recreational, virtual). However, job burnout appears to be a stronger predictor of cyberslacking behaviors ($\beta = 0.47$) than activities ($\beta = 0.28$). It is evident that burnt-out employees tend to disengage from work and exhibit deviant or counterproductive work behaviors. In summary, exhaustion and burnout are significant predictors of procrastination at work, which is characterized by engaging in non-work-related activities both offline and online. Procrastination behavior appears to be an employee's strategy for coping with fatigue and emotional exhaustion at work.

Job Satisfaction: Job satisfaction is commonly defined as a positive emotional state as a result of the evaluation of one's job or job experiences (Locke, 1978). Scholars emphasized the role of job satisfaction in predicting citizenship and counterproductive work behavior (Judge et al., 2021). Lonergan and Maher (2000) found that a decrease in employee satisfaction increases the risk of dysfunctional behaviors, such as withdrawal and procrastination, while an increase in satisfaction may contribute to an employee's commitment and performance. However, empirical findings on the relationship between procrastination and job satisfaction have not been conclusive. Some studies suggest that procrastination at work leads to lower job satisfaction (see Section 2.2.3). As Steel (2007) suggested, these relationships may reflect a mechanism based on a vicious cycle that reinforces employees' procrastination. However, there is no convincing empirical evidence for an inverse relationship. While job satisfaction has been well-documented as a predictor of counterproductive work behavior, one can assume that job satisfaction also predicts procrastination and cyberslacking behavior at work. Some studies have found a negative correlation between job satisfaction and procrastination at work (Cadena et al., 2011; Hen et al., 2021; Wang et al., 2021). Job satisfaction also has been found a significant predictor of high procrastination at work (Sunarta et al., 2023). This implies that job satisfaction can help reduce procrastination behavior.

Some empirical evidence indicates that employee satisfaction was negatively associated with cyberslacking (O'Neill et al., 2014a). The research conducted by Vitak et al. (2011) found a weak but significant relationship between job dissatisfaction and excessive use of two specific online activities, such as communication via short text messages and browsing social networking sites. Wang et al. (2021) found that job satisfaction significantly moderated the negative correlation between electronic monitoring of Internet use and cyberslacking at work. Employees dissatisfied with their jobs tended to engage in more cyberslacking when there were no policies in place to control Internet usage or when electronic monitoring was not present. Nonetheless, these effects are more effective in reducing cyberslacking of employees with higher job satisfaction. However, the meta-analysis comprising 14 studies (Mercado et al., 2017b) and later research (Giordano & Mercado, 2023; Mosquera et al., 2022) consistently indicated a nonsignificant relationship between the two variables ($\bar{r} = -0.04$). A considerable body of research has found that non-work-related Internet use is related to high job satisfaction (Andel et al., 2019; Farivar & Richardson, 2021; Lim & Chen, 2012; Mohammad et al., 2019; Stanton, 2002). However, it is not clear which direction this relationship is likely to take. These results may correspond to a restorative approach to cyberslacking (Lim & Teo, 2024), which suggests positive consequences of non-work-related Internet use (see Section 2.2.3). In addition, job satisfaction was mediated relationship between workload and cyberloafing (Korzynski & Protsiuk, 2022). It suggests that nom-work-related Internet use may be a response to employees dissatisfaction due to high workload.

In summary, the presented research findings indicated complex associations of job satisfaction with employees' procrastination and cyberslacking. They suggest that job satisfaction is both a predictor and a result of non-work-related behavior offline and online.

Boredom: Among the emotional predictors of cyberslacking, boredom at work ranks relatively high. Individuals with higher levels of susceptibility to boredom as an individual trait (Tam et al., 2021) experience it more frequently and more intensely. In search of more stimulation, these individuals are also more likely to engage in risky behaviors (e.g. reckless driving, binge eating, drug, and alcohol abuse) or dysfunctional behaviors (e.g. problematic Internet use). Like procrastination, cyberslacking can be triggered by boredom at work. When the work situation is not sufficiently stimulating and employees feel bored, they begin to seek more attractive activities at work to alleviate this unpleasant state. Consequently, they willingly engage in various non-work-related online activities, such as browsing websites or social networks for entertainment (Koessmeier & Büttner, 2021; Sümer & Büttner, 2022).

Boredom is also considered a state commonly attributed to external factors. This notion is supported by research indicating that boredom resulting from underload at work often leads to cyberslacking (Pindek et al., 2018). A meta-analysis of seven studies (Mercado et al., 2017b) showed that boredom as a negative affective state determined by underloaded work was moderately associated with Internet abuse at work ($\bar{r} = 0.24$). Similarly, in other studies, those individuals who experience greater boredom at work show greater engagement in a variety of non-work-related online activities; as employees' boredom increases, the frequency of browsing social networks, instant messaging, and online shopping increases (0.17–0.34) (Sümer & Büttner, 2022). Boredom at work was directly found to influence non-work online activities among US computer workers (Eastin et al., 2007) and Portuguese employees (Mosquera et al., 2022). Researchers have speculated that the tendency for cyberslacking in a situation of boredom at work can explain the mechanism of insufficient self-regulation and habitual dysfunctional use of work technology, such as personal e-mailing, instant messaging, or gaming (Fichtner & Strader, 2014). Thus, any personal or recreational activity on the Internet increases the attractiveness and stimulation of the work situation and allows the employee to distract from work tasks. Therefore, using the Internet at work for personal purposes seems to be a strategy to reduce boredom (Pindek et al., 2018). Eastin et al. (2007) suggested that cyberslacking is the result of a self-reactive incentive to overcome boredom at work. On the other hand, Vitak et al. (2011) found that employees who performed repetitive tasks at work were just as likely to engage in non-work-related online activities.

2.3.2.2 Motivational Factors

Work motivation is considered a set of internal psychological mechanisms that activate and organize human behavior oriented toward work performance (Bakker & Demerouti, 2007; Edgar, 2020), and may diminish deviant work behavior (Robinson & Bennett, 1995). Researchers have also argued that procrastinators tend to avoid occupations and types of work that require intrinsic motivation and choose lower-demanding jobs (Nguyen et al., 2013), which in turn can reinforce their procrastination tendency. The relationship between employees' motivation to work and procrastination offline and online at work appears to be complex due to various sources and types of motivation. Extrinsic motivation is induced by external work-related stimuli, such as relationships with colleagues, working conditions, or the reward system (e.g. money, extra incentives, security). Intrinsic motivation stems from the internal desire derived from the work content, such as interesting and challenging tasks, autonomy, responsibility, variation, creativity, opportunities to use one's skills, and feedback on work outcomes (Ryan & Deci, 2000). Weak intrinsic motivation to work can foster the tendency to engage in procrastination behaviors. On the other hand, strengthening intrinsic motivation will promote the avoidance of procrastination at work.

Work Engagement: Work engagement is defined as a positive, work-related state of mind characterized by vigor, dedication, and absorption of work (Bakker & Schaufeli, 2014) and was found to be a strong predictor of work-related outcomes. Employees who are actively engaged in performing their tasks likely have limited free time for extracurricular activities. These individuals exceed their designated work hours and continually strive to enhance the organization and their performance. Previous research has shown that low work engagement is associated with various dysfunctional and counterproductive work behaviors (Chen et al., 2020), while high work engagement can lead to resource depletion, work–family conflict, and burnout in the long run.

Studies have shown that soldiering and cyberslacking as work procrastination dimensions were associated with low work engagement (Metin et al., 2018; Metin et al., 2020; van den Berg & Roosen, 2018; Wang et al., 2021). Studies conducted in seven European countries (i.e. Slovenia, Croatia, Czech Republic, Turkey, Ukraine, Finland, and the United Kingdom) confirmed negative associations between work engagement and soldiering (−0.31 to −0.45) except for the Czech Republic and Ukraine, and between work engagement and cyberslacking in Turkey (Metin et al., 2020). A meta-analysis of seven studies (Mercado et al., 2017b) and further studies (Elrehail et al., 2021; O'Neill et al., 2014; Oosthuizen et al., 2018) supported a moderately negative correlation between employee engagement and cyberslacking ($\bar{r} = -0.18$). These results suggest that highly engaged employees are less likely to engage in non-work-related activities offline and online. Probably, highly engaged employees are active and enthusiastic about their work and avoid potential distractions at work, which results in a reduced tendency to procrastinate work. Individuals with weaker work engagement are more likely to avoid work. Consequently, they are more likely to engage in non-work-related activities, such as soldiering or cyberslacking. These findings correspond to the Job Demands–Resources model (JD–R) (Bakker et al., 2023) where work engagement has been found to mediate the relationship between job characteristics and cyberslacking. In Oosthuizen et al. (2018) study organizational trust (as a resource) increased work engagement, which diminished the tendency to cyberslacking. A study carried out in India found that work engagement (parallelly with organizational identification) mediated the relationship between bureaucracy and cyberslacking (Soral et al., 2020). Coercive bureaucracy in the organization reduces organizational identification while enabling bureaucracy leads to increased organizational identification. This enhances work engagement and, in turn, reduces cyberslacking at work. Moreover, work engagement mediated the effect of the supervisor's communication style on cyberslacking (Khattak et al., 2020). Aggressive and passive communication of leaders reduced employees' work engagement, thus increasing cyberslacking. Conversely, assertive leader communication enhances work engagement and weakens subordinates' cyberslacking. Another motivating factor contributing to employee cyberslacking is job involvement (Sampat & Basu, 2017; Tandon et al., 2022). Job involvement as the cognitive and emotional identification with work, expressing the belief that work can fulfill one's most important needs and expectations, was found to be related to cyberslacking at work (Karimi Mazidi et al., 2021; Liberman et al., 2011; Lim, 2002; Tandon et al., 2022). Employees who identify strongly with their jobs, tend to care about their work role, put forth increased effort, and are less likely to engage in non-work-related Internet use. They also tend to spend more time on work than on non-work-related activities.

Summarizing, the presented research consistently indicated significant negative relationships between work engagement and employee procrastination, as well as soldiering and cyberslacking as their subdimensions. Much less is known about the possible direction of the relationship. Moreover, there is evidence for the mediating effect of motivational mechanisms in the links between work characteristics and non-work-related Internet at work.

Organizational Commitment: Organizational commitment is defined as the identification with an organization and loyalty to an organization and is viewed as a multidimensional construct comprising three types: affective, normative, and continuance (Allen & Meyer, 1990). *Affective commitment* refers to an employee's emotional attachment to the organization and their willingness to identify with it and participate in its affairs and issues. *Normative commitment* refers to a moral obligation or a type of obligation to maintain employment within a particular organization. *Continuance commitment* is related to the belief that leaving a job within a given organization is too costly and involves the loss of resources invested by the individual or the inability to secure alternative employment. Research has shown a negative relationship between organizational commitment and procrastination at work (Akhtar & Faisal Malik, 2016; Wang et al., 2021). Employees who are actively involved in achieving organizational goals are less likely to engage in non-work-related activities and procrastinate work tasks. Multiple studies have demonstrated a negative correlation between organizational commitment and cyberslacking (Garrett & Danziger, 2008a; Hensel & Kacprzak, 2020; Liberman et al., 2011; Usman et al., 2021). Researchers have suggested that employees who are highly committed to their organization view cyberslacking as incongruent with their self-image and work involvement style, which could potentially damage the workplace's reputation. Other studies showed that affective commitment was linked to a reduced tendency to cyberslacking and simultaneously mediated the relationship between highly meaningful work and cyberslacking (Usman et al., 2021). This means that having a strong emotional attachment or moral obligation to the organization results in less non-work-related Internet use during work hours. Furthermore, organizational commitment moderated the relationship between emotional exhaustion and cyberslacking (Lim et al., 2021). When employees were highly committed to the organization, emotional exhaustion weakened cyberloafing. Employees can feel a strong commitment to their work and organization, which is related to financial benefits and their desire to work within the organization. Thus, organizational commitment could serve as a valuable resource for employees in managing stress and non-work-related Internet use.

Summarizing, the role of emotional and motivational factors, such as negative affect, boredom, stress, exhaustion, burnout, job satisfaction, work engagement, and organizational commitment, is important in explaining procrastination at work. Specifically, it plays a mediational role in the relationship between job characteristics and procrastination behavior. Previous research has primarily focused on the negative effects of procrastination or cyberslacking in the workplace. Motivational mechanisms have been identified as key in redirecting employees from unproductive non-work-related activities to efficient work performance. A growing body of research in this area is gradually expanding the understanding of procrastination at work in relation to other constructs.

2.3.3 Sociodemographic Factors

To fully comprehend the phenomenon of procrastination both offline and online in the workplace, it is necessary to investigate its potential sociodemographic predictors. Studies have shown that employee procrastination and cyberslacking vary in the dependence of sociodemographic variables such as gender, age, education, and marital status. This chapter presents the relevant findings.

Gender: Research has shown that men are significantly more likely to procrastinate at work than women (Nguyen et al., 2013; Shrivastava et al., 2016). As researchers suggested, women's lower propensity to procrastinate at work may indirectly contribute to their higher performance and lower organizational labor costs. However, other studies have not found significant gender differences in the level of procrastination at work (He et al., 2021; Hen et al., 2021; Legood et al., 2018; Lin, 2018; Sarwat et al., 2021). This means that in certain working conditions, gender may moderate the effects of other variables in uncovering employee procrastination. Therefore, it is worth controlling the effect of gender in studies on procrastination at work. Previous research has yielded inconsistent results regarding the influence of gender on cyberslacking. Many studies in this field have revealed that men engage in non-work-related Internet use at work more frequently than women. A meta-analysis of 23 studies (Mercado et al., 2017b) confirmed a weak effect of gender ($\bar{r} = -0.07$). Moreover, the annual Internet productivity survey of 5,000 people in the United States from 2015 (CorpMagazine, 2015) showed that men were more likely than women to engage in non-work activities at work. Specifically, men spent 59 minutes a day on their mobile devices and women spent 52 minutes. Furthermore, men spent 45 minutes on personal tasks, while women spent 38 minutes. The top three non-work digital activities that employees engage in are replying to personal e-mails, visiting social networks, and browsing sports websites. However, some studies found no significant differences in non-work-related Internet abuse between women and men (Garrett & Danziger, 2008b; Lavoie & Pychyl, 2001; Lim & Chen, 2012).

Age: The majority of studies have consistently found a significant effect of age on employees' procrastination (Beutel et al., 2016; Hen et al., 2021; Rehman et al., 2019; Saman & Wirawam, 2021). Similarly, age is negatively associated with cyberslacking. Thus, the tendency to procrastinate at work seems to be higher among younger people, who are more engaged in non-work-related activities than older employees, especially in activities online. This effect was confirmed by a meta-analysis of 23 studies ($\bar{r} = -0.08$) (Mercado et al., 2017b), and a review by Tandon et al. (2022). According to surveys conducted by salary.com in 2014, the frequency of wasting work time on online activities daily decreases slightly with age; 91% of people aged 18–25, 95% of people aged 26–32, 92% of people aged 33–39, 90% of people aged 40–50, 85% of people aged 51–60, and 78% of people over 60 years of age.

Education and Marital Status. Some studies have also shown significant, but weak differences in the level of procrastination and cyberslacking depending on the level of education. Furthermore, employees with higher education tend to procrastinate (Göncü Köse & Metin, 2018; Hammer & Ferrari, 2002) and engage in non-work-related Internet use at work for private purposes (Garrett & Danziger, 2008a). A meta-analysis of six studies (Mercado et al., 2017b) confirmed a small positive effect of education level ($\bar{r} = 0.11$) on cyberslacking. Employees with high education typically hold senior positions and perform more complex, divergent, and less-structured work tasks, without time constraints and quantitative performance standards. High autonomy in the organization and methods of performing work contributes to a greater propensity for procrastination of tasks at work. The empirical facts presented above are in line with the results of numerous studies on the role of sociodemographic variables in explaining dispositional procrastination in general (e.g. Steel & Ferrari, 2013), which are described in detail in Section 1.3.2. Furthermore, a review of studies on the role of sociodemographic factors in explaining procrastination and cyberslacking indicated inconsistent results. Therefore, it is worth controlling these variables in future research.

2.4 Work-Related Antecedents of Procrastination at Work

According to the situational approach, work-related factors may be a significant source of procrastination, as evidenced by numerous studies (Feyzi Behnagh & Ferrari, 2022; Steel, 2007). However, limited research exists on procrastination in work and organizational settings. Most studies focused mainly on identifying the work environment's characteristics that contribute to the activation and intensification of general tendency to procrastination. Previous research confirmed that particular characteristics of tasks and work settings encourage employees to procrastinate the tasks and engage in non-work-related activities. This chapter presents some theoretical models and research results explaining the phenomenon of procrastination in the workplace. Among the situational factors that contribute to procrastination at work are employment-related factors and job characteristics. The initial set of predictors pertains to professional status and job type, encompassing profession, employment status, tenure, pay level, organizational hierarchy position, task specificity, career advancement limitations, and attitudes toward work and procrastination. The second group relates to job characteristics and organizational factors.

2.4.1 Theoretical Approaches to Procrastination at Work

Various theoretical frameworks were developed or adopted to clarify employee procrastination behavior its sources and mechanisms. These include the task procrastination model (Harris & Sutton, 1983), the job characteristics model (JCM) (Hackman & Oldham, 1976, 1980), the interactive model of procrastination at work (van Eerde, 2016), and the Job Demands–Resources model (Bakker & Demerouti, 2014).

2.4.1.1 Task Procrastination Model

Harris and Sutton (1983) presented one of the first conceptualizations of organizational determinants of procrastination in the workplace, focusing on several situational, task-related, and environmental characteristics that predict employee procrastination at work. The model includes the focal task features (such as difficulty, ambiguity, appeal, and deadline pressure), relationships of the focal task to other tasks, and organizational context features (Figure 2.1).

The focal task attributes include difficulty, dimension of interest, ambiguity, and deadline pressure. Task difficulty is linked to qualitative overload of the professional role, which may result from competence deficits or insufficient organizational resources to execute tasks at work. Employees may postpone the start of difficult tasks to prevent frustration and failure. The task appeal suggests

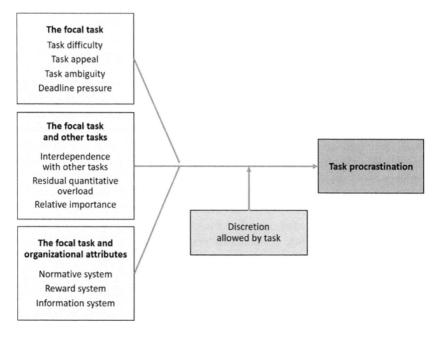

Figure 2.1 Task procrastination model in the organizational setting
(Source: Harris and Sutton, 1983, p. 989).

that interesting and challenging tasks can help maintain a high level of engagement and reduce procrastination among employees. Unclear and ambiguous
tasks can contribute significantly to procrastination, as employees may avoid
or delay tasks that are not well defined or prioritized. Furthermore, the absence
of deadlines can also lead to procrastination in the workplace, as tasks are more
likely to be postponed if they lack a strict or distant deadline. Conversely, tasks
with specific deadlines or those that cannot be postponed are more difficult to
delay. Among the predictors of employee procrastination in the workplace, the
authors identified the relationship between the focal task and other tasks, including interdependence, residual quantitative overload, and the relative importance
of a task. A focal task that is independent of other tasks makes it easier for
employees to postpone its completion. Furthermore, individuals are more likely
to procrastinate on the main task when overwhelmed with additional tasks that
require significant time and energy to complete. Procrastination behavior is also
influenced by the relative importance of the task compared to other tasks. The
higher the task's importance, the less likely it is to be postponed. The authors
indicated three components of organizational culture contributing to task procrastination in the workplace, i.e. the normative system, the reward system, and

the information system. Procrastination behavior in the workplace is contingent upon the system of organizational norms, which grants 'tacit' or overt uncon-scious authorization to postpone tasks at work in certain organizations. In addi-tion, the system of penalties and rewards used in the workplace can strengthen the tendency to procrastinate. If procrastination does not have consequences or is rewarded, the likelihood of repeating this behavior increases. Additionally, tasks that are not adequately compensated by the employer are more likely to be procrastinated by employees. Task procrastination can also be determined by an ineffective information system. When task instructions and information are inac-curate, incomplete, or ambiguous, working conditions become more unpredicta-ble and difficult to control. This leads to increased levels of stress and frustration for employees, which in turn results in procrastination. The discretion allowed by task can significantly influence the relationship between task characteristics and procrastination. Workers with a high level of discretion allowed by task are more likely to procrastinate, while its low level can limit or prevent task delay. Therefore, discretion can significantly moderate the association between task characteristics and employee procrastination.

In summary, Harris and Sutton (1983) conceptualized procrastination at work as a situational form of procrastination, accentuating situational, task-related, and organizational characteristics contributing to explaining the phenomenon of task procrastination in the workplace. However, this approach is limited by its failure to consider personality factors and its lack of comprehensive empirical verification.

2.4.1.2 Job Characteristics Model

Researchers attempted to adopt Hackman and Oldham's (1976, 1980) job char-acteristic model (JCM) to identify predictors and mechanisms underlying pro-crastination in the workplace. The JCM specifies core job characteristics, such as *skill variety* – referring to the quantity and diversity of competencies required for performing the tasks; *task significance* – a degree of influence of the job on other individuals; *task identity* – the employee's sense of involvement in performing the entire task; *autonomy* – the level of independence an employee experiences when performing the job; *feedback* – indicating how much the job contributes to receiving specific information about job performance (see Figure 2.2).

Hackman and Oldham (1980) proposed that the *core job characteristics* influence three psychological states, such as the experienced meaningfulness of the work, the experienced responsibility, and the knowledge of the results of the work activity. These *critical psychological states* are important factors in determining work-related *outcomes*, such as high internal work motivation, high-quality work performance, high work satisfaction, and low absenteeism and turnover. This may suggest that work tasks possess a significant moti-vational capacity when specific job conditions are fulfilled that establish an

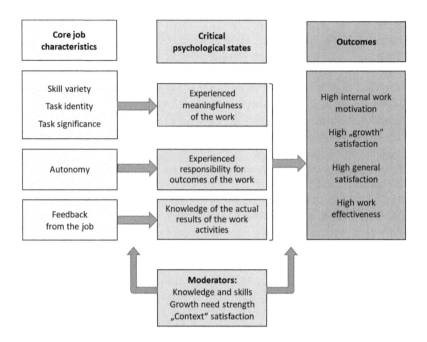

Figure 2.2 Job characteristic model
(Source: Hackman and Oldham, 1976, p. 256).

experience of meaningfulness, responsibility, and knowledge of work results, leading to enhanced internal motivation, job satisfaction, and work performance. According to the JCM, high levels of job characteristics are additive and contribute to positive work outcomes (Hackman & Oldham, 1980). The JCM offers a framework for designing or enriching jobs that improve work behavior and outcomes. It provides valuable insights and strategies for creating more satisfying and motivating work environments. Additionally, specific aspects of the work environment can enhance work performance and satisfaction but also diminish the risk of counterproductive or deviant work behavior (Spector & Jex, 1991). Thus, it is reasonable to include workplace procrastination in the model as one symptomatic aftereffect of the job context on employees.

One of the weaknesses of the model is that it does not encompass the role of interpersonal relationships in work outcomes. Several studies have tested the JCM to explain procrastination at work. Lonergan and Maher (2000) confirmed the usefulness of the model in the study conducted among 147 corporate employees. The results showed that high feedback, job autonomy, and task significance effectively predicted decreased employees' decisional procrastination. Thus, it was found that the greater the presence of job enrichment elements, the less likely people are willing to procrastinate. Employees who lack a sense of purpose and effective organizational skills may experience feelings of uselessness, potentially leading to increased procrastination. Receiving feedback on one's work performance can decrease fear of failure and uncertainty regarding future performance, thus reducing the likelihood of work procrastination. Some individuals may procrastinate to avoid feedback from others and protect their self-esteem (Ferrari, 1991). Meaningful tasks can provide a greater sense of purpose and direction. Autonomy at work can also promote positive outcomes, including job satisfaction, commitment, motivation, and performance, which may reduce the tendency to procrastinate. However, the freedom to organize tasks and set deadlines, or the lack of constant supervision, may also be linked to increased procrastination. Therefore, the relationship between autonomy and procrastination is not straightforward. Lonergan and Maher (2000) found an interaction effect between autonomy and locus of control in predicting procrastination. Specifically, increasing autonomy was linked to a decrease in procrastination, which was stronger among internals. However, among externals, both low and high autonomy may increase employee motivation to procrastinate and avoid work. Low autonomy tasks may cause fear of evaluation and failure, while high autonomy tasks can lead to anxiety and uncertainty. A study following the JCM framework examined the relationship between work environment characteristics and overall procrastination (measured by GPS; Lay, 1986) in a group of nurses in Iran (Khoshouei, 2017). The study did not confirm the role of the factors postulated in the JCM model, except for feedback from the job factor. The study tested the effect of locus of control on job characteristics and found a positive relationship between external locus of control and procrastination. Some job characteristics, such as skill diversity, have limited verification. Furthermore, core job characteristics are often linked to various psychological states and work outcomes through different psychological states. Arshad et al. (2016) tested the JCM in the context of cyberloafing. Their study found that job characteristics, specifically skill variety and job autonomy, as well as stressors, such as role ambiguity and role conflict, were contributing factors to engaging in non-work-related activities. Based on these empirical findings, it seems that the JCM has not been fully verified through empirical means. One issue is that the factors tested in the model were highly interdependent, despite being postulated as orthogonal by the authors. Additionally, studies did not examine the mediating role of psychological states, which may play a key role in explaining procrastination. However, there is research that has revealed the significant role of job characteristics (which are the elements of the model) as potential contextual antecedents of work procrastination. Despite the inconclusive results presented above, the JCM framework has the potential to explain procrastination in the workplace as a phenomenon determined by the characteristics of the job and, thereby, activate psychological states. However, the JCM challenges the notion that work characteristics are solely extrinsic. Future research should expand the model to include additional job-related and individual predictors, as well as investigate other mechanisms that contribute to procrastination in the workplace.

2.4.1.3 Interactional Model of Procrastination

Wandelin van Eerde (2016) proposed a more comprehensive, interactive model, in which the phenomenon of procrastination at work can be understood as the result of the interaction of personal and contextual work-related factors that trigger various aspects of employee well-being (Figure 2.3).

Personal factors contributing to procrastination at work include a personality tendency to avoid and sleep quality that may intensify procrastination behavior. Individuals with high avoidance tendencies are more likely to exhibit procrastination behavior, even in work settings. Additionally, sleep as a means of regenerating energy resources necessary for self-regulation may influence employees' procrastination. Therefore, procrastination may be a tactic for avoiding difficult work situations and a manifestation of the limited resources needed for self-regulation. Sleep may be a buffer of negative consequences for well-being (van Eerde, 2016). Personal characteristics serve as the foundational basis for procrastination tendencies, although they may be enhanced or weakened by situational factors. The author highlighted the role of situational factors in determining the intensity and frequency of procrastination behavior in the workplace. Among the work-related characteristics, autonomy, time demands, self-control, and support contribute to employee procrastination (van Eerde, 2016). High *autonomy* in the workplace can be appealing to procrastinators, allowing for revealing

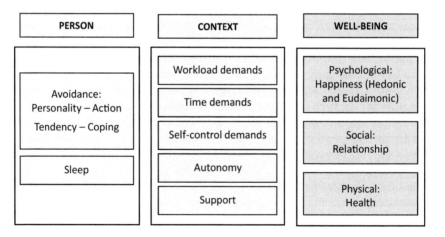

Figure 2.3 Interactional model of procrastination at work
(Source: van Eerde, 2016, p. 237).

procrastination tendencies. On the contrary, insufficient autonomy can result in an inability to manage work demands and overload. Autonomy restrictions are often recognized as a workplace stressor, potentially triggering procrastination as a strategy of work avoidance, but also reducing the tendency to procrastinate.

Workload demands as a crucial contextual factor in differentiating work performance can contribute to the frequency of work-related procrastination, including quantitative, qualitative, and time demands. In general, high workload and well-organized work tasks do not provide possibilities for procrastination. However, a high workload can also increase procrastination at work (see Section 2.4.3). Furthermore, procrastination in work settings appears to be significantly decreased by external factors of self-control demands, such as impulse control, managing distractions, and overcoming task resistance. Some jobs require impulse control in the form of inhibiting impulsive reactions interfering with work performance. Many occupations also have high potential distractions, which hinder work performance. Therefore, employers often set employees' self-control demands to concentrate on their tasks and refrain from being sidetracked by competing activities. Additionally, employees often have to overcome internal reluctance or resistance when it comes to executing unattractive work. Another factor contributing to procrastination at work is the extent of *support* from colleagues and supervisors. Team interdependence and the ability to monitor others' behaviors can lower avoidance-based procrastination tendencies. However, supported employees may still procrastinate on their work. Then the support from coworkers can serve as a buffer to alleviate the excessive demands that may lead individuals to procrastinate. Additionally, supervisor support can also predict procrastination in work settings. Probably, leadership-related behavior, such as transformational, oriented toward satisfying employees' needs, plays an essential role in mitigating employee procrastination, whereas a passive-avoidant, insufficient, or excessively controlling style may enhance employee procrastination.

The interactive model of work-related procrastination suggests that personal and contextual factors interact to predict procrastination in the workplace and its impact on well-being. The proposed framework accentuates the role of *situational strength* of work in reinforcing procrastination behavior. According to the trait activation theory (Mischel & Shoda, 1995), every work situation affects the manifestation of an employee's personality traits in the work context. Work situations regarded as 'weak' allow employees to freely express their personality at work, leading to a stronger personality-based determination of behavior. On the other hand, 'strong' situations do not give much freedom in personality traits and individual preferences, which are likely suppressed by situational factors. Thus, 'strong' situations characterized by clearly defined goals, well-structured and supervised work, and adequate incentives to achieve outcomes weaken the inclination to procrastinate. On the contrary, 'weak' situations provide some degree of flexibility in work environments, increasing the potential to select behaviors based on personality traits, including an expression of their dispositional tendency to procrastinate. In this vein, employees with a high disposition to procrastinate are likely to seek positions and work settings that allow them to delay tasks (Nguyen et al., 2013; van Eerde, 2016).

2.4.1.4 Job Demand–Resources Model

The Job Demands–Resources model (JD–R) (Bakker & Demerouti, 2007, 2014) is a useful framework to understand procrastination in the workplace. The JD–R model is a heuristic approach to explain an individual's functioning in work conditions through the interaction of job demands and resources (Figure 2.4).

Job demands refer to the physical, psychological, social, or organizational aspects of a job that require sustained effort and may cause stress or strain. Job demands that can contribute to procrastination at work include high workload, time pressure, task difficulty, ambiguity, monotony, or complexity, lack of clarity of expectations and conflicting priorities, poor working conditions, poor interpersonal relationships, or organizational constraints. Job demands express the level of quantitative, qualitative, and emotional workload, and can have direct and detrimental effects on performance and various forms of counterproductive work behavior (Balducci et al., 2011), including procrastination at work (Metin et al., 2016). When employees face both excessive and low demands, they may procrastinate more. These opposing effects of demands are likely to depend on the nature of the demands and the employee's subjective interpretation of them. Demands can be perceived as hindrances or challenges. Although both types of job demands are very loaded and imply exploitation of high effort and energy, they have distinct effects. *Challenge demands* include quantitative and

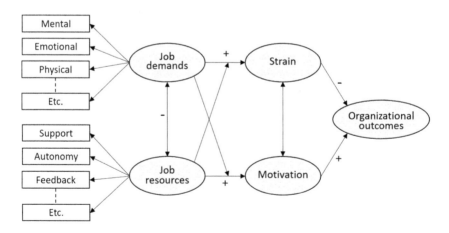

Figure 2.4 Job demands–resources model
(Source: Bakker & Demerouti, 2007, p. 313).

qualitative work demands and emotional, cognitive, and time pressures. They can induce positive emotions and cognitive responses, facilitate the achievement of goals, the development or acquisition of knowledge and skills, and stimulate engagement and work performance. *Hindrance demands* include demands related to role conflict, job insecurity, and negative interpersonal relationships. They do not have any developmental potential for the employee but elicit negative emotions and cognitive reactions and can undermine engagement and work performance (Bakker & Demerouti, 2014). Therefore, an employee's subjective interpretation of job demands holds significance for organizational behavior (Li et al., 2020). As the researchers suggested, employees can rate the same type of demands as either stimulating or hindering, and associated with both positive and negative organizational outcomes. Thus, in the case of predicting procrastination at work, both hypotheses seem likely. Both low and high job demands can be associated with a high propensity to engage in procrastination behavior at work.

Job resources encompass the physical, psychological, social, or organizational aspects of work that facilitate the achievement of work-related goals, reduce job demands and their physiological and psychological costs, and stimulate personal growth and development. According to the JD–R model (Bakker & Demerouti, 2014), job resources include resources related to job content and work organization (such as autonomy, development opportunities, variation, and meaning of work), as well as organizational resources (such as a sense of control, job security, quantity and quality of information, participation in decision-making), or social factors (such as support from colleagues or supervisors at the workplace, a good atmosphere at work). The JD–R model was extended by including personal resources (Bakker et al., 2023). These individual aspects refer to resilience and a sense of ability to control and impact the environment successfully. Personal resources include resilience, optimism, self-efficacy, and other dispositions, which play a similar role as job resources. The JD–R model posits that the interplay between job demands and resources influences well-being and performance in two distinct manners. They can have both protective (*buffering*) and enhancing (*boosting*) effects on employee well-being and performance.

First, job resources have the *buffering effect* of the negative impact of job demands on well-being and performance. When employees have access to job resources, they reduce the strain caused by overwhelming job demands, enhance intrinsic work motivation, and subsequently increase well-being and work performance. Besides, low job resources may diminish work outcomes and activate deviant work behaviors. To summarize, the buffering effect of job resources helps employees to cope with work challenges and pressures, thereby protecting them from the detrimental effects of excessive job demands. Second, the *boosting effect* of job demands enhances the positive effect of job resources on motivation, well-being, and work performance. When employees face high job demands, job resources become particularly beneficial in increasing work engagement, satisfaction, and performance. In general, the interaction between job demands and resources can have both protective and enhancing effects on employee work-related outcomes (Bakker & Demerouti, 2014).

The JD–R model integrates two psychological processes. The first process is an *energetic process* that is triggered by job demands and refers to the allocation and exhaustion of personal resources, such as physical and mental energy. High job demands increase stress and exhaustion, which lead to negative work outcomes. The second process is a *motivational process* that is induced by job resources. High job resources stimulate work engagement and, thus, promote positive organizational outcomes. Furthermore, the absence of job resources can lead to exhaustion, whereas high resources can buffer the impact of job demands on exhaustion (Bakker & Demerouti, 2014). Following the JD–R model, procrastination can be seen as a behavioral response to specific or high job demands and the availability or lack of job resources. When job demands are high and resources are limited, procrastination may be a strategy for avoiding aversive tasks and coping with stress. When employees experience fatigue, stress, or exhaustion, they can procrastinate work tasks due to a lack of energy to initiate or sustain effort. Procrastination can temporarily alleviate immediate discomfort but can lead to increased stress, reduced job satisfaction, and lower performance in the long run. When employees are faced with high job demands without sufficient resources to handle them, they may be more likely to procrastinate due to feelings of overwhelm or lack of confidence in their ability to meet the demands.

On the other hand, when employees have sufficient job resources, such as supportive colleagues, clear guidelines, or adequate time and tools to complete tasks, they are more likely to feel capable and motivated to proactively perform their work, reducing the tendency to procrastinate. Examples of job resources that can mitigate work-related procrastination include social support, autonomy, feedback, training and development opportunities, and access to necessary tools and information (Metin et al., 2016; see Table 3.1). When employees have adequate resources, they are more likely to feel capable and motivated to complete tasks promptly, reducing the likelihood of procrastination. Organizations must recognize the importance of balancing work demands and resources to promote work engagement and minimize procrastination among employees. Thus, high intrinsic motivation and work engagement can help overcome the tendency to procrastinate and increase task performance.

The JD–R model as a framework explaining procrastination in the workplace was adopted in several studies (Edmondson et al., 2024; Elrehail et al., 2021; Metin et al., 2016; Sarwat et al., 2021; Zhang et al., 2023). However, the results only partially supported hypotheses based on propositions of the JD–R model. Research revealed significant effects of various job demands in predicting procrastination, such as hindrance and challenge demands (Huang et al., 2023; Zhou et al., 2021), workload, cognitive demands (Metin et al., 2016;

Sarwat et al., 2021), work–life conflict, and grit (Edmondson et al., 2024). Cyberslacking was found to be determined by job demands, such as role ambiguity, role conflict, and work overload (Elrehail et al., 2021). Among job resources, skill variety, task significance, task identity, autonomy, feedback, and harmonious passion contributed to procrastination (Elrehail et al., 2021; Zhang et al., 2023). Furthermore, energetic (via stress or exhaustion) and motivational (engagement, motivation) processes were established as mediational mechanisms to predict cyberloafing (Bajcar & Babiak, 2020; Elrehail et al., 2021), while the motivational process was revealed in predicting productive procrastination (Edmondson et al., 2024). Moreover, other emotional states such as boredom, stress-related presenteeism, well-being, or resilience were tested as mediators in the associations of job demands and resources with procrastination (Metin et al., 2016; Sarwat et al., 2021; Zhang et al., 2023). Among motivational mediators between job resources on cyberslacking, resilience had a nonsignificant effect (Zhou et al., 2021). Another study revealed positive indirect effects of public and private social media use for work-related and social-related purposes on employees' social cyberloafing through work engagement, negative impact of work-related private social media use, and positive effect of social-related private social media on employees exhaustion (Ma et al., 2021).

The JD–R model was also used in research on cyberslacking consequences for work outcomes. Work performance was determined by work-Internet leisure activities (Mohammad et al., 2019) and by procrastination (Ahmad et al., 2021). Mental distractions, ergonomics-related factors, and information overload as a result of personal use of technology cyberslacking contributed to stress, while mental breaks, work–life balance, and creativity as cyberslacking resources were related to motivation (Kim & Christensen, 2017). Authors have established neuroticism, job technology requirements, and support climate as boundary conditions, which can decrease or enhance the associations of job demands with strain, and resources with motivation. Previous studies relatively rarely examined the moderating effect of variables for the effects of job demands and resources on procrastination behavior. Zhang et al. (2023) have found that interpersonal conflict alleviated the impact of harmonious passion on procrastination, while work motivation strengthened the effect of job stress on cyberloafing (Elrehail et al., 2021).

Summarizing, the JD–R model seems to be a suitable framework to explain procrastination behavior in the workplace and the mechanisms underlying it. Although numerous studies in this area provide incomplete and inconsistent insight into the role of individual and work-related predictors of procrastination at work, the JD–R model has the potential to extend the understanding of procrastination at work. Based on the assumptions of the JD–R model, it can be inferred that motivational processes play a role in how work-related factors influence cyberloafing.

2.4.2 Employment-Related Factors

Previous research has shown that non-work-related Internet use at work also depends on various professional and organizational factors, such as employment status, position in the organizational hierarchy, seniority, and remuneration.

Employment Status: Some studies revealed the effect of employment status on procrastination in the workplace. Specifically, part-time and unemployed workers were more prone to procrastination at work than full-time employees (DeArmond et al., 2014; Metin et al., 2016; Nguyen et al., 2013; Wan et al., 2014). Additionally, Nguyen et al. (2013) found that 57% of unemployed individuals and 44% of full-time individuals demonstrated a high level of procrastination. This association can potentially be explained by the greater attachment and commitment of full-time employees. An individual who is employed part-time may feel not fully integrated into the organization and may not share its goals. Hence, there is a higher likelihood of engaging in non-work-related activities that detract from professional duties. A study conducted among full-time US employees found a significant association between job status and Internet abuse behavior at work. A 2019 survey of 2,219 working Americans conducted by Darius Foroux (2019), showed that self-employed entrepreneurs (76%) browsed the Internet slightly less (1–4 hours a day), compared to contracted employees (80%). Comparable results were discovered by Garrett and Danzinger (2008a).

Remuneration: Remuneration may influence employee procrastination, but the direction of this relationship is unclear. Evidence suggests a negative and relatively low correlation ($r = -0.26$) between employees' procrastination and remuneration for work. Researchers have also found that procrastination significantly predicted low pay (Nguyen et al., 2013). It can also be assumed that an employee's remuneration affects their tendency to procrastinate at work. Thus, paying employees below or above the market rate (i.e. underpaying or overpaying) may lead to high levels of procrastination behavior. Procrastination is a critical variable that can adversely affect an employee's earnings. Employee remuneration is positively associated with cyberslacking, indicating that higher income promotes a greater tendency to engage in this behavior at work (Garrett & Danziger, 2008b; Rajah & Lim, 2011). However, other studies have not found a significant relationship between income and cyberslacking (e.g. Vitak et al., 2011), which was supported by a meta-analysis of eight studies ($\bar{r} = 0.05$) conducted by Mercado et al. (2017b).

Job Tenure: Previous studies indicated a significant negative association between work experience and the intensity of employee procrastination (Nguyen et al., 2013; Göncü Köse & Metin, 2018). It is possible that individuals with higher tenure have developed strategies to cope with difficult conditions and therefore do not need to avoid work tasks. There was, however, evidence for a nonsignificant correlation between work experience and procrastination (DeArmond et al., 2014; Uysal & Yilmaz, 2020). A meta-analysis of 10 studies (Mercado et al., 2017b) clearly showed that tenure had a negligible negative effect on explaining cyberslacking ($\bar{r} = -0.07$), indicating that employees younger in terms of tenure are particularly interested and exposed to Internet abuse at work. The latest research confirmed that the relationship between cyberslacking and job experience is weak (Alharthi et al., 2021) or nonsignificant (Zhang et al., 2020; Zhou et al., 2021).

Working Hours: A meta-analysis of six studies (Mercado et al., 2017b) indicated a significant (though weak) correlation between weekly work and non-work-related Internet use during work hours ($\bar{r} = 0.12$). This may imply that individuals engage in such behaviors as their work time increases. Furthermore, extensive technology access at work poses a risk of increased cyberslacking among workers. There is a positive correlation between the time spent on the Internet for work purposes and the level of Internet misuse for private purposes ($\bar{r} = 0.20$). Employees who demonstrate proficiency in Internet usage are more likely to engage in cyberslacking, specifically e-mailing and browsing websites (Blanchard & Henle, 2008). The present state of knowledge does allow to conclusively determine the influence of factors associated with professional status on procrastination. Therefore, it is important to systematically control the effects of these variables in conjunction with other potential predictors of cyberslacking.

Position in the Organization: Procrastination at work can be determined by the position in the organization. Employees in higher positions within the organizational structure exhibit lower levels of procrastination than those who are lower in the hierarchy (Ferrari et al., 2005). Top managers exhibited a lower tendency to procrastinate than middle managers (Aziz & Tariq, 2013; Chevrenidi & Bolotova, 2018). This could be attributed to higher job resources available to individuals in higher positions, such as autonomy, remuneration, power, and prestige, which allow them to handle their work more effectively and discourage procrastination at work. Researchers have also posited that cyberslacking is more prevalent in office jobs than in low-status occupations (Garrett & Danziger, 2008a; Ugrin et al., 2007). As one ascends the organizational hierarchy, the incidence of using the Internet at work for non-work purposes increases. For example, Ugrin et al. (2007) study revealed that managers engage in non-work-related online activities at work significantly more frequently than employees at lower levels of the organization. These disparities likely result from reduced oversight and increased independence and adaptability in the administration of work. Nevertheless, a meta-analysis of eight studies indicated that cyberslacking is nonsignificantly linked to the position occupied within the organization ($\bar{r} = 0.07$) (Mercado et al., 2017b). This finding suggests that engaging in non-work-related activities online and offline is prevalent among distinct workforce categories and across organizational hierarchies.

Industry/occupation: The specificity of occupations as a factor contributing to employee procrastination seems to be well documented empirically. Certain occupations can systematically increase the tendency to procrastinate (Hammer & Ferrari, 2002; Ferrari et al., 2005; Lonergan & Maher, 2000; Metin et al., 2018; Singh & Singh, 2018). Research results consistently reported that office workers exhibit higher levels of procrastination on work tasks than non-office workers (Hammer & Ferrari, 2002; Harriott & Ferrari, 1996; Hen et al., 2021). The authors attributed these differences to the lower job security of blue-collar workers, which may promote less procrastination behavior at work. In addition, people with a high tendency to procrastinate, whether in decision-making or everyday life, probably well adapt to office work, which is often perceived as less demanding and less challenging (Hammer & Ferrari, 2002). Moreover, a higher level of procrastination was also declared by individuals employed in education (Laybourn et al., 2019), higher education (Harriott & Ferrari, 1996), health care (Harriott & Ferrari, 1996; Ma et al., 2021), sales (Ferrari et al., 2005), IT (Slashdot, 2009), as compared to other occupations. According to a survey conducted by Slashdot (2009), approximately 40% of IT workers spend half of their work time on non-work-related activities, and only 17% of them perform work through the required 8 hours per day. Significantly lower levels of procrastination were found among business-related occupations (Harriot & Ferrari, 1996), non-office (Hammer & Ferrari, 2002; Harriott & Ferrari, 1996; Hen et al., 2021), military officers (Nguyen et al., 2013), and self-employed such as doctors and lawyers (Ferrari et al., 2005).

Nguyen et al. (2013) compared occupational groups in terms of the frequency of procrastination behaviors and identified three occupational groups exposed to significantly different levels of risk of procrastination. *High-risk occupations* included waiters, legal secretaries, computer systems administrators, library assistants, and sales representatives. *Moderate-risk occupations* included teachers, photographers, writers ($M = 3.66$, $SD = 0.05$), lawyers, university lecturers, and operations managers, while *low-risk occupations* included top managers, librarians, economists, loan officers, and military officers. Furthermore, public sector employees exhibited higher procrastination at work than their private sector counterparts (Ahmad et al. 2021). Employees reported increased procrastination at work due to the lack of connection between their performance and the reward, job insecurity, an excess of staff, or unclear delineation of job responsibilities.

Similarly, cyberslacking occurs predominantly in office work settings. Occupations in management, finance, or business were found to have a higher occurrence of cyberslacking (Garrett & Danziger, 2008a, 2008b). As research results showed, office employees often engaged in non-work-related Internet use during work time than in other occupations (Blanchard & Henle, 2008; Moody & Siponen, 2013). This finding is likely due to the specifics of modern office work, which is inextricably linked to computer use and increased exposure to online procrastination, called cyberslacking. The OfficeTeam service (2017) survey results showed that office workers spent an average of 8 hours per week on non-work activities, and most of this time (i.e. about 5 hours per week) is spent browsing the Internet. Additional confirmation of the high cyberslacking among office workers can indicate that non-work-related Internet use at work was higher in occupations that require the use of a computer. A meta-analysis of nine studies (Mercado et al., 2017b) confirmed that computer use at work was moderately associated with employees' cyberslacking ($\bar{r} = 0.17$). Especially, employees in the information technology industry manifested higher levels of problematic Internet browsing for non-work purposes than employees in other industries (Koay et al., 2017a; Shrivastava et al., 2016). Cyberslacking is a product of the modern reality of flexible work time, remote work with permanent Internet access, bringing work home, and blurring the lines between work and non-work (Lim & Teo, 2005). Moreover, private mobile devices with Internet access create broad opportunities to use Web resources for non-work purposes during work time. This makes cyberslacking no longer just the domain of office workers working on a computer with company Internet access. Still, certain features of the work environment may be conducive to increasing or reducing cyberslacking.

Researchers have proposed a potential explanation for differences in procrastination susceptibility across jobs and occupations in the light of the gravitational hypothesis, which explains why people choose and keep jobs compatible with their predispositions (Rogelberg, 2007). This allows employees to select jobs that best fit their personality profiles. According to this hypothesis, procrastinators likely prefer work that does not require high energy expenditure, self-control, conscientiousness, and persistence and therefore is conducive to procrastination. The gravitational hypothesis may also explain why employers are less likely to retain procrastinators in positions that require high motivation or engagement (Nguyen et al., 2013). When recruiting employees for specific positions, organizations take care of the best job-person to maximize employees' and organizational productivity. For this reason, organizations prefer candidates with a high level of procrastination. Thus, procrastination is often either a negative criterion or is not included in the employee profile at all. Additionally, high procrastination under certain work conditions may be explained by the situational strength of work (Meyer et al., 2020), which justifies the effect of personality traits on behavior in the work context. In 'strong' work situations, a dispositional tendency to procrastinate does not have the opportunity to manifest, whereas 'weak' situations create favorable conditions for employees to easily procrastinate at work. For example, a job with major demands and constraints and close supervision will likely weaken procrastination behavior at work. Other occupations that have low workloads, autonomy, or computer use allow for the free expression of dispositional procrastination.

In conclusion, the research presented above showed differences in the level of employee procrastination depending on the specifics of the profession. It seems that occupations typically occupied by procrastinators seems especially suited to promote procrastination. Procrastinators are more likely to do work that is less engaging and satisfying. Thus, the tendency to procrastinate can be induced by an arrangement of working conditions. Thus, one can recognize that procrastination at work is dependent on situational factors.

2.4.3 Job Characteristics

As theoretical models suggest, procrastination at work is determined by various characteristics of the work environment. This chapter provides a review of empirical findings on work-related contextual factors contributing to procrastination and cyberslacking, such as factors related to (1) workload and demands, job content and organization, interpersonal relationships, leadership, and organizational characteristics.

2.4.3.1 Workload and demads

Workload: Previous research showed inconclusive results on the role of workload in relation to procrastination behavior at work. Some studies indicate that a propensity for procrastination or cyberslacking is associated with a high workload, while others have found the opposite relationship. On the one hand, high workload was directly related to high procrastination (DeArmond et al., 2014; Metin et al., 2016; Prem et al., 2018). However, these relationships were relatively weak. High workload has also been found to be associated with procrastination via reduced levels of psychological detachment from work and then increased fatigue (DeArmond et al., 2014). Studies also revealed that workload directly promotes an increase in cyberslacking at work (Henle & Blanchard, 2008; Varghese & Barber, 2017). Overloaded employees escape from their work by engaging in various unproductive work behaviors, including cyberslacking. For example, a study of emergency department workers found that as the workload increased (i.e. the number and severity of medical cases), the frequency of browsing Facebook increased (Black et al., 2013). Moreover, high workloads lead to non-work-related online activities at work through emotional exhaustion (Zhou et al., 2021) or burnout (Aghaz & Sheikh, 2016). Excessive workload can cause employees to be overburdened and unable to complete their tasks within a given time frame. This can lead to increased fatigue, depletion of personal resources, and a desire to detach from work. As a result, employees may turn to non-work-related offline or online activities as a way to cope with stress. However, there is also empirical evidence to support a negative relationship between workload and procrastination. When employees have more work to do, they are less likely to procrastinate. In a low-workload situation, employees may seek shorter or longer breaks from work or more enjoyable activities during work hours. This was supported by research findings indicating associations of procrastination behavior in situations of understimulation at work (Metin et al., 2016). This study also found that the low cognitive demands at work are highly correlated with procrastination. Thus, the more difficult and intellectually demanding the tasks, the less an employee engages in procrastination behaviors. According to the subjective appraisal of job demands, challenge demands were negatively associated while hindrance demands were positively associated with cyberslacking (Zhou et al., 2021). Henle and Blanchard (2008) were among the first to postulate that high workload or role overload may lead to less personal Internet abuse. Subsequently, numerous investigations have confirmed this relationship (Tandon et al., 2022). Too much work likely requires employees to exert great effort and resources to increase work performance and meet tight deadlines, which discourages employees from taking too many breaks. Probably, the overloaded employees do not have time for cyberloafing. Moreover, high workload affects employee procrastination through decreasing job satisfaction (Korzynski & Protsiuk, 2022). On the other hand, low workload was associated with a greater propensity to cyberslacking, which may suggest that low-stimulus work promotes the search for more attractive and enjoyable activities in work settings. Additionally, underload is associated with excessive engagement in non-work-related activities at work indirectly through a state of boredom (Metin et al., 2016). Researchers have explained these relations by pointing out that in the situation of understimulation at work, employees use less physical–cognitive energy and feel less engaged in their work (Tam et al., 2021). For this reason, they may actively seek enjoyable distractions from work, such as instant messaging, excessively long breaks, or active online entertainment seeking, to fill the emptiness in work activity. To summarize, the workload has an ambivalent effect in predicting procrastination and cyberslacking, suggesting the U-shaped relationship between them, according to the curvilinear relationship of the workload with work outcomes.

Time Demands and Time Pressure: An important factor that can influence procrastination is time demands. Indeed, working under time pressure is directly associated with high procrastination behavior (Prem et al., 2018; Weymann, 1988), but it is also mediated by positive appraisal of demands (as challenges) and negative appraisal of demands at work (as hindrances). This may mean that time pressure at work is perceived as a threat leading to high procrastination or as a challenge, enhancing work motivation and thus diminishing procrastination behavior. Furthermore, the findings of Roster and Ferrari (2020) on the relatively strong relationship between perceived time control and low propensity may support these results.

Role Conflict and Ambiguity: Job features including role ambiguity and role conflict are linked to cyberslacking, but were not examined in relation to procrastination. Role ambiguity (related to uncertainty about the performance of job tasks) or role conflict (i.e. inconsistency between numerous job demands) fosters job stress and uncertainty (Katz & Kahn, 1978), which can make employees become disengaged from their work and resort to counterproductive activities as a coping mechanism. Cyberslacking is also becoming more popular as a stress-relieving strategy that lets workers take a little break from demanding tasks (Henle & Blanchard, 2008). Prior studies have repeatedly demonstrated positive correlations between role conflict, role ambiguity, and non-work-related online activities during work time (Arshad et al., 2016; Henle & Blanchard, 2008; Varghese & Barber, 2017). Additionally, role conflict amplified the effect of high neuroticism and low agreeableness on cyberslacking. Under conditions of high role ambiguity, employees with high levels of neuroticism were less likely to engage in personal online use (Varghese & Barber, 2017). Furthermore, personal Web usage at work was found to buffer the negative effect of experiencing role conflict on employees' well-being (Gözü et al., 2015). Arguably, cyberslacking allows employees to cope more effectively with role conflict. In summary, the level of cyberslacking can be determined by the level and type of job demands.

2.4.3.2 Job Content and Organization of Work

Numerous studies have shown that procrastination and cyberslacking at work are determined by characteristics of the work environment related to the job content and work organization (Berthelsen et al., 2018), such as autonomy, feedback on work, meaning of work, variety of work, opportunities for development, innovation, and feedback. There is also empirical evidence of no relationship between job autonomy and procrastination (Khoshouei, 2017; Metin et al., 2016; Singh & Singh, 2018).

Autonomy at Work: Autonomy at work is defined as the extent to which an employee has the freedom to plan, prioritize, and perform his or her work in his or her way (Spector, 1986). Autonomy gives employees the freedom and possibility to choose work priorities, plan their work, and reduce work fatigue by allowing them to self-direct their efforts at work. According to self-determination theory (Deci & Ryan, 2008), autonomy and a sense of influence at work can contribute to higher work outcomes, as emphasized in the JCM (Hackman & Oldham, 1980). The role of autonomy in explaining procrastination behavior in work settings was also postulated in theoretical models (van Eerde, 2016) and it was empirically verified (Arshad et al., 2016; Khoshouei, 2017; Lonergan & Maher, 2000; Metin et al., 2016; Nguyen et al., 2013; Singh & Singh, 2018). Research in this area showed that low autonomy at work is associated with high levels of employee procrastination (Metin et al., 2016). It is likely that employees with higher autonomy at work perceive greater responsibility for their tasks and are less likely to engage in personal Internet use at work. However, some studies showed a positive relationship between them (Arshad et al., 2016; Garrett & Danziger, 2008b; Ugrin et al., 2007). Employees with high ability to self-organize their work spent significantly more time on non-work-related online activities for personal purposes. This is especially true for employees in higher positions, whose work allows for higher autonomy, while employees in lower positions tend to have less autonomy and fewer possibilities to cyber-slack. This effect seems to be justified in light of the gravitational hypothesis. Procrastinators pursue occupations allowing procrastination. In addition, pro-crastination at work may also depend on an individual need for autonomy, show-ing that some people need a lot of autonomy, while others do not (Nguyen et al., 2013). However, nonsignificant relationships between autonomy and personal Internet use at work were also revealed (König & La Caner de Guardia, 2014).

Meaning of Work: When work is meaningful, it is of high importance to the employee's professional and personal life, serves the greater good, and is mean-ingful to others. High task significance (Lonergan & Maher, 2000) and instru-mentality of the work (Weymann, 1988) were associated with procrastination at work. On the contrary, other research findings have shown nonsignificant associations of procrastination at work with task significance and task identity at work (Khoshouei, 2017). Previous studies have found a negative association of job meaning with cyberslacking (Jia et al., 2013; Usman et al., 2021). This suggests that employees perceive their work as valuable to others and engage in the organization's pursuit of their goals rather than misuse the Internet at work (which conflicts with interests within the organization). Furthermore, research has shown that meaningful work is linked to a decrease in cyberslacking due to increased affective commitment. This means that when employees find their work meaningful, they are more likely to identify with their job and dedicate effort toward achieving the organization's goals, which in turn discourages cyberslacking. Additionally, this negative relationship is influenced by leader–member exchange and is more pronounced under favorable leader–member exchange conditions (Usman et al., 2021). Individuals who strongly identify with their work may not even think about engaging in any non-work activities. To summarize, a high sense of meaningful work and responsibility can reduce dysfunctional behavior at work, including misusing the Internet.

Variation of Work: High levels of work variation can reduce work outcomes and promote dysfunctional work behavior (Hackman & Oldham, 1980). There is empirical evidence that low work variation, low skills needed to do the job, low job importance, and difficulty identifying the task to be performed are associated with cyberslacking (Elrehail et al., 2021). These characteristics make working conditions responsible for creating feelings of monotony and boredom at work, which can induce or exacerbate cyberslacking at work (Elrehail et al., 2021). However, it should be noted that in other studies these variables have not shown a significant effect in explaining cyberslacking (Arshad et al., 2016). In addition, sometimes employees are overqualified in relation to the qualifications required to perform the assigned tasks. Such a mismatch between the individual and the job can lead to an increase in various forms of work avoidance, including cyber-slacking (Zhang et al., 2020; Cheng et al., 2020; Tandon et al., 2022).

Feedback: The negative association between feedback and low procrastination has been well verified in research (Khoshouei, 2017; Lonergan & Maher, 2000; Weymann, 1988). Feedback increases employees' self-worth at work and in the organization, and thereby can reduce procrastination tendencies. In addition, systematic feedback on outcomes allows an employee to strengthen self-efficacy and reduce anxiety and uncertainty about their future outcomes, thus decreasing procrastination. In contrast, procrastination may be high, when employees avoid feedback from others to protect their self-esteem (Ferrari & Tice, 2000). Some other studies found no significant relationship between feedback and cyberslacking (Arshad et al., 2016).

2.4.3.3 Social Capital Factors

The phenomenon of procrastination in work settings is also related to social capital factors. Good interpersonal relationships with coworkers, recognition (Nguyen et al., 2013), and effective communication between people (expressed by receiving feedback from coworkers) (Lonergan & Maher, 2000) reduce procrastination behavior, while workplace ostracism increases employee procrastination (He et al., 2021). Team cohesion is not related to team members' procrastination (Singh & Singh, 2018). Interpersonal relationships can also influence an employee indirectly by modeling behavior. Employees may adopt procrastination behaviors if they see that it is allowed or they perceive the positive effects of these behaviors.

Social Support: The role of relationships with coworkers at work in explaining procrastination and cyberslacking at work is relatively poorly recognized by researchers. Studies have revealed that team acceptance plays a particularly important role in explaining Internet misuse at work (Askew et al., 2014; Tandon et al., 2022), sense of justice (Lim, 2002; Tandon et al., 2022), and management support (Liberman et al., 2011). Good relationships are most often accompanied by trust and social support within the organization and have positive effects on the functioning of employees and the organization as a whole, while any disruptive factors in social interactions can foster counterproductive or deviant behavior at work, resulting in lower performance. Specifically, low mutual support from coworkers and supervisors contributed to a high tendency to cyberslacking (Bajcar & Babiak, 2020), or engage in computer games during work time (Reinecke, 2009). However, other studies have revealed that positive interpersonal relationships and social acceptance in the organization simultaneously predict high levels of non-work-related Internet misuse at work (Askew et al., 2019; Betts et al., 2014). It seems that the more an employee feels accepted by coworkers, the more she engages in cyberslacking in work settings.

Ostracism: As research has shown, workplace ostracism is related to procrastination at work. Workplace ostracism refers to the experience of being ignored, excluded, or socially isolated by coworkers. In the workplace, ostracism can lead to feelings of loneliness and rejection, and sense of lack of belonging. These negative emotions may increase stress and reduce motivation, making it difficult to perform work effectively. Potentially, they also promote procrastination of work tasks due to resource depletion. Furthermore, ostracism at work more strongly influences procrastination at work under conditions of low psychological detachment because the associated negative emotions require more resources to cope with the difficult situation of ostracism (He et al., 2021). Unsatisfactory or dysfunctional social interactions in organizations, such as workplace ostracism (Hu et al., 2021; Koay, 2018b; Yang et al., 2023), and exposure to physical or verbal aggression (Andel et al., 2019), can increase cyberslacking at work. Probably, employees experiencing ostracism in the workplace may be prone to excessive browsing of social networks to satisfy their needs for belonging (Hu et al., 2021; Koay, 2018b; Yang et al., 2023). The relationship between ostracism at work and Internet abuse at work was mediated through emotional detachment (Koay, 2018b). Employees subjected to ostracism may experience emotional exhaustion, which in turn leads to 'escape' to the Internet to recover depleted resources and prevent further loss of resources. Thus, it seems that for excluded employees, cyberslacking is a strategy to prevent the loss of personal resources and emotional exhaustion. Furthermore, the relationship between workplace ostracism and cyberslacking was mediated by loneliness at work (Hu et al. (2021). Excessive browsing of the social media networks at work may be a strategy to cope with workplace ostracism, but at the same time may promote employees' isolation, cutting them off from future interactions with coworkers and perpetuating their loneliness (Tandon et al., 2022).

Organizational Justice: Organizational justice is defined as the perception of fairness or justice in the workplace in three aspects: distributive (fairness in the distribution of performance or rewards), procedural (fairness of the distribution of rewards or performance), and interactional (treating employees fairly and respectfully) (Colquitt et al., 2001). There were limited findings on the relationships between organizational justice and employee procrastination. The study conducted by Sunarta et al. (2023) showed that organizational justice indirectly influenced employee procrastination by decreasing job satisfaction.

The role of organizational justice in predicting cyberslacking has been particularly well documented. Although various justice-related constructs have been tested, the results of studies quite clearly indicated weak negative associations between organizational justice and cyberslacking at work, revealed in different samples of employees (Akin et al., 2017; Betts et al., 2014; Garrett & Danziger, 2008a; Lim, 2002; Lim & Teo, 2006; Oosthuizen et al., 2018). When an employee meets his or her job demands but does not receive adequate resources in return, it is perceived by the employee as an unfair employee–employer relationship. If a company or its members have treated an employee unfairly, she will be more likely to engage in deviant or counterproductive work behavior, including cyber-slacking. The meta-analysis of the studies (Mercado et al., 2017b) confirmed a weak effect of organizational, procedural, and interactional justice ($\bar{r} = -0.09$ to -0.10), while a nonsignificant effect of distributive justice in explaining cyber-slacking at work. The effect of procedural justice on cyberslacking was fully mediated by normative conflict (Zoghbi-Manrique-de-Lara, 2009). Furthermore, research suggests that the justice–cyberslacking relationship is weakened by high levels of self-control (Restubog et al., 2011). In another study, organizational justice was a moderator of the relationship between personality traits (neuroticism and agreeableness) and cyberslacking at work (Kim et al., 2016). This implies that a sense of social justice increases the effect of conscientiousness on reducing Internet misuse behavior at work. However, the link between justice and cyberslacking is not always obvious. In a study conducted among hospital employees, all organizational justice dimensions predicted minor cyberloafing activities (such as e-mailing, communicating with friends, browsing the Web), while procedural and interactive justice predicted major cyberloafing activities (such as browsing adult content, gaming, watching movies, gambling).

Social exchange theory provides some explanation for this relationship. By engaging in cyberslacking, employees seek to equalize the inputs versus the benefits of their work (Lim, 2002). More often than not, they reduce their performance levels in line with the small gratifications they receive from their work. Therefore, cyberslacking is a way to equalize or restore equity among workers (Jamaluddin et al., 2015; Lim, 2002). Henle et al. (2009) found that the perceived fairness of US workers and students' application of policies to reduce cyberslacking is associated with reduced actual Internet misuse at work. Another hypothesis assumes that cyberslacking coping strategy for stress is exacerbated by feelings of injustice at work (Lim & Chen, 2012; Ugrin & Pearson, 2013). However, in some studies, justice was not significantly related to cyberslacking (Akin et al., 2017; Yildiz et al., 2015).

Support from Supervisors: Studies commonly examine whether a supervisor's behavior affects employee procrastination. However, the results indicate that supervisor support remains unrelated to subordinates' procrastination (Nguyen et al., 2013) and cyberslacking (Mercado et al., 2017b). One study has found that organizational support was related to low cyberslacking indirectly through increasing employees' work engagement (Oosthuizen et al., 2018). On the other hand, the support of supervisors for increasing non-work-related Internet misuse seems to be far more significant. The support of supervisors appears to make employees feel that their work is meaningful and contributes to the organization, leading to increased work motivation and performance. However, employees who are supported by their supervisors and encouraged to use the Internet for their work may interpret this as a type of permission for both work-related and non-work-related Internet use (Garrett & Danziger, 2008b; Liberman et al., 2011; Vitak et al., 2011). Therefore, the effect of organizational support can be counterproductive. Additionally, the supervisor's compassion and mindfulness (Zoghbi-Manrique-de-Lara et al., 2020) are important factors in reducing cyberslacking. The mindfulness of leaders has a positive impact on the attitudes, well-being, and behavior of employees (Reb & Atkins, 2017); it fosters a climate of mindfulness and concern among employees for the goals of the organization. Supervisors can communicate their expectations, support, and rewards to subordinates more effectively. This can help employees identify cyberslacking as an obstacle to organizational goals and make it harder to engage in cyberslacking automatically. Mindfulness increases awareness, which can prevent or reject habitual non-work-related Internet use during work. The researchers found that compassion played a mediating role in the relationship between supervisor mindfulness and employee Internet abuse. Mindfulness promotes empathic concern in the workplace, reducing the likelihood of engaging in cyberslacking, a behavior that harms the organization (Zoghbi-Manrique-de-Lara et al., 2020).

2.4.3.4 *Leadership Behaviors*

Among the work-related determinants of employee procrastination is leadership style as a pattern of behavior that a leader adopts when influencing the behavior of his subordinates. Leadership style may influence employees' citizenship or deviant work behavior, including procrastination at work. There was empirical evidence for the role of leadership in predicting subordinates' procrastination and cyberslacking. Transformational, transactional, paternalistic, inclusive, and abusive leadership are related to procrastination at work, while cyberslacking is related to ethical, responsible, empowered, participative, transformational, authoritarian, paternalistic, and abusive leadership.

Inclusive Leadership: Studies have shown that inclusive leadership negatively affects employees' procrastination behavior (Lin, 2018). Inclusive leadership is defined as a style of influencing subordinates by including and recognizing their input in decision-making and expressing their views and ideas in the organization (Ryan, 2006). An inclusive style allows subordinates to develop their work experience and the effectiveness of groups and organizations. Among the behaviors of an inclusive leader are: (1) behaviors that foster a sense of belonging, such as supporting group members, ensuring that fairness and equality are part of each member's experience, and providing opportunities for collective deci-sion-making on important issues; and (2) a sense of uniqueness by encouraging diverse contributions to the group's work and helping group members fully offer their unique talents and perspectives to enhance the group's work. Consequently, Lin (2018) revealed that inclusive leadership is also associated with subordinate procrastination through intrinsic motivation. This suggests that inclusive leader-ship can provide employees with a supportive and satisfying work environment that facilitates their needs and strengthens intrinsic motivation, which in turn reduces their procrastination behavior. However, this relationship was stronger under conditions of strong employee identification with the organization.

Transformational Leadership: The effects of transformational leadership were significant in predicting low subordinates' procrastination, including soldier-ing and cyberslacking (Göncü Köse & Metin, 2018). Transformational lead-ership involves the interaction of a leader and employees and the creation of an engaged team-based relationship and emotional ties. Transformational style involves visionary inspiration of subordinates to act as well as to solve prob-lems independently and creatively, motivating subordinates by fostering a sense of value and importance of their tasks at the expense of financial incentives, encouraging active participation of the team in realizing the company's vision, and going beyond self-interest and needs in achieving organizational goals (Bass & Riggio, 2006). Through inspiration and vision, a transformational leader undermines deviant organizational behavior (Uddin et al., 2017), as well as pro-crastination of work (Göncü Köse & Metin, 2018). The authors suggest that employees may procrastinate (by engaging in soldiering and cyberslacking) less often under conditions of effective motivation by a supervisor to work together on group goals, even at the expense of their personal goals and benefits (e.g. engagement in personal and organizational goals). The authors suggested that transformational leaders inspire and stimulate subordinates' behaviors for the benefit of the group and the organization and are also likely to motivate them to focus on achieving goals and avoid any behaviors that detract from work, such as soldiering and cyberslacking. It seems that the supportive work environment created by the transformational leader encourages subordinates to positive work behavior for the organization rather than engaging in soldiering or cyberslack-ing. However, a study conducted in a Taiwanese sample found a positive direct relationship between transformational leadership style and procrastination at work (Singh & Singh, 2015), speculating about the positive consequences of employee procrastination for the organization.

Paternalistic Leadership: Göncü Köse and Metin (2018) examined the relation-ship between paternalistic and procrastination at work represented by soldiering and cyberslacking. Paternalistic leadership is negatively perceived in Western cultures as excessive control and an authoritarian approach to subordinates, while in Eastern cultures it expresses a hierarchical relationship, in which the role of the leader is to provide care, protection, and guidance in work and non-work areas of employees' lives, and the role of the subordinate is loyalty and submission to the leader (Aycan, 2006). Hence, some studies have found associations of paternalistic leadership with increased organizational citizenship behavior, high levels of trust in the supervisor, strong identification with the organization, and high job satisfaction (e.g. Bedi, 2020; Cheng et al., 2004). The study results showed significant negative correlations of paternalistic leadership with soldiering (−0.25) and cyberslacking (−0.21), but in the regression model with controlling other variables, the effects of paternalistic leadership were found to be statistically nonsignificant.

Abusive Supervision: Abusive supervision is defined as 'the perception by subordinates of the degree to which superiors engage in continuous displays of hostile verbal and nonverbal behavior, excluding physical contact' (Tepper, 2000; p. 178). He et al. (2021) showed that abusive supervision is associated with subordinates' procrastination, directly and indirectly through workplace ostracism. The abusive leader creates an unfriendly (even hostile) atmosphere at work, which reduces subordinates' willingness to establish and maintain proper interpersonal relationships. Research also found that the detected indirect relationship between power abuse, ostracism, and procrastination at work is moderated by psychological resilience and psychological detachment. Among employees with low psychological strength, abuse of power by superiors more strongly determines ostracism in the workplace due to greater sensitivity to difficult emotional situations and interpersonal conflicts. On the other hand, ostracism more strongly influences procrastination at work under conditions of low psychological detachment because the associated negative emotions require more resources to cope with the difficult situation of ostracism (He et al., 2021).

Recent studies have systematically confirmed a significant relationship between abusive supervision and cyberslacking at work (Agarwal & Avey, 2020; Koay et al., 2022; Lim et al., 2021). This effect is part of a broader stream of research indicating that employees exposed to unfair and humiliating treatment by a superior tend to engage in a variety of deviance that often goes undetected and and not subject to any sanctions (Tepper et al., 2008). Cyberslacking appears to meet these criteria. Abusive leader behavior promotes employees' cyberslacking, which is a form of retaliation and helps them relieve stress and regain a sense of control. Abusive supervision interacts with other variables in predicting subordinates' non-work-related Internet use. For example, this relationship is moderated by negative reciprocity beliefs, moral disengagement, psychological contract breach, or organizational commitment. Koay and colleagues (2022) revealed that the relationship between abusive supervision and a subordinate's cyberloafing is stronger among employees with high levels of negative reciprocity beliefs and moral disengagement. Additionally, the psychological contract breach reinforced non-work-related Internet abuse at work (Agarwal & Avey, 2020). This relationship is also moderated by negative reciprocity beliefs. In addition, support was found for the three-way interaction effect of abusive supervision, moral disengagement, and negative reciprocity beliefs on cyberslacking, such that the positive relationship between abusive supervision and cyberslacking is strongest at high levels of moral disengagement and negative reciprocity beliefs.

Other studies have found that the effect of abusive supervision on cyberslacking was mediated by emotional exhaustion (Lim et al., 2021) and psychological capital (Agarwal & Avey, 2020). Abusive supervision affected cyberslacking through the mediation of emotional or psychological capital (Agarwal & Avey, 2020). In a study by Lim et al. (2021), abusive supervision was observed to promote emotional exhaustion in subordinates, which in turn led to an increase in cyberslacking. The negative behavior of a supervisor may lead to lower support for subordinates, which in turn can cause employees to engage in cyberslacking as a way to recover their depleted psychological resources. This effect is more likely to occur when employees have low organizational attachment. In a study conducted by Agarwal and Avey (2020), the relationship between abusive supervision and misuse of the Internet at work was found to be mediated by psychological capital, which is represented by optimism, self-efficacy, hope, and resilience. Additionally, the relationship was found to be moderated by breach of psychological contract between the supervisor and the subordinate. Therefore, it can be concluded that the stronger effect of abusive supervision on the misuse of the Internet at work is justified under conditions of a serious breach of contract.

Ethical Leadership: Only one article has found a significant effect of ethical leadership in weakening employee cyberloafing (Zoghbi-Manrique-de-Lara & Viera-Armas, 2017). Ethical leadership can influence employees through leader behavior and interpersonal relationships with a high degree of morality and by promoting such behavior among subordinates (Brown et al., 2005). Ethical leadership is associated with positive attitudes and behaviors of employees (such as satisfaction, motivation, commitment, ethical choices, and prosocial behavior) and low levels of counterproductive behavior, such as non-work-related Internet activities at work. Furthermore, the relationship between ethical leadership and cyberslacking was mediated by the culture of adhocracy (Zoghbi-Manrique-de-Lara & Viera-Armas, 2017). Strong relationships of ethical leadership to the values of the adhocracy culture (related to innovation and progress, willingness to take risks, and flexibility) appear to be an effective mechanism for reinforcing subordinates' concern and commitment to the organization and thereby curbing unacceptable cyberslacking behavior.

Responsible Leadership: Responsible leadership is values-based, defined as a relationship between leaders and subordinates who share a common sense of meaning and purpose and foster greater motivation and commitment to achieving sustainable values and creating social change (Pless & Maak, 2011). As researchers have found, the relationship between responsible leadership and cyberslacking is mediated by stress and a felt obligation (Zhu et al., 2021). A responsible leadership style may increase feelings of obligation and restore self-regulatory resources, which may reduce the tendency to engage in non-work-related Internet activities during work hours. However, it can also increase stress levels at work, leading to the depletion of employees' self-regulation resources, which can intensify subordinates' cyberslacking (Zhu et al., 2021). This result is inconsistent with previous findings in this area.

Authoritarian Leadership: Authoritarian leadership is a negative leadership style exhibited by autocratic, dictatorial, scolding, distancing, and other actions, which can be a source of stress for employees. As a result, employees may excessively exploit personal resources to cope with authoritarian leaders, leading to the exhaustion of resources among employees. To regain depleted resources, employees may avoid contact with supervisors, avoid work, and over-use the Internet for non-work-related purposes. Zhang et al. (2022) have found a positive effect of authoritarian leadership on subordinates' cyberslacking in the Chinese sample. This relationship was mediated by emotional exhaustion, implying that leaders' authoritarian behavior may increase emotional exhaustion, which in turn, contributed to a higher level of cyberloafing among subordinates. Furthermore, this relationship was negatively moderated by power distance orientation. This suggests that when employees have a higher power distance orientation, the negative impact of authoritarian leadership on emotional exhaustion is weakened.

Empowering Leadership: Empowering leadership is defined as the leader's behavior oriented toward sharing power and allocating autonomy and responsibilities among employees (Cheong et al., 2019). It may promote positive work behavior, but also negative outcomes among employees. Empowering leadership may simultaneously enhance resources and induce stress. Similarly, empowering leadership may affect cyberslacking positively and negatively by two competing mechanisms. The study conducted in the hospitality industry (Peng et al., 2023b) showed that empowering leadership was positively related to cyberslacking through role ambiguity, as well as negatively through organization-based self-esteem. When leaders empower employees by providing them autonomy, responsibility, and resources, they are more likely to be engaged in work-related tasks than non-work-related Internet use. On the other hand, the same work conditions may be perceived as high expectations for employees, leading to feelings of stress and avoiding work by cyberslacking. These mediational relationships were moderated by power distance orientation. Specifically, empowering leadership decreased cyberslacking by strengthening organization-based self-esteem among employees with lower power distance, while it enhanced cyberslacking by increasing their role ambiguity. However, the non-significant effect of empowering leadership was found in the personal use of social network sites at work (Andreassen et al., 2014a).

Participative Leadership: Participative leadership style increases employees' feelings of importance, meaningfulness, and worth by including them in decision-making, inviting them to express their opinions, and ensuring them greater discretion at work (Lam et al., 2014). A study by Peng et al. (2023a) showed that participative leadership was related to cyberloafing indirectly through organization-based self-esteem. This leadership behavior fosters high organization-based self-esteem understood as high self-consistency between self-concept and behavior, which increases employees' engagement in work and reduces non-work-related Internet use. Furthermore, the indirect relationship between participative leadership and employee cyberloafing through their organization-based self-esteem was significant when employees' needs for power were high, and nonsignificant when their power needs were low.

Supervisor's Communication Style: One of the factors related to employees' cyberslacking is the supervisor's communication style perceived by subordinates (Agarwal, 2019). The study showed that an aggressive and passive top-down communication style increases employees' cyberslacking, while an assertive style decreases the level of employees' Internet misuse. An aggressive communication style is associated with less emotional support and inaccessibility of the supervisor to employees. A passive style means that the supervisor does not make his thoughts, ideas, and expectations clear, and employees have to guess their intentions. The aggressive and passive communication styles can cause employees to avoid difficult relationships with their supervisors and engage in non-work-related Internet abuse (Agarwal, 2019).

In conclusion, it can be stated that leaders' behaviors contributed to employees' tendency to engage in non-work-related activities offline and online. Procrastination and cyberslacking at work may be reduced by constructive leadership styles, which focus on employees' motivation to achieve organizational goals and tasks and supportive relationships with subordinates. On the other hand, destructive leadership can increase employees' inclination to procrastinate by setting a bad example of their procrastination for followers to follow. Therefore, managers need to comprehend the influence their leadership styles have on how employees perform their duties.

2.4.3.5 Organizational Factors

Among the organizational factors that are relevant to non-work-related Internet misuse at work are social and organizational norms, company policies, sanctions, and organizational justice.

Social Norms: There is ample empirical evidence that indicate that social norms are a strong predictor of Internet abuse in various work environments. The issue of the relationship between norms and cyberslacking behavior is complex and nuanced. A study by Blanchard and Henle (2008) found that norms for Internet use at work were more conducive to reducing minor forms of cyberloafing among employees (handling private e-mails, using instant messaging for private contacts), while serious forms of Internet abuse, such as playing online games, visiting adult sites, and gambling online, did not depend on organizational norms.

Previous research indicated that different norms (*prescriptive vs. descriptive*) are associated with cyberslacking behavior (Askew et al., 2014; Askew et al., 2019; Blanchard & Henle, 2008; Liberman et al., 2011). *Prescriptive norms* refer to behavior that is socially expected, while *descriptive norms* describe the behavior that is commonly observed. This distinction is based on different sources of human motivation. Descriptive norms influence behavior by providing cues about what others are doing, while prescriptive norms drive behavior by indicating social rewards or punishments for conforming to social expectations. Regarding cyberloafing, prescriptive norms dictate the extent to which coworkers and supervisors approve of employees engaging in non-work-related online activities, while descriptive norms express the degree to which coworkers and supervisors themselves use the Internet for non-work purposes during work hours (Askew et al., 2019). Both types of norms may refer to the same individual and manifest as disapproval of Internet abusers at work and violation of the norms by engaging in non-work-related online activities. A meta-analysis of 12 studies (Mercado et al., 2017b) concluded that norms have a significant impact on the emergence and maintenance of cyberslacking behavior ($\bar{r} = 0.32$), although descriptive norms explained a larger proportion of the variance in cyberslacking than prescriptive norms. This research stream investigates and synthesizes attitudes toward cyberslacking among coworkers and supervisors, as well as the cyberslacking behaviors of employees and supervisors (Tandon et al., 2022).

Coworkers' Attitudes toward Cyberslacking: Regarding prescriptive and descriptive norms for Internet usage within an organization, the approval of cyberslacking by supervisors and their actual participation in cyberslacking are important factors in the spread of this behavior. Studies have shown that employee cyberloafing is linked to the cyberslacking of their colleagues (Askew et al., 2019; Liberman et al., 2011). The correlation between employee and coworker cyberslacking was 0.45 measured at the same point in time and 0.38 when the measurements were taken at different time points (Khansa et al., 2017). However, a slightly different picture of the phenomenon was revealed when evaluating and justifying the cyberslacking of others. Typically, employees evaluate associates' Internet abuse more negatively than their own (Hernández et al., 2016). Positive attitudes toward Internet abuse at work seem to create favorable organizational conditions for the rise of cyberslacking in organizations. Employees may believe that browsing the Internet for non-work-related purposes is harmless and therefore more tempting to engage in such activities.

Employees who observed cyberslacking in other employees and supervisors were more prone to non-work-related Internet use (Askew et al., 2019). According to the assumptions of social learning theory (Bandura, 2023), employees may learn to use the Internet for non-work purposes by observing the behavior of their colleagues. Additionally, the approval of non-work-related Internet use by coworkers and supervisors may influence an employee's decision to engage in cyberslacking. This social justification of cyberslacking can lead to unethical behavior. The minor cyberslacking behaviors among employees, such as receiving and sending personal e-mails or instant messaging at work, are higher when supervisors approve of Internet browsing at work. This can be attributed to employees finding it easier to justify their cyberslacking when they perceive their supervisors to approve of Internet browsing at work. However, this perceived endorsement of supervisors' cyberslacking may be due to a subjective overinterpretation of support for work-related Internet use and an emerging belief that the boss condones cyberslacking (Liberman et al., 2011). At the same time, it was revealed that employees' attitudes toward cyberslacking can also enhance their non-work-related online activities (Khansa et al., 2018). Similarly, those with more positive attitudes toward computers were more likely to use computers at work for personal reasons. Furthermore, engaging in cyberslacking behavior in the past is associated with a greater propensity for such behavior in the future (Khansa et al., 2017). Accordingly, the more employees have used cyberloafing in the past, the stronger their intentions to cyberloafing in the future. A meta-analysis of the results confirmed a strong relationship between attitudes and behavior related to cyberslacking ($\bar{r} = 0.37$), as well as between intention and cyberslacking behavior ($\bar{r} = 0.53$; Mercado et al., 2017b).

Leader Attitudes toward Procrastination: When leaders procrastinate at work, they may unknowingly encourage their subordinates to do the same. Even if supervisors disapprove of procrastination, they might inadvertently display this behavior themselves. According to social learning theory (Bandura, 2023), employees often mimic their superiors' actions, interpreting them as acceptable. This can lead to a cycle where procrastination or similar unproductive behaviors are adopted by subordinates. Studies have also shown that leader procrastination indirectly contributes to subordinates' deviant behavior by causing frustration among employees (Legood et al., 2018). Essentially, a leader's procrastination can hinder employees' resources and abilities needed to complete tasks, leading to increased frustration. This link between leader procrastination, frustration, and deviant behavior is influenced by the quality of the relationship between supervisors and subordinates. A strong relationship mitigates the impact of leader procrastination on frustration and reduces the likelihood of deviant behavior. Supervisor procrastination is a form of negative leadership akin to the laissez-faire style, where decisions and actions are deferred or neglected, albeit with less direct influence over subordinates (Legood et al., 2018).

Policy and Sanctions: Due to the prevalence of cyberslacking behaviors, many organizations are implementing intervention and prevention measures to curb the practice. These measures include control over the work of subordinates, and the implementation of Internet use policies, rules, and guidelines for electronic device use. The most common tools used are regulatory and technological which help to organize Internet access, monitor usage, and detect abuse. Researchers have noted that having a formal Internet use policy in an organization serves as a countermeasure to cyberloafing (Jia et al., 2013), and the lack of sanctions and monitoring of employees' online activity result in abuse of the Internet for non-work-related purposes (Ugrin & Pearson, 2013; Zoghbi-Manrique-de-Lara & Olivares-Mesa, 2010). In the absence of sanctions, cyberloafing can easily become a habitual activity (Lim & Teo, 2005; Moody & Siponen, 2013). This may suggest that the lack of regulation of Internet misuse for non-work purposes promotes the escalation of the phenomenon and its serious consequences for organizations. A meta-analysis of eight studies (Mercado et al., 2017b) indicated that the regulation of Internet use at work is negatively associated with cyber-slacking at work ($\bar{r} = -0.12$), although monitoring of this practice *per se* does not affect online abuse at work ($\bar{r} = -0.05$).

Many organizations use various sanctions for cyberslacking activities. Previous studies have shown that the use of organizational sanctions for Internet misuse at work reduces this behavior. Employees who perceive little or no sanctions are more likely to engage in cyberslacking. However, formal penalty systems have been found to increase cyberslacking (Zoghbi-Manrique-de-Lara, 2006). Henle and Blanchard (2008) emphasized that the high severity of sanctions can undermine their regulatory power. A meta-analysis of five studies concluded that the threat of sanctions for cyberslacking at work was not related to cyberslacking ($p = 0.01$; Mercado et al., 2017b). This effect corresponds to the assumptions of social learning theory (Bandura, 2023), indicating that cyberslacking is lower when it involves the risk of negative consequences of imposed sanctions.

Cheng and colleagues (2014) found that the severity of sanctions was not a significant predictor of cyberslacking. Instead, low perceived benefits and a high risk of detection were associated with lower levels of cyberslacking. This could be due to employees never having been punished for cyberslacking before (due to undetected abuse) or because the perceived benefits outweigh the costs of sanctions (Khansa et al., 2017). The severity of sanctions may not have the intended impact and could neutralize the negative consequences of cyberslacking behavior at work. Employees who engage in sanctionable behavior may ignore the potential threat of sanctions and underestimate the likelihood of them being imposed (Cheng et al., 2014). Banning or restricting Internet use at work may be ineffective for employers. Subordinates often ignore these norms. Additionally, the combination of organizational control mechanisms with sanction systems for Internet abuse at work may reinforce the tendency to hide cyberslacking. Research has also found that the application of policies supporting Internet use for non-work-related purposes leads to an increase in this behavior in employees (Askew et al., 2014). Thus, the introduction of formal controls to regulate Internet abuse behavior at work could be controversial. According to the deterrence approach, sanctions- and detection-oriented controls affect (albeit small) reducing engagement in cyberslacking at work (Cheng et al., 2014; Moody & Siponen, 2013).

Recently, researchers have suggested that systemic measures should not be limited to the use of deterrence strategies or ignoring the phenomenon of regulation of cyberslacking in organizations. Studies have confirmed that monitoring employees' Internet use reduces cyberslacking behavior (e.g. Jiang et al., 2020), but also reduces employee loyalty, intrinsic motivation, and citizenship behavior at work. In conclusion, the findings presented shed some light on the complex picture of cyberslacking and the effectiveness of systemic measures to regulate this phenomenon in the organization.

References

Abbas, A. A., & Al Hasnawi, H. H. (2020). Role of psychological contract breach and violation in generating emotional exhaustion: The mediating role of job procrastination. *Cuadernos de Gestión, 20*(3), 15–28. https://doi.org/10.5295/cdg.181021aa

Adeel, A., Sarminah, S., Jie, L., Kee, D. M. H., Qasim Daghriri, Y., & Alghafes, R. A. (2023). When procrastination pays off: Role of knowledge sharing ability, autonomous motivation, and task involvement for employee creativity. *Heliyon, 9*(10), e19398. https://doi.org/10.1016/j.heliyon.2023.e19398

Agarwal, U. A. (2019). Impact of supervisors' perceived communication style on subordinate's psychological capital and cyberloafing. *Australasian Journal of Information Systems, 23*, 1–27. https://doi.org/10.3127/ajis.v23i0.1759

Agarwal, U. A., & Avey, J. B. (2020). Abusive supervisors and employees who cyberloaf. *Internet Research, 30*(3), 789–809. https://doi.org/10.1108/INTR-05-2019-0208

Aghaz, A., & Sheikh, A. (2016). Cyberloafing and job burnout: An investigation in the knowledge-intensive sector. *Computers in Human Behavior, 62*, 51–60. https://doi.org/10.1016/j.chb.2016.03.069

Ahmad, Z., Munir, N., & Hussain, M. (2021). Procrastination and job performance of employees working in public and private sector organizations. *Pakistan Social Sciences Review, 5*(2), 1166–1176. https://doi.org/10.35484/pssr.2021(5-II)89

Akbulut, Y., Dönmez, O., & Dursun, Ö. Ö. (2017). Cyberloafing and social desirability bias among students and employees. *Computers in Human Behavior, 72*, 87–95. https://doi.org/10.1016/j.chb.2017.02.043

Akhtar, S., & Faisal Malik, M. (2016). Effect of boredom and flexible work practices on the relationship of WFC with procrastination and affective commitment: Mediation of non-work-related presenteeism. *Global Journal of Flexible Systems Management*, *17*(4), 343–356. https://doi.org/10.1007/s40171-016-0132-6

Akin, A., Ulukök, E., & Arar, T. (2017). Analyzing the relationship between organizational justice and cyberloafing: A study in a public university. *RSEP International Conferences on Social Issues and Economic Studies, Prague, Czechia, 29–30 June, 2017*, 9–19. https://doi.org/10.19275/rsepconferences088

Alharthi, S., Levy, Y., Wang, L., & Hur, I. (2021). Employees' mobile cyberslacking and their commitment to the organization. *Journal of Computer Information Systems*, *61*(2), 141–153. https://doi.org/10.1080/08874417.2019.1571455

Allen, N. J., & Meyer, J. P. (1990). The measurement and antecedents of affective, continuance and normative commitment to the organization. *Journal of Occupational Psychology*, *63*(1), 1–18. https://doi.org/10.1111/j.2044-8325.1990.tb00506.x

Anandarajan, M., & Simmers, C. A. (2004). Constructive and dysfunctional personal web usage in the workplace: Mapping employee attitudes. In M. Anandarajan & C. A. Simmers (Eds.), *Personal web usage in the workplace: A guide to effective human resources management* (pp. 1–27). Information Science Publishing.

Anandarajan, M., Simmers, C. A., & D'Ovidio, R. (2011). Exploring the underlying structure of personal Web usage in the workplace. *Cyberpsychology, Behavior, and Social Networking*, *14*(10), 577–583. https://doi.org/10.1089/cyber.2010.0136

Andel, S. A., Kessler, S. R., Pindek, S., Kleinman, G., & Spector, P. E. (2019). Is cyberloafing more complex than we originally thought? Cyberloafing as a coping response to workplace aggression exposure. *Computers in Human Behavior*, *101*, 124–130. https://doi.org/10.1016/j.chb.2019.07.013

Anderson, J. H. (2016). Structured nonprocrastination: Scaffolding efforts to resist the temptation to reconstrue unwarranted delay. In F. M. Sirois & T. A. Pychyl (Eds.), *Procrastination, health, and well-being* (pp. 43–63). Academic Press. https://doi.org/10.1016/B978-0-12-802862-9.00003-7

Andreassen, C. S., Torsheim, T., & Pallesen, S. (2014a). Predictors of use of social network sites at work - A specific type of cyberloafing. *Journal of Computer-Mediated Communication*, *19*(4), 906–921. https://doi.org/10.1111/jcc4.12085

Andreassen, C. S., Torsheim, T., & Pallesen, S. (2014b). Use of online social network sites for personal purposes at work: Does it impair self-reported performance? *Comprehensive Psychology*, *3*(1), Article 18. https://doi.org/10.2466/01.21.CP.3.18

Arshad, M., Aftab, M., & Bukhari, H. (2016). The impact of job characteristics and role stressors on cyberloafing: The case of Pakistan. *International Journal of Scientific and Research Publications*, *6*(12), 244–252.

Askew, K. L., Buckner, J. E., Taing, M. U., Ilie, A., Bauer, J. A., & Coovert, M. D. (2014). Explaining cyberloafing: The role of the theory of planned behavior. *Computers in Human Behavior*, *36*, 510–519. https://doi.org/10.1016/j.chb.2014.04.006

Askew, K. L., & Buckner, J. E. (2017). The role of the work station: Visibility of one's computer screen to coworkers influences cyberloafing through self-efficacy to hide cyberloafing. *The Psychologist-Manager Journal*, *20*(4), 267–287. https://doi.org/10.1037/mgr0000061

Askew, K. L., Ilie, A., Bauer, J. A., Simonet, D. V., Buckner, J. E., & Robertson, T. A. (2019). Disentangling how coworkers and supervisors influence employee cyberloafing: What normative information are employees attending to? *Journal of Leadership & Organizational Studies*, *26*(4), 526–544. https://doi.org/10.1177/1548051818813091

Aziz, S., & Tariq, N. (2013). Role of organization type, job tenure, and job hierarchy in decisional procrastination and perceived locus of control among executives. *Pakistan Journal of Psychological Research, 28*(1), 25–50.

Aycan, Z. (2006). Paternalism. Towards conceptual refinement and operationalization. In U. Kim, K. S. Yang, & K. K. Hwang (Eds.), *Indigenous and cultural psychology. International and cultural psychology* (pp. 445–466). Springer. https://doi.org/10 .1007/0-387-28662-4_20

Bajcar, B., & Babiak, J. (2020). Job characteristics and cyberloafing among polish IT professionals: Mediating role of work stress. In K. S. Soliman (Ed.), *Proceedings of the 36th International Business Information Management Association Conference* (pp. 6565–6578). The IBIMA Conference, 4–5 November, Granada, Spain.

Bakker, A. B., & Demerouti, E. (2007). The job demands-resources model: State of the art. *Journal of Managerial Psychology, 22*(3), 309–328. https://doi.org/10.1108 /02683940710733115

Bakker, A. B., & Demerouti, E. (2014). Job demands-resources theory. In P. Y. Chen & C. L. Cooper (Eds.), *Wellbeing: A complete reference guide* (pp. 1–28). John Wiley & Sons Inc. https://doi.org/10.1002/9781118539415.wbwell019

Bakker, A. B., Demerouti, E., & Sanz-Vergel, A. (2023). Job demands–resources theory: Ten years later. *Annual Review of Organizational Psychology and Organizational Behavior, 10*(1), 25–53. https://doi.org/10.1146/annurev-orgpsych-120920-053933

Bakker, A. B., & Schaufeli, W. B. (2014). Work engagement. In C. L. Cooper (Ed.), *Wiley online library. Wiley encyclopedia of management* (3rd ed., pp. 1–5). Wiley. https://doi.org/10.1002/9781118785317.weom110009

Balducci, C., Schaufeli, W. B., & Fraccaroli, F. (2011). The job demands–resources model and counterproductive work behaviour: The role of job-related affect. *European Journal of Work and Organizational Psychology, 20*(4), 467–496. https://doi.org/10 .1080/13594321003669061

Bandura, A. (2023). *Social cognitive theory: An agentic perspective on human nature.* John Wiley & Sons, Inc.

Baskaran, S., Nedunselian, N., Mahadi, N., & Mahmood, Z. (2019). An epidemic phenomenon of workplace cyberloafing: Investigations and implications. *International Journal of Work Organisation and Emotion, 10*(4), Article 10027828, 1. https://doi .org/10.1504/ijwoe.2019.10027828

Bass, B. M., & Riggio, R. (2006). *Transformational leadership* (2nd ed.). Lawrence Erlbaum Associates Publishers. https://doi.org/10.4324/9781410617095

Bauer, J. A., & Spector, P. E. (2015). Discrete negative emotions and counterproductive work behavior. *Human Performance, 28*(4), 307–331. https://doi.org/10.1080 /08959285.2015.1021040

Bedi, A. (2020). A meta-analytic review of paternalistic leadership. *Applied Psychology, 69*(3), 960–1008. https://doi.org/10.1111/apps.12186

Beheshtifar, M., Hoseinifar, H., & Moghadam, M. N. (2011). Effect procrastination on work-related stress. *European Journal of Economics, Finance and Administrative Sciences, 38*, 59–64.

Belanger, F., & van Slyke, C. (2002). Abuse or learning? *Communications of the ACM, 45*(1), 64–65. https://doi.org/10.1145/502269.502299

Berthelsen, H., Hakanen, J. J., & Westerlund, H. (2018). Copenhagen psychosocial questionnaire - A validation study using the job demand-resources model. *PLoS One, 13*(4), e0196450. https://doi.org/10.1371/journal.pone.0196450

Betts, T. K., Setterstrom, A. J., Pearson, J. M., & Totty, S. (2014). Explaining cyberloafing through a theoretical integration of theory of interpersonal behavior and theory of organizational justice. *Journal of Organizational and End User Computing, 26*(4), 23–42. https://doi.org/10.4018/joeuc.2014100102

Beutel, M. E., Klein, E. M., Aufenanger, S., Brähler, E., Dreier, M., Müller, K. W., Quiring, O., Reinecke, L., Schmutzer, G., Stark, B., & Wölfling, K. (2016). Procrastination, distress and life satisfaction across the age range - A German representative community study. *PLoS One, 11*(2), e0148054. https://doi.org/10.1371/journal.pone.0148054

Black, E., Light, J., Black, N. P., & Thomson, L. (2013). Online social network use by health care providers in a high traffic patient care environment. *Journal of Medical Internet Research, 15*(5), e94. https://doi.org/10.2196/jmir.2421

Blanchard, A. L., & Henle, C. A. (2008). Correlates of different forms of cyberloafing: The role of norms and external locus of control. *Computers in Human Behavior, 24*(3), 1067–1084. https://doi.org/10.1016/j.chb.2007.03.008

Blau, G., Yang, Y., & Ward-Cook, K. (2006). Testing a measure of cyberloafing. *Journal of Allied Health, 35*(1), 9–17.

Bock, G.-W., & Ho, S. L. (2009). Non-Work Related Computing (NWRC). *Communications of the ACM, 52*(4), 124–128. https://doi.org/10.1145/1498765.1498799

Breems, N., & Basden, A. (2014). Understanding of computers and procrastination: A philosophical approach. *Computers in Human Behavior, 31*, 211–223. https://doi.org/10.1016/j.chb.2013.10.024

Brinthaupt, T. M., & Shin, C. M. (2001). The relationship of academic cramming to flow experience. *College Student Journal, 35*(3), 457–471.

Brown, M. E., Treviño, L. K., & Harrison, D. A. (2005). Ethical leadership: A social learning perspective for construct development and testing. *Organizational Behavior and Human Decision Processes, 97*(2), 117–134. https://doi.org/10.1016/j.obhdp.2005.03.002

Bruursema, K., Kessler, S. R., & Spector, P. E. (2011). Bored employees misbehaving: The relationship between boredom and counterproductive work behaviour. *Work & Stress, 25*(2), 93–107. https://doi.org/10.1080/02678373.2011.596670

Cadena, X., Schoar, A., Cristea, A., & Delgado-Medrano, H. (2011). *Fighting procrastination in the workplace: An experiment.* https://doi.org/10.3386/w16944

CareerBuilder. (2015). *Over half of employers lose 1–2 hours of productivity a day.* https://resources.careerbuilder.com/news-research/employers-battle-workforce-distraction

Carpenter, N. C., & Berry, C. M. (2017). Are counterproductive work behavior and withdrawal empirically distinct? A meta-analytic investigation. *Journal of Management, 43*(3), 834–863. https://doi.org/10.1177/0149206314544743

Chauhan, R. S., MacDougall, A. E., Buckley, M. R., Howe, D. C., Crisostomo, M. E., & Zeni, T. (2020). Better late than early? Reviewing procrastination in organizations. *Management Research Review, 43*(10), 1289–1308. https://doi.org/10.1108/MRR-09-2019-0413

Chen, H., Richard, O. C., Dorian Boncoeur, O., & Ford, D. L. (2020). Work engagement, emotional exhaustion, and counterproductive work behavior. *Journal of Business Research, 114*, 30–41. https://doi.org/10.1016/j.jbusres.2020.03.025

Chen, J. V., Chen, C. C., & Yang, H.-H. (2008). An empirical evaluation of key factors contributing to Internet abuse in the workplace. *Industrial Management & Data Systems, 108*(1), 87–106. https://doi.org/10.1108/02635570810844106

Cheng, B. S., Zhou, X., Guo, G., & Yang, K. (2020). Perceived overqualification and cyberloafing: A moderated-mediation model based on equity theory. *Journal of Business Ethics, 164*, 565–577. https://doi.org/10.1007/s10551-018-4026-8

Cheng, B.-S., Chou, L.-F., Wu, T.-Y., Huang, M.-P., & Farh, J.-L. (2004). Paternalistic leadership and subordinate responses: Establishing a leadership model in Chinese organizations. *Asian Journal of Social Psychology, 7*(1), 89–117. https://doi.org/10.1111/j.1467-839X.2004.00137.x

Cheng, L., Li, W., Zhai, Q., & Smyth, R. (2014). Understanding personal use of the Internet 0at work: An integrated model of neutralization techniques and general deterrence theory. *Computers in Human Behavior, 38*, 220–228. https://doi.org/10.1016/j.chb.2014.05.043

Cheong, M., Yammarino, F. J., Dionne, S. D., Spain, S. M., & Tsai, C.-Y. (2019). A review of the effectiveness of empowering leadership. *The Leadership Quarterly, 30*(1), 34–58. https://doi.org/10.1016/j.leaqua.2018.08.005

Chevrenidi, A., & Bolotova, A. (2018). Relationships between time perspectives and procrastination of employees with different job titles. *Psychology. Journal of the Higher School Economics, 15*(3), 573–589. https://doi.org/10.17323/1813-8918-2018-3-573-589

Chowdhury, S. F., & Pychyl, T. A. (2018). A critique of the construct validity of active procrastination. *Personality and Individual Differences, 120*, 7–12. https://doi.org/10.1016/j.paid.2017.08.016

Cohen, A., & Özsoy, E. (2024). The Dark Triad and Cyberloafing: Unveiling the Shadowy Nexus. *Academy of Management Proceedings*, 2024(1). https://doi.org/10.5465/AMPROC.2024.1011

Coker, B. L. (2011). Freedom to surf: The positive effects of workplace Internet leisure browsing. *New Technology, Work and Employment, 26*(3), 238–247. https://doi.org/10.1111/j.1468-005X.2011.00272.x

Colquitt, J. A., Conlon, D. E., Wesson, M. J., Porter, C. O., & Ng, K. Y. (2001). Justice at the millennium: A meta-analytic review of 25 years of organizational justice research. *Journal of Applied Psychology, 86*(3), 425–445. https://doi.org/10.1037/0021-9010.86.3.425

CorpMagazine. (2015). *Survey finds 68% of workers distracted by Internet on the job*. https://www.corpmagazine.com/industry/technology/survey-finds-68-of-workers-distracted-by-Internet-on-the-job/

D'Abate, C. P., & Eddy, E. R. (2007). Engaging in personal business on the job: Extending the presenteeism construct. *Human Resource Development Quarterly, 18*(3), 361–383. https://doi.org/10.1002/hrdq.1209

DeArmond, S., Matthews, R. A., & Bunk, J. (2014). Workload and procrastination: The roles of psychological detachment and fatigue. *International Journal of Stress Management, 21*(2), 137–161. https://doi.org/10.1037/a0034893

Deci, E. L., & Ryan, R. M. (2008). Self-determination theory: A macrotheory of human motivation, development, and health. *Canadian Psychology / Psychologie Canadienne, 49*(3), 182–185. https://doi.org/10.1037/a0012801

Derin, N., & Gökçe, S. G. (2016). Are cyberloafers also innovators? A study on the relationship between cyberloafing and innovative work behavior. *Procedia - Social and Behavioral Sciences, 235*, 694–700. https://doi.org/10.1016/j.sbspro.2016.11.070

Eastin, M. S., Glynn, C. J., & Griffiths, R. P. (2007). Psychology of communication technology use in the workplace. *Cyberpsychology & Behavior: The Impact of the*

Internet, Multimedia and Virtual Reality on Behavior and Society, 10(3), 436–443. https://doi.org/10.1089/cpb.2006.9935

Edgar, F. (2020). The behavioral model logic: A micro-level examination of competitive strategies, HR practices and employee outcomes. *Personnel Review, 49*(9), 1919–1944. https://doi.org/10.1108/PR-03-2019-0110

Edmondson, D., Matthews, L., & Ward, C. (2024). The role of grit, engagement and exhaustion in salesperson productive procrastination. *Journal of Business & Industrial Marketing, 39*(1), 29–36. https://doi.org/10.1108/JBIM-01-2023-0030

Elrehail, H., Rehman, S. U., Chaudhry, N. I., & Alzghoul, A. (2021). Nexus among cyberloafing behavior, job demands and job resources: A mediated-moderated model. *Education and Information Technologies, 26*(4), 4731–4749. https://doi.org/10.1007/s10639-021-10496-1

Farivar, F., & Richardson, J. (2021). Workplace digitalisation and work-nonwork satisfaction: The role of spillover social media. *Behaviour & Information Technology, 40*(8), 747–758. https://doi.org/10.1080/0144929X.2020.1723702

Ferrari, J. R. (1991). Self-handicapping by procrastinators: Protecting self-esteem, social-esteem, or both? *Journal of Research in Personality, 25*(3), 245–261. https://doi.org/10.1016/0092-6566(91)90018-L

Ferrari, J. R. (1992). Procrastination in the workplace: Attributions for failure among individuals with similar behavioral tendencies. *Personality and Individual Differences, 13*(3), 315–319. https://doi.org/10.1016/0191-8869(92)90108-2

Ferrari, J. R. (2001). Procrastination as self-regulation failure of performance: Effects of cognitive load, self-awareness, and time limits on 'working best under pressure'. *European Journal of Personality, 15*(5), 391–406. https://doi.org/10.1002/per.413

Ferrari, J. R., Doroszko, E., & Joseph, N. (2005). Exploring procrastination in corporate settings: Sex, status, and settings for arousal and avoidance types. *Individual Differences Research, 3*(2), 140–149.

Ferrari, J. R., Swanson, H. L., & Patel, D. A. (2021). The impact of office clutter on remote working: "I can't work with all this stuff!". *North American Journal of Psychology, 23*(1), 155–171.

Ferrari, J. R., & Tice, D. M. (2000). Procrastination as a self-handicap for men and women: A task-avoidance strategy in a laboratory setting. *Journal of Research in Personality, 34*(1), 73–83. https://doi.org/10.1006/jrpe.1999.2261

Feyzi Behnagh, R., & Ferrari, J. R. (2022). Exploring 40 years on affective correlates to procrastination: A literature review of situational and dispositional types. *Current Psychology, 41*(2), 1097–1111. https://doi.org/10.1007/s12144-021-02653-z

Fichtner, J. R., & Strader, T. J. (2014). Non-work-related computing and job characteristics: Literature review and future research directions. *Journal of Psychological Issues in Organizational Culture, 4*(4), 65–79. https://doi.org/10.1002/jpoc.21122

Fida, R., Paciello, M., Tramontano, C., Barbaranelli, C., & Farnese, M. L. (2015). "Yes, I can": The protective role of personal self-efficacy in hindering counterproductive work behavior under stressful conditions. *Anxiety, Stress, and Coping, 28*(5), 479–499. https://doi.org/10.1080/10615806.2014.969718

Foroux, D. (2019). *Procrastination study: 88% of the workforce procrastinates.* https://dariusforoux.com/procrastination-study/

Fox, S., & Spector, P. E. (Eds.). (2005). *Counterproductive work behavior: Investigations of actors and targets* (1st ed.). American Psychological Association. https://doi.org/10.1037/10893-000

Galletta, D., & Polak, P. (2003). An empirical investigation of antecedents of Internet abuse in the workplace. *SIGHCI 2003 Proceedings, 14*, 47–51. https://aisel.aisnet.org/sighci2003/14/

Garrett, R. K., & Danziger, J. N. (2008a). Disaffection or expected outcomes: Understanding personal Internet use during work. *Journal of Computer-Mediated Communication, 13*(4), 937–958. https://doi.org/10.1111/j.1083-6101.2008.00425.x

Garrett, R. K., & Danziger, J. N. (2008b). On cyberslacking: Workplace status and personal Internet use at work. *CyberPsychology & Behavior, 11*(3), 287–292. https://doi.org/10.1089/cpb.2007.0146

Giordano, C., & Mercado, B. K. (2023). Cyberloafing: Investigating the importance and implications of new and known predictors. *Collabra: Psychology, 9*(1), Article 57391, 1–18. https://doi.org/10.1525/collabra.57391

Göncü Köse, A., & Metin, U. B. (2018). Linking leadership style and workplace procrastination: The role of organizational citizenship behavior and turnover intention. *Journal of Prevention & Intervention in the Community, 46*(3), 245–262. https://doi.org/10.1080/10852352.2018.1470369

Gözü, C., Anandarajan, M., & Simmers, C. A. (2015). Work–family role integration and personal well-being: The moderating effect of attitudes towards personal web usage. *Computers in Human Behavior, 52*, 159–167. https://doi.org/10.1016/j.chb.2015.05.017

Gruys, M. L., & Sackett, P. R. (2003). Investigating the dimensionality of counterproductive work behavior. *International Journal of Selection and Assessment, 11*(1), 30–42. https://doi.org/10.1111/1468-2389.00224

Güğerçin, U. (2020). Does techno-stress justify cyberslacking? An empirical study based on the neutralisation theory. *Behaviour & Information Technology, 39*(7), 824–836. https://doi.org/10.1080/0144929X.2019.1617350

Hackman, J. R., & Oldham, G. R. (1976). Motivation through the design of work. Test of a theory. *Organizational Behavior and Human Performance, 16*(2), 250–279. https://doi.org/10.1016/0030-5073(76)90016-7

Hackman, J. R., & Oldham, G. R. (1980). *Work redesign.* Addison-Wesley.

Hall, N. C., Lee, S. Y., & Rahimi, S. (2019). Self-efficacy, procrastination, and burnout in post-secondary faculty: An international longitudinal analysis. *PLoS One, 14*(12), e0226716. https://doi.org/10.1371/journal.pone.0226716

Hammer, C. A., & Ferrari, J. R. (2002). Differential incidence of procrastination between blue and white-collar workers. *Current Psychology, 21*(4), 333–338. https://doi.org/10.1007/s12144-002-1022-y

Harriott, J., & Ferrari, J. R. (1996). Prevalence of procrastination among samples of adults. *Psychological Reports, 78*(2), 611–616. https://doi.org/10.2466/pr0.1996.78.2.611

Harris, N. N., & Sutton, R. I. (1983). Task procrastination in organizations: A framework for research. *Human Relations, 36*(11), 987–995. https://doi.org/10.1177/001872678303601102

He, Q., Wu, M., Wu, W., & Fu, J. (2021). The effect of abusive supervision on employees' work procrastination behavior. *Frontiers in Psychology, 12*, 596704. https://doi.org/10.3389/fpsyg.2021.596704

Hen, M., Goroshit, M., & Viengarten, S. (2021). How decisional and general procrastination relate to procrastination at work: An investigation of office and non-office workers. *Personality and Individual Differences, 172*, 110581. https://doi.org/10.1016/j.paid.2020.110581

Henle, C. A., & Blanchard, A. L. (2008). The interaction of work stressors and organizational sanctions on cyberloafing. *Journal of Managerial Issues, 20*(3), 383–400. https://www.jstor.org/stable/40604617

Henle, C. A., Kohut, G., & Booth, R. (2009). Designing electronic use policies to enhance employee perceptions of fairness and to reduce cyberloafing: An empirical test of justice theory. *Computers in Human Behavior, 25*(4), 902–910. https://doi.org/10.1016/j.chb.2009.03.005

Hensel, P. G., & Kacprzak, A. (2020). Job overload, organizational commitment, and motivation as antecedents of cyberloafing: Evidence from employee monitoring software. *European Management Review, 17*(4), 931–942. https://doi.org/10.1111/emre.12407

Hernández, W., Levy, Y., & Ramim, M. M. (2016). An empirical assessment of employee cyberslacking in the public sector: The social engineering threat. *Online Journal of Applied Knowledge Management, 4*(2), 93–109.

Hobfoll, S. E. (2012). *Conservation of resources theory: Its Implication for stress, health, and resilience.* Oxford University Press. https://doi.org/10.1093/oxfordhb/9780195375343.013.0007

Hobfoll, S. E., Halbesleben, J., Neveu, J.-P., & Westman, M. (2018). Conservation of resources in the organizational context: The reality of resources and their consequences. *Annual Review of Organizational Psychology and Organizational Behavior, 5*(1), 103–128. https://doi.org/10.1146/annurev-orgpsych-032117-104640

Hu, Y., Chen, Y., & Ye, M. (2021). Eager to belong: Social cyberloafing as a coping response to workplace ostracism. *Current Psychology.* Advance online publication. https://doi.org/10.1007/s12144-021-01690-y

Huang, Q., Zhang, K., Huang, Y., Bodla, A. A., & Zou, X. (2023). The interactive effect of stressor appraisals and personal traits on employees' procrastination behavior: The conservation of resources perspective. *Psychology Research and Behavior Management, 16*, 781–800. https://doi.org/10.2147/PRBM.S399406

Huma, Z., Hussain, S., Thurasamy, R., & Malik, M. I. (2017). Determinants of cyberloafing: A comparative study of a public and private sector organization. *Internet Research, 27*(1), 97–117. https://doi.org/10.1108/IntR-12-2014-0317

Ivarsson, L., & Larsson, P. (2011). Personal Internet usage at work: A source of recovery. *Journal of Workplace Rights, 16*(1), 63–81. https://doi.org/10.2190/WR.16.1.e

Jamaluddin, H., Ahmad, Z., Alias, M., & Simun, M. (2015). Personal Internet use: The use of personal mobile devices at the workplace. *Procedia - Social and Behavioral Sciences, 172*, 495–502. https://doi.org/10.1016/j.sbspro.2015.01.391

Janssen, O., Lam, C. K., & Huang, X. (2010). Emotional exhaustion and job performance: The moderating roles of distributive justice and positive affect. *Journal of Organizational Behavior, 31*(6), 787–809. https://doi.org/10.1002/job.614

Jia, H., Jia, R., & Karau, S. (2013). Cyberloafing and personality. *Journal of Leadership & Organizational Studies, 20*(3), 358–365. https://doi.org/10.1177/1548051813488208

Jiang, H., Siponen, M., & Tsohou, A. (2021). Personal use of technology at work: A literature review and a theoretical model for understanding how it affects employee job performance. *European Journal of Information Systems*, 1–15. https://doi.org/10.1080/0960085X.2021.1963193

Jiang, H., Tsohou, A., Siponen, M., & Li, Y. (2020). Examining the side effects of organizational Internet monitoring on employees. *Internet Research, 30*(6), 1613–1630. https://doi.org/10.1108/INTR-08-2019-0360

Judge, T. A., Zhang, S., & Glerum, D. R. (2021). Job satisfaction. In V. I. Sessa & N. A. Bowling (Eds.), *Essentials of industrial and organizational psychology. Essentials of job attitudes and other workplace psychological constructs* (First published, pp. 207–241). Routledge. https://doi.org/10.4324/9780429325755-11

Jung, H.-S., & Yoon, H.-H. (2022). The effect of social undermining on employees' emotional exhaustion and procrastination behavior in deluxe hotels: Moderating role of positive psychological capital. *Sustainability, 14*(2), 931. https://doi.org/10.3390/su14020931

Karimi Mazidi, A., Rahimnia, F., Mortazavi, S., & Lagzian, M. (2021). Cyberloafing in public sector of developing countries: Job embeddedness as a context. *Personnel Review, 50*(7/8), 1705–1738. https://doi.org/10.1108/PR-01-2020-0026

Katz, D., & Kahn, R. L. (1978). *The social psychology of organizations* (2nd ed.). Wiley.

Khansa, L., Barkhi, R., Ray, S., & Davis, Z. (2018). Cyberloafing in the workplace: Mitigation tactics and their impact on individuals' behavior. *Information Technology and Management, 19*(4), 197–215. https://doi.org/10.1007/s10799-017-0280-1

Khansa, L., Kuem, J., Siponen, M., & Kim, S. S. (2017). To cyberloaf or not to cyberloaf: The impact of the announcement of formal organizational controls. *Journal of Management Information Systems, 34*(1), 141–176. https://doi.org/10.1080/07421222.2017.1297173

Khattak, S. R., Ullah, H., & Awaz, M. Z. (2020). Does supervisor communication styles reduce cyberloafing? Important roles of work engagement and psychological capital. *Global Social Sciences Review, 5*(1), 562–571. https://doi.org/10.31703/gssr.2020(V-I).57

Khoshouei, M. S. (2017). Prediction of procrastination considering job characteristics and locus of control in nurses. *Journal of Holistic Nursing and Midwifery, 27*(2), 27–35. https://doi.org/10.18869/acadpub.hnmj.27.2.27

Kim, J., Hong, H., Lee, J., & Hyun, M.-H. (2017). Effects of time perspective and self-control on procrastination and Internet addiction. *Journal of Behavioral Addictions, 6*(2), 229–236. https://doi.org/10.1556/2006.6.2017.017

Kim, K., Del Carmen Triana, M., Chung, K., & Oh, N. (2016). When do employees cyberloaf? An interactionist perspective examining personality, justice, and empowerment. *Human Resource Management, 55*(6), 1041–1058. https://doi.org/10.1002/hrm.21699

Kim, S. J., & Christensen, A. L. (2017). The dark and bright sides of personal use of technology at work: A job demands–resources model. *Human Resource Development Review, 16*(4), 425–447. https://doi.org/10.1177/1534484317725438

Kim, S. J., & Byrne, S. (2011). Conceptualizing personal web usage in work contexts: A preliminary framework. *Computers in Human Behavior, 27*(6), 2271–2283. https://doi.org/10.1016/j.chb.2011.07.006

Klingsieck, K. B. (2013). Procrastination in different life-domains: Is procrastination domain specific? *Current Psychology, 32*(2), 175–185. https://doi.org/10.1007/s12144-013-9171-8

Koay, K. Y. (2018a). Assessing cyberloafing behaviour among university students: A validation of the cyberloafing scale. *Pertanika Journal of Social Sciences & Humanities, 26*(1), 409–424.

Koay, K. Y. (2018b). Workplace ostracism and cyberloafing: A moderated–mediation model. *Internet Research, 28*(4), 1122–1141. https://doi.org/10.1108/IntR-07-2017-0268

Koay, K. Y., Lim, V. K., Soh, P. C.-H., Ong, D. L. T., Ho, J. S. Y., & Lim, P. K. (2022). Abusive supervision and cyberloafing: A moderated moderation model of moral disengagement and negative reciprocity beliefs. *Information & Management*, *59*(2), 103600. https://doi.org/10.1016/j.im.2022.103600

Koay, K. Y., & Soh, P. C.-H. (2018). Does cyberloafing really harm employees' work performance? An overview. In J. Xu, F. L. Cooke, M. Gen, & S. E. Ahmed (Eds.), *Proceedings of the Twelfth International Conference on Management Science and Engineering Management. ICMSEM 2018. Lecture notes on multidisciplinary industrial engineering* (pp. 901–912). Springer International Publishing. https://doi .org/10.1007/978-3-319-93351-1_71

Koay, K. Y., Soh, P. C.-H., & Chew, K. W. (2017a). Antecedents and consequences of cyberloafing: Evidence from the Malaysian ICT industry. *First Monday*, *22*(3). https://doi.org/10.5210/fm.v22i3.7302

Koay, K. Y., Soh, P. C.-H., & Chew, K. W. (2017b). Do employees' private demands lead to cyberloafing? The mediating role of job stress. *Management Research Review*, *40*(9), 1025–1038. https://doi.org/10.1108/MRR-11-2016-0252

Koessmeier, C., & Büttner, O. B. (2021). Why are we distracted by social media? Distraction situations and strategies, reasons for distraction, and individual differences. *Frontiers in Psychology*, *12*, 711416. https://doi.org/10.3389/fpsyg.2021.711416

König, C. J., & La Caner de Guardia, M. E. (2014). Exploring the positive side of personal Internet use at work: Does it help in managing the border between work and nonwork? *Computers in Human Behavior*, *30*, 355–360. https://doi.org/10.1016/j.chb.2013.09.021

Korzynski, P., & Protsiuk, O. (2022). What leads to cyberloafing: the empirical study of workload, self-efficacy, time management skills, and mediating effect of job satisfaction. *Behaviour & Information Technology*, *43*(1), 200–211. https://doi.org/10 .1080/0144929X.2022.2159525

Lam, C. K., Huang, X., & Chan, S. C. H. (2014). The threshold effect of participative leadership and the role of leader information sharing. *Academy of Management Journal*, *58*(3), 836–855. https://doi.org/10.5465/amj.2013.0427

Lavoie, J. A. A., & Pychyl, T. A. (2001). Cyberslacking and the procrastination superhighway. *Social Science Computer Review*, *19*(4), 431–444. https://doi.org/10 .1177/089443930101900403

Lay, C. H. (1986). At last, my research article on procrastination. *Journal of Research in Personality*, *20*(4), 474–495. https://doi.org/10.1016/0092-6566(86)90127-3

Laybourn, S., Frenzel, A. C., & Fenzl, T. (2019). Teacher procrastination, emotions, and stress: A qualitative study. *Frontiers in Psychology*, *10*, 2325. https://doi.org/10.3389 /fpsyg.2019.02325

Le Blanc, P., Jonge, J. de, & Schaufeli, W. B. (2000). Job stress and health. In N. Chmiel (Ed.), *Introduction to work and organizational psychology: A European perspective* (pp. 148–177). Blackwell Publishing.

Legood, A., Lee, A., Schwarz, G., & Newman, A. (2018). From self-defeating to other defeating: Examining the effects of leader procrastination on follower work outcomes. *Journal of Occupational and Organizational Psychology*, *91*(2), 430–439. https://doi .org/10.1111/joop.12205

Li, P., Taris, T. W., & Peeters, M. C. W. (2020). Challenge and hindrance appraisals of job demands: One man's meat, another man's poison? *Anxiety, Stress, and Coping*, *33*(1), 31–46. https://doi.org/10.1080/10615806.2019.1673133

Li, S.-M., & Chung, T.-M. (2006). Internet function and Internet addictive behavior. *Computers in Human Behavior*, *22*(6), 1067–1071. https://doi.org/10.1016/j.chb.2004 .03.030

Liberman, B., Seidman, G., McKenna, K. Y., & Buffardi, L. E. (2011). Employee job attitudes and organizational characteristics as predictors of cyberloafing. *Computers in Human Behavior*, *27*(6), 2192–2199. https://doi.org/10.1016/j.chb.2011.06.015

Lim, P. K., Koay, K. Y., & Chong, W. Y. (2021). The effects of abusive supervision, emotional exhaustion and organizational commitment on cyberloafing: A moderated-mediation examination. *Internet Research*, *31*(2), 497–518. https://doi.org/10.1108/ INTR-03-2020-0165

Lim, V. K. G. (2002). The IT way of loafing on the job: Cyberloafing, neutralizing and organizational justice. *Journal of Organizational Behavior*, *23*(5), 675–694. https:// doi.org/10.1002/job.161

Lim, V. K. G., & Chen, D. J. Q. (2012). Cyberloafing at the workplace: Gain or drain on work? *Behaviour & Information Technology*, *31*(4), 343–353. https://doi.org/10.1080 /01449290903353054

Lim, V. K. G., & Teo, T. S. (2005). Prevalence, perceived seriousness, justification and regulation of cyberloafing in Singapore. *Information & Management*, *42*(8), 1081–1093. https://doi.org/10.1016/j.im.2004.12.002

Lim, V. K. G., & Teo, T. S. H. (2006). Cyberloafing and organizational justice: The moderating role of neutralization technique. In M. Anandarajan, C. Simmers, & T. Teo (Eds.), *Advances in management information systems. The Internet and workplace transformation* (pp. 241–258). Routledge. https://doi.org/10.4324/9781315699530 -18

Lim, V. K. G., & Teo, T. S. H. (2024). Cyberloafing: A review and research agenda. *Applied Psychology*, *73*(1), 441–484. https://doi.org/10.1111/apps.12452

Lim, V. K. G., Teo, T. S. H., & Loo, G. L. (2002). How do I loaf here? Let me count the ways. *Communications of the ACM*, *45*(1), 66–70. https://doi.org/10.1145/502269 .502300

Lin, H. (2018). The effect of inclusive leadership on employees' procrastination. *Psychology*, *9*(4), 714–727. https://doi.org/10.4236/psych.2018.94045

Liu, H., Ji, Y., & Dust, S. B. (2021). "Fully recharged" evenings? The effect of evening cyber leisure on next-day vitality and performance through sleep quantity and quality, bedtime procrastination, and psychological detachment, and the moderating role of mindfulness. *Journal of Applied Psychology*, *106*(7), 990–1006. https://doi.org/10 .1037/apl0000818

LiveCareer. (2021). *Prokrastynacja: Czym jest i jak z nią walczyć [Procrastination: What it is and how to fight it]*. https://www.livecareer.pl/porady-zawodowe/ prokrastynacja

Locke, E. A. (1978). "Job satisfaction reconsidered": Reconsidered. *American Psychologist*, *33*(9), 854–855. https://doi.org/10.1037/0003-066X.33.9.854

Lonergan, J. M., & Maher, K. J. (2000). The relationship between job characteristics and workplace procrastination as moderated by locus of control. *Journal of Social Behavior & Personality*, *15*(5), 213–224.

Lowe-Calverley, E., & Grieve, R. (2017). Web of deceit: Relationships between the dark triad, perceived ability to deceive and cyberloafing. *Cyberpsychology: Journal of Psychosocial Research on Cyberspace*, *11*(2). https://doi.org/10.5817/CP2017-2-5

Ma, H., Zou, J.-M., Zhong, Y., & He, J.-Q. (2021). The influence of mobile phone addiction and work procrastination on burnout among newly graduated Chinese nurses. *Perspectives in Psychiatric Care*, *57*(4), 1798–1805. https://doi.org/10.1111/ppc.12752

Mahatanankoon, P., Anandarajan, M., & Igbaria, M. (2004). Development of a measure of personal web usage in the workplace. *CyberPsychology & Behavior*, *7*(1), 93–104. https://doi.org/10.1089/109493104322820165

Mastrangelo, P. M., Everton, W., & Jolton, J. A. (2006). Personal use of work computers: Distraction versus destruction. *Cyberpsychology & Behavior: The Impact of the Internet, Multimedia and Virtual Reality on Behavior and Society*, *9*(6), 730–741. https://doi.org/10.1089/cpb.2006.9.730

McCrae, R. R., & Costa, P. T. (2003). *Personality in adulthood: A five-factor theory perspective* (2nd ed.). Guilford Press. https://doi.org/10.4324/9780203428412

Meier, A., Reinecke, L., & Meltzer, C. E. (2016). Facebocrastination? Predictors of using Facebook for procrastination and its effects on students well-being. *Computers in Human Behavior*, *62*, 65–76. https://doi.org/10.1016/j.chb.2016.06.011

Meng, X., Pan, Y., & Li, C. (2024). Portraits of procrastinators: A meta-analysis of personality and procrastination. *Personality and Individual Differences*, *218*, 112490. https://doi.org/10.1016/j.paid.2023.112490

Mercado, B. K., Dilchert, S., Giordano, C., & Ones, D. S. (2017a). Counterproductive work behaviors. In D. S. Ones, N. Anderson, C. Viswesvaran, & H. K. Sinangil (Eds.), *The SAGE handbook of industrial, work and organizational psychology: Personnel psychology and employee performance* (pp. 109–210). SAGE Publications Ltd. https://doi.org/10.4135/9781473914940.n7

Mercado, B. K., Giordano, C., & Dilchert, S. (2017b). A meta-analytic investigation of cyberloafing. *Career Development International*, *22*(5), 546–564. https://doi.org/10.1108/CDI-08-2017-0142

Metin, U. B., Peeters, M. C. W., & Taris, T. W. (2018). Correlates of procrastination and performance at work: The role of having "good fit". *Journal of Prevention & Intervention in the Community*, *46*(3), 228–244. https://doi.org/10.1080/10852352.2018.1470187

Metin, U. B., Taris, T. W., & Peeters, M. C. W. (2016). Measuring procrastination at work and its associated workplace aspects. *Personality and Individual Differences*, *101*, 254–263. https://doi.org/10.1016/j.paid.2016.06.006

Metin, U. B., Taris, T. W., Peeters, M. C. W., Korpinen, M., Smrke, U., Razum, J., Kolářová, M., Baykova, R., & Gaioshko, D. (2020). Validation of the procrastination at work scale. *European Journal of Psychological Assessment*, *36*(5), 767–776. https://doi.org/10.1027/1015-5759/a000554

Meyer, R. D., Kelly, E. D., & Bowling, N. A. (2020). Situational strength theory. In D. C. Funder, J. F. Rauthmann, & R. Sherman (Eds.), *Oxford library of psychology. The Oxford handbook of psychological situations* (pp. 78–95). Oxford University Press. https://doi.org/10.1093/oxfordhb/9780190263348.013.7

Mischel, W., & Shoda, Y. (1995). A cognitive-affective system theory of personality: Reconceptualizing situations, dispositions, dynamics, and invariance in personality structure. *Psychological Review*, *102*(2), 246–268. https://doi.org/10.1037/0033-295X.102.2.246

Michielsen, H. J., Croon, M. A., Willemsen, T. M., & de Vries, J. van Heck, G. L. (2007). Which constructs can predict emotional exhaustion in a working population? A study into its determinants. *Stress and Health*, *23*(2), 121–130.

Mishra, D., & Tageja, N. (2022). Cyberslacking for coping stress? Exploring the role of mindfulness as personal resource. *International Journal of Global Business and Competitiveness.* Advance online publication. https://doi.org/10.1007/s42943-022 -00064-w

Mohammad, J., Quoquab, F., Halimah, S., & Thurasamy, R. (2019). Workplace Internet leisure and employees' productivity. *Internet Research, 29*(4), 725–748. https://doi .org/10.1108/IntR-05-2017-0191

Mohsin, F. Z., & Ayub, N. (2014). The relationship between procrastination, delay of gratification, and job satisfaction among high school teachers. *Japanese Psychological Research, 56*(3), 224–234. https://doi.org/10.1111/jpr.12046

Moody, G. D., & Siponen, M. (2013). Using the theory of interpersonal behavior to explain non-work-related personal use of the Internet at work. *Information & Management, 50*(6), 322–335. https://doi.org/10.1016/j.im.2013.04.005

Moor, L., & Anderson, J. R. (2019). A systematic literature review of the relationship between dark personality traits and antisocial online behaviours. *Personality and Individual Differences, 144*, 40–55. https://doi.org/10.1016/j.paid.2019.02.027

Mosquera, P., Soares, M. E., Dordio, P., & Melo, L. A. E. (2022). The thief of time and social sustainability: Analysis of a procrastination at work model. *Revista De Administração De Empresas, 62*(5), Article e2021-0313. https://doi.org/10.1590/s0034-759020220510

Munjal, S., & Mishra, R. (2019). Associative impact of personality orientation and levels of stress on procrastination in middle-level managers. *Indian Journal of Public Administration, 65*(1), 53–70. https://doi.org/10.1177/0019556118820456

Ng, J. C. Y., Shao, I. Y. T., & Liu, Y. (2016). This is not what I wanted. *Employee Relations, 38*(4), 466–486. https://doi.org/10.1108/ER-12-2015-0216

Nguyen, B., Steel, P., & Ferrari, J. R. (2013). Procrastination's impact in the workplace and the workplace's impact on procrastination. *International Journal of Selection and Assessment, 21*(4), 388–399. https://doi.org/10.1111/ijsa.12048

O'Neill, T. A., Hambley, L. A., & Bercovich, A. (2014a). Prediction of cyberslacking when employees are working away from the office. *Computers in Human Behavior, 34*, 291–298. https://doi.org/10.1016/j.chb.2014.02.015

O'Neill, T. A., Hambley, L. A., & Chatellier, G. S. (2014b). Cyberslacking, engagement, and personality in distributed work environments. *Computers in Human Behavior, 40*, 152–160. https://doi.org/10.1016/j.chb.2014.08.005

OfficeTeam. (2017, July 19). *Working hard or hardly working? Employees waste more than one day a week on non-work activities* [Press release]. https://www.roberthalf .com/officeteam

Oosthuizen, A., Rabie, G. H., & de Beer, L. T. (2018). Investigating cyberloafing, organisational justice, work engagement and organisational trust of South African retail and manufacturing employees. *SA Journal of Human Resource Management, 16.* https://doi.org/10.4102/sajhrm.v16i0.1001

Oravec, J. C. (2018). Cyberloafing and constructive recreation. In M. Khosrow-Pour (Ed.), *Encyclopedia of information science and technology* (4th ed., pp. 4316–4325). IGI Global. https://doi.org/10.4018/978-1-5225-2255-3.ch374

Paulhus, D. L., & Williams, K. M. (2002). The Dark Triad of personality: Narcissism, machiavellianism, and psychopathy. *Journal of Research in Personality, 36*(6), 556– 563. https://doi.org/10.1016/S0092-6566(02)00505-6

Paulsen, R. (2015). Non-work at work: Resistance or what? *Organization, 22*(3), 351– 367. https://doi.org/10.1177/1350508413515541

Pearlman-Avnion, S., & Zibenberg, A. (2018). Prediction and job-related outcomes of procrastination in the workplace. *Journal of Prevention & Intervention in the Community, 46*(3), 263–278. https://doi.org/10.1080/10852352.2018.1470418

Peng, J., Hou, N., Zou, Y., & Long, R. (2023a). Participative leadership and employees' cyberloafing: A self-concept-based theory perspective. *Information & Management, 60*(8), 103878. https://doi.org/10.1016/j.im.2023.103878

Peng, J., Nie, Q., & Chen, X. (2023b). Managing hospitality employee cyberloafing: The role of empowering leadership. *International Journal of Hospitality Management, 108*, 103349. https://doi.org/10.1016/j.ijhm.2022.103349

Pindek, S., Krajcevska, A., & Spector, P. E. (2018). Cyberloafing as a coping mechanism: Dealing with workplace boredom. *Computers in Human Behavior, 86*, 147–152. https://doi.org/10.1016/j.chb.2018.04.040

Pless, N. M., & Maak, T. (2011). Responsible leadership: Pathways to the future. In N. M. Pless (Ed.), *Responsible leadership* (pp. 3–13). Springer. https://doi.org/10.1007/978-94-007-3995-6_2

Prasad, S., Lim, V. K., & Chen, D. J. (2010). Self-regulation, individual characteristics and cyberloafing. *ACIS 2010 Proceedings, 159*, 1641–1648. https://aisel.aisnet.org/pacis2010/159/

Prem, R., Scheel, T. E., Weigelt, O., Hoffmann, K., & Korunka, C. (2018). Procrastination in daily working life: A diary study on within-person processes that link work characteristics to workplace procrastination. *Frontiers in Psychology, 9*, 1087. https://doi.org/10.3389/fpsyg.2018.01087

Pychyl, T. A., & Sirois, F. M. (2016). Procrastination, emotion regulation, and well-being. In F. M. Sirois & T. A. Pychyl (Eds.), *Procrastination, health, and well-being* (pp. 163–188). Academic Press. https://doi.org/10.1016/B978-0-12-802862-9.00008-6

Rahman, M. S., & Muldoon, J. (2020). Dark side of technology: Investigating the role of dark personality traits and technological factors in managing cyberloafing behavior. *Journal of Strategic Innovation and Sustainability, 15*(3). https://doi.org/10.33423/jsis.v15i3.2947

Rajah, R., & Lim, V. K. G. (2011). Cyberloafing, neutralization, and organizational citizenship behavior. *PACIS 2011 Proceedings, 152*, 1–15. https://aisel.aisnet.org/pacis2011/152

Ramayah, T. (2010). Personal web usage and work inefficiency. *Business Strategy Series, 11*(5), 295–301. https://doi.org/10.1108/17515631011080704

Reb, J., & Atkins, P. W. B. (2017). *Mindfulness in organizations*. Cambridge University Press.

Rehman, S., & Qamar-ul-islam, Z. A. (2019). Predictive relationship between procrastination, pork stress and mental well-being among bank employees of Gujranwala. *International Journal of Scientific Research in Multidisciplinary Studies, 5*(12), 79–85.

Reinecke, L. (2009). Games and recovery. *Journal of Media Psychology, 21*(3), 126–142. https://doi.org/10.1027/1864-1105.21.3.126

Restubog, S. L. D., Garcia, P. R. J. M., Toledano, L. S., Amarnani, R. K., Tolentino, L. R., & Tang, R. L. (2011). Yielding to (cyber)-temptation: Exploring the buffering role of self-control in the relationship between organizational justice and cyberloafing behavior in the workplace. *Journal of Research in Personality, 45*(2), 247–251. https://doi.org/10.1016/j.jrp.2011.01.006

Restubog, S. L. D., Garcia, P. R. J. M., Wang, L., & Cheng, D. (2010). It's all about control: The role of self-control in buffering the effects of negative reciprocity beliefs and trait anger on workplace deviance. *Journal of Research in Personality*, *44*(5), 655–660. https://doi.org/10.1016/j.jrp.2010.06.007

Robinson, S. L., & Bennett, R. J. (1995). A typology of deviant workplace behaviors: A multidimensional scaling study. *Academy of Management Journal*, *38*(2), 555–572. https://doi.org/10.5465/256693

Rogelberg, S. G. (2007). *Encyclopedia of industrial and organizational psychology* (Vol. 1–2). Sage. https://doi.org/10.4135/9781412952651

Roster, C. A., & Ferrari, J. R. (2020). Time is on my side-or is it? Assessing how perceived control of time and procrastination influence emotional exhaustion on the job. *Behavioral Sciences (Basel, Switzerland)*, *10*(6). https://doi.org/10.3390/bs10060098

Ryan, J. (2006). Inclusive leadership. *Education Review.* Advance online publication. https://doi.org/10.14507/er.v0.687

Ryan, R. M., & Deci, E. L. (2000). Intrinsic and extrinsic motivations: Classic definitions and new directions. *Contemporary Educational Psychology*, *25*(1), 54–67. https://doi.org/10.1006/ceps.1999.1020

Şahin, M. D. (2021). Effect of item order on certain psychometric properties: A demonstration on a cyberloafing scale. *Frontiers in Psychology*, *12*, 590545. https://doi.org/10.3389/fpsyg.2021.590545

Salary. (2013). *Wasting time at work survey.* https://www.salary.com/chronicles/2013-wasting-time-at-work-survey/

Salary. (2014). *Wasting time at work survey.* https://www.salary.com/chronicles/2014-wasting-time-at-work/

Saman, A., & Wirawan, H. (2021). Examining the impact of psychological capital on academic achievement and work performance: The roles of procrastination and conscientiousness. *Cogent Psychology*, *8*(1), Article 1938853. https://doi.org/10.1080/23311908.2021.1938853

Sampat, U., & Basu B. S. (2017). Cyberloafing: The di(sguised)gital way of loafing on the job. *Journal of Organizational Behavior*, *16*(1), 19–37.

Sarwat, N., Ali, R., & Khan, T. I. (2021). Cognitive job demands, presenteeism and procrastination: The moderating role of psychological capital. *Sir Syed Journal of Education & Social Research*, *4*(1), 193–203. https://doi.org/10.36902/sjesr-vol4-iss1-2021(193-203)

Sawitri, H. S. R., & Mayasari, D. (2017). Keeping up with the cyberloafer: how do cyberloafing and creative self-efficacy bear with creativity? *Journal for Global Business Advancement*, *10*(6), Article 91931, 652. https://doi.org/10.1504/JGBA.2017.091931

Senécal, C., & Guay, F. (2000). Procrastination in job-seeking: An analysis of motivational processes and feelings of hopelessness. *Journal of Social Behavior & Personality*, *15*(5), 267–282.

She, Z., & Li, Q. (2023). When too little or too much hurts: Evidence for a curvilinear relationship between cyberloafing and task performance in public organizations. *Journal of Business Ethics*, *183*(4), 1141–1158. https://doi.org/10.1007/s10551-022-05038-9

Sheikh, A., Aghaz, A., & Mohammadi, M. (2019). Cyberloafing and personality traits: an investigation among knowledge-workers across the Iranian knowledge-intensive sectors. *Behaviour & Information Technology*, *38*(12), 1213–1224. https://doi.org/10.1080/0144929X.2019.1580311

Shin, J., & Grant, A. M. (2021). When putting work off pays off: The curvilinear relationship between procrastination and creativity. *Academy of Management Journal*, *64*(3), 772–798. https://doi.org/10.5465/amj.2018.1471

Shrivastava, A., Sharma, M. K., & Marimuthu, P. (2016). Internet use at workplaces and its effects on working style in Indian context: An exploration. *Indian Journal of Occupational and Environmental Medicine*, *20*(2), 88–94. https://doi.org/10.4103/0019-5278.197531

Singh, S., & Bala, R. (2020). Mediating role of self-efficacy on the relationship between conscientiousness and procrastination. *International Journal of Work Organisation and Emotion*, *11*(1), Article 109422, 41. https://doi.org/10.1504/IJWOE.2020.109422

Singh, S., & Singh, D. R. (2015). Procrastination patterns of transactional and transformational leaders. *Pacific Business Review International*, *8*(1), 33–40.

Singh, S., & Singh, D. R. (2018). Perceived performance and procrastination in hospitality industry: Examining the mediator role of work environment. *Journal of Hospitality Application and Research*, *13*(2), 44.

Sirois, F. M. (2022). *Procrastination: What it is, why it's a problem, and what you can do about it.* American Psychological Association.

Sirois, F. M. (2023). Procrastination and stress: A conceptual review of why context matters. *International Journal of Environmental Research and Public Health*, *20*(6), 5031. https://doi.org/10.3390/ijerph20065031

Skowronski, M., & Mirowska, A. (2013). A manager's guide to workplace procrastination. *Advanced Management Journal*, *78*(3), 4–9, 27.

Slashdot.org. (2009). *How many hours do you really work each day?* https://slashdot.org/pollBooth.pl?qid=1719&aid=-1

Soral, P., Arayankalam, J., & Pandey, J. (2020). The impact of ambivalent perception of bureaucratic structure on cyberloafing. *Australasian Journal of Information Systems*, *24*. https://doi.org/10.3127/ajis.v24i0.2087

Spector, P. E. (1986). Perceived control by employees: A meta-analysis of studies concerning autonomy and participation at work. *Human Relations*, *39*(11), 1005–1016. https://doi.org/10.1177/001872678603901104

Spector, P. E. (2010). The relationship of personality to Counterproductive Work Behavior (CWB): An integration of perspectives. *Human Resource Management Review*, *21*(4), 342–352. https://doi.org/10.1016/j.hrmr.2010.10.002

Spector, P. E. (2024). The dual nature of cyberloafing. *Applied Psychology*, *73*(1), 502–505. https://doi.org/10.1111/apps.12472

Spector, P. E., & Jex, S. M. (1991). Relations of job characteristics from multiple data sources with employee affect, absence, turnover intentions, and health. *Journal of Applied Psychology*, *76*(1), 46–53. https://doi.org/10.1037/0021-9010.76.1.46

Spyridaki, E., & Galanakis, M. (2022). Locus of control theory, productivity, job satisfaction, and procrastination: A systematic literature review in the organizational context of the 21st century. *Journal of Psychology Research*, *12*(12). https://doi.org/10.17265/2159-5542/2022.12.008

Stajkovic, A. D., & Luthans, F. (1998). Self-efficacy and work-related performance: A meta-analysis. *Psychological Bulletin*, *124*(2), 240–261. https://doi.org/10.1037/0033-2909.124.2.240

Stanton, J. M. (2002). Company profile of the frequent Internet user. *Communications of the ACM*, *45*(1), 55–59. https://doi.org/10.1145/502269.502297

Statista. (2019). *Type of areas of life in which French people procrastinate 2019.* Statista Research Department. https://www.statista.com/statistics/987270/procrastination-areas-life-france/#statisticContainer

Steel, P. (2007). The nature of procrastination: A meta-analytic and theoretical review of quintessential self-regulatory failure. *Psychological Bulletin, 133*(1), 65–94.

Steel, P., & Ferrari, J. (2013). Sex, education and procrastination: An epidemiological study of procrastinators' characteristics from a global sample. *European Journal of Personality, 27*(1), 51–58. https://doi.org/10.1002/per.1851

Steel, P., & Klingsieck, K. B. (2016). Academic procrastination: Psychological antecedents revisited. *Australian Psychologist, 51*(1), 36–46. https://doi.org/10.1111/ap.12173

Sümer, C., & Büttner, O. B. (2022). I'll do it - after one more scroll: The effects of boredom proneness, self-control, and impulsivity on online procrastination. *Frontiers in Psychology, 13*, 918306. https://doi.org/10.3389/fpsyg.2022.918306

Sunarta, S., Tjahjono, H. K., Muafi, M., & Prajogo, W. (2023). Organizational justice on employee procrastination: A moderated-mediation model of job satisfaction and psychological contract breach. *International Journal of Professional Business Review, 8*(5), e01881. https://doi.org/10.26668/businessreview/2023.v8i5.1881

Tam, K. Y. Y., van Tilburg, W. A. P., & Chan, C. S. (2021). What is boredom proneness? A comparison of three characterizations. *Journal of Personality, 89*(4), 831–846. https://doi.org/10.1111/jopy.12618

Tandon, A., Kaur, P., Ruparel, N., Islam, J. U., & Dhir, A. (2022). Cyberloafing and cyberslacking in the workplace: Systematic literature review of past achievements and future promises. *Internet Research, 32*(1), 55–89. https://doi.org/10.1108/INTR -06-2020-0332

Tepper, B. J. (2000). Consequences of abusive supervision. *Academy of Management Journal, 43*(2), 178–190. https://doi.org/10.5465/1556375

Tepper, B. J., Henle, C. A., Lambert, L. S., Giacalone, R. A., & Duffy, M. K. (2008). Abusive supervision and subordinates' organization deviance. *Journal of Applied Psychology, 93*(4), 721–732. https://doi.org/10.1037/0021-9010.93.4.721

Thatcher, A., Wretschko, G., & Fridjhon, P. (2008). Online flow experiences, problematic Internet use and Internet procrastination. *Computers in Human Behavior, 24*(5), 2236–2254. https://doi.org/10.1016/j.chb.2007.10.008

Tsai, H.-Y. (2023). Do you feel like being proactive day? How daily cyberloafing influences creativity and proactive behavior: The moderating roles of work environment. *Computers in Human Behavior, 138*, 107470. https://doi.org/10.1016/j.chb.2022.107470

Tudose, C.-M., & Pavalache-Ilie, M. (2021). Procrastination and work satisfaction. *Social Science and Law, 14*(63), 37–46. https://doi.org/10.31926/but.ssl.2021.14.63.1.4

Uddin, M. A., Rahman, M. S., & Howladar, M. H. R. (2017). Empirical study on transformational leadership, deviant behaviour, job performance, and gender: Evidence from a study in Bangladesh. *Portuguese Journal of Management Studies, 22*(2), 77–97. https://ideas.repec.org/a/pjm/journl/vxxiiy2017i2p77-97.html

Ugrin, J. C., & Pearson, J. M. (2013). The effects of sanctions and stigmas on cyberloafing. *Computers in Human Behavior, 29*(3), 812–820. https://doi.org/10.1016/j.chb.2012 .11.005

Ugrin, J. C., Pearson, J. M., & Odom, M. D. (2007). Profiling cyber-slackers in the workplace: Demographic, cultural, and workplace Factors. *Journal of Internet Commerce, 6*(3), 75–89. https://doi.org/10.1300/J179v06n03_04

Usman, M., Javed, U., Shoukat, A., & Bashir, N. A. (2021). Does meaningful work reduce cyberloafing? Important roles of affective commitment and leader-member exchange. *Behaviour & Information Technology, 40*(2), 206–220. https://doi.org/10 .1080/0144929X.2019.1683607

Uysal, H. T., & Yilmaz, F. (2020). Procrastination in the workplace: The role of hierarchical career plateau. *Upravlenets*, *11*(3), 82–101.

van Daalen, G., Willemsen, T. M., Sanders, K., & van Veldhoven, M. J. P. M. (2009). Emotional exhaustion and mental health problems among employees doing "people work": The impact of job demands, job resources and family-to-work conflict. *International Archives of Occupational and Environmental Health*, *82*(3), 291–303. https://doi.org/10.1007/s00420-008-0334-0

van den Berg, J., & Roosen, S. (2018). Two faces of employee inactivity: Procrastination and recovery. *Journal of Prevention & Intervention in the Community*, *46*(3), 295–307. https://doi.org/10.1080/10852352.2018.1470423

van Doorn, O. N. (2011). *Cyberloafing: A multi-dimensional construct placed in a theoretical framework* [Unpublished MBA Thesis]. Eindhoven University of Technology.

van Eerde, W. (2003). Procrastination at work and time management training. *The Journal of Psychology*, *137*(5), 421–434. https://doi.org/10.1080/00223980309600625

van Eerde, W. (2004). Procrastination in academic settings and the big five model of personality: A meta-analysis. In H. C. Schouwenburg, C. H. Lay, T. A. Pychyl, & J. R. Ferrari (Eds.), *Counseling the procrastinator in academic settings* (pp. 29–40). American Psychological Association. https://doi.org/10.1037/10808-003

van Eerde, W. (2016). Procrastination and well-being at work. In F. M. Sirois & T. A. Pychyl (Eds.), *Procrastination, health, and well-being* (pp. 233–253). Academic Press. https://doi.org/10.1016/B978-0-12-802862-9.00011-6

van Eerde, W., & Venus, M. (2018). A daily diary study on sleep quality and procrastination at work: The moderating role of trait self-control. *Frontiers in Psychology*, *9*, 2029. https://doi.org/10.3389/fpsyg.2018.02029

Varghese, L., & Barber, L. K. (2017). A preliminary study exploring moderating effects of role stressors on the relationship between big five personality traits and workplace cyberloafing. *Cyberpsychology: Journal of Psychosocial Research on Cyberspace*, *11*(4). https://doi.org/10.5817/CP2017-4-4

Verešová, M. (2013). Procrastination, stress and coping among primary school teachers. *Procedia - Social and Behavioral Sciences*, *106*, 2131–2138.

Vitak, J., Crouse, J., & LaRose, R. (2011). Personal Internet use at work: Understanding cyberslacking. *Computers in Human Behavior*, *27*(5), 1751–1759. https://doi.org/10.1016/j.chb.2011.03.002

Wan, H. C., Downey, L. A., & Stough, C. (2014). Understanding non-work presenteeism: Relationships between emotional intelligence, boredom, procrastination and job stress. *Personality and Individual Differences*, *65*, 86–90. https://doi.org/10.1016/j.paid.2014.01.018

Wang, J., Li, C., Meng, X., & Liu, D. (2021). Validation of the Chinese version of the procrastination at work scale. *Frontiers in Psychology*, *12*, 726595. https://doi.org/10.3389/fpsyg.2021.726595

Weatherbee, T. G. (2010). Counterproductive use of technology at work: Information & communications technologies and cyberdeviancy. *Human Resource Management Review*, *20*(1), 35–44. https://doi.org/10.1016/j.hrmr.2009.03.012

Weymann, E. C. (1988). Procrastination in the workplace: Dispositional and situational determinants of delay behavior at work. *Academy of Management Proceedings*, *1988*(1), 226–230. https://doi.org/10.5465/ambpp.1988.4980589

Wong, G. Y.-L., Kwok, R. C.-W., Zhang, S., Lai, G. C.-H., & Cheung, J. C.-F. (2023). Mutually complementary effects of cyberloafing and cyber-life-interruption on employee exhaustion. *Information & Management, 60*(2), 103752. https://doi.org/10.1016/j.im.2022.103752

Wright, J. D. (Ed.). (2015). *The international encyclopedia of the social & behavioral sciences* (2nd ed.). Elsevier. https://doi.org/10.1093/obo/9780199828340-0140

Wu, J., Mei, W., Liu, L., & Ugrin, J. C. (2020). The bright and dark sides of social cyberloafing: Effects on employee mental health in China. *Journal of Business Research, 112*, 56–64. https://doi.org/10.1016/j.jbusres.2020.02.043

Yan, J., & Yang, J. (2014). Trait procrastination and compulsive Internet use as predictors of cyberloafing. In *Proceedings of ICSSSM '14: June 25–27, 2014, Beijing, China* (pp. 1–4). IEEE. https://doi.org/10.1109/ICSSSM.2014.6874119

Yang, H., Lin, Z., Chen, X., & Peng, J. (2023). Workplace loneliness, ego depletion and cyberloafing: Can leader problem-focused interpersonal emotion management help? *Internet Research, 33*(4), 1473–1494. https://doi.org/10.1108/intr-01-2021-0007

Yildiz, H., Yildiz, B., & Ateş, H. (2015). Is there a role of organizational justice perceptions onrganizational justice perceptions on cyberslacking activities? *The Journal of Knowledge Economy & Knowledge, 10*(2), 55–66.

Zhang, H., Zhao, H., Liu, J., Xu, Y., & Lu, H. (2015). The dampening effect of employees' future orientation on cyberloafing behaviors: The mediating role of self-control. *Frontiers in Psychology, 6*, Article 1482. https://doi.org/10.3389/fpsyg.2015.01482

Zhang, J., Akhtar, M. N., Zhang, Y., & Sun, S. (2020). Are overqualified employees bad apples? A dual-pathway model of cyberloafing. *Internet Research, 30*(1), 289–313. https://doi.org/10.1108/INTR-10-2018-0469

Zhang, Y., Wang, J., Akhtar, M. N., & Wang, Y. (2022). Authoritarian leadership and cyberloafing: A moderated mediation model of emotional exhaustion and power distance orientation. *Frontiers in Psychology, 13*, 1010845. https://doi.org/10.3389/fpsyg.2022.1010845

Zhang, Z., Shen, Y., Yang, M., & Zheng, J. (2023). Harmonious passion and procrastination: An exploration based on actor–partner interdependence model. *International Journal of Contemporary Hospitality Management, 35*(12), 4407–4427. https://doi.org/10.1108/IJCHM-09-2022-1054

Zhou, B., Li, Y., Hai, M., Wang, W., & Niu, B. (2021). Challenge-hindrance stressors and cyberloafing: A perspective of resource conservation versus resource acquisition. *Current Psychology.* Advance online publication. https://doi.org/10.1007/s12144-021-01505-0

Zhou, Z. E., Meier, L. L., & Spector, P. E. (2014). The role of personality and job stressors in predicting counterproductive work behavior: A three-way interaction. *International Journal of Selection and Assessment, 22*(3), 286–296. https://doi.org/10.1111/ijsa.12077

Zhu, J., Wei, H., Li, H., & Osburn, H. (2021). The paradoxical effect of responsible leadership on employee cyberloafing: A moderated mediation model. *Human Resource Development Quarterly, 32*(4), 597–624. https://doi.org/10.1002/hrdq.21432

Zoghbi-Manrique-de-Lara, P. (2006). Fear in organizations. *Journal of Managerial Psychology, 21*(6), 580–592. https://doi.org/10.1108/02683940610684418

Zoghbi-Manrique-de-Lara, P. (2009). Inequity, conflict, and compliance dilemma as causes of cyberloafing. *International Journal of Conflict Management, 20*(2), 188–201. https://doi.org/10.1108/10444060910949630

Zoghbi-Manrique-de-Lara, P. (2012). Reconsidering the boundaries of the cyberloafing activity: The case of a university. *Behaviour & Information Technology, 31*(5), 469–479. https://doi.org/10.1080/0144929X.2010.549511

Zoghbi-Manrique-de-Lara, P., & Viera-Armas, M. (2017). Corporate culture as a mediator in the relationship between ethical leadership and personal Internet use. *Journal of Leadership & Organizational Studies, 24*(3), 357–371. https://doi.org/10.1177/1548051817696877

Zoghbi-Manrique-de-Lara, P., & Olivares-Mesa, A. (2010). Bringing cyber loafers back on the right track. *Industrial Management & Data Systems, 110*(7), 1038–1053. https://doi.org/10.1108/02635571011069095

Zoghbi-Manrique-de-Lara, P., Viera-Armas, M., & de Blasio García, G. (2020). Does supervisors' mindfulness keep employees from engaging in cyberloafing out of compassion at work? *Personnel Review, 49*(2), 670–687. https://doi.org/10.1108/PR-12-2017-0384

3   Modeling Procrastination at Work
Individual and Work-Related Antecedents

Procrastination has been thoroughly researched and documented in the literature. However, empirical studies that focus on procrastination in the work context are scarce. Recent research has begun to explore the idea that procrastination may manifest differently in different work environments. Consequently, scholars have begun to investigate the nature of procrastination in the workplace, its predictors, and outcomes (Göncü Köse & Metin, 2018; Hen et al., 2021; Hutmanová et al., 2022; Metin et al., 2016, 2018, 2020; Mosquera et al., 2022; Rehman et al., 2019; Saman & Wirawan, 2021; Tudose & Pavalache-Ilie, 2021; van den Berg & Roosen, 2018; Wang et al., 2021; Yao et al., 2023). Research has evidenced (see Table 3.1) that general procrastination, decisional procrastination, work engagement, work stress, work satisfaction, conscientiousness, mental health, well-being, psychological capital, and recovery are all correlates of work procrastination. Furthermore, procrastination at work is associated with work-related factors, such as workload, mental demands, job resources, autonomy, possibilities for development, counterproductive work behavior, authenticity at work, job crafting, boredom, citizenship work behavior, turnover intention, transformational paternalistic leadership and work, and contextual performance. Although previous research has improved our comprehension of predictors and potential mechanisms of procrastination in the workplace, it remains incomplete. More research is needed to fully grasp the phenomenon of work-related procrastination, including its individual and work-related determinants, as well as the underlying mechanisms. This chapter presents empirical studies aimed at (1) verifying the nature and structure of procrastination at work measurement tool, the Procrastination at Work Scale (PAWS), (2) establishing associations of procrastination at work with similar psychological constructs (e.g. trait procrastination and counterproductive work behavior), (3) expanding the set of individual and work-related sources of procrastination, and (4) identifying potential mechanisms explaining procrastination at work. Empirical results contribute to a better understanding of procrastination as a work-specific phenomenon.

Procrastination at work can be examined within the framework of the JD–R model (Bakker & Demerouti, 2014; Bakker et al., 2023), which focuses on the interaction between job demands and job resources in influencing positive employee outcomes or negative work behavior. Job resources buffer the negative

DOI: 10.4324/9781003422860-4

Table 3.1 Research results on procrastination at work measured by PAWS – a systematic review

Authors	Sample	Measure	Correlates		Direct indirect effects
			Workplace demographic factors	*Individual characteristics behavior*	
Metin et al. 2016	The Netherlands $N = 384/200$ White-collar employees	PAW as an endogenous variable	Workload ↔ PAW: *ns*; SOL: 0.13; CBL: −0.09	Boredom ↔ PAW: 0.62; SOL: 0.55; CBL: 0.49	Job resources ↑ PAW ($\beta = 0.34$)
		Soldiering	Mental demands: PAW: −0.10; SOL: *ns*; CBL: −0.11	General procrastination ↔ PAW: 0.46; SOL: 0.49; CBL: 0.23	Workload ↑ PAW ($\beta = 0.22$)
		Cyberslacking	Autonomy ↔ PAW: *ns*; SOL: *ns*; CBL: −0.10	WE: Vigor ↔ PAW: −0.29; SOL: −0.31; CBL: −0.14	CWB total: ↔ PAW: 0.79
			Opport. for development ↔ PAW: *ns*; SOL: *ns*; CBL: *ns*	WE: Dedication ↔→PAW: −0.28; SOL: −0.28; CBL: −0.18	Workload ↑ boredom ↑ PAW ($\beta = -0.28$)
				WE: Absorption ↔→PAW: −0.27; SOL: −0.27; CBL: −0.17	Job resources ↑ boredom ↑ PAW *ns*
				CWB: Withdrawal ↔ PAW: 0.50; SOL: 0.50, CBL: 0.32	
				CWB: Abuse ↔ PAW: 0.55, SOL: 0.52; CBL: 0.38	
Metin et al. 2016	Turkey $N = 243$ White-collar employees	PAW as an endogenous variable	Workload ↔ PAW: *ns*; SOL: 0.11; CBL: −0.17	Boredom ↔ PAW: 0.54; SOL: 0.53; CBL: 0.33	CWB total ↔ PAW: 0.76
		Soldiering	Mental demands ↔ PAW: −0.17; SOL: −0.17; CBL: −0.11	General procrastination ↔ PAW: 0.55; SOL: 0.63; CBL: 0.21	Job resources ↑ PAW *ns*
		Cyberslacking	Autonomy ↔ PAW: −0.12; SOL: −0.20; CBL: *ns*	WE: Vigor ↔ PAW: −0.27; SOL: −0.31; CBL: *ns*	Workload ↑ PAW ($\beta = 0.14$)
			Opport. for development ↔ PAW: *ns*; SOL: −0.12; CBL: *ns*	WE: Dedication ↔→PAW: −0.28; SOL: −0.30; CBL: −0.13	Workload ↑ boredom ↑ PAW *ns*
				WE: Absorption ↔→PAW: −0.26; SOL: −0.31; CBL: *ns*	Job resources ↑ boredom ↑ PAW *ns*
				CWB: Withdrawal ↔ PAW: 0.46; SOL: 0.39; CBL: 0.37	
				CWB: Abuse ↔ PAW: 0.54; SOL: 0.54, CBL: 0.33	

(Continued)

Table 3.1 (Continued)

Authors	Sample	Measure	Correlates		Direct indirect effects
			Workplace/demographic factors	*Individual characteristics behavior*	
Metin et al. (2018)	The Netherlands $N = 380$ White-collar full-time employee	PAW as an endogenous variable	Self-alienation ↔ SOL: −0.27, CBL: *ns*	WE: Vigor ↔ SOL: −0.27; CBL: −0.14	WE total → PAW (β = −0.19)
		Soldiering	Authentic living ↔ SOL: −0.11; CBL: *ns*	WE: Dedication ↔ SOL: −0.21; CBL: *ns*	JP ↔ PAW: −0.23
		Cyberslacking	Social influence ↔ SOL: −0.26; CBL: −0.15	WE: Absorption ↔ SOL: −0.13; CBL: *ns*	Authenticity at work → PAW *ns*
				Task performance ↔ SOL: −0.24; CBL: −0.13	Job crafting → PAW *ns*
				Context. performance ↔ SOL: −0.11; CBL: *ns*	Authenticity → Work engagement → PAW *ns*
					Job crafting → Work engagement → PAW *ns*
Göncü Köse & Metin (2018)	Turkey $N = 126$ Full-time white-collar employees	PAW as an endogenous variable	Paternalistic leadership ↔ SOL: −0.25; CBL: −0.21	Turnover intention ↔ SOL: −0.23; CBL: *ns*	Turnover intention → PAW *ns*
		Soldiering	Transformational leadership ↔ SOL: −0.32; CBL: −0.30	OCB: civic virtue ↔ SOL: −0.23; CBL: *ns*	Transformational leadership → PAW (β = −0.27)
		Cyberslacking	Age ↔ SOL: −0.18; −CBL: −0.25	OCB: conscientiousness ↔ SOL: −0.41; CBL: −0.30	OCB → PAW (β = −0.55)
			Education ↔ SOL: −0.18; CBL: *ns*		Paternalistic leadership → turnover intention → PAW *ns*
			Tenure ↔ SOL: −0.19; CBL: −0.19		Transformational leadership → turnover intention → PAW *ns*
			Tenure with the supervisor ↔ SOL: *ns*; CBL: *ns*		Paternalistic leadership → OCB → PAW *ns*
			Overwork hours ↔ SOL: *ns*; CBL: *ns*		Transformational leadership → OCB → PAW *ns*
Van den Berg & Roosen (2018)	The Netherlands $N = 116$ Full time office employees	Soldiering		Recovery at work ↔ PAW: *ns*; SOL: *ns*; CBL: *ns*	
		Cyberslacking		WE ↔ PAW: *ns*; SOL: −0.22; CBL: *ns*	
		PAW (total)		WE: Vigor ↔ PAW: −0.19; SOL: 0.28; CBL: *ns*	

(Continued)

Table 3.1 (Continued)

Authors	Sample	Measure	Correlates		Direct indirect effects
			Workplace demographic factors	*Individual characteristics behavior*	
				WE: Dedication ↔ PAW: *ns*; SOL: *ns*; CBL: *ns*	
				WE: Absorption ↔ PAW: *ns*; SOL: −0.19; CBL: *ns*	
				JP total ↔ PAW: *ns*; SOL: *ns*; CBL: 0.30	
				JP: Task performance ↔ PAW: *ns*; SOL: −0.27; CBL: *ns*	
				JP: Contextual performance ↔ PAW: 0.18; SOL: *ns*; CBL: 0.30	
Metin et al. (2020)	*N* = 1028	Soldiering		*Correlations over 0.17 are significant at p < 0.05*	*For total sample:*
	Full-time white-collar employees from Great Britain, Slovenia, Czech Republic, Croatia, Finland, Turkey, Ukraine	Cyberslacking		'WE total ↔ SOL: −0.13 to −0.45; CBL: 0.09 to −0.22	WE: Vigor ↔ SOL: −0.22; CBL: *ns*
				WE: Vigor ↔ SOL: −0.11 to −0.39; CBL: 0.09 to −0.12	WE: Dedication ↔ SOL: −0.19; CBL: *ns*
				WE: Dedication ↔ SOL: −0.14 to −0.40; CBL: −0.15 to 0.11	WE: Absorption ↔ SOL: −0.19; CBL: −0.07
				WE: Absorption ↔ SOL: −0.09 to −0.43; CBL: 0.03 to −0.30	JP: Task performance ↔ SOL: −0.21; CBL: *ns*
				JP total ↔ SOL: −0.12 to −0.55; CBL: 0.10 to −0.26	JP: Contextual performance ↔ SOL: −0.08; CBL: *ns*
				JP: Task performance ↔ SOL: −0.08 to −0.60; CBL: −0.03 to 0.24	
				JP: Contextual performance ↔ SOL: −0.04 to −0.41; CBL: 0.12 to −0.31'	
Hen et al. (2021)	Israel *N* = 204 Office and non-office employees of public corporation	PAW (total)	Education: −0.05 Gender: −0.13 Age: −0.14		*Office workers:* Decisional procrastination ↑ PAW (β = 0.57) General procrastination ↑ PAW (β = 0.31)

(Continued)

Table 3.1 (Continued)

Authors	Sample	Measure	Correlates Workplace demographic factors	Individual characteristics behavior	Direct indirect effects
Mosquera et al. (2022)	Portugal N = 287 Employees	Soldiering Cyberslacking		Work stress ↔ SOL: 0.37; CBL: ns Job satisfaction ↔ SOL: −0.20; CBL: ns Boredom ↔ SOL: −0.58; CBL: 0.43	*Non-office workers:* Decisional procrastination → PAW (β = 0.18) General procrastination → PAW (β = 0.09) Boredom → SOL (β = 0.60) Boredom → CBL (β = 0.48) SOL → Work stress (β = 0.41) SOL → Job satisfaction (β = −0.23) CBL → Work stress *ns* CBL → Job satisfaction *ns* PAW → Performance (β = −0.41)
Saman & Wirawan (2021)	N = 400 Indonesia Employees from different countries	PAW (total)	Age: −0.25 Marital status: −0.15 Education: *ns* Tenure: −0.19	Performance ↔ PAW: −0.53 Psychological capital ↔ PAW: −0.33 Conscientiousness ↔ PAW: 0.24	
Wang et al. (2021)	China N = 227 Workers in different industries	PAW (total)		Work engagement ↔ PAW: −0.23 Counterproductive work behavior ↔ PAW: 0.44 Task performance ↔ PAW: −14 Workplace well-being ↔ PAW: −0.23 Organizational commitment ↔ PAW: −0.29	
Rehman et al. (2019)	Pakistan N = 110 Bank employees	PAW (total) Soldiering Cyberslacking		Mental health ↔ PAW: −0.44; SOL: 0.50; SOL ↔ Mental well-being *ns* CBL: −0.40 General work stress ↔ PAW: 0.64; SOL: 0.59; CBL: 0.56	CBL → Mental well-being *ns* CBL → Mental well-being (β = −0.26)

(Continued)

Table 3.1 (Continued)

Authors	Sample	Measure	Correlates		Direct indirect effects
			Workplace demographic factors	*Individual characteristics behavior*	
Hutmanova et al. (2022)	Slovakia $N = 153$ Small and medium-sized enterprises	PAW (total)		Intrinsic motivation ↔ PAW: −0.68 Introjected motivation ↔ PAW: −0.21 Identified regulation ↔ PAW: −0.39 Integrated regulation ↔ PAW: −0.49 Amotivation ↔ PAW: 0.79	
Yao et al. (2023)	China $N = 450$ Teleworkers	PAW (total)	Age: 0.23 Industry: *ns* Position level: −0.16 Position: *ns* Education: *ns* Seniority: −0.17 Marital status: *ns* Professional title: *ns* Children: *ns* Organization: *ns*	Work connectivity behavior ↔ PAW: 0.14 Role stress ↔ PAW: 0.27 RWSE ↔ PAW: 0.44	Work connectivity behavior → work stress → PAW (β = 0.11) Direct and indirect effects are weaker for employees with higher RWSE

Note. PAW – procrastination at work; SOL – soldiering; CBL – cyberslacking; JP – job performance, WE – work engagement, OCB – organizational citizen behavior, CWB – counterproductive work behavior, RWSE – remote work self-efficacy; *ns* – statistically nonsignificant impact of high demands. However, when job resources are available, high job demands can boost the positive impact of job resources, increasing levels of work engagement, which ultimately can lead to achieving higher work-related outcomes (Bakker et al., 2023). Analogous effects between job demands and job resources may be expected in the prediction of procrastination at work. Procrastination can be seen as a response to overwhelming job demands and the availability or lack of job resources. Furthermore, job demands and resources can affect employees through two different regulatory processes: an energetic and a motivational process (Bakker & Demerouti, 2014; Bakker et al., 2023). In the energetic process, high job demands and excessive resource depletion lead to greater mobilization of the employee's strength and effort needed to maintain optimal levels of job performance. Alternatively, the motivational process maintains a balance between the negative effects of excessive demands and resources at work. The available job resources can help employees cope effectively with job demands, leading to increased work engagement and subsequently achieving higher work-related outcomes, while also reducing the risk of negative health effects. Therefore, it is likely that the effect of job demands and resources on procrastination at work can also be explained by mechanisms related to energetic and motivational processes.

For this research, a general conceptual model was developed to explain the procrastination phenomenon at work (Figure 3.1), according to the assumptions of the JD–R model (Bakker et al., 2023). This model proposes to examine the predictive role of personal resources and job demands, job resources, and leadership resources in explaining procrastination at work. The effects of the interaction of job resources and leadership resources with job demands were also tested.

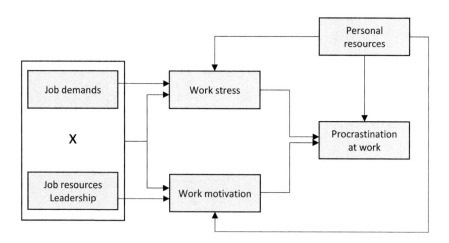

Figure 3.1 A general conceptual model of relationships tested in studies 1–5.

Additionally, the mediational effects of work stress and work motivation in the relationship between predictors and procrastination at work were investigated.

Before testing the conceptual model, the empirical verification of the procrastination at work measure (PAWS; Metin et al., 2016; Metin et al., 2020) – in terms of its reliability and theoretical validity in the context of trait procrastination and counterproductive work behavior, as reported in Section 3.1. Next, five studies were conducted to examine the conceptual model of the relationships presented in Figure 3.1. The results of these studies are presented in Section 3.2. This research project was approved by the Scientific Research Committee of the Wroclaw University of Science and Technology.

3.1 Empirical Verification of the Procrastination at Work Construct

For a long time, studies on procrastination at work often used measures of general procrastination. Some research (Ferrari et al., 2005; Lonergan & Maher, 2000) interpreted procrastination at work as a broad dispositional tendency to procrastinate in specific work situations. However, many experts argue that procrastination in the workplace is a distinct issue requiring a specific assessment tool (Ferrari, 1992a; Ferrari et al., 2005; Klingsieck, 2013; Metin et al., 2016; van Eerde, 2016).

3.1.1 Measuring Procrastination at Work

There are a variety of techniques, such as objective measurements, experimental approaches, or self-reports that are used in research on procrastination. Almost all studies have used previously validated self-report measures, which typically involve participants completing questionnaires or surveys that assess their subjective experiences and perceptions of procrastination. These instruments often rate the frequency, severity, and reasons for their procrastination behavior.

3.1.1.1 Self-Reported Measures of Procrastination

Commonly used self-report procrastination measures (Svartdal & Steel, 2017) include the General Procrastination Scale (GPS) (Lay, 1986), the Tuckman Procrastination Scale (TPS) (Tuckman, 1991), the Pure Procrastination Scale (PPS) (Steel, 2010), the Adult Inventory of Procrastination Scale (AIP) (McCown et al., 1989), and the Decisional Procrastination Scale (DPS) (Mann et al., 1997). There are also questionnaires assessing more specific aspects of procrastination, such as Metacognitive Beliefs about Procrastination (Fernie et al., 2009), the Irrational Procrastination Scale (IPS) (Steel, 2010), Pure Procrastination Scale (PPS) (Steel, 2010), the Unintentional Procrastination Scale (UPS) (Fernie et al., 2017), or the Active Procrastination Scale (Choi & Moran, 2009). The scales that were used most frequently in research are briefly described below.

General Procrastination Scale (GPS) (Lay, 1986) measures global trait-like tendencies toward procrastination across a variety of tasks. It consists of 20 items that focus primarily on implemental delay. The GPS demonstrated very good reliability and validity (Lay, 1997; Sirois et al., 2019). So far, this scale has been used most frequently to measure workplace procrastination (Chevrenidi & Bolotova, 2018; Gupta et al., 2012; Hammer & Ferrari, 2002; Khoshouei, 2017; Legood et al., 2018; Ma et al., 2021; Mohsin & Ayub, 2014; Munjal & Mishra, 2019; Pearlman-Avnion & Zibenberg, 2018; Uysal & Yilmaz, 2020).

Adult Inventory of Procrastination (AIP) (McCown et al., 1989) is a 15-item unidimensional measure of avoidance procrastination of tasks or situations that could reveal a lack of competence or motivation and result in failure. The AIP demonstrates very good reliability (Ferrari & Patel, 2004; McCown et al., 1989) and criterion validity related to the behavioral tendency to procrastinate (Ferrari et al., 2007).

Decisional Procrastination Scale (DPS) (Mann et al., 1997) contains five items that primarily focus on delay in planning, decision-making, and implementation. The DPS was confirmed as a unidimensional measure (e.g. Mariani & Ferrari, 2012), with very good reliability and validity in various samples.

Tuckman Procrastination Scale (TPS) (Tuckman, 1991) is a 16-item instrument to assess the likelihood of postponing the start of tasks, delaying making tough decisions, and waiting until the last minute. The TPS was often used to measure employee procrastination, achieving a satisfactory level of reliability and predictive validity (Ahmad et al., 2021; Barabanshchikova et al., 2018; Huang et al., 2023; Kühnel et al., 2016; Kühnel et al., 2018; Prem et al., 2018; Sarwat et al., 2021; van Eerde & Venus, 2018; Wan et al., 2014).

Irrational Procrastination Scale (IPS) (Steel, 2010) contains nine items designed to assess the tendency to engage in irrational or dysfunctional delay of tasks during the implementation phase or beyond what is reasonable or to postpone important responsibilities. The IPS demonstrates good internal reliability and validity (Steel, 2010; Svartdal & Steel, 2017).

Pure Procrastination Scale (PPS) (Steel, 2010) is a 12-item instrument used to measure purely irrational aspects of delay combining items derived from the DPQ, GPS, and AIP aggregated in three subscales of decisional, arousal, and avoidant procrastination. This three-dimensional structure of procrastination proposed by Ferrari (1992b) was not confirmed, indicating a unidimensional tendency to delay with a high level of reliability and validity (Steel, 2010).

Many scholars emphasize that self-report measures of procrastination indicate high levels of reliability, but moderate levels of concurrent validity, and often relatively low levels of predictive validity (e.g., Vangsness et al., 2022). The major weakness of these scales is the lack of representation of work-related procrastination behaviors, such as extending breaks, dealing with private matters, browsing the Internet, computer games, or communicating via social media during working hours. However, the findings of these studies significantly contributed to the knowledge of postponement behavior in the workplace and provided a basis for further investigation of procrastination in the context of work and organizations.

3.1.1.2 Behavioral Measures of Procrastination

In addition to self-reported measures, researchers also use behavioral measures to capture evidence of procrastination behaviors related to lateness or timeliness of the intended behavior, such as late submission of assignments and peer ratings of procrastination. These measures often involve observing individual actual actions or lack thereof, such as the timing of task completion, implementation delay, avoidance, and engagement in unrelated activities. However, there is a scarcity of research results based on behavioral measures of procrastination at work. Most studies that have examined behavioral delay have focused on lateness/timeliness in completing the intended behavior (e.g. Howell et al., 2006; Lay, 1986; McCown et al., 1989; Tice & Baumeister, 2018), onset delay (Moon & Illingworth, 2005; Senécal et al., 1997; Steel, 2010), or the initial delay of planned action and preferences for onset delay (Svartdal et al., 2018). Studies have revealed in the experiment the effect of increased procrastination in the workplace on creativity (Shin & Grant, 2021), as well as the impact of decreased procrastination with rational work planning on performance, satisfaction, and compensation (Cadena et al., 2011). Furthermore, a negative relationship has been found between leader decisional procrastination and employee innovation among those who were low in resistance to change (Haesevoets et al., 2022). Behavioral measures of procrastination involve assessing delays or prolonged periods of inaction based on task initiation and completion time. Additionally, they may assess adherence to deadlines or the tendency to delay task completion until the last minute. The researchers also monitored instances of task switching and engagement in distracting activities while working on a task through observations or video recordings. One commonly used measure for recording procrastination behaviors is the diary. Additionally, task monitoring software or apps can be used to assess behavioral indicators of procrastination by tracking an individual's completion time, delay, and time spent on non-task-related activities online.

Procrastination at work appears to be a different phenomenon from general procrastination. Consequently, the best way to obtain information about employees' procrastinating tendencies is to employ a measure specifically tailored to the work context.

3.1.2 Procrastination at Work Scale: A Validation of Measure

To advance research on procrastination in the workplace, Metin et al. (2016) developed the Procrastination at Work Scale (PAWS) to measure this specific phenomenon. PAWS has been adapted in seven different language zones, including the Netherlands, Croatia, Czech Republic, Finland, Slovenia, Ukraine, Turkey, and the United Kingdom (Metin et al., 2020), and has also been used in many cross-sectional studies on individual and work-related predictors and consequences of procrastination in various cultural contexts (see Table 3.1). Consistent with ongoing research, the current study aims to validate PAWS in the Polish context and investigate its individual and work-related determinants. This contributes to a broader understanding of the phenomenon of procrastination in the workplace.

The validation process was conducted on PAWS in a sample of Polish employees. The process included multiple stages, such as examining the reliability, factorial validity, and theoretical validity of the instrument. The two-factor structure of procrastination at work was confirmed. The first factor, *soldiering*, refers to the tendency to delay and avoid work tasks in exchange for non-work activities. The second factor, *cyberslacking,* entails online activities at the expense of work responsibilities. These two dimensions reflect workplace procrastination, which is characterized by delaying work and avoiding work tasks in favor of more pleasurable non-work-related activities (see Section 2.1.2).

3.1.2.1 Participants and Measure

The validity of PAWS was tested in a total sample comprising 1,805 participants (946 women, 859 men) between 25 and 70 years ($M = 39.4$, $SD = 10.7$) of various occupations, organizations, and types of work. The average job tenure in the sample was 15.0 years ($SD = 10.9$). The 12-item PAWS (Metin et al., 2016) was used to measure procrastination at work. The PAWS contains two subscales of *soldiering* containing eight items and *cyberslacking* represented by four items. Respondents rated items on a 7-point scale (1 – strongly disagree, 7 – strongly agree). Before applying the PAWS measure, two independent native English translators translated the items into Polish (forward translation). Subsequently, two bilingual individuals back-translated the questionnaire into English. This new English version was then re-translated into Polish by two professionals with a high command of English who were blind to the original version of the PAWS (Beaton et al., 2000).

3.1.2.2 Factorial Structure of Procrastination at Work Construct

First, a confirmatory factor analysis of the PAWS items was performed to verify the internal validity of the measure. The analysis was performed, using structural equation modeling (SEM) (Byrne, 2016) with AMOS 27.0 software. Due to the large number of controlled variables, structural equation modeling with the maximum likelihood method was used. This approach enables the simultaneous detection of numerous directional relationships among many variables while estimating measurement errors. The fit of the SEM models was evaluated with the χ^2/df statistic and other fit indices, such as the root mean square error of approximation (RMSEA), the standardized root mean square residual (SRMR), Tucker Lewis Index (TLI), and Comparative Fit Index (CFI) (Byrne, 2016). According to the recommended criteria, the model was fitted to the data at an acceptable level, if the fit indices achieved the following values: χ^2/df < 8; RMSEA and SRMR < 0.08; and TLI and CFI > 0.90.

Three alternative factorial solutions were tested. *Model 1* with one first-order factor to which was loaded all the 12 items. In *Model 2*, two first-order factor solution was tested. The first factor included eight items representing the soldiering dimension, and the second factor contained four items expressing the cyberslacking dimension. *Model 3* included a one-second-order factor, combining soldiering and cyberslacking as first-order factors.

Model 1 did not fit the data well (χ^2/df = 15.67, RMSEA = 0.132, SRMS = 0.085, CFI = 0.84, TLI = 0.80), whereas *Model 2* and *Model 3* obtained acceptable fit indices (*Model 2*: χ^2/df = 6.09, RMSEA = 0.078, SRMS = 0.052, CFI = 0.95, TLI = 0.93; *Model 3*: χ^2/df = 5.44, RMSEA = 0.072, SRMS = 0.045, CFI = 0.96, TLI = 0.94), and significantly better compared to *Model 1* ($\Delta\chi^2$ = 43.17, $p < 0.01$; $\Delta\chi^2$ = 58.50, $p < 0.01$). The path regression coefficients were statistically significant at a level of 0.51 to 0.80 and the correlation between factors was 0.61. Therefore, it appears that procrastination at work is a unified construct consisting of two interrelated dimensions: soldiering and cyberslacking. The validation of PAWS in the sample of Polish employees confirmed the two-dimensional structure procrastination at work extracted by Metin et al. (2016). Therefore, in subsequent analyses, procrastination at work was considered as a two-dimensional construct.

3.1.2.3 Reliability of Procrastination at Work Measure

The reliability of PAWS was analyzed at the item level (including the item-total, inter-item, and intraclass correlations) and the scale level (including internal consistency, split-half reliability, differences between extreme score groups, and short- and long-term temporal stability). The results of the item-level analysis showed acceptable correlations between the items and the total score, with correlation coefficients ranging from 0.42 to 0.75, exceeding the recommended threshold of 0.3. The intraclass correlations also achieved a high level. Furthermore, the inter-item mean correlations supported the discriminatory power of the PAWS items.

The reliability of the PAWS at the scale level was also satisfactory. Internal consistency estimated using Cronbach's α coefficient (Cronbach, 1951; Peterson, 1994) was high. Composite reliability split-half reliability was examined by estimating Spearman–Brown split-half correlations between two random two-item divisions (Cronbach, 1951). The correlation coefficients achieved a high level, supporting the high reliability of the PAWS. The composite reliability of the latent constructs of the PAWS was estimated, indicating that the shared variance among items in subscales was very high (Hair et al., 2020). Additionally, the average variance extracted (AVE) as the amount of variance captured by a construct in relation to the amount of variance because of measurement error was acceptable for the PAWS measures (Hair et al., 2020). The results of the analysis of the variance of the extreme measurement scores (27% of the participants with the highest scores and 27% with the lowest scores) revealed significant differences between the low and high scores on the subscales and the total score (see Table 3.2). Additionally, short- and long-term stability analyses (Polit, 2014) of the PAWS were performed. To estimate short-term stability, procrastination at work was measured twice with a two-week interval in a group of 124 individuals (69 women and 55 men) aged 26 to 55 years ($M = 37.2$; $SD = 9.5$). The correlation between the two measurements indicated a high level of stability of the PAWS measures over time (Peterson, 1994). To assess the long-term stability of the measure, measurements were taken in a sample of 510 respondents (269 women, 241 men; $M = 44.6$, $SD = 9.7$). A high correlation between both measurements (cf. Table 3.3) indicates the high long-term stability of the PAWS (Polit, 2014), although they were lower compared to the short-term stability. Thus, the procrastination at work measured by the PAWS is relatively stable both in the short term and in the long term and insensitive to situational factors. In general, the reliability of a PAWS measure is at a satisfactory level.

Table 3.2 Item- and scale-level reliability parameters for the PAWS measure

Parameters	Soldiering	Cyberslacking	Procrastination at work (total)
M(SD)	2.70(1.06)	2.90(1.33)	2.80(1.04)
Scale-level			
Internal consistency (Cronbach α)	0.89	0.80	0.89
Composite reliability (CR)	0.90	0.80	0.93
Average Variance Extracted (AVE)	0.53	0.51	0.52
Split-half reliability (Spearman– Brown formula)[a]	0.87	0.72	0.70
Test-retest correlation (two-week interval[a])	0.79**	0.82**	0.83**
Test-retest correlation (six-month interval[b])	0.63**	0.68**	0.70**
Extreme-scores group differences[a]	−47.90***	−56.53***	52.14***
Item-level			
Intraclass correlation (ICC)[a]	0.89	0.80	0.89
Inter-item mean correlation[a]	0.51	0.50	0.42
Inter-item correlations[a]	0.34–0.66	0.30–0.63	0.15–0.66
Item-total correlations[a]	0.57–0.75	0.48–0.71	0.42–0.71

Note. $N = 1805$; [a] $n = 124$; [b] $n = 510$; **$p < 0.01$; ***$p < 0.001$.

Table 3.3 Correlations between general procrastination and procrastination at work

General procrastination measurement	Soldiering	Cyberslacking	Procrastination at work (total)
General Procrastination Scale (GPS-9)[a]	0.59**	0.34**	0.50**
Adult Inventory Procrastination (AIP)[b]	0.62**	0.32**	0.51**
Pure Procrastination Scale (PPS)[c]	0.67**	0.34**	0.56**

Note. $^*p < 0.05$; $^{**}p < 0.01$. [a] $n = 587$; [b] $n = 561$; [c] $n = 657$

Additionally, a total score of procrastination at work was weakly and positively correlated with age (0.23). Slightly older age is associated with the dimension of cyberslacking (0.29) and lower with the dimension of soldiering (0.12). These results correspond to previous results, which showed low correlations (Hen et al., 2021; Mercado, Giordano et al., 2017; Rehman et al., 2019; Saman & Wirawam, 2021; Tandon et al., 2022). Procrastination scores were significantly higher among men than among women, in cyberslacking, ($F(1,1803) = 16.68$, $p < 0.001$), and a total score of procrastination at work ($F(1,1803) = 11.20$, $p < 0.04$). A nonsignificant difference in soldiering dimension was observed in soldiering ($F(1,1803) = 2.66$, ns). Previous research provided a nonsignificant effect of gender on procrastination at work or cyberslacking (He et al., 2021; Hen et al., 2021; Legood et al., 2018; Lin, 2018; Sarwat et al., 2021) or a weak effect of gender on cyberslacking (Mercado, Giordano et. al., 2017).

To summarize, the PAWS measure achieved satisfactory reliability, both at the item- and the scale-level. At the item level, item-total, inter-item, and intraclass correlations were moderate to high, suggesting good discrimination of the PAWS items. The PAWS subscales achieved a high level of internal consistency, split-half reliability, differences between extreme score groups, as well as short- and long-term stability of the measure over time. It should be noted that a moderate level of stability in procrastination at work over-time suggests that it may be susceptible to the effects of various situational work-related factors. These analyses provided strong evidence for PAWS as a reliable tool to measure procrastination at work consisting of soldiering and cyberslacking behavior in the Polish organizational setting.

3.1.3 Theoretical Validity of Procrastination at Work Measure

In the following stage, a theoretical validity analysis of the PAWS was carried out. To improve understanding of the broader context of procrastination phenomena in the workplace, the correlation between soldiering, cyberslacking, and other theoretical constructs was explored. The convergent and divergent validity of the procrastination measure at work was verified in relation to procrastination as a trait and counterproductive work behavior. It was predicted that the dimensions of procrastination would strongly relate to procrastination as a trait and to passive counterproductive work behavior, but not to active counterproductive work behavior.

3.1.3.1 Procrastination at Work in Relation to General Procrastination

The PAWS validity test included an examination of the relationship between procrastination at work and general procrastination. According to previous findings, a moderate association between these constructs was revealed.

Participants and Measure: In this study, procrastination at work and general procrastination were measured. General procrastination was measured in three different subsamples using three different scales.

Procrastination at Work: The PAWS (Metin et al., 2016; Metin et al., 2020) was used to measure procrastination at work in terms of soldiering and cyber-slacking dimensions. The details of the PAWS are described in Section 3.1.2. Procrastination at work was measured in the total sample of 1,805 respondents (946 women, 859 men), aged 25 and 70 ($M = 39.4$, $SD = 10.7$).

General Procrastination Scale (GPS–9) (Sirois et al., 2019) was used in a subsample of 587 (312 women, 275 men), aged 20 to 67 years ($M = 34.1$, $SD = 9.2$). The GPS–9 assesses the dispositional tendency to procrastinate on various tasks. It includes nine items (e.g. 'I keep saying, I'll do it tomorrow'.), which are rated on a 5-point scale (1 – strongly disagree; 5 – strongly agree). The GPS–9 in this study achieved a high level of reliability (0.83).

Adult Inventory of Procrastination (AIP) (McCown et al., 1989) was used in a subsample of 561 (282 women, 279 men) aged 25 to 65 years ($M = 35.5$, $SD = 9.2$). The 15-item AIP measures procrastination in terms of the frequency of postponing performing everyday tasks or activities (e.g. 'I often fail to complete tasks on time'.). It was rated on a 5-point scale (1 – strongly disagree, 5 – strongly agree). The internal consistency was satisfactory in this study (0.81).

Pure Procrastination Scale (PPS) (Steel, 2010) was used in a subsample of 657 participants (336 women, 321 men), aged 30 to 70 years ($M = 32.2$, $SD = 9.8$). The 12-item PPS assesses the general tendency to dysfunctional delay in any activities. Participants rated items on a 5-point scale (1 – strongly disagree, 5 – strongly agree). In this study, a total mean score was considered. The internal consistency of the measure was satisfactory in this study (0.91).

To minimize common method bias (Podsakoff et al., 2003), general procrastination and procrastination at work were measured in separate sessions of 2 or 4 weeks apart.

Results: Correlation analysis showed that soldiering was strongly correlated with all measures of general procrastination (see Table 3.3). The highest correlation was below 0.70 (0.67), indicating no collinearity between the analyzed variables.

Significant correlations between soldering and procrastination were revealed. Cyberslacking was moderately correlated with different measures of dispositional procrastination, suggesting that cyberslacking differs from general procrastination to a greater extent than soldiering. These results are in line with previous studies, which found moderate associations between general procrastination and procrastination at work (Hen et al., 2021; Metin et al., 2016).

Due to the content similarity between general procrastination and procrastination at work measures, it was examined whether these constructs are semantically different but intercorrelated. To this end, a confirmatory factor analysis was used to examine different factor solutions that included the PAWS items and one of three questionnaires measuring general procrastination (PPS, AIP, GPS). For each of the questionnaires measuring general procrastination (PPS, AIP, GPS), four models were tested, with one, two, and three first-order factors and two second-order factors (see Table 3.4).

As Table 3.4 shows, one-factor solutions (*Models 1, 4, 7*) obtained acceptable, but the lowest values of fit indices. Comparisons between tested models ($\Delta\chi^2$) showed statistically significant differences. Two-factor solutions (*Models 2, 5, 8*) were significantly better fitted into the data than one-factor models. However, three-factor models (*Models 3, 6, 9*) achieved significantly higher fit

Table 3.4 Fit indices of factor solutions for measures of general procrastination and procrastination at work

Tested model	χ^2/df	RMSEA	SRMS	CFI	TLI	$\Delta\chi^2$
Model 1. One first-order factor 1: PAWS+PPS	6.66	0.061	0.053	0.95	0.93	–
Model 2. Two first-order factors: 1:PAWS; 2:PPS	4.22	0.059	0.035	0.97	0.96	452.43***
Model 3. Three first-order factors: 1:SOL; 2:CBL; 3:PPS	3.62	0.041	0.029	0.98	0.97	129.43***
Model 4. One first-order-factor: 1: PAWS+AIP	3.92	0.068	0.064	0.90	0.88	–
Model 5. Two first-order factors: 1:PAWS; 2:AIP	3.20	0.056	0.059	0.92	0.91	191.44***
Model 6. Three first-order-factors: 1:SOL; 2:CBL; 3:AIP	2.97	0.056	0.053	0.93	0.92	65.32***
Model 7. One first-order-factor: 1: PAWS+GPS	6.05	0.089	0.082	0.89	0.87	–
Model 8. Two first-order factors: 1:PAWS, 2:GPS	3.59	0.064	0.069	0.94	0.93	405.26***
Model 9. Three first-order-factors: 1:SOL; 2:CBL; 3:GPS	3.10	0.058	0.064	0.95	0.94	88.77***

Note. PAWS – Procrastination at Work Scale, SOL – Soldiering subscale, CBL – Cyberslacking subscale, PPS – Pure Procrastination Scale, AIP – Adult Inventory of Procrastination, GPS – General Procrastination Scale. ***$p < 0.001$.

indices, confirming the high degree of homogeneity of the subscales (Byrne, 2016). The results indicated that despite the semantic similarity/relatedness, general procrastination and procrastination at work may be considered as different constructs, albeit highly intercorrelated. Procrastination at work and its dimensions of soldering and cyberslacking appear to be a specific manifestation of general procrastination (Klingsieck, 2013; van Eerde, 2016), and therefore, require separate empirical investigation in the work environment. Measuring procrastination at work is more relevant than making inferences about work procrastination based on general procrastination measures.

In conclusion, a high convergent validity of procrastination at work in relation to dispositional general procrastination was supported. Due to the strong correlation between general procrastination and dimensions of procrastination at work, the measurement of soldiering at work will be used in further analysis without controlling for general procrastination.

3.1.3.2 *Procrastination at Work and Counterproductive Work Behavior*

This study examined the relationship between procrastination at work and counterproductive work behavior in the context of validity testing. Counterproductive work behavior is defined as volitional acts that carry out the intention to harm the organization or people associated with it (Fox & Spector, 2005). Counterproductive behavior and procrastination at work have common features, but also differences. Procrastination at work refers to intentionally delaying tasks, but without the intention of causing harm to the organization (Metin et al., 2016). However, the outcomes of procrastination are still counterproductive. The literature emphasizes the similarity of procrastination to withdrawal as passive counterproductive behavior because both involve a deliberate and voluntary reduction in the amount of time and energy spent on work and the freedom to decide whether to undertake or postpone tasks at work (van den Berg & Roosen, 2018). Only one study found positive links between soldiering and cyberslacking, with abuse and withdrawal (Metin et al., 2016), which shed light on the relationship between both types of behavior. Therefore, it was assumed that procrastination and its dimensions will be correlated with passive forms of behavior (e.g. intentional reduction in productivity and organizational withdrawal) and will be distinct from active counterproductive behavior at work (e.g. theft, sabotage, and workplace abuse).

Participants and Measures: The study was carried out online among 587 employees (312 women and 275 men), aged 20 to 67 years ($M = 34.1$, $SD = 9.2$), who worked in various industries and occupations. Respondents had an average job tenure of 14.5 years ($SD = 10.7$) and completed questionnaires measuring procrastination at work and counterproductive work behavior.

Procrastination at Work: The PAWS (Metin et al., 2016, 2020) was used to measure procrastination at work and its dimensions of soldiering and cyber-slacking. Details of PAWS are described in Section 3.1.2. Procrastination at work achieved high internal consistency in this study (0.86–0.89).

Counterproductive Work Behavior: The Polish version of the Counterproductive Work Behavior – Checklist (CWB–C; Baka et al., 2015) comprised four sub-scales: *sabotage* (e.g. 'You intentionally destroy tools or equipment belonging to your employer'.), *abuse* (e.g. 'You insult someone because of how they do their job'.), *theft* (five items; e.g. 'You take your employer's money without permission'.), and *withdrawal* (e.g. 'You take longer breaks than you're allowed'.). Respondents rated items on a 5-point scale (1 – never, 5 – every day). The internal consistency of CWB–C dimensions and total procrastination score was satisfactory (0.72–0.93).

Results: As depicted in Table 3.5, a total score of counterproductive work behavior was moderately correlated with procrastination at work and its dimensions of soldiering and cyberslacking. Furthermore, procrastination at work and soldiering are closely correlated, while cyberslacking is moderately correlated with withdrawal. Collinearity and multicollinearity were not problematic in this analysis, because the highest correlation was below 0.70 (0.52) and the variance inflation factor (VIF = 1.56) scores did not exceed 6 (Tabachnick et al., 2019). Procrastination at work and its dimensions were weakly correlated with sabotage, abuse, and theft. The results indicate that soldiering and cyber-slacking, as dimensions of procrastination, are strongly related to passive counterproductive work behavior and, to a lesser extent, active counterproductive work behavior.

To determine the relationship between procrastination dimensions and counterproductive work behavior, four-factor models were tested using a confirmatory factor analysis: *Model 1* with one first-order factor solution includes

Table 3.5 Correlations between procrastination at work and counterproductive work behavior

Counterproductive work behaviors	Soldiering	Cyberslacking	Procrastination at work (total)
Sabotage	0.31**	0.21**	0.27**
Abuse	0.28**	0.18**	0.23**
Withdrawal	0.57**	0.42**	0.52**
Theft	0.31**	0.16**	0.25**
Total score	0.44**	0.29**	0.39**

Note. **$p < 0.01$.

dimensions of counterproductive behavior and procrastination at work; *Model 2* with two first-order factor solutions – in which the first factor included abuse, theft, sabotage, and withdrawal, while the second factor – soldiering and cyberslacking; *Model 3* with two first-order factor solutions – in which the first factor covered abuse, theft, sabotage, and the second factor included withdrawal, soldiering, and cyberslacking; *Model 4* with two second-order factor solution, in which the first factor included abuse, theft, sabotage, and second factor covered withdrawal and second-order factor of procrastination at work (combining soldiering and cyberslacking as first-order factors). According to the criteria (Byrne, 2016), *Models 1* and *2* achieved unsatisfactory fit parameters to the empirical data, whereas *Models 3* and *4* obtained acceptable indices of fit to the data (see Table 3.6). Therefore, it should be noted that in *Model 3* soldiering and cyberslacking were first-order factors, while in *Model 4* procrastination at work as a second-order factor consisted of soldiering and cyberslacking.

These results showed that procrastination at work is associated with counterproductive withdrawal behavior. Specifically, soldiering and cyberslacking were strongly related to passive withdrawal and weaker to theft, abuse, and sabotage considered as active counterproductive behavior. Thus, it may indicate that inactivity is a common component of procrastination and withdrawal from work, which results in reduced job performance by not engaging in productive behavior. The study's results supported a strong relationship between dimensions of procrastination at work, i.e. soldiering cyberslacking and withdrawal. Through analyzing counterproductive and procrastination behaviors, two related groups of active (theft, abuse, sabotage) and passive (withdrawal, soldiering, cyberslacking) work behaviors were identified (Balducci et al., 2011). Connections of procrastination dimensions with withdrawal may arise from some similarities between both behaviors. These are forms of voluntary

Table 3.6 Fit indices of factor solutions for dimensions of procrastination at work and counterproductive work behavior

Tested model	χ^2/df	RMSEA	SRMS	CFI	TLI	$\Delta\chi^2$
Model 1. One first-order factor: 1: PAW+CWB	19.52	0.158	0.089	0.88	0.85	–
Model 2. Two first-order factors: 1: AB+SA+TH+WI; 2: SOL+CBL	16.44	0.169	0.064	0.93	0.82	41.87**
Model 3. Two first-order factors: 1: AB+SAB+TH; 2: SOL+CBL+WI	4.46	0.080	0.041	0.98	0.96	23.89**
Model 4. Two second-order factors: 1: AB+SA+TH+WI; 2: PAW(SOL+CBL)	2.20	0.047	0.016	0.99	0.99	32.45**

Note. **$p<0.01$. PAW – procrastination at work, SOL – soldiering, CBL – cyberslacking, CWB – counterproductive work behavior, AB – abuse, SA – sabotage, TH – theft, WI – withdrawal.

work avoidance behavior. In addition, both have negative consequences for both the employee and the organization by reducing the amount of time and energy devoted to work. However, employees who procrastinate do not intend to harm the organization but only avoid unfavorable situations. Similarly, cyberslacking is considered a form of organizational withdrawal (Lim & Chen, 2012). The results of the study partially confirmed that procrastination and counterproductive work behavior have common and distinct characteristics (Mercado et al., 2017). Thus, it can be assumed that procrastination at work fits into the definitional scope of passive counterproductive work behavior because misuse of work time and resources was observed (Gruys & Sackett, 2003). These behaviors seem to create a qualitatively different form of counterproductive work behavior resulting from self-regulation deficits and employing dysfunctional strategies for coping with stress or restoring resources (Balducci et al., 2011; Fox & Spector, 2005).

In summary, the results of this study provided strong evidence for PAWS as a valid and reliable tool for measuring procrastination at work, consisting of soldiering and cyberslacking behavior in Polish work-related settings. Both dimensions and the total score achieved high reliability and convergent validity in relation to general procrastination and counterproductive work behavior.

3.2 Individual and Work-Related Predictors of Procrastination at Work

Building upon previous empirical findings and scholarly postulations on the need for investigation of procrastination at work (Klingsieck, 2013; van Eerde, 2016), there were explored the individual and work-related characteristics contributing to employee procrastination and the mechanisms that explained it. Based on the JD–R model assumptions (Bakker & Demerouti, 2014; Bakker et al., 2023), the conceptual model was proposed, assuming the various job demands, job resources, leadership resources, their interactions, and various personal resources as predictors of procrastination at work. Furthermore, the mediational role of work stress and work motivation (represented by various indicators) in the associations of individual and work-related factors with procrastination at work (see Figure 3.2).

To verify a conceptual model, a series of five studies were designed. Studies 1–4 tested: (1) indirect effects of job demands, job resources, leadership resources, and personal resources on procrastination at work through work stress and/or work motivation as mediators (mediation models), (2) interaction effects of job demands with job resources and leadership resources on procrastination through stress and/or work motivation (moderated mediation model), and (3) relationships between job demands, resources, and personal resources and procrastination at work under conditions of low- vs. high-job demands (conditional mediation model). However, the conceptual model tested in these studies varied

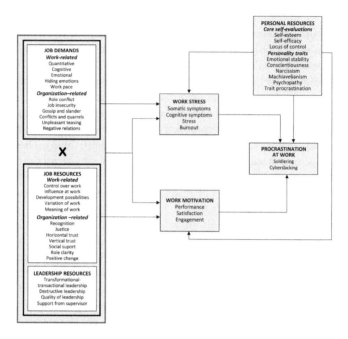

Figure 3.2 Details of the general conceptual model of procrastination at work – predictors and mediators.

in the arrangement of variables within each category. Study 5 focused on the role of work-related factors in predicting weekly procrastination behaviors. The study investigated whether procrastination at work varies from week to week and what work-related factors that predict weekly fluctuations in employee procrastination behavior. Furthermore, Study 5 aimed to uncover the mechanisms through which job demands, job resources, and leadership resources influence weekly procrastination at work represented by weekly soldiering and cyberslacking behaviors.

Analytical Strategy: Statistical analyses were performed using IBM SPSS Statistics 27.0, SPSS AMOS 27, and Mplus. As preliminary analyses, Pearson's correlations between the study variables were calculated. In addition, collinearity and multicollinearity were assessed before testing structural relationship models. If the highest correlation among study variables was below 0.70 and the variance inflation factor (VIF) values exceeded 6 (Tabachnick et al., 2019), both collinearity and multicollinearity may affect regression inferences. In each study, Harman's single-factor test was also performed to examine potential common method variance among the study variables. This was done by performing a factor analysis of all study items with a fixed single factor without rotation. According to the recommendations of Podsakoff et al. (2003), common method variance exists when one factor explains more than 50% of the covariance among the variables in the study.

To test hypotheses assuming the effects of individual and work-related factors in predicting procrastination at work, mediation and moderated mediation analyses were conducted in each of the studies. Mediation analysis was used to determine how the mediator variable influences or explains the relationship between the independent variable (X) and the dependent variable (Y), by including a mediator variable (M). By including a mediator in the analysis, researchers can better understand the underlying process or mechanisms by which X affects Y. Moderated mediation analysis allows researchers to test the indirect effect of X on Y through M, while also taking into account the effect of the moderating variable (Rucker et al., 2011). This method can shed light on the complex interactions among predictors that may be meaningful in a given model. By testing for moderation effects, researchers can determine whether the strength or direction of the relationship between X and Y is influenced by the third variable. This can help provide a more complete and accurate understanding of the underlying mechanisms at work in a given model.

To estimate mediation and moderated mediation models of relationships between analyzed variables, structural equation modeling (SEM) with maximum likelihood method estimation was applied. The SEM is as a statistical technique that allows the examination of complex patterns of relationships between observed variables and latent constructs, by estimating path regression, loadings, covariance parameters, and measurement errors (Byrne, 2016). The goodness of fit of the SEM models was evaluated using various fit indices, including the χ^2/df statistic, the root mean square error of approximation (RMSEA), the standardized root mean square residual (SRMR), Tucker Lewis index (TLI), and comparative fit index (CFI) (Byrne, 2016). Based on the recommended criteria (Hu & Bentler, 1999), the model will be considered adequately fitted to the data if the following fit indices are achieved: χ^2/df < 8, RMSEA and SRMR < 0.08, and TLI and CFI > 0.90.

The direct effect in the SEM was represented by the regression coefficient of the path between two associated variables in the model (e.g. X $\rightarrow$ M, M $\rightarrow$ Y, or X $\rightarrow$ Y). The indirect effect is determined by the product of the coefficients of direct effects for pathways X $\rightarrow$ M and M $\rightarrow$ Y. To estimate the statistical significance of the indirect effects, a bootstrapping procedure with error correction on 10,000 samples was used. The indirect effect is considered statistically significant if its 95% confidence interval does not include 0 (Hayes, 2022).

In moderated mediation, significant two-way interactions were decomposed into conditional models of tested relationships for two groups with low and high levels of the moderator variable, divided according to the median of the moderator scores. Multigroup analyses (MGA) were then conducted to examine whether structural models were invariant between the compared groups (Byrne, 2016). Multigroup analysis enables the estimation of parameters in separate structural models for each of the groups. These models have identical structures in each group and can provide separate estimates of within-group parameters such as loadings, paths, and correlations. To test the difference between the models in a multigroup analysis, the χ^2 change ($\Delta\chi^2/\Delta df$) and the fit index change (ΔCFI and ΔTLI) were used. A change in the goodness-of-fit index greater than 0.01 indicates a difference between the models (Vandenberg & Lance, 2000). Furthermore, the Z test was used to assess the equality of direct effects between groups. Furthermore, following Cohen's (1992) recommendations, a value of $r = 0.10$ was used as the cut-off criterion for small effect size in all tested models. Based on this assumption, effects lower than 0.10 were considered as practically not meaningful and were not taken into account in the interpretation.

In Study 5, multilevel modeling was used to examine the direct, indirect, and interactive effects of job demands and resources on weekly changes in procrastination behavior at work. This method is useful for the analysis of data that have nested hierarchical structure. There are two basic types of prediction equations in multilevel analyses. At the level 1 – the within-person variability of procrastination behavior at work and at the level 2 – the between-person of procrastination were examined. To test hypotheses, the nested moderated mediation model was examined, using structural equation analysis with MPlus (Byrne, 2016; Muthén et al., 2017). Analogically to studies 1–4, the fit of the model parameters was estimated, as well as the indirect effects using the bootsrapping procedure with 10,000 samples.

3.2.1 Core Self-Evaluations, Job Demands, Job Resources, Transformational– Transactional Leadership, and Work Motivation – Study 1

Study 1 sought to determine whether procrastination at work is associated with job demands, job resources, leadership resources, and personal resources. Simultaneously, it looked at whether work motivation mediated the links between individual and work-related factors and procrastination at work, thereby identify the the the motivational regulatory mechanism of procrastination at work postulated in the JD–R model (Bakker et al., 2023). These investigations were conducted on the assumption that job resources and demands interact and that employee procrastination is correlated with indicators of job motivation.

The conceptual model of Study 1 included job demands (represented by quantitative demands and negative social relationships), job resources (represented by control at work, role clarity, support, and change), leadership resources (represented by transformational–transformational style), personal resources in terms of core self-evaluations (represented by self-esteem and self-efficacy) as predictors, and work motivation (represented by work performance, work satisfaction,

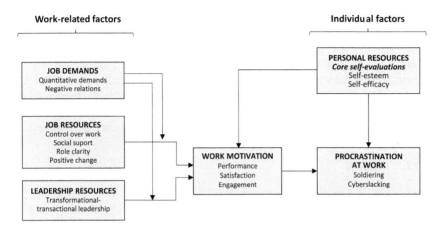

Figure 3.3 A conceptual model of the relationships between the variables tested in Study 1.

and work engagement) as mediator in relationships with procrastination at work. A detailed conceptual model is presented in Figure 3.3.

The following specific research hypotheses were formulated:

H.1.1. Core self-evaluations are directly associated with low procrastination at work

H.1.2. Core self-evaluations are indirectly associated with procrastination at work through work motivation

H.1.3. High job resources are indirectly associated with low procrastination at work through work motivation

H.1.4. Transformational–transactional leadership is indirectly associated with low procrastination at work through work motivation

H.1.5. The interaction of job demands and job resources is indirectly associated with procrastination at work through work motivation, such that the indirect effect of job resources on procrastination at work via work motivation is stronger in high than low job demands conditions

H.1.6. The interaction of job demands with transformational–transformational leadership is indirectly related to procrastination at work through work motivation, such that the indirect effect of transformational–transforma-tional leadership on procrastination at work via work motivation is stronger in high than low job demands conditions

3.2.1.1 Participants and Procedure

The study was conducted online in three sessions. In Study 1, 624 employees participated ($M = 45.7$, $SD = 9.3$), with 501 participants taking part in all three sessions (259 women, 242 men). The age of participants ranged from 30 to 70 years ($M = 44.6$, $SD = 9.7$), and their average job tenure was 2.6 years ($SD = 10.6$). The participants worked in various industries and performed various job functions. To avoid common-method bias (Podsakoff et al., 2003), participants completed different surveys in each session. In the first session, they assessed procrastination at work and leadership styles. In the second session (after 16 weeks), they rated self-efficacy, job demands, and resources. In the third session (after 8 weeks), participants assessed their global self-esteem and work motivation (including work performance, work satisfaction, and work engagement).

3.2.1.2 Measures

Procrastination at Work: To assess procrastination at work consisting of two dimensions, i.e. soldiering and cyberslacking, PAWS was used (Metin et al., 2020), described in detail in Section 3.1.2. The internal consistency of the measures in this study was high (0.83–0.91).

Job Demands and Resources: To measure job demands and job resources, the 35-item Health and Safety Executive – HSE Indicator Tool (Edwards et al., 2008) was used. This tool measures various work aspects as potential stressors: *demands (quantitative)* – represented by task overload, time pressure, task difficulty at work, (8 items; e.g. 'I am given impossible deadlines'.); *control* – assessing the extent to which an employee has control over her work and organization (6 items, e.g. 'I can decide on my own about my breaks'.); *social support* – identifying the level of support, assistance from superiors and co-workers (9 items; e.g. 'I receive constructive comments and feedback on the work I do'.), *social relationships* (negative) – assessing the atmosphere and quality of interpersonal relationships in the workplace (4 items; e.g. 'I experience unpleasantness at work in the form of rude remarks or behavior'.); *role* – measuring the clarity of the performed role and the perception of role conflict (5 items; e.g. 'I know how to perform the role assigned to me'.); *change* – identifying how change is managed and communicated in the organization (3 items, e.g. 'When changes are made at work, I know how they will translate into daily activities'.). Respondents rated items on a 5-point scale (1 – never, 5 – always). The internal consistency of the dimensions ranged from 0.78 to 0.82.

Transformational–Transactional Leadership: To measure transformational and transactional leadership, two subscales of the Multifactor Leadership Questionnaire (MLQ–5X) (Bass & Avolio, 1994) were used. Since both dimensions have a strong correlation in the Polish setting (Bajcar & Babiak, 2022), in this study they were aggregated and considered a transformational-transactional leadership. Respondents rated their immediate leader's behavior on a 5-point scale (1 – not at all, 5 – very often). The internal consistency of transformational–transactional leadership was high (0.95).

Work Motivation: To measure work motivation, three indicators, i.e. employee subjective assessment of work performance, work satisfaction, and work engagement were used. *Work performance* was assessed using a single item 'How would you rate your performance at work?' *Work satisfaction* by item 'How do you rate your satisfaction with your job?' on a 5-point scale (1 = very low, 5 – very high). *Work engagement* was rated using the 9-item Utrecht Work Engagement Scale (UWES–9) (; Schaufeli et al., 2006). It includes three sub-scales: *vigor* (e.g. 'I feel energized at work'.), *dedication* (e.g. 'I am devoted to my work'.), and *absorption* (e.g. 'I am absorbed in my work'.), rated on a 7-point scale (0 – never, 6 – always). In this study, work engagement is represented by the total average score. The internal consistency of work engagement dimensions ranged from 0.83 to 0.94.

Personal resources were evaluated through self-esteem and self-efficacy, which represent core self-evaluations. To assess global *self-esteem,* the Rosenberg Self-Esteem Questionnaire (RSES) (Rosenberg, 1965) was used. Respondents rated 10 items expressing positive and negative feelings about themselves on a 4-point scale (1 – completely disagree, 4 – completely agree). A high RSES score represents high self-esteem. The internal consistency of the measure was 0.90. *Self-efficacy* was measured using the Generalized Self-Efficacy Scale (GSES) (Schwarzer & Jerusalem, 1995), which assesses an individual's general belief that she is effective in dealing with difficult situations and obstacles in life. Ten GSES items were rated on a 5-point scale (1 – completely disagree, 5 – completely agree) and achieved high internal consistency (0.92).

3.2.1.3 Test of Common-Method Variance

Although the variables were assessed in three sessions at intervals of 16 and 8 weeks, Harman's single-factor test was conducted to estimate the common-method variance (Podsakoff et al., 2003). A one-factor model was tested in the confirmatory factor analysis, but the fit parameters were unacceptable (χ^2/df = 6.79; RMSEA = 0.108; SMRS = 0.040; GFI = 0.89; AGFI = 0.82; TLI = 0.83; CFI = 0.87). Subsequently, a five-factor model was tested, in which the variables were separated according to their content: (1) soldiering and cyberslacking; (2) job demands; (3) job and leadership resources; (4) work engagement, job satisfaction, job effectiveness; and (5) self-esteem and self-efficacy. The model obtained acceptable fit parameters (χ^2/df = 34.266; RMSEA = 0.080; SMRS = 0.079; TLI = 0.92; CFI = 0.95). These results suggest that the relationships between constructs are not affected by the timing of measurements in this study.

3.2.1.4 Results

Bivariate Correlations: In search of individual and work-related sources of procrastination at work, the correlations between the measured variables were analyzed. As the highest correlation was below 0.70 (0.61) and the variance inflation factor scores (VIF = 0.81) did not exceed 2.20, neither collinearity nor multicollinearity was a problem in the study (Tabachnick et al., 2019). Job demands were correlated with work procrastination (0.27), specifically slightly stronger with soldiering (0.29) than with cyberslacking (0.22). Among the work motivation dimensions, work performance exhibited the highest negative correlation with procrastination at work (−0.26) but was stronger with soldiering (−0.30) than with cyberslacking (−0.17). Work satisfaction and work engagement were weak but significantly correlated with the total procrastination score (−0.12 to −0.13). A more substantial association was observed between work satisfaction and work engagement with soldiering (−0.14 to −0.18), while the relationships with cyberslacking were nonsignificant (0.06–0.08). The correlations between the total score of job resources and its dimensions, and procrastination at work were close to 0, except for the role clarity dimension, which was weakly correlated with procrastination at work (−0.17), soldiering (−0.21), and cyberslacking (−0.10). Job demands (represented by quantitative demands and negative social relationships) were associated with procrastination (0.22–0.29). Transformational–transactional leadership did not correlate significantly with the dimensions of procrastination at work (0.04–0.06).

Test of the Mediation Model: To simplify the relationship model tested in this study, job characteristics were aggregated into two second-order factor solutions, as revealed in the confirmatory factor analysis: (1) factor of job resources containing control, roles, support, and change, and (2) factor of job demands that included quantitative demands and negative relationships. The two-factor solution was well fitted to the data (χ^2/df = 3.63; RMSEA = 0.073; SMRS = 0.020; TLI = 0.97; CFI = 0.99) and will be examined in further analyses in this study. Job demands, job resources, and transformational–transformational leadership as observed variables were entered into the model. Procrastination at work was a latent outcome variable including soldiering and cyberslacking, while work motivation, as the latent mediator variable, contained work performance, satisfaction, and engagement.

The initial model was estimated with assumed all paths and covariances (Figure 3.4.A) but it did not achieve an acceptable fit to the data (χ^2/df = 7.29; RMSEA = 0.112; SMRS = 0.054; TLI = 0.82; CFI = 0.91). All path coefficients estimated in the model are shown in Table 3.7. Furthermore, the nonsignificant path 'job demands ➡ work motivation' and path 'transformational–transactional leadership to work motivation' with β coefficient equal to 0.10 were removed from the model. Simultaneously, additional constraints suggested by the modification indices were imposed. As a result, the final model obtained better fit indices (χ^2/df = 3.62; RMSEA = 0.072; SMRS = 0.040; TLI = 0.93; CFI = 0.97), explaining 26% of the variance in procrastination at work (Figure 3.4.B).

A. Initial model

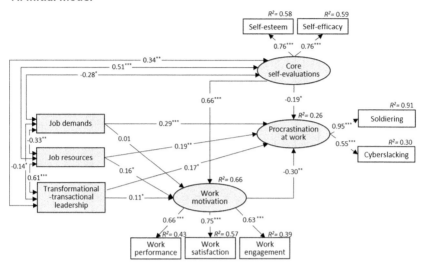

B. Final model

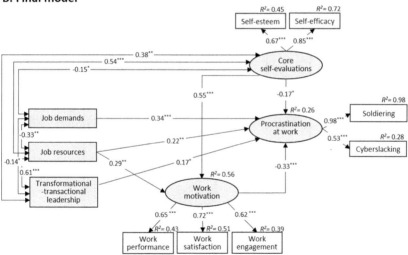

Figure 3.4 Initial (A) and final (B) mediation models tested in Study 1.

Note. $^*p < 0.05$, $^{**}p < 0.01$, $^{***}p < 0.001$. Path values are standardized regression coefficients β. Statistically nonsignificant paths are gray.

Table 3.7 Direct Effects In The Initial Mediation And Moderated Mediation Models Tested In Study 1

Direct path		Mediation model	Moderated mediation model
		$\beta(se)$	$\beta(se)$
Core self-evaluations	→ Work motivation	0.66(0.08)***	0.67(0.08)***
Job demands	→ Work motivation	−0.01(0.06)	−0.01(0.06)
Job resources	→ Work motivation	0.16(0.07)**	0.16(0.08)**
Transformational–transactional leadership	→ Work motivation	0.11(0.06)*	0.11(0.06)*
Core self-evaluations	→ Procrastination at work	−0.19(0.14)*	−0.15(0.14)*
Job demands	→ Procrastination at work	0.29(0.07)**	0.26(0.06)**
Job resources	→ Procrastination at work	0.19(0.08)*	0.15(0.08)*
Transformational–transactional leadership	→ Procrastination at work	0.17(0.06)*	0.18(0.06)*
Work motivation	→ Procrastination at work	−0.30(0.15)***	−0.35(0.15)***
Job resources x job demands	→ Work motivation		0.002(0.07)
Job resources x job demands	→ Procrastination at work		0.001(0.07)
Transformational–transactional leadership x job demands	→ Work motivation		0.02(0.07)
Transformational–transactional leadership x job demands	→ Procrastination at work		0.27(0.09)**

Note. *$p < 0.05$, **$p < 0.01$, ***$p < 0.001$. β – standardized regression coefficient.

As depicted in Figure 3.4.B, core self-evaluations, job demands, job resources, and transformational–transactional leadership were found to be significant predictors of procrastination at work. Specifically, core self-evaluations weakly predicted low procrastination at work, insufficiently supporting hypothesis H.1.1. High job demands (represented by quantitative demands and negative relationships) were directly associated with high procrastination at work. This result is consistent with previous findings, suggesting that excessive workload leads to various forms of work avoidance (Metin et al., 2016), including procrastination at work. Furthermore, high job resources (represented by control over work, role clarity, change, and social support) and transformational–transactional leadership were weakly related to high procrastination at work.

Core self-evaluations also showed relatively strong indirect effects on procrastination through work motivation, supporting H.1.2 (see Table 3.8). Potentially, high levels of core self-evaluations promote intrinsic work motivation, leading to low procrastination behavior at work (such as offline and online activities). Furthermore, the indirect effects of work motivation in the relationships between job resources and procrastination at work were significant, supporting hypothesis H.1.3. However, work motivation was a nonsignificant mediator of the effects of transformational–transactional leadership on procrastination at work. As a result, hypothesis H.1.4 was not supported.

Test of Moderated Mediation Model: In the next step, the moderated mediation model was examined. This model extended the previous mediation model by including two-way interactions: (1) between job resources and job demands, and (2) between transformational–transactional leadership and job demands. These interactions were represented in the model as the multiplied standardized scores of both variables. First, a moderated mediation model was tested with assumed all paths between variables and covariances between predictors, but did not fit the data (χ^2/df = 6.19; RMSEA = 0.102; SMRS = 0.054; TLI = 0.83; CFI = 0.92). Therefore, the nonsignificant path and covariance coefficients were removed from the model, thus improving the goodness-of-fit indices (χ^2/df = 3.44; RMSEA = 0.070; SMRS = 0.045; TLI = 0.92; CFI = 0.96). The final moderated mediation model supported the direct and indirect effects revealed in the mediation model (Tables 3.7 and 3.8). Furthermore, the effect of interaction 'job resources x job demands' on work motivation and procrastination at work was statistically nonsignificant. The interaction of 'leadership x job demands' was also nonsignificant in explaining work motivation, but significant in predicting procrastination at work. This indicates that the effect of the predictor on the outcome variable is conditional and depends on the level of the moderator. In the next step, an interaction effect between transformational–transformational leadership and job demands was therefore decomposed into conditional effects in low vs. high job demands, extracted based on the median score (Me = 2.92). The model fitted well to the data (χ^2/df = 2.95; RMSEA = 0.063; SMRS = 0.057;

Table 3.8 Indirect effects in the empirical models tested in Study 1

Tested model	Effect(se)	BC 95% CI
Mediation model		
Core self-evaluations→work motivation→procrastination at work	−0.20(0.08)	[−0.47, −0.02]
Job demands→work motivation→procrastination at work	−0.003(0.02)	[−0.04, 0.05]
Job resources→work motivation→procrastination at work	−0.05(0.04)	[−0.14, −0.001]
Transformational-transactional leadership→work motivation→procrastination at work	−0.03(.02)	[−0.09, 0.001]
Moderated mediation model		
Core self-evaluations→work motivation→procrastination at work	−0.23(0.12)	[−0.51, −0.05]
Job demands→work motivation→procrastination at work	−0.001(0.02)	[−0.05, 0.05]
Job resources→work motivation→procrastination at work	−0.06(0.04)	[−0.15, −0.01]
Transformational-transactional leadership→work motivation→procrastination at work	−0.04(0.03)	[−0.12, 0.001]
Job resources x job demands→work motivation→procrastination at work	−0.001(0.03)	[−0.06, 0.06]
Transformational-transactional leadership x job demands→work motivation→procrastination at work	−0.008(0.03)	[−0.08, 0.04]
Conditional mediation model		
Low job demands (n = 257)		
Core self-evaluations→work motivation→procrastination at work	−0.19(0.07)	[−0.40, −0.02]
Job resources→work motivation→procrastination at work	−0.15(0.04)	[−0.30, −0.01]
Transformational-transactional leadership→work motivation→procrastination at work	−0.13(0.04)	[−0.25, −0.01]
High job demands (n = 244)		
Core self-evaluations→work motivation→procrastination at work	−0.18(0.01)	[−0.39, −0.03]
Job resources→work motivation→procrastination at work	−0.05(0.01)	[−0.13, −0.01]
Transformational-transactional leadership→work motivation→procrastination at work	−0.01(0.01)	[−0.01, 0.01]

Note. BC 95% CI – Bias-corrected 95% confidence interval.

TLI = 0.90; CFI = 0.95). Based on the fit indices change, the model comparison between the groups with low ($n = 257$) and high ($n = 244$) job demands showed a statistically significant difference ($\Delta\chi^2 = 28.18$; $p < 0.001$; ΔCFI = 0.02, ΔTLI = 0.02). The results showed that job demands moderated the relationship between job resources, transformational–transactional leadership, core self-evaluations, work motivation, and procrastination at work (Figure 3.5).

The Z test, which assumes the equality of direct effects between the low vs. high job demands, revealed statistically significant differences in the path of 'transformational–transactional style ➡ procrastination at work' ($Z = -2.32$; $p < 0.05$). This relationship was statistically significant only when job demands were high. Furthermore, the path of transformational–transactional leadership to work motivation differed significantly between low and high job demand conditions ($Z = 3.02$; $p < 0.01$), such that there were significant positive effects of transformational–transactional leadership on work motivation in low job demands conditions, while in high job demands, this relationship was not significant. These results did not support hypothesis H.1.6. Furthermore, there were significant differences between conditions on the path of work motivation ➡ procrastination at work ($Z = 2.54$, $p < 0.05$), such that this relationship was stronger in low than high job demands conditions. Furthermore, core self-evaluations were associated with work motivation to a greater extent in conditions of high job demands than in low job demands ($Z = -3.36$, $p < 0.01$). The effects of core self-evaluations on procrastination at work ($Z = -0.57$, *ns*), as well as job resources on procrastination and motivation at work ($Z = 0.30$, *ns*; $Z = 1.70$, *ns*; respectively), were significant and did not differ depending on job demands level, thus did not support hypothesis H.1.5.

Multigroup analysis resulted in a distinct pattern of mediation effects moderated by a level of job demands. Under *low job demands*, both work-related and individual factors were directly associated with procrastination at work, as well as indirectly through work motivation. Low core self-evaluations, high job resources, and high transformational–transactional leadership were directly related to high procrastination at work. Work motivation was to be a significant mediator in the relationships of core self-evaluations and job resources with decreased employee procrastination (Figure 3.5.A). In *high job demands* conditions, the pattern of relationships was slightly different. Low core-self-evaluations and high job resources were directly related to high employee procrastination. Although work motivation mediated the effects of core self-evaluations and transformational–transactional leadership, it did not mediate the effects of job resources on procrastination at work (Figure 3.5.B).

Because not all paths in the multigroup analysis were significant, conditional mediation models were estimated separately under conditions of low and high job demands. The model in low job demands conditions yielded an acceptable level-of-fit indices (χ^2/df = 2.19; RMSEA = 0.068; SRMR = 0.037; TLI = 0.93; CFI = 0.97). The alternative model for high job demands was fitted to the data at

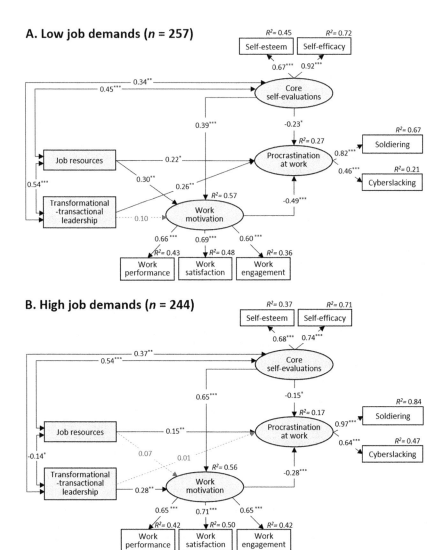

Figure 3.5 A conditional mediation model in low (A) and high (B) job demands conditions tested in Study 1.

Note. $^{*}p < 0.05$, $^{**}p < 0.01$, $^{***}p < 0.001$. Path values are standardized regression coefficients β. Statistically nonsignificant paths are gray.

an acceptable level (χ^2/df = 2.54; RMSEA = 0.080; SRMR = 0.060; TLI = 0.92; CFI = 0.96). As a result, except for the nonsignificant direct effect of core self-evaluations on procrastination at work, the pattern of relationships detected in the multigroup analysis was confirmed.

3.2.1.5 Summary of Study 1

Study 1 investigated the relationships between job demands, job resources, leadership resources, personal resources, and procrastination at work. Furthermore, the study examined the mediating role of work motivation in these relationships.

Direct Effects: In this study, low *core self-evaluations* represented by self-esteem and self-efficacy directly and weakly predicted procrastination at work. This finding aligned with previous empirical research, which found negative associations of self-esteem and self-efficacy with both general and academic procrastination (Flett et al., 1995; Hajloo, 2014; Klassen et al., 2008; Steel, 2007; van Eerde, 2003). Moreover, high *job demands* represented by quantitative demands and negative interpersonal relationships directly and moderately affected procrastination at work. High levels of excessive workload and negative interpersonal relationships in an organization create unfavorable working conditions that may trigger procrastination at work. Engaging in non-work-related, but pleasurable activities like private talks with coworkers (i.e. soldiering) or browsing the Internet for pleasure (i.e. cyberslacking) can alleviate the aversiveness caused by high job demands. This is probably one way by which employees deal with demands on their time and unfavorable work relationships while still maintaining a balanced emotional state. High *job resources* (represented by high control over work, role clarity, positive change, and support from supervisors and colleagues) were associated with high procrastination at work. Probably, employees with high job resources perceive such work environment as permissive of cyberslacking or soldering, believing that these behaviors would not adversely affect their work outcomes. There was also revealed a very weak positive effect of *transformational–transactional leadership* on employee procrastination. This result was skeptically considered in the overall pattern of relationships because it is inconsistent with previous findings (Göncü Köse & Metin, 2018) showing a negative association between transformational leadership and employee procrastination. These low effects require further empirical verification. However, it should be noted that the effects of core self-evaluations, job resources, and transformational–transactional leadership on procrastination at work were statistically significant, but at a relatively low level.

Indirect Effects: Study 1 also revealed the mediating effect of *work motivation* in the relationship of core self-evaluations as personal resources with procrastination at work. Employees with high core self-evaluations, represented by high self-efficacy and self-esteem, are often highly self-motivated to work, providing challenges and self-actualization. It seems that high level of intrinsic motivation can help direct an employee's resources toward completing work-related tasks while reducing their non-work-related activities. Furthermore, high job resources indirectly impacted procrastination at work through work motivation. It implies that a highly resourceful work environment empowers employees, enhancing their work motivation, which is effective in mitigating procrastination at work. Thus, high job resources and high intrinsic work motivation may prevent employees' procrastination behavior. This mechanism represents a regulatory mechanism, which potentially explains how the workplace can reduce procrastination at work. Following the proposition of the JD–R model (Bakker et al., 2023), job resources increase positive outcomes and decrease negative outcomes through the motivational regulatory process. However, transformational–transactional leadership did not affect procrastination at work indirectly through employee work motivation. This effect was unexpected in the light of the metaanalysis of findings showing that constructive leadership relates positively to followers' work engagement (K = 588, ρ =.467) (Pletzer et al., 2024). Transformational and transactional leaders *ex-definitione* influence employee motivation at work, albeit in slightly different ways.

Interaction Effects: The moderated mediation model tested in Study 1, revealed that the interaction between *job resources* and *job demands* did not significantly affect procrastination at work, but the interaction between leadership and job demands had an impact only on work motivation. Thus, different patterns of relationships were revealed in the low and high job demands conditions.

In *low job demands* conditions, procrastination at work was directly determined by low core self-evaluations and high job resources. Additionally, transformational–transactional leadership and job resources reduced work procrastination through high work motivation, but these effects were weak compared to the indirect effect of core self-evaluations. This may indicate that when *job demands* are low, high personal resources, as well as job and leadership resources, stimulate work motivation, which reduces employee tendency to soldiering and cyberslacking. When *job demands* are *high*, core self-evaluations have a direct impact and an indirect impact through work motivation on work procrastination. This result partially supported the *boosting effect* of job demands on the relationship between personal resources and procrastination at work, because personal resources determine work motivation significantly more in high than low job demands conditions. Furthermore, the indirect effect of job resources on procrastination at work was not boosted by high job demands, but rather by low job demands. Overly demanding work can reduce the motivational function of job resources, while low job demands can improve the role of job resources in reducing work procrastination. Additionally, in high job demands situations, transformational–transactional leadership only weakly affected high procrastination at work, but not indirectly through work motivation. Presumably, excessive quantitative and emotional demands cause transformational–transactional leadership to trigger procrastination behavior to protect depleted resources or as a form of retaliation against a highly stressful work environment.

Individual and Work-related Antecedents. The results of Study 1 suggest that core self-evaluations as dispositional factors have a relatively high impact on procrastination at work, while work-related factors have a slightly lower impact. Furthermore, this study supported the assumption that individual characteristics, such as core self-evaluations and work motivation, can serve as protective factors against procrastination at work. Conversely, work-related factors such as job demands, job resources, and leadership can be considered as risk factors that directly trigger or intensify procrastination at work. However, providing adequate job resources and leadership can positively influence employee motivation, ultimately leading to reduced procrastination behaviors.

3.2.2 Trait Procrastination, Job Demands, Job Resources, and Work Stress – Study 2

Study 2 aimed to investigate the associations of trait procrastination, job demands, and job resources with procrastination at work. Job resources were divided into work-related and organization-related resources in the conceptual model (Figure 3.6). *Job demands* were represented by quantitative demands, cognitive demands, emotional demands, hiding emotions, and work pace, as well as job insecurity, role conflict, gossip and slander, conflicts, quarrels, and unpleasant teasing. *Work-related resources* included influence at work, variation, meaning of work, and possibilities for development. *Organization-related resources* contained recognition, justice, and vertical and horizontal trust. Study 2 also examined the mediating role of work stress in the tested relationships, reflecting the energetic process in the JD–R model (Bakker et al., 2023). Furthermore, the study tested the interaction effects of job demands with work-related or organization-related resources in predicting work procrastination. A conceptual model of the tested relationships is presented in Figure 3.6.

The following hypotheses were formulated:

H.2.1. Trait procrastination is directly related to high procrastination at work

H.2.2. Trait procrastination is indirectly related to procrastination at work through work stress

H.2.3. High job demands are indirectly associated with high procrastination at work through work stress

H.2.4. High work-related resources are indirectly associated with low procrastination at work through work stress

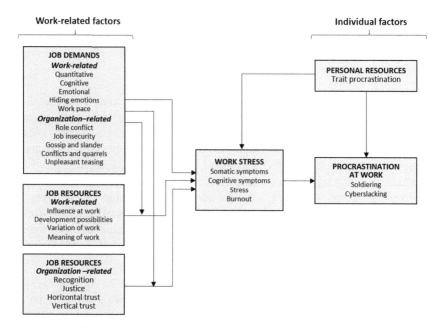

Figure 3.6 A conceptual model of the relationships between the variables tested in Study 2.

H.2.5. High organization-related resources are indirectly associated with low procrastination at work through work stress

H.2.6. The interaction of job demands and work-related resources is indirectly related to procrastination at work through work stress, such that the indirect effect of work-related resources on procrastination at work via work stress is stronger in high than in low job demands conditions

H.2.7. The interaction of job demands and organization-related resources is indirectly associated with procrastination at work through work stress, such that the indirect effect of organization-related resources on procrastination at work via work stress is stronger in high than in low job demands conditions

3.2.2.1 Participants and Procedure

Data collection was conducted online, using the snowball method. A total of 657 adults (336 women and 321 men), aged 24 to 63 years ($M = 32.2$; $SD = 9.8$) participated in the study. They were employed in diverse industries and professions, with an average job tenure of 8.5 ($SD = 9.1$).

To avoid common-method bias (Podsakoff et al., 2003), the study was conducted in two sessions separated by a two-week interval. Job demands, job resources, and trait procrastination were assessed in session 1 and work stress and procrastination at work were measured in session 2. Participants agreed to participate voluntarily and were ensured anonymity.

3.2.2.2 Measures

Procrastination at Work: The PAWS (Metin et al., 2020) was used to assess procrastination at work and its two subdimensions (i.e. soldiering and cyber-slacking). It was described in detail in Section 3.1.1. The internal consistency of the measures was satisfactory and ranged from 0.74 to 0.89.

Job Demands and Resources: The Copenhagen Psychosocial Questionnaire (COPSOQ II subscales) (Pejtersen et al., 2010) was used to assess selected aspects of the workplace, such as *quantitative demands* (e.g. 'Do you have enough time for your work tasks?'), *cognitive demands* (e.g. 'Does your work require you to make difficult decisions?'), *emotional demands* (e.g. 'Do you get emotionally involved in your work?'), *demands for hiding emotions* (e.g. 'Does your work require that you hide your feelings?'), *work pace* (e.g. 'Do you have to work very fast?'), *job insecurity* (e.g. 'Are you worrying about becoming unemployed?'), *role conflict* (e.g. 'Are contradictory demands placed on you at work?'), *unpleasant teasing* (e.g. 'Have you been exposed to unpleasant teasing at your workplace during the last 12 months?'), *conflicts and quarrels* (e.g. 'Have you been involved in quarrels or conflicts at your workplace during the last 12 months?'), *gossip and slander* (e.g. 'Have you been exposed to gossip and slander at your workplace during the last 12 months?'), *influence at work* (e.g. 'Do you have any influence on what you do at work?'), *possibilities for development* (e.g. 'Do you have the possibility of learning new things through your work?'), *variation of work* (e.g. 'Is your work varied?'), *meaning of work* (e.g. 'Is your work meaningful?'), *recognition* (e.g. 'Is your work recognized and appreciated by the management?'), *justice* (e.g. 'Is the work distributed fairly?'), *horizontal trust* (e.g. 'Do the employees in general trust each other?'), and *vertical trust* (e.g. 'Does the management trust the employees to do their work well?'). The participants rated items on two different 5-point Likert-type scales (1 – never, 5 – always; and 1 – to a very small extent, 5 – to a very large extent). The reliability coefficients of the measures in this study ranged from 0.60 to 0.75.

In the tested model, the COPSOQ II dimensions were aggregated into job demands and two types of resources (Berthelsen et al., 2018): (1) *job demands* included demands regarding the overall workload and difficult organizational conditions, such as quantitative, cognitive, emotional demands, demands for hiding emotions, work pace, job insecurity, role conflict, conflicts and quarrels, unpleasant teasing, as well as gossip and slander; (2) *work-related resources*, which refer to the content and organization of work, i.e. influence at work, possibilities for development, variety of work, and meaning of work; and (3) *organization-related resources* represented by recognition, justice, vertical, and horizontal trust, which express social and organizational capital. The three-factor structure of the job characteristics was confirmed in the confirmatory factor analysis, achieving acceptable fit indices to the data (χ^2/df = 3.63; RMSEA = 0.063; SMSR = 0.080; CFI = 0.95; TLI = 0.91). The internal consistency of the factors in this study was satisfactory (0.66–0.79).

Work Stress: To measure stress at work, four subscales from the COPSOQ II (Pejtersen et al., 2010) were used: (1) *somatic symptoms* scale that expresses the frequency of somatic stress symptoms experienced by an employee, such as abdominal pain, headaches, heart palpitations, or muscle pain (e.g. 'How often have you had a headache in the workplace?'), (2) *cognitive symptoms* reflecting the frequency of experiencing problems with memory, concentration, clear thinking, and decision-making at work. (e.g. 'How often have you had problems concentrating?'), (3) *stress* concerning the frequency of experiencing tension, nervousness, and problems with rest at work (e.g. 'How often have you been tense?'), and (4) *burnout,* describing lack of strength, fatigue, and physical and emotional exhaustion at work (e.g. 'How often have you been physically exhausted?'). Participants assessed their stress symptoms in the workplace during the last 4 weeks on a 5-point scale (1 – not at all, 5 – all the time). The internal consistency for the stress measures in this study ranged from 0.67 to 0.81.

Trait Procrastination: To measure trait procrastination, PPS (Steel, 2010) was used (see Section 3.1.3.1). The internal consistency of the scale in this study was high (0.91).

3.2.2.3 Test of Common-Method Variance

To determine whether there was a risk of common-method variance (Podsakoff et al., 2003) in this study, Harman's single-factor test was performed. The confirmatory factor analysis tested a one-factor model that included all measured variables but did not yield satisfactory fit indices (χ^2/df = 9.13; RMSEA = 0.111; SMSR = 0.066; CFI = 0.77; TLI = 0.69). However, a six-factor model was fitted to the data at an acceptable level (χ^2/df = 2.92; RMSEA = 0.054; SMSR = 0.123; CFI = 0.95; TLI = 0.93). Therefore, it can be assumed that the measurement of the variables in this study was not a source of explained variance in the results.

3.2.2.4 Results

Bivariate Correlations: A preliminary analysis of correlations among study variables showed that job demands were significantly correlated with procrastination at work (0.30) and soldiering (0.36), but weakly with cyberslacking (0.16). Analogous relationships occurred between procrastination at work and specific job-related demands (i.e. quantitative, cognitive, emotional demands, demands for hiding emotions, work pace, job insecurity, role conflict, conflicts and quarrels, unpleasant teasing, and gossip and slander). Soldiering was most strongly correlated with quantitative demands, role conflict, job insecurity, unpleasant teasing, conflicts, and quarrels (0.31–0.37), but weakly with cognitive and emotional demands, and work pace. Cyberslacking was significantly and weakly correlated with job insecurity, role conflict, unpleasant teasing, conflicts and quarrels, gossip and slander (0.16–0.23), and did not correlate significantly with job demands related to workload, such as quantitative, cognitive, or emotional demands, demand for hiding emotions, and work pace. No significant relationships were observed between work-related resources, including influence at work, possibilities for development, variation of work, and meaning of work, and the total mean score and dimensions of procrastination at work. Organization-related resources, such as recognition, justice, vertical, and horizontal trust poorly correlated with procrastination at work. Work stress symptoms (somatic symptoms, cognitive symptoms, stress, and burnout) were moderately correlated with soldiering (0.32–0.46) and weakly with cyberslacking. It is worth noting that both job demands were correlated with work-related resources (0.32) and low with organization-related resources (−0.18). General procrastination was strongly correlated with procrastination dimensions and total score (0.55–0.67). Both collinearity and multicollinearity were not a problem in the study, because the highest correlation was below 0.70 (0.67) and the variance inflation factor (VIF = 1.64) scores did not exceed 6 (Tabachnick et al., 2019).

Test of Mediation Model: The tested model included four aggregated observable variables of job demands, work-related resources, organization-related resources, and trait procrastination with work stress as a latent mediating variable in predicting the latent variable of procrastination at work. The initial model tested with all paths between variables and covariances between predictors (Figure 3.7.A) achieved an acceptable fit to the data (χ^2/df = 5.18; RMSEA = 0.080; SMRS = 0.073; TLI = 0.94; CFI = 0.97). The high positive effects of trait procrastination were revealed, but relatively low effects of work-related factors on procrastination at work (Table 3.9). To increase the parsimony of the model, the statistically nonsignificant path 'organization-related resources → work stress' and the paths 'work-related resources → procrastination at work' and 'organization-related resources → procrastination at work' with $\beta < 0.10$ as practically not meaningful, were removed. Moreover, additional constraints suggested by the modification indices were imposed. The final model was very well fitted to the data (χ^2/df = 2.22; RMSEA = 0.043; SMRS = 0.027; TLI = 0.98; CFI = 0.99), explaining 53% of the variance (Figure 3.7.B).

As depicted in Figure 3.7, trait procrastination was directly and strongly related to procrastination at work, supporting hypothesis H.2.1. Job demands and resources also significantly predicted procrastination at work, but at a low level. Using the bootstrapping procedure with 10,000 samples, three significant indirect effects in the model were estimated because their 95% confidence

A. Initial model

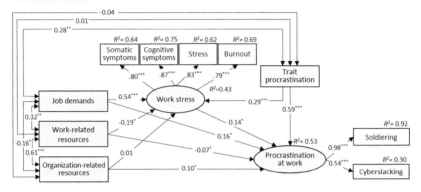

B. Final model

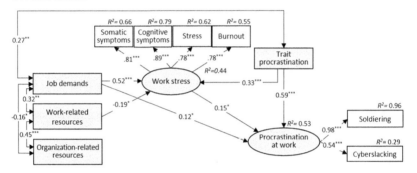

Figure 3.7 Initial (A) and final (B) mediation models tested in Study 2.

Note. $^*p < 0.05$, $^{**}p < 0.01$, $^{***}p < 0.001$. Path values are standardized regression coefficients β. Statistically nonsignificant paths are gray.

intervals did not include 0 (Hayes, 2022). Work stress significantly mediated the relationship between dispositional procrastination and procrastination at work, thus supporting hypothesis H.2.2. Additionally, work stress mediated the associations of job demands and work-related resources with procrastination at work, supporting hypotheses H.2.3 and H.2.4. However, the significant indirect effect of organization-related resources on procrastination at work through work stress was not observed, which did not support hypothesis H.2.5. Highly demanding work was related to elevated work stress, which subsequently led to increased soldiering and cyberslacking as manifestations of procrastination. Conversely, high work-related resources were associated with lower work stress, which then led to low procrastination at work (Table 3.10).

Table 3.9 Direct effects in the initial mediation and moderated mediation models tested in Study 2

Direct path			Mediation model	Moderated mediation model
			β(se)	β(se)
Trait procrastination	→	Work stress	0.29(0.04)***	0.27(0.04)***
Job demands	→	Work stress	0.54(0.04)***	0.52(0.01)***
Work-related resources	→	Work stress	−0.19(0.04)**	−0.19(0.04)**
Organization-related resources	→	Work stress	−0.01(0.04)	−0.01(0.04)
Trait procrastination	→	Procrastination at work	0.59(0.03)***	0.58(0.03)***
Organization-related resources	→	Procrastination at work	0.09(0.03)*	0.09(0.04)*
Work-related resources	→	Procrastination at work	−0.07(0.03)*	−0.07(0.04)*
Job demands	→	Procrastination at work	0.16(0.04)*	0.13(0.04)*
Work stress	→	Procrastination at work	0.14(0.04)*	0.14(0.05)*
Work-related resources x job demands	→	Work stress		0.03(0.05)
Work-related resources x job demands	→	Procrastination at work		0.11(0.04)*
Organization-related resources x job demands	→	Work stress		0.05(0.05)
Organization-related resources x job demands	→	Procrastination at work		0.02(0.03)

Note. * $p < 0.05$, ** $p < 0.01$, *** $p < 0.001$. β − standardized regression coefficient.

Table 3.10 Indirect effects in the empirical models tested in Study 2

Tested model	Effect(se)	BC 95% CI
Mediation model		
Trait procrastination → work stress → procrastination at work	0.04(0.01)	[0.02, 0.07]
Job demands → work stress → procrastination at work	0.08(0.02)	[0.03, 0.13]
Work-related resources → work stress → procrastination at work	-0.03(0.01)	[-0.06, -0.01]
Organization-related resources → work stress → procrastination at work	-0.001(0.01)	[-0.01, 0.01]
Moderated mediation model		
Trait procrastination → work stress → procrastination at work	0.04(0.01)	[0.01, 0.07]
Job demands → work stress → procrastination at work	0.07(0.02)	[0.03, 0.13]
Work-related resources → work stress → procrastination at work	-0.03(0.01)	[-0.05, -0.01]
Organization-related resources → work stress → procrastination at work	-0.002(0.01)	[-0.02, 0.01]
Work-related resources x job demands → work stress → procrastination at work	0.003(0.01)	[-0.008, 0.02]
Organization-related resources x job demands → work stress → procrastination at work	0.007(0.01)	[-0.005, 0.02]
Conditional mediation model		
Low job demands (n = 334)		
Trait procrastination → work stress → procrastination at work	0.001(0.01)	[-0.009, 0.014]
Work-related-resources → work stress → procrastination at work	0.001(0.01)	[-0.001, 0.001]
Organization-related resources → work stress → procrastination at work	0.001(0.01)	[-0.003, 0.003]
High job demands n = 323		
Trait procrastination → work stress → procrastination at work	0.14(0.01)	[0.08, 0.21]
Work-related resources → work stress → procrastination at work	-0.03(0.01)	[-0.07, -0.01]
Organization-related resources → work stress → procrastination at work	0.001(0.01)	[-0.003, 0.004]

Note. BC 95% CI – Bias-corrected 95% confidence interval.

Test of Moderated Mediation Model: The model was then expanded to include the interactions between job demands and work-related resources, and between job demands and organization-related resources. The interactions were represented by the product of standardized scores of both variables. The moderated mediation model with assumed all paths and covariances between predictors produced a good fit to the data (χ^2/df = 4.87; RMSEA = 0.077; SMRS = 0.033; TLI = 0.93; CFI = 0.96), accounting for 56% of the variance in procrastination at work. To enhance the model fit indices, statistically nonsignificant paths and those with the smallest coefficients were removed, and changes in the covariance structure suggested by the modification indices were entered. Thus, the final moderated mediation model achieved a well fit to the data (χ^2/df = 2.47; RMSEA = 0.047; SMRS = 0.027; TLI = 0.97; CFI = 0.98), explaining 55% of the variance in procrastination at work.

The moderated mediation model revealed significant direct and indirect effects (Tables 3.9 and 3.10). Additionally, a significant interaction effect between job demands and work-related resources on procrastination at work and nonsignificant on work stress was observed. The interaction effects between job demands and organization-related resources on stress and procrastination at work were also nonsignificant. This suggests that the effect of predictors on the outcome variable depends on the moderator's level. Therefore, the interaction between work-related resources and job demands was decomposed into conditional models in low and high job demands. Conditions were distinguished according to the median of job demands scores (*Me* = 2.66). Multigroup analysis revealed that the model achieved excellent fit indices of fit (χ^2/df = 1.99; RMSEA = 0.039; SMRS = 0.038; TLI = 0.97; CFI = 0.99) and was significantly in the low vs. high job demands groups ($\Delta\chi^2$ = 14.62; $p < 0.05$), accounted for 35% of the variance in procrastination at work in low job demands and 63% of the variance in high job demands conditions. The Z test, assuming the equality of the path coefficients between groups, revealed significant differences between low vs. high job demands conditions (Figure 3.8.A and B).

The results showed a significant effect of organization-related resources on work stress in low job demands, but not significant in high job demands ($Z = 3.80$, $p < 0.01$). Moreover, organization-related resources nonsignificantly affected procrastination at work regardless of the level of job demands ($Z = 0.72$, *ns*). Trait procrastination was associated with work stress significantly lower in low than high job demands conditions ($Z = -3.07$, $p < 0.05$), while the effect of trait procrastination on procrastination at work did not differ between low vs. high job demands conditions ($Z = 1.30$, *ns*). Work-related resources were significantly associated with procrastination at work in low job demands conditions, while nonsignificantly in high job demands conditions ($Z = -2.56$, $p < 0.05$). Moreover, the effect of work-related resources on work stress did not differ significantly between low and high job demands conditions ($Z = -1.78$, *ns*). Additionally, in high job demand conditions, work stress had a significant

A. Low job demands (*n* = 334)

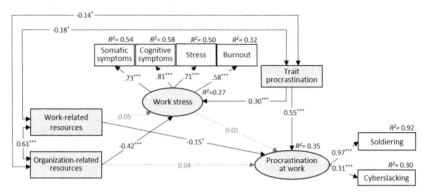

B. High job demands (*n* = 323)

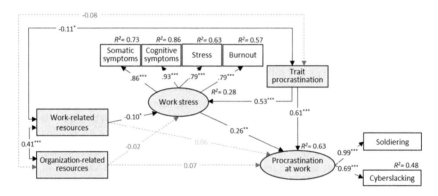

Figure 3.8 A conditional mediation model in low (A) and high (B) job demands conditions tested in Study 2.

Note. $^*p < 0.05$, $^{**}p < 0.01$, $^{***}p < 0.001$. Path values are standardized regression coefficients β. Statistically nonsignificant paths are gray.

effect on procrastination ($Z = -3.25$, $p < 0.01$), but was not significant in low demands conditions. Due to differences in the pattern of relationships between low and high job demands conditions, different models were tested separately. After removing statistically nonsignificant paths, the models showed better fit to the data (low job demand: $\chi2/df = 21.82$; RMSEA = 0.050; SMRS = 0.036; TLI = 0.97; CFI = 0.98; high job demands: $\chi^2/df = 2.03$; RMSEA = 0.057; SMRS = 0.054; TLI = 0.98; CFI = 0.99), confirming relationship patterns revealed in multigroup analysis. Additionally, the significant indirect effect of work-related resources on procrastination through work stress was observed in high job demands, which supported hypothesis H.2.6.

In the *low job demands* conditions, procrastination at work was predicted by high trait procrastination and low work-related resources. Procrastination at work was not determined by organization-related resources and work stress. Therefore, work stress did not mediate the effects of tested individual and work-related factors on procrastination at work. In *high job demands* conditions, the effects of trait procrastination and work-related resources on procrastination at work were significantly mediated by work stress. The indirect effect of organization-related resources on procrastination through work stress was nonsignificant, thus hypothesis H.2.7 was not supported.

3.2.2.5 Summary of Study 2

Study 2 examined the relationships between job demands, work-related resources, organization-related resources, trait procrastination, work stress, and procrastination at work.

Direct Effects: The results indicated that dispositional general procrastination moderately predicted procrastination behavior at work. This supported previous findings that indicate that general procrastination promotes the tendency to procrastinate in professional contexts (Hen & Goroshit, 2018; Hen et al., 2021; Metin et al., 2016, 2018; van Eerde, 2016). Individuals with an high disposition to delay will also be more likely to engage in soldiering or cyberslacking at work. Additionally, predictive effects of work-related factors on procrastination were observed. *Job demands* were weakly associated with high procrastination behavior. Presumably, high job demands represented by various work- and organization-related characteristics may create an unfavorable work environment, ultimately leading to a slight increase in employee procrastination. These findings are in line with prior research indicating that high workloads contribute to the escalation of non-work-related activities (Arshad et al., 2016; Black et al., 2013; Blanchard & Henle, 2008; DeArmond et al., 2014; Metin et al., 2016; Varghese & Barber, 2017). Study 2 found very weak direct effect of *work-related* and *organization-related resources* on employee procrastination. This suggests that influence at work, possibilities for development, variation of work, and meaning of work foster diligent work conduct rather than non-work-related activities. Similarly, previous findings revealed that employee procrastination is reduced in the highly resourceful workplace with high possibilities for development (Metin et al., 2016, 2018), autonomy (Metin et al., 2020), and a sense of purpose and meaning of work (Lonergan & Maher, 2000; Weymann, 1988). A high level of job resources was also found to be associated with reduced levels of cyberslacking at work (Garrett & Danziger, 2008; Jiang et al., 2021; Liberman et al., 2011). Furthermore, organization-related resources, represented by recognition, justice, vertical, and horizontal trust, predicted elevated procrastination at work, although this effect was very weak. Consistent with Study 1, job resources related to social capital create conditions for engaging in non-work-related activities. Employees working in comfortable social environments appeared to be more likely to engage in non-work-related activities such as cyberslacking and soldering. However, these effects were very weak and may be questionable. Therefore, they are not included in the overall summary of results, as they require further verification.

Indirect Effects: Study 2 revealed the mediational role of *work stress* in the relationships between individual and work-related factors and employee procrastination. For example, a general tendency to procrastinate was associated with high stress, which encourages soldiering and cyberslacking behaviors at work. Previous studies also revealed that the general tendency to procrastinate is often accompanied by stress at work. Probably, individuals struggle to regulate aversive stimuli, most likely as a result of self-regulation issues (Steel, 2007).

Furthermore, *work stress* acted as a mediating factor between of job demands and procrastination at work. The implication is that demanding jobs could lead to work-related stress that drains one's resources (Hobfoll, 1989). As a result, people participate in extracurricular activities both online and offline to relieve work-related stress, find relief from work overload, and replenish their exhausted resources. This finding is consistent with meta-analytical research showing that different job demands affect workers' emotional exhaustion, burnout, and strain (Aronsson et al., 2017). Other studies found a direct relationship between stress or exhaustion and employee procrastination (Lavoie & Pychyl, 2001; Roster & Ferrari, 2020; Wan et al., 2014), and cyberloafing in the workplace (Elrehail et al., 2021; Lim & Teo, 2024). There is also empirical evidence suggesting that perceived stress mediates the association between job demands and procrastination (DeArmond et al., 2014; Laybourn et al., 2019) or cyberloafing at work (Bajcar & Babiak, 2020; Elrehail et al., 2021; Koay et al., 2017; Zhou et al., 2021). In this study, work stress mediated the impact of work-related resources on employees procrastination, although this effect is weak. As suggested by other researchers, job resources enable employees to cope with threatening circumstances and protect them against health-impairing consequences. The lack of resources may affect burnout (Hakanen et al., 2008; Schaufeli et al., 2009). Therefore, job resources likely contribute to successful work performance at lower psychological costs, thus reducing work stress and exhaustion (Bakker & Demerouti, 2007). High resources related to job content and work organization (i.e. influence at work, opportunities for development, variety, and meaning of work) may help create a positive work environment that reduces stress and, in turn, reduces procrastination at work.

Interaction Effects: The moderated mediation test revealed a statistically significant interaction effect of job demands and work-related resources on procrastination at work. This suggests that the pattern of observed relationships depends on the job demands level.

In the *low job demands* conditions, high general procrastination affected procrastination, and low work-related resources directly affected procrastination at work, while organization-related resources did not affect procrastination at work. Moreover, work stress had no effect in triggering procrastination at work, therefore, it did not mediate any effects of individual or work-related factors in job demands conditions. It can be assumed that a low workload creates a conducive working environment where general procrastination is the strongest predictor of high employee procrastination with the weak impact of low work-related resources. In the *high job demands* conditions, only trait procrastination was strongly related to employee procrastination directly and indirectly through perceived work stress. Furthermore, high work-related resources such as possibilities for development, influence at work, variation, and meaning of work may slightly mitigate stress and thereby reduce procrastination at work. Thus, employees may engage in these behaviors to cope with overload and to recover personal resources necessary to maintain or increase performance at work. Taking small breaks from work to engage in cyberloafing may help employees cope with stress caused by high job overload (Tandon et al., 2022; Varghese & Barber, 2017; Wu et al., 2020). However, this effect was weak and did not provide sufficient evidence for these relationships. It is important to note that a weak statistical effect does not necessarily mean that the observed difference or relationship is not meaningful. It suggests that the evidence is not strong enough to confidently conclude the existence of these relationships. The results of this study correspond to the proposition of the JD–R model (Bakker et al., 2023) that job demands in interaction with work-related resources influence organizational outcomes through exhaustion or strain as energetic regulatory process. Thus, this study expanded the knowledge about energetic mechanisms clarifying the impact of individual and job characteristics on procrastination at work.

Individual and Work-related Antecedents: In summary, general procrastination as an individual characteristic had a direct and indirect impact on procrastination at work through work stress. Among contextual factors, job demands strongly and work-related resources relatively weakly determined procrastination at work indirectly through work stress. Organization-related resources were not significantly affected by procrastination at work. Therefore, trait procrastination and job demands may be considered as risk factors to induce and increase employee soldiering and cyberslacking, whereas work-related resources can be seen as protective factors against increasing stress and procrastination at the workplace. Simultaneously, work stress may potentially explain the enhancing effect of general procrastination and job demands on procrastination at work and the diminishing impact of work-related resources on procrastination at work.

3.2.3 *Personality Traits, Job Demands, Job Resources, Destructive Leadership, and Work Engagement – Study 3*

Study 3 aimed to investigate effects of job demands, job resources, destructive leadership, as well as positive and negative personality traits on employee procrastination. The mediating role of work motivation in these relationships was also examined. Based on the JD–R theory (Bakker et al., 2023), a conceptual model was proposed, which offers a plausible motivational mechanism explaining the associations between individual and work-related factors and procrastination at work (Figure 3.9).

Job demands included quantitative demands, cognitive demands, emotional demands, role conflict, and job insecurity. Job resources were related to job content and work organization, such as influence at work, possibilities for development, variation, and meaning of work. Destructive leadership was represented by abusive supervision (Tepper, 2000). Personal resources were represented by personality traits, including emotional stability and conscientiousness (McCrae & Costa, 2003), as well as narcissism, Machiavellianism, and psychopathy (Paulhus & Williams, 2002). Previous research has shown that these personality traits are important predictors of general procrastination (Lyons & Rice, 2014; Markiewicz & Dziewulska, 2018; Meng et al., 2024; Sanecka, 2022; Steel, 2007; Steel et al., 2001; van Eerde, 2004). The configuration of low levels of positive and high levels of dark traits was conceptualized as a negative personality profile. Work motivation as a mediating variable was represented by work engagement. The following hypotheses were formulated:

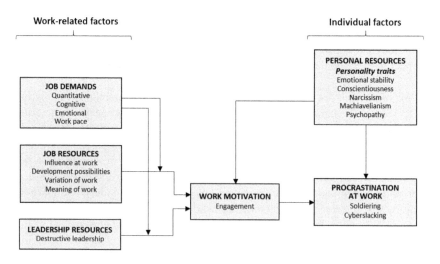

Figure 3.9 A conceptual model of the relationships between the variables tested in Study 3.

H.3.1. The negative profile of personality traits is directly related to high procrastination at work

H.3.2. The negative profile of personality traits is indirectly associated with high procrastination at work through work engagement

H.3.3. High job resources are indirectly associated with low procrastination at work through work engagement

H.3.4. Destructive leadership is indirectly associated with high procrastination at work through work engagement

H.3.5. The interaction of job demands and job resources is indirectly associated with procrastination at work through work engagement, such that the indirect effect of job resources on procrastination at work via work engagement is stronger in high than low job demands conditions

H.3.6. The interaction of job demands and destructive leadership is indirectly associated with procrastination at work through work engagement such that the indirect effect of destructive leadership on procrastination at work via work engagement is stronger in high than low job demand conditions

3.2.3.1 Participants and Procedure

Study 3 was conducted online in two four-week interval sessions. A total of 463 adults from a variety of occupations (207 women, 256 men), aged between 24 and 69 years ($M = 36.7$; $SD = 9.2$) with a mean job tenure of 13.4 years ($SD = 8.2$) participated in both sessions. In the first session, participants assessed job demands and resources, destructive leadership, and procrastination at work, and 4 weeks later rated work engagement and personality traits.

3.2.3.2 Measures

Procrastination at Work: As in previous studies, PAWS was used to measure procrastination at work and its dimensions of soldiering and cyberslacking (Metin et al., 2020), described in detail in Section 3.1.2. The internal consistency of this measure in Study 3 achieved a high level (soldiering: 87; cyberslacking: 0.80; total average score: 0.89).

Job Demands and Resources: Job demands and resources were measured using the COPSOQ II subscales (Pejtersen et al., 2010), aggregated into broader and consistent constructs of job demands and resources (Berthelsen et al., 2018). *Job demands* included quantitative demands, cognitive demands, emotional demands, and work pace. *Job resources* included influence at work, possibilities for development, variation, and meaning of work. The internal consistency of the measure in this study ranged from 0.69 to 0.80. The confirmatory factor analysis confirmed a two-factor solution of job demands and resources, achieving good fit indices ($\chi^2/df = 5.20$; RMSEA = 0.049; SRMR = 0.013; CFI = 0.99; TLI

= 0.99). The internal consistency for aggregated job demands and job resources was high (0.84 and 0.87, respectively).

Destructive Leadership: Destructive leader behavior was measured using the 15-item abusive supervision scale (Tepper, 2000) assessing psychological and verbal violence toward subordinates (e.g. 'My boss humiliates me in front of others'.). Respondents rated items on a 7-point scale (1 – never, 7 – always). The internal consistency of the measure in this study was high (0.90).

Work Engagement: The UWES-9 (Schaufeli et al., 2006) was used to assess work engagement. It was described in detail in Section 3.2.1.2. The internal consistency of the measure was high (0.89).

Personality Traits: Two subscales of the Ten Items Personality Inventory (TIPI) (Gosling et al., 2003) were used to assess emotional stability and conscientiousness. Respondents rated items on a 7-point scale (1 – strongly disagree, 7 – strongly agree). The internal consistency of the measure in this study was 0.71 and 0.75, respectively. Moreover, the 12-item Dark Triad Dirty Dozen (DTDD) questionnaire (Jonason & Webster, 2010) was used to assess narcissism (e.g. 'I tend to want others to admire me'.), Machiavellianism (e.g. 'I have used deceit or lied to get my way'.), and psychopathy (e.g. 'I tend to lack remorse'.). Participants rated items on a 5-point scale (1 – strongly disagree, 5 – strongly agree). In this study, the internal consistency of the measures was high (0.75–0.82).

All variables were included in the analysis as total average scores.

3.2.3.3 Test of Common-Method Variance

Due to the simultaneous measurement of multiple variables, Harman's single-factor test was performed to rule out common-method variance (Podsakoff et al., 2003). In the confirmatory factor analysis, a one-factor model was tested that included all measured variables. The model turned out not well fitted to the data (χ^2/df = 5.39; RMSEA = 0.097; SRMR = 0.131; CFI = 0.80; TLI = 0.76). The six-factor model, including separate work engagement, procrastination at work, job resources, job demands, personality traits, and destructive leadership, was confirmed and obtained acceptable fit indices (χ^2/df = 3.80; RMSEA = 0.074; SMRS = 0.067; TLI = 0.92; CFI = 0.97). Thus, it seems that common-method bias can be ruled out in this study.

3.2.3.4 Results

Bivariate Correlations: Preliminary analysis showed that the dimensions of procrastination at work (i.e. soldiering and cyberslacking) were moderately intercorrelated (0.47). Both dimensions and the total score of procrastination at work were weakly correlated with job demands (−0.15–0.12) and job resources (−0.20–0.01), as well as with work engagement (−0.13 to −0.20). Procrastination at work had a slightly higher correlation with personality traits. The strongest associations were observed for psychopathy and Machiavellianism with soldiering (0.39–0.41), while the weakest associations were with cyberslacking (0.24–0.32). Narcissism was positively correlated with both dimensions of procrastination at work (0.21–0.25). Similarly, emotional stability and conscientiousness were moderately correlated with soldiering (−0.23 and 0.25, respectively), but slightly less with cyberslacking (−0.09, −0.15). Moreover, destructive leadership was quite weakly correlated with soldiering (0.16) and nonsignificantly with cyberslacking (−0.01). The highest correlation between the variables analyzed was below 0.70 (0.61) and the variance inflation factor scores did not exceed 6 (VIF = 1.35), neither collinearity nor multicollinearity was a problem in the study (Tabachnick et al., 2019).

Test of Mediation Model: The tested mediation model included job demands, job resources, and destructive leadership as observable variables, with a latent outcome variable of procrastination at work represented by soldiering and cyberslacking. Personality traits were entered into the model as a latent variable including emotional stability, conscientiousness, narcissism, Machiavellianism, and psychopathy, whereas work engagement as a potential mediator in the relationship between the above predictors and procrastination at work. Using the SEM with the maximum likelihood method, the initial model with all assumed paths and covariances between predictors was estimated (Figure 3.10.A). However, it did not achieve an acceptable level of fit indices (χ^2/df = 4.51; RMSEA = 0.087; SMRS = 0.078; TLI = 0.83; CFI = 0.90). For the sake of parsimony of the model, statistically nonsignificant paths and those with the smallest values ($\beta < 0.10$) were removed. Additionally, constraints suggested by the modification indices were imposed. Thus, the final model (Figure 3.10.B) was a better fit to the data (χ^2/df = 3.43; RMSEA = 0.072; SMRS = 0.077; TLI = 0.90; CFI = 0.92). The negative profile of personality traits had a strong direct effect on work procrastination, supporting hypothesis H.3.1. Job demands, job resources, and destructive leadership were nonsignificantly related to procrastination at work (see Table 3.11 and Figure 3.10.B).

To estimate the indirect effects in the model, an error-corrected bootstrapping procedure with 10,000 samples was employed (Hayes, 2022). As a result, only one significant indirect effect of job resources on procrastination at work through work engagement was observed (see Table 3.12). High job resources were associated with work engagement, which in turn negatively affected procrastination behavior at work, supporting hypothesis H.3.3. These findings indicate that when work is enriched with high levels of autonomy, variation, meaning, and opportunities for development, it improves work engagement. This, in turn,

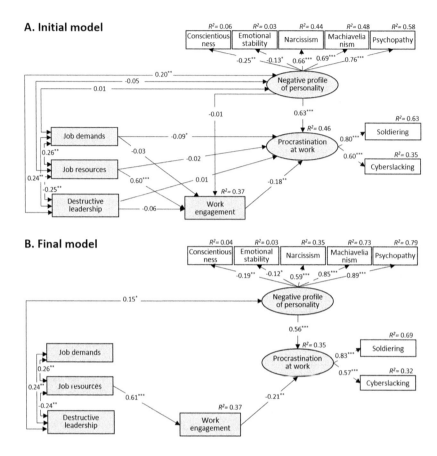

Figure 3.10 Initial (A) and final (B) mediation models tested in Study 3.

Note. $^*p < 0.05$, $^{**}p < 0.01$, $^{***}p < 0.001$. Path values are standardized regression coefficients β. Statistically nonsignificant paths are gray.

leads to a reduction in procrastination at work. The indirect effects of personality traits, job demands, and destructive leadership were statistically nonsignificant, not supporting hypotheses H.3.2 and H.3.4.

Test of Moderated Mediation Model: Next, the moderating role of job demands in the relationship between job resources, destructive leadership, work engagement, and procrastination at work was examined. In the tested model, two interactions of job resources with job demands and destructive leadership with job demands were introduced. As in studies 1 and 2, the interactions were represented in the model as the product of standardized scores of the interacting

Table 3.11 Direct effects in the initial mediation and moderated mediation models tested in Study 3

Direct path		Mediation model β(se)	Moderated mediation model β(se)
Negative personality traits	→ Work engagement	−0.01(0.04)	−0.01(0.05)
Job demands	→ Work engagement	−0.03(0.04)	−0.03(0.04)
Job resources	→ Work engagement	0.60(0.04)***	0.59(0.04)***
Destructive leadership	→ Work engagement	−0.06(0.06)	−0.11(0.04)*
Negative personality traits	→ Procrastination at work	0.62(0.06)***	0.63(0.07)***
Job demands	→ Procrastination at work	−0.09(0.06)*	−0.09(0.06)*
Destructive leadership	→ Procrastination at work	0.01(0.06)	0.005(0.07)
Work engagement	→ Procrastination at work	−0.18(0.08)**	−0.18(0.08)**
Job resources x job demands	→ Work engagement		−0.004(0.04)
Job resources x job demands	→ Procrastination at work		0.06(0.06)
Destructive leadership x job demands	→ Work engagement		0.10(0.07)*
Destructive leadership x job demands	→ Procrastination at work		0.002(0.06)

Note. $^*p < 0.05$, $^{**}p < 0.01$, $^{***}p < 0.001$. β – standardized regression coefficient.

Table 3.12 Indirect effects in the empirical models tested in Study 3

Tested model	Effect(se)	BC 95% CI
Mediation model		
Negative profile of personality→work engagement→procrastination at work	0.003(0.01)	[−0.02, 0.02]
Job demands→work engagement→procrastination at work	0.005(0.01)	[−0.01, 0.03]
Job resources→work engagement→procrastination at work	−0.11(0.05)	[−0.21, −0.02]
Destructive leadership→work engagement→procrastination at work	0.01(0.01)	[−0.01, 0.04]
Moderated mediation model		
Negative profile of personality→work engagement→procrastination at work	0.002(0.009)	[−0.02, 0.02]
Job demands→work engagement→procrastination at work	0.005(0.01)	[−0.01, 0.03]
Job resources→work engagement→procrastination at work	−0.10(0.05)	[−0.21, −0.01]
Destructive leadership→work engagement→procrastination at work	0.02(0.01)	[0.002, 0.05]
Job resources x job demands→work engagement→procrastination at work	0.001(0.01)	[−0.02, 0.02]
Destructive leadership x job demands→work engagement→procrastination at work	−0.02(0.02)	[−0.06, 0.002]
Conditional mediation model		
Low job demands (n = 243)		
Negative profile of personality→work engagement→procrastination at work	−0.003(0.02)	[−0.03, 0.03]
Job resources→work engagement→procrastination at work	−0.17(0.06)	[−0.32, −0.07]
Destructive leadership→work engagement→procrastination at work	0.04(0.02)	[0.01, 0.07]
High job demands (n = 220)		
Negative profile of personality→work engagement→procrastination at work	−0.001(0.01)	[−0.01, 0.01]
Job resources→work engagement→procrastination at work	−0.04(0.06)	[−0.18, 0.06]
Destructive leadership→work engagement→procrastination at work	0.003(0.01)	[−0.01, 0.04]

Note. BC 95% CI – Bias-corrected 95% confidence interval.

variables. The moderated mediation model with assumed paths from all predictors to the outcome variable and covariances between predictors was not fitted to the data at an acceptable level (χ^2/df = 6.98; RMSEA = 0.114; SMRS = 0.069; TLI = 0.71; CFI = 0.82). To improve the model fit indices, all nonsignificant paths and covariances between variables were removed and additional constraints suggested by the modification indices were imposed (see Table 3.11). Finally, the model achieved a good fit to the data (χ^2/df = 3.08; RMSEA = 0.067; SMRS = 0.073; TLI = 0.90; CFI = 0.93), which explained 44% of the variance in procrastination.

The pattern of relationships revealed in the mediation model (Table 3.11) was also supported in the moderated mediation model. Furthermore, the interaction effect of job resources and job demands turned out to be statistically not significant on both work engagement and procrastination. The second effect of interaction between destructive leadership and job demands was nonsignificant in explaining procrastination at work, but significant in predicting the mediator of work engagement (Table 3.12). The significant interaction effect of destructive leadership with job demands on work engagement was decomposed into conditional mediation models in groups with low job demands (n = 243) and high job demands (n = 220). The groups were distinguished based on the median value (Me = 3.08) in the job demands scores. Multigroup analysis showed that the estimated model was able to fit the data well (χ^2/df = 2.86; RMSEA = 0.064; SMRS = 0.066; TLI = 0.88; CFI = 0.90) but did not reveal statistically significant differences between the mediation models in conditions of low vs. high job demands ($\Delta\chi^2$ = 7.91; ns). Despite this, the Z test, assuming the equality of the path coefficients between groups, showed significant differences between low vs. high job demands conditions, in two paths 'work engagement ➞ procrastination at work' (Z = 2.05, p < 0.05) and 'destructive leadership ➞ work engagement' (Z = 1.93, p < 0.10).

Due to nonsignificant differences in conditional models between the groups with low and high job demands, separate models for each condition were not estimated. After eliminating nonsignificant paths, both models showed an acceptable fit to the data (low job demands: χ^2/df = 2.167; RMSEA = 0.069; SMSR = 0.063; CFI = 0.95; TLI = 0.91; high job demands condition: χ^2/df = 2.08; RMSEA = 0.070; SMRS = 0.078; TLI = 0.89; CFI = 0.91), supporting the results of the multigroup analysis. In *low job demands* conditions, high job resources strongly, whereas low destructive leadership very weakly are associated with procrastination at work indirectly through work engagement (Figure 3.11.A). In *high job demands* conditions, the indirect effect of job resources on procrastination at work through work engagement was not observed (Figure 3.11.B). In both conditions, the negative profile of personality traits strongly affected procrastination at work. These results did not support hypotheses H.3.5 and H.3.6.

A. Low job demands (*n* = 243)

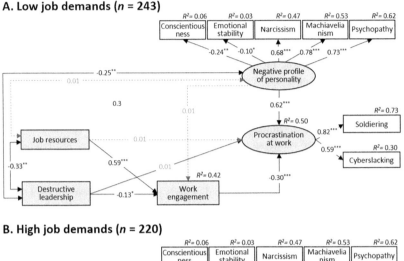

B. High job demands (*n* = 220)

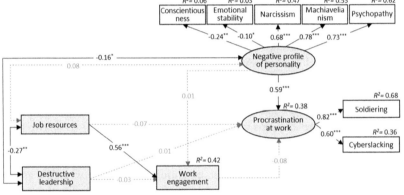

Figure 3.11 A conditional mediation model in low (A) and high (B) job demands
          conditions tested in Study 3.

Note. $^{*}p < 0.05$, $^{**}p < 0.01$, $^{***}p < 0.001$. Path values are standardized regression coefficients β.
Statistically nonsignificant paths are gray.

3.2.3.5 Summary of Study 3

Compared to studies 1 and 2, Study 3 analyzed a distinct combination of individual
and work-related factors in the prediction of procrastination at work. These factors
included personality traits, job demands, job resources, destructive leadership, and
the mediating role of work engagement in the relationships under examination.

Direct Effects: This study revealed that the *negative profile of personality traits*
had a strong direct impact on employee procrastination. A *negative personality*

profile, represented by low emotional stability, low conscientiousness, high narcissism, high Machiavellianism, and high psychopathy, determined a high tendency to engage in soldiering and cyberslacking at work. These results are consistent with research on personality factors contributing to procrastination at work (Pearlman-Avnion & Zibenberg, 2018; Singh & Bala, 2020), as well as dispositional procrastination (Steel, 2007; van Eerde, 2004). Individuals with low emotional stability are more susceptible to experiencing high stress, negative emotions, and impulsive behavior, which may lead to a greater tendency to irrational delay in work. Furthermore, low conscientiousness, represented by distraction, poor organization, and low achievement motivation, was also associated with dispositional procrastination (Steel, 2007; van Eerde, 2004). Similarly, low emotional stability and conscientiousness were associated with cyberslacking at work (Lim & Teo, 2024; Mercado, Giordano, et al., 2017; Tandon et al., 2022). The role of dark personality traits in explaining procrastination at work is not yet well established. Previous studies have demonstrated an association of dark personality traits with deviant work behavior (Ellen et al., 2021), as well as problematic Internet use (Kircaburun & Griffiths, 2018; Moor & Anderson, 2019), and cyberslacking in the workplace (Lowe-Calverley & Grieve, 2017; Tandon et al., 2022). Individuals with elevated levels of dark personality traits may engage in excessive online activities, such as cyberslacking, due to their negative motives. The presented results demonstrate the association of negative personality traits with procrastination at work, especially with its online component. Effects of work-related factors on procrastination behavior at work were very weak or statistically nonsignificant. *Job demands* represented by quantitative demands, cognitive demands, emotional demands, role conflict, and job insecurity, affected low procrastination at work very weak. *Job resources* (i.e., influence at work, possibilities for development, variation, and meaning of work) and *destructive leadership* did not significantly predict procrastination at work. The weak or nonsignificant direct effects of *job demands*, *job resources*, and *destructive leadership* correspond to the JD–R proposition that job demands and resources do not directly influence work outcomes but rather indirectly through exhaustion and stress or motivation (Bakker & Demerouti, 2014). Therefore, they were not included in the general discussion of the results.

Indirect Effects: This study also revealed a significant mediating role of *work engagement* in the relationships between job resources and procrastination at work. Job resources were closely related to work engagement, which leads to low employee procrastination. It seems that a resourceful work environment promotes employee work engagement, which reduces the tendency to spend too much time on non-work-related activities. This strong indirect effect can be represent the motivational regulatory mechanism underlying the effect of job resources on procrastination at work. According to the JD–R postutates (Bakker & Demerouti, 2014), resources influence work-related behavior and outcomes through work motivation. To summarize, the mediational effects of work engagement can suggest a motivational mechanism explaining the impact of job resources on procrastination at work. The same motivational mechanism may justify how destructive leadership improves procrastination at work by decreasing work engagement, but this study did not provide sufficient support for this effect. Therefore, it requires further examination.

Interaction Effects: The study revealed a significant effect of the interaction between destructive leadership and job demands on work engagement. However, the overall mediation models did not differ significantly between the low and high job demand conditions. It implies that the revealed pattern of relationships becomes relatively independent of job demands level, except for two paths from destructive leadership to work motivation and from work motivation to procrastination at work.

In *low job demands* conditions, a negative profile of personality traits directly and strongly predicted procrastination at work. Additionally, high job resources strongly impacted procrastination indirectly through high work engagement. Destructive leadership affected increased employee procrastination through decreased work engagement, but this effect was very weak. One can assume that low job demands create unstimulating work conditions prompting employees to engage personal resources in non-work-related activities offline (Metin et al., 2016; Mosquera et al., 2022) and online activities (Mercado, Giordano, et al., 2017; Pindek et al., 2018; Sümer & Büttner, 2022). Low job demands may create favorable conditions, in which high job resources and low destructive leadership enhance work engagement, thus decreasing soldiering and cyberslacking. In *high job demands* conditions, the negative profile of personality traits also strongly directly determined procrastination at work. Job resources directly predicted high work engagement. Due to the nonsignificant impact of work engagement on procrastination, indirect effect of job resources on procrastination at work through high work engagement was not observed. Destructive leadership was nonsignificantly related to employees procrastination. This result supported the JD–R hypothesis about the boosting effect of job demands on the relationship between job resources and work engagement but did not determine procrastination as a negative work-related outcome (Bakker et al., 2023). The independence of procrastination from work engagement in high workload conditions can suggest that employees engage in non-work-related activities for various reasons beyond low work engagement. Perhaps there are additional mechanisms explaining the variance in job procrastination beyond the motivational process pathway as defined by JD–R. The energetic process may serve as a complementary mechanism, explaining the effects of job demands and resources on work-related outcomes through exhaustion, strain, and burnout. However, these results provided insufficient evidence to support this hypothesis.

Individual and Work-Related Antecedents: Summarizing, this study provided evidence that both personal and work-related factors predicted procrastination at work. A negative personality profile was revealed to be a strong direct antecedent of work procrastination. Among work-related factors, low job demands had a weak direct effect on procrastination behavior at work. Moreover, job resources are strongly indirectly associated with procrastination through increased work engagement, while destructive leadership contributes to high procrastination by diminishing work engagement only in low job demands. Taking into account this pattern of relationships, negative personality traits and destructive leadership can be viewed as risk factors for inducing or enhancing employee procrastination. Conversely, job demands and job resources may serve as protective factors against procrastination at work. However, the weak effects of destructive leadership and job demands require further investigation.

3.2.4 Personality Traits, Core Self-Evaluations, Job Demands, Job Resources, Leadership Resources, Work Stress, and Work Motivation – Study 4

This study aimed to investigate the parallel mediational role of work stress and work motivation in the associations between individual and work-related factors, and procrastination at work. The proposed conceptual model (Figure 3.12) included various factors, including personality traits and core self-evaluations as personal resources, as well as aggregated job demands, job resources, and

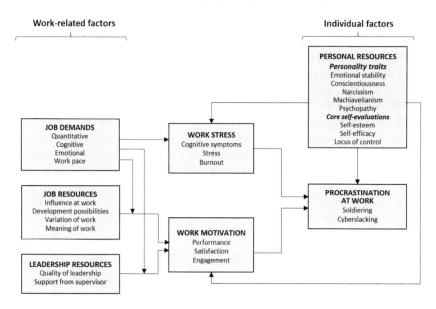

Figure 3.12 A conceptual model of the relationships between the variables tested in Study 4.

leadership resources to predict procrastination at work. Job demands were represented by quantitative demands, cognitive demands, emotional demands, and work pace. Job resources related to job content and work organization have included influence at work, possibilities for development, variation, and meaning of work, whereas leadership resources – support from supervisors and quality of leadership. Following the JD–R theory (Bakker et al., 2023), it was assumed that job resources and leadership resources in interaction with job demands are associated with elevated work stress, which consequently would result in increased procrastination at work. Simultaneously, job resources interacting with job demands can increase work motivation, thereby reducing procrastination at work. Therefore, the following hypotheses were formulated:

H.4.1. Core self-evaluations are directly related to low procrastination at work

H.4.2. The negative profile of personality traits is directly related to high procrastination at work

H.4.3. Core self-evaluations are indirectly associated with low procrastination at work parallelly through stress and work motivation

H.4.4. The negative profile of personality traits is indirectly associated with low procrastination at work parallelly through stress and work motivation

H.4.5. High job demands are indirectly related to high procrastination at work through work stress

H.4.6. High job resources are indirectly associated with low procrastination at work through work motivation

H.4.7. High leadership resources are indirectly associated with low procrastination at work through work motivation

H.4.8. The interaction of job demands and job resources is indirectly related to procrastination at work through work motivation, such that the indirect effect of job resources on procrastination at work via work motivation is stronger in high- than low job demands conditions

H.4.9. The interaction of job demands and leadership resources is indirectly related to procrastination at work through work motivation, such that the indirect effect of leadership resources on procrastination at work via work motivation is stronger in high than low job demands conditions

The pattern of hypothesized relationships between individual and work-related factors and procrastination at work is presented in Figure 3.12.

3.2.4.1 Participants and Procedure

This study was conducted in two two-week online interval sessions. A total of 470 individuals participated, consisting of 261 women and 209 men aged between 19 and 76 years ($M = 36.9$; $SD = 10.4$). Participants were employed in various professions and industries with an average job tenure of 12.0 years ($SD = 10.7$). To reduce the common method variance (Podsakoff et al., 2003), the following variables were measured during the first session: procrastination at work, job demands, leadership resources, emotional stability, conscientiousness, work performance, and job satisfaction. In the second session, job resources, work stress, work engagement, negative personality traits, and core self-evaluations were assessed.

3.2.4.2 Measures

Procrastination at Work: Procrastination at work was measured using the PAWS (Metin et al., 2016, 2020) described in detail in Section 3.1.2. The reliability of the *soldiering* and *cyberslacking* dimensions in this study was high (0.83 and 0.87, respectively).

Job Demands and Job Resources: The COPSOQ II (Pejtersen et al., 2010) was used to measure *job demands* (i.e. quantitative demands, cognitive demands, emotional demands, and work pace) and job resources (including influence at work, possibilities for development, variation of work, and meaning of work). Section 3.2.2.2 presents a description of the COPSOQ II subscales. Leadership resources. This study measured also two aspects of leadership resources, such as support from supervisors, and quality of leadership. *Support from supervisors* represents the frequency of help and support when difficulties arise (e.g. 'How often do you get help and support from your nearest superior?'). Items were rated on a 5-point scale (1 – very little, 5 – to a very large extent). *Quality of leadership* expresses the subordinate's evaluation of supervisor leadership effects (e.g. 'Your immediate superior gives high priority to job planning'.), assessed on a 5-point scale (1 – never, 5 – always). In this study, the internal consistency of the measures was satisfactory (0.68–0.83).

The confirmatory factor analysis confirmed the three second-order factor solution, achieving a good fit to the data (χ^2/df = 3.55; RMSEA = 0.074; SMSR = 0.046; CFI = 0.92; TLI = 0.96). Thus, in the study the aggregated job demands, job resources, and leadership resources, were analyzed as different types of job characteristics.

Work Stress: Stress in the workplace was measured using the COPSOQ II subscales (Pejtersen et al., 2010): cognitive symptoms, stress, and burnout, which were described at length in Section 3.2.2.2. The reliability of the scales in this study was satisfactory (0.75–0.89).

Motivation to Work: The same tool as in Study 1 was used to measure work motivation, which is represented by work engagement, work performance, and work satisfaction. A detailed description of motivation to work is presented in Section 3.2.1.2.

Personal Resources: Personal resources were represented by positive and nega-tive personality traits and core self-evaluations.

(1) *Personality Traits*: As in Study 3, emotional stability and conscientious-ness were measured using the TIPI (Gosling et al., 2003), while narcissism, Machiavellianism, and psychopathy were measured using the DTDD (Jonason & Webster, 2010), respectively (described in Section 3.2.3.2). The internal consistency of these measures was satisfactory and ranged from 0.74 to 0.82.
(2) *Core Self-evaluations:* The Core Self-Evaluations Scale (CSES) (Judge et al., 2002) was used to measure three three-item dimensions of self-efficacy, self-esteem, and locus of control.

Self-esteem subscale refers to an approval of oneself and the degree to which one sees oneself as capable, significant, successful, and worthy (e.g. 'Overall, I am satisfied with myself'.).
Self-efficacy subscale expresses general belief about effective handling of dif-ficult situations and obstacles (e.g. 'I complete tasks successfully'.), and the locus of control subscale measures the belief in one's ability to control one's environment (e.g. 'I determine what will happen in my life'.). Items were assessed on a 5-point scale (1 – strongly disagree, 5 – strongly agree). The internal consistency of the subscales in this study was high (0.81–0.83).

3.2.4.3 Test of Common Method Variance

To avoid the common method variance arising from the simultaneous measure-ment of multiple variables (Podsakoff et al., 2003), the study was conducted in two sessions. Each session was designed to measure variables that did not overlap in meaning with other variables in that session. Nevertheless, to check whether the measurement could have been a source of an error, Harman's single-factor test was performed. The 1-factor model including all measured variables was estimated but did not fit satisfactory to the data (χ^2/df = 6.72; RMSEA = 0.110; SMSR = 0.084; CFI = 0.75; TLI = 0.69). In the next step, a 9-factor model achieved acceptable fit indices (χ^2/df = 2.49; RMSEA = 0.056; SMSR = 0.051; CFI = 0.94; TLI = 0.91).

3.2.4.4 Results

Bivariate Correlations: The analysis showed that there is a low or very low cor-relation between personality traits and self-evaluations with soldiering (−0.18 to −0.28) but nonsignificantly with cyberslacking. Dark personality traits were correlated with procrastination dimensions and the total score (0.18–0.24), while conscientiousness was stronger (−0.24 to −0.42) and emotional stabil-ity weaker (−0.08 to −0.19). Additionally, low job demands dimensions (i.e.

cognitive, emotional demands, and pace) were negatively associated (−0.12 to −0.21), while quantitative demands were positively associated with procrastination at work dimensions (0.11–0.21). Among the dimensions of job resources, development opportunities and the meaning of work were negatively related to work procrastination and its dimensions (−0.11 to −0.23), while the influence and variation at work did not show any correlation with procrastination at work. Similarly, leadership quality and managerial support were very weakly correlated with employee procrastination dimensions or not at all (−0.03 to −0.11). The highest correlation was found between work procrastination and work stress (0.14–0.48) and work motivation (−0.09 to −0.41). Both collinearity and multicollinearity were not a problem in the study, because the highest correlation was below 0.70 (0.63) and the variance inflation factor (VIF = 1.59) scores did not exceed 6 (Tabachnick et al., 2019).

Test of Mediation Model: In the next step, a mediation model of relationships among dispositional predictors (i.e. personality traits, and core self-evaluations) and work-related predictors (i.e. job demands, job resources, leadership resources) and procrastination at work mediated by work stress and work motivation was examined. Job demands, job resources, and leadership resources (as observable variables), personality traits and core self-evaluations (as latent variables), work stress and work motivation (as latent mediating variables), as well as procrastination at work (as latent outcome variable) encompassing soldiering and cyberslacking, were entered into the model.

The initial model was estimated with assumed all paths between the variables analyzed and covariances between the predictors (Figure 3.13.A), achieving acceptable fit indices (χ^2/df = 3.67; RMSEA = 0.075; SMRS = 0.076; TLI = 0.90; CFI = 0.93). To increase the parsimony of the model, in the *post hoc* modifications nonsignificant paths were removed and constraints suggested by the modification indices were imposed (Figure 4.14.B). As a result, the final model was better fitted to the data (χ^2/df = 2.87; RMSEA = 0.063; SMRS = 0.066; TLI = 0.90; CFI = 0.93). Finally, the model explained 59% of the variance in procrastination at work (Figure 3.13.B).

The model revealed a high direct effect of core self-evaluations and negative profile of personality traits on procrastination at work. Thus, hypotheses H.4.1 and H.4.2 were supported. Moreover, job demands and job resources were weakly related to procrastination at work, while the effect of leadership resources was statistically nonsignificant (Table 3.13).

Using the bootstrapping procedure with error correction on 10,000 samples (Hayes, 2022), the significant indirect effects of individual and work-related factors were revealed (Table 3.14). Core self-evaluations had parallel indirect effects on procrastination at work through work stress and motivation, supporting hypothesis H.4.3. However, the relationship between personality traits and procrastination was mediated by work stress but not by work motivation.

A. Initial model

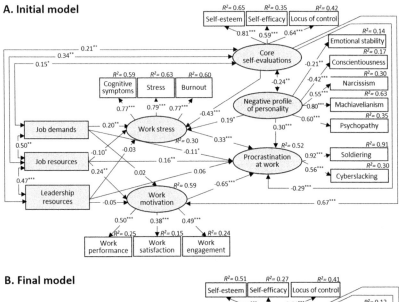

B. Final model

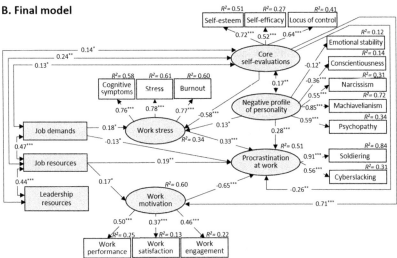

Figure 3.13 Initial (A) and final (B) mediation models tested in Study 4.

Note. $^*p < 0.05$, $^{**}p < 0.01$, $^{***}p < 0.001$. Path values are the standardized regression coefficients β. Statistically nonsignificant paths are gray.

Thus, hypothesis H.4.4 was partially supported. Furthermore, significant indirect effects of job demands and resources were observed in the tested model. Specifically, high job demands were related to high work stress, leading to high procrastination at work, which supported hypothesis H.4.5. Moreover, the

Table 3.13 Direct effects in the initial mediation and moderated mediation models tested in Study 4

Direct path		Mediation model	Moderated mediation model
		β(se)	β(se)
Core self-evaluations	→ Work stress	−0.43(0.08)***	−0.38(0.09)***
Negative profile of personality	→ Work stress	0.19(0.06)*	0.23(0.09)*
Job demands	→ Work stress	0.20(0.05)*	0.21(0.05)*
Job resources	→ Work stress	−0.10(0.05)*	−0.11(0.05)*
Leadership resources	→ Work stress	−0.03(0.07)	−0.03(0.07)
Core self-evaluations	→ Work motivation	0.67(0.02)***	0.65(0.02)***
Negative profile of personality	→ Work motivation	0.01(0.01)	0.04(0.01)
Job demands	→ Work motivation	0.02(0.01)	0.003(0.01)
Job resources	→ Work motivation	0.24(0.01)**	0.23(0.01)**
Leadership resources	→ Work motivation	−0.05(0.01)	−0.04(0.01)*
Core self-evaluations	→ Procrastination at work	0.29(0.09)***	0.36(0.09)***
Negative profile of personality	→ Procrastination at work	0.30(0.03)***	0.40(0.05)***
Job demands	→ Procrastination at work	−0.11(0.02)*	−0.10(0.02)*
Job resources	→ Procrastination at work	0.16(0.03)*	−0.14(0.03)*
Leadership resources	→ Procrastination at work	0.06(0.03)	0.04(0.03)
Work stress	→ Procrastination at work	0.33(0.03)***	0.31(0.03)***
Work motivation	→ Procrastination at work	−0.65(0.68)***	−0.63(0.65)***
Job resources x job demands	→ Work stress		0.02(0.09)
Job resources x job demands	→ Work motivation		0.05(0.02)
Job resources x job demands	→ Procrastination at work		−0.01(0.04)
Leadership resources x job demands	→ Work stress		−0.03(0.09)
Leadership resources x job demands	→ Work motivation		−0.17(0.02)*
Leadership resources x job demands	→ Procrastination at work		−0.02(0.05)

Note. *p < 0.05, ***p < 0.001. β – standardized regression coefficient.

Table 3.14 Indirect effects in the empirical models tested in Study 4

Tested model	Effect(se)	BC 95% CI
Mediation model		
Core self-evaluations→work stress→procrastination at work	-0.14(0.04)	[-0.27, -0.02]
Core self-evaluations→work motivation→procrastination at work	-0.44(0.10)	[-0.96, -0.07]
Personality traits→work stress→procrastination at work	0.06(0.01)	[0.01, 0.12]
Personality traits→work motivation→procrastination at work	-0.001(0.01)	[-0.03, 0.02]
Job demands→work stress →procrastination at work	0.07(0.03)	[0.02, 0.15]
Job demands→work motivation→procrastination at work	-0.01(0.01)	[-0.09, 0.04]
Job resources→ work stress→procrastination at work	-0.03(0.02)	[-0.06, 0.001]
Job resources→work motivation→procrastination at work	-0.16(0.07)	[-0.30, -0.02]
Leadership resources→work stress procrastination at work	-0.02(0.01)	[-0.03, 0.02]
Leadership resources→work motivation→ procrastination at work	0.03(0.02)	[-0.04, 0.05]
Moderated mediation model		
Core self-evaluations→work stress→procrastination at work	-0.11(0.04)	[-0.21, -0.02]
Core self-evaluations→work motivation→procrastination at work	-0.41(0.10)	[-0.60, -0.01]
Personality traits→ work stress→procrastination at work	0.07(0.02)	[0.02, 0.14]
Personality traits→ work motivation→procrastination at work	0.02(0.01)	[-0.04, 0.05]
Job demands→work stress→procrastination at work	0.06(0.03)	[0.01, 0.09]
Job demands→work motivation→procrastination at work	-0.01(0.06)	[-0.03, 0.04]
Job resources→work stress→procrastination at work	-0.03(0.03)	[-0.05, 0.003]
Job resources→ work motivation→procrastination at work	-0.14(0.07)	[-0.29, -0.02]
Leadership resources→work stress→procrastination at work	-0.01(0.04)	[-0.03, 0.02]
Leadership resources→work motivation→procrastination at work	0.02(0.07)	[-0.01, 0.04]
Job resources x job demands→work stress→procrastination at work	0.01(0.02)	[-0.02, 0.03]
Job resources x job demands→work motivation→procrastination at work	-0.03(0.02)	[-0.001, 0.05]
Leadership resources x job demands →work stress→procrastination at work	-0.01(0.08)	[-0.03, 0.02]
Leadership resources x job demands→work motivation→procrastination at work	0.11(0.05)	[0.03, 0.21]

(Continued)

Table 3.14 (Continued)

Tested model	Effect(se)	BC 95% CI
Conditional mediation model		
Low job demands (n = 231)		
Core self-evaluations→work stress→procrastination at work	−0.15(0.06)	[−0.25, −0.04]
Core self-evaluations→work motivation→procrastination at work	−0.18(0.06)	[−0.36, −0.04]
Personality traits→ work stress→procrastination at work	0.04(0.02)	[0.006, 0.08]
Personality traits→ work motivation→procrastination at work	−0.003(0.02)	[−0.03, 0.02]
Job resources→work stress procrastination at work	0.003(0.01)	[−0.02, 0.03]
Job resources→work motivation→ procrastination at work	−0.04(0.01)	[−0.07, −0.01]
Leadership resources→work stress→procrastination at work	0.03(0.04)	[−0.01, 0.05]
Leadership resources→work motivation→procrastination at work	−0.02(0.01)	[−0.04, 0.01]
High job demands (n = 239)		
Core self-evaluations→work stress→procrastination at work	−0.26(0.07)	[−0.45, −0.07]
Core self-evaluations→work motivation→procrastination at work	−0.34(0.10)	[−0.48, −0.08]
Personality traits→ work stress→procrastination at work	0.02(0.01)	[−0.02, 0.04]
Personality traits→ work motivation→procrastination at work	0.11(0.05)	[0.01, 0.23]
Job resources→work stress→procrastination at work	0.02(0.02)	[−0.01, 0.03]
Job resources→work motivation→procrastination at work	−0.08(0.04)	[−0.14, −0.02]
Leadership resources→work stress→procrastination at work	0.02(0.03)	[−0.02, 0.04]
Leadership resources→work motivation→procrastination at work	−0.10(0.04)	[0.02, 0.18]

Note. BC 95% CI – Bias-corrected 95% confidence interval.

indirect effects of job resources on work procrastination through work motivation were significant, supporting hypothesis H.4.6. However, the relationship between leadership resources and procrastination at work was not mediated by work stress and work motivation, thereby hypothesis H.4.7 was not confirmed.

Test of Moderated Mediation Model. In the next step, a moderated mediation model was examined. Two interactions between job demands and job resources and between job demands and leadership resources were entered into the model. Interactions were represented as the product for standardized scores of both variables. The model with assumed all paths and covariances between variables did not achieve an acceptable fit to the data (χ^2/df =4.34; RMSEA = 0.084; SMRS = 0.08; TLI = 0.73; CFI = 0.81). When nonsignificant paths were removed, the final moderated mediation model was better fitted to the data (χ^2/df = 2.67; RMSEA = 0.052; SMRS = 0.057; TLI = 0.90; CFI = 0.92), explaining 60% of the variance in procrastination at work. The moderated mediation model supported the pattern of relationships revealed in the mediation model (Table 3.14). The effects of the interaction between job demands and job resources were nonsignificant on mediators of work stress and work motivation, as well as on procrastination at work (outcome). Although the interaction between job demands and leadership resources had a nonsignificant effect on work stress and procrastination at work, there was a significant one on work motivation. Additionally, the interaction effect between leadership resources and job demands was associated with procrastination at work indirectly through work motivation (Table 3.15). This suggests that the effect of leadership resources on the level of work motivation may be conditional and depends on the level of job demands.

Therefore, the significant interaction effect between leadership resources and job demands on work motivation was decomposed into conditional effects for low ($n = 231$) and high ($n = 239$) job demands conditions, extracted based on the median score ($Me = 12.08$). Multigroup analysis revealed that the conditional mediation model achieved an excellent fit to the data (χ^2/df = 2.07; RMSEA = 0.042; SMRS = 0.048; TLI = 0.90; CFI = 0.92) but did not differ significantly between low and high job demands conditions ($\Delta\chi^2$/df = 12.17, *ns*). However, the Z test assuming the equality of path coefficients between groups revealed a statistically significant weak difference between low and high job demands for the paths of core self-evaluations on work stress ($Z = 2.56$, $p < 0.05$) and procrastination at work ($Z = -3.86$, $p < 0.01$); work motivation on procrastination at work ($Z = 2.72$, $p < 0.05$), as well as negative personality traits and leadership resources on motivation to work ($Z = -3.11$, $p < 0.01$; $Z = -3.45$, $p < 0.01$, respectively), but not significant differences for the effects of negative personality traits, job and leadership resources on work stress ($Z = 1.01$, *ns*; $Z = 0.41$, *ns*; $Z = 1.72$, *ns*, respectively), as well as on procrastination at work ($Z = -0.41$, *ns*; $Z = 0.23$, *ns*; $Z = -0.78$, *ns*, respectively). There were also nonsignificant differences between the conditions of low vs. high job demands in the effects of job resources and core self-evaluations (Z = -0.41, *ns*; Z = -1.30, *ns,* respectively) on work motivation, as well as work stress (Z = -1.07, *ns*) on procrastination.

In both *low* and *high job demands* conditions, a negative profile of personality traits was directly and strongly related to procrastination at work. Core self-evaluations were also strongly related to procrastination at work directly and indirectly through high work motivation and low work stress. Additionally, a relatively weak indirect effect of job resources on procrastination through work motivation was observed (Figure 3.14.A). In *low job demands* conditions, the effect of core self-evaluations on procrastination was lower than in high job demands. In *high job demands* conditions, leadership resources had a weak indirect effect on procrastination at work through work motivation, such that leadership resources led to reducing procrastination through enhancing work motivation (Figure 3.14.B). These results did not support hypothesis H.4.8 but supported hypothesis H.4.9. Due to nonsignificant differences in the conditional mediation model revealed in the multigroup analysis, separate models in the conditions of low and high job demands were not estimated.

3.2.4.5 Summary of Study 4

Similarly to studies 1, 2, and 3, Study 4 examined the impact of individual and work-related factors of job demands and leadership resources on procrastination at work parallely through work stress and work motivation.

Direct Effects: The results of this study demonstrated the important role of individual characteristics in predicting procrastination at work. Personality traits and core self-evaluations were directly associated with procrastination at work. A *negative profile of personality traits*, including low emotional stability, low conscientiousness, high narcissism, high Machiavellianism, and high psychopathy, promoted a high tendency to procrastinate behavior at work. These results are consistent with the findings of Study 3 and with previous research on the effects of conscientiousness and emotional stability in predicting procrastination at work (Pearlman-Avnion & Zibenberg, 2018; Singh & Bala, 2020) and cyberslacking (Lim & Teo, 2024; Mercado, Giordano, et al., 2017; Tandon et al., 2022). Dark personality traits are associated with problematic, unethical, and antisocial behavior (Ellen et al., 2021) and cyberloafing at work (Lowe-Calverley & Grieve, 2017). However, so far, there are no findings on associations between dark traits and procrastination at work. The results of Study 4 may suggest that people exhibiting elevated dark personality traits tend to engage in excessive non-work-related activities. Study 4 revealed the important role of *core self-evaluations* in explaining procrastination at work. According to previous findings, core self-evaluations as a stable meta-trait is associated with job performance and job satisfaction, but also with job stress or health problems (Judge et al., 2012). In this study, core self-evaluations represented by high self-esteem,

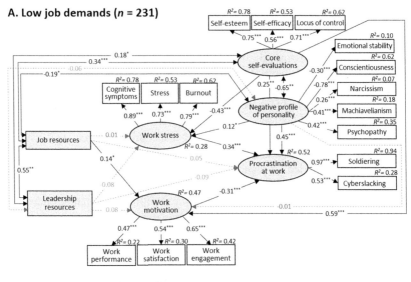

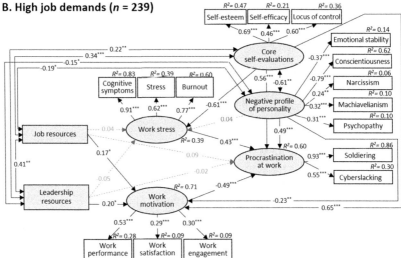

Figure 3.14 A conditional mediation model in low (A) and high (B) job demands conditions tested in Study 4.

Note. $^*p < 0.05$, $^{**}p < 0.01$, $^{***}p < 0.001$. Path values are standardized regression coefficients β. Statistically nonsignificant paths are gray.

high self-efficacy, and internal locus of control determined low procrastination at work. Research on the relationship between core self-evaluations and procrastination or cyberslacking at work is lacking. However, there are findings supporting relationships between procrastination at work and components of core self-evaluation, i.e. self-esteem, self-efficacy (Pearlman-Avnion & Zibenberg, 2018; Singh & Bala, 2020), and locus of control (Khoshouei, 2017; Lonergan & Maher, 2000). Other studies also showed that all components of core self-evaluations can be associated with non-work-related computing (Blanchard & Henle, 2008; Chen et al., 2011). Additionally, low *job demands*, including quantitative, cognitive, emotional demands, work pace, and role conflict, have contributed to increased employee procrastination. Although this effect was weak, it is consistent with prior research indicating that unstimulating work can lead to boredom and subsequently to engaging in soldiering and cyberslacking behaviors at work (Metin et al., 2016). Employees insufficiently stimulated at work likely have less physical and cognitive energy, and motivation to complete work and perform at a higher level. Consequently, they tend to seek frequent work breaks or more enjoyable activities during work hours (Elpidorou, 2018; Metin et al., 2016; Reijseger et al., 2013), or engage in online activities (Mercado, Giordano, et al., 2017; Tandon et al., 2022). Similar to the results of Study 1, high job resources (represented by influence at work, possibilities for development, variation of work, and meaning of work) were weakly related to high procrastination at work. This finding contradicts the assumptions of the JD–R model (Bakker et al., 2023), which posits that job resources enhance positive and diminish negative organizational behavior. However, the high availability of various job resources related to job content and work organization seems to create favorable work conditions that promote employees' procrastination possibly due to the belief that their work is clear, under their control, and rich in organizational support.

Indirect Effects: The study results revealed that work stress and work motivation are mediators of the relationships between individual characteristics, work-related factors, and procrastination at work. Core self-evaluations affected procrastination at work parallelly through *work stress* and *work motivation*. Specifically, high core self-evaluations can simultaneously reduce stress and enhance work motivation, which in turn can lead to lower procrastination at work. These effects may represent two parallel self-regulation mechanisms (through work stress and work motivation) in explaining procrastination at work. This corresponds to findings on the impact of core self-evaluations on different motivations and different levels of self-regulation resources, influencing procrastination. Individuals with low core self-evaluation tend to have less approach motivation and more avoidance motivation, which depletes self-regulatory resources, leading to greater work avoidance and lower work outcomes compared to approach motivation (Ferris et al., 2011). Employees with low core self-evaluations have also inadequate regulatory resources, and therefore often engage in non-work-related activities such as soldering or cyberslacking. Furthermore, the relationship between the negative profile of personality traits and procrastination at work was amplified by high work stress. This finding corresponds with a high tendency to stress determined by personality traits, such as low emotional stability and conscientiousness.

Furthermore, the indirect effects of *work stress* and *work motivation* were observed in the relationship between work-related factors and procrastination at work. Specifically, work stress mediated the relationship between job demands and procrastination at work, while work motivation mediated the relationship between job resources and procrastination at work. Although these effects were weak, they supported the JD–R model propositions (Bakker et al., 2023) that job demands affect organizational outcomes through high strain, exhaustion, or burnout, while job resources, through work engagement or motivation. The identified relationships suggest two parallel mechanisms that clarify the procrastination at work, analogously to the regulatory processes (i.e. energetic and motivational) posited in the JD–R model. The indirect effect of 'job demands → work stress → procrastination at work' alludes to an energetic process, suggesting that high job demands generate increased physical and mental costs and encourage the exhaustion of psychological resources. This can lead to the conservation of employees' resources in different ways, like engaging in various non-work-related activities. Leadership resources did not affect procrastination by decreasing work stress. This not corresponds with the results of the meta-analysis (Pletzer et al., 2024) suggesting that constructive leadership related to low burnout. The indirect effect of 'job resources → work motivation → procrastination at work' corresponds to the motivational process, in which high job resources entail enhancing work engagement and subsequently decreasing the tendency to engage in non-work-related activities offline or/and online. However, an indirect effect of leadership resources on procrastination at work through work motivation has not been confirmed. According to previous research, it was assumed that high leadership resources can influence subordinates' motivation to work, which reduces soldiering and cyberslacking at work. The dominant trend in existing research suggests that constructive leadership decreases procrastination at work (Göncü Köse & Metin, 2018; Singh & Singh, 2015; Zhu et al., 2021; Zoghbi-Manrique-de-Lara et al., 2020), while destructive leadership increases the risk of soldiering (He et al., 2021) and cyberslacking (Agarwal & Avey, 2020; Koay et al., 2022; Lim et al., 2021). The role of leadership resources in predicting employee procrastination appears to be more complex and requires further exploration.

To summarize, the indirect effects of job demands and resources may suggest parallel processes (energetic and motivational), potentially explaining procrastination at work. The energetic process could serve as a plausible mechanism to increase procrastination at work through work stress processes, while the underlying motivational process clarifies the decline in procrastination at work by work motivation. This study sheds light on these mechanisms, although the revealed effects were weak and need further investigation.

Interaction Effects: In this study, significant interaction effects of job demands and leadership resources on work motivation were observed. However, the conditional mediation models did not significantly differ depending on the level of job demands.

In both conditions of *low* vs. *high job demands*, individual factors represented by negative personality traits and low core self-evaluations were strongly and directly related to high procrastination at work. The relationship between the negative personality profile and procrastination at work was also amplified by high stress. Additionally, the effect of core self-evaluations on employee procrastination was mediated parallelly by work stress and motivation. Among work-related factors, job resources weakly impacted the reduction of procrastination at work indirectly through high work motivation both in low and high job demands conditions. In low *job demands* conditions, the relationship between the negative personality profile and procrastination at work was mediated by high stress. In *low job demands* conditions, additional indirect effect of the negative personality profile, on procrastination at work through work stress, whereas in high *job demands* conditions through work motivation was observed. When work is underloaded, the negative profile of personality traits indirectly increases procrastination at work through increased employees' strain. In *high job demands* negative personality traits also increase procrastination behavior by decreased work motivation. At the same time, in the case of overloaded work high availability of job resources and supportive leader behaviors slightly diminish employee work motivation and subsequently enhance procrastination behavior.

In conclusion, employee procrastination was strongly determined by individual characteristics, such as negative personality traits and core self-evaluations. Furthermore, core self-evaluations may reduce procrastination at work by activating work motivation and simultaneously alleviating work stress. Also, the high availability of job resources may enhance work motivation and then diminish employee procrastination. Procrastination may also be increased by the negative profile of personality, although differently in low vs. high job demands. Leadership resources, which indirectly affects procrastination through high work motivation, especially when the work environment is highly demanding. The results of this study only partially support the boosting effects of job demands for the relationship between job resources and work engagement, postulated in the JD–R model (Bakker & Demerouti, 2007; Bakker et al., 2007). Job demands weakly improve the impact of job resources on work motivation and, subsequently, on lower employee procrastination.

Individual and Work-Related Antecedents: Summarizing results of Study 4, individual factors play an important role in predicting procrastination at work. The negative profile of personality traits directly determines procrastination, while low core self-evaluations contribute to a high tendency to soldiering and cyberslacking at work indirectly through reducing work stress and enhancing work motivation. Work-related factors, such as job demands and job resources affected employees' procrastination behavior much weaker than individual characteristics, whereas leadership resources did not significantly relate with employees' procrastination. Nevertheless, it is important to acknowledge that situational factors play an important role in explaining procrastination at work. Job demands indirectly increased procrastination at work through elevated work stress, whereas job resources, indirectly weakened procrastination at work through high work motivation. Additionally, job demands moderated only the indirect impact of negative personality traits and leadership resources on lowering procrastination behavior through enhanced work motivation. These effects were observed only under high job demands conditions. In low job demands, indirect effect of personality traits on procrastination via high work stress was observed. From a different perspective, Study 4 supported that negative personality traits can be a risk factor for procrastination in the workplace. Conversely, core self-evaluations as well as job resources and leadership resources are the protective factors, which indirectly mitigate procrastination through work stress reduction or work motivation improvement. Leadership resources may play a role as a risk factor, especially in high job demands conditions.

3.2.5 Job Demands, Job Resources, Leadership Resources, Work Stress, and Work Motivation – Study 5

To obtain a more comprehensive understanding of work procrastination, it is important to identify factors that account for within-person fluctuations in work procrastination (van Eerde & Venus, 2018). As research results suggest, a substantial part of the variance in procrastination is explained by fluctuations in procrastination over time (Kühnel et al., 2016; Prem et al., 2018; van Eerde & Venus, 2018). Therefore, Study 5 aimed to investigate the weekly variation of procrastination behavior at work (at the within-person level) and its work-related predictors (at the between-person level). Specifically, there was investigated whether job demands, job resources, leadership resources, and their interactions predicted the weekly variation in procrastination behavior represented by soldiering and cyberslacking at work. In addition, the mediating effects of work stress and work motivation, which would explain the associations between work-related factors and weekly procrastination behaviors at work, were also examined in this study. Using behavioral measures of soldiering and cyberslacking ensures a more accurate and more objective assessment of procrastination at work. As previous research suggested, high job demands have been found to induce employee burnout, which can result in a variety of deviant work behaviors (Schaufeli et al., 2009). Excessive workloads have the potential to deplete human resources, which are essential to achieve high-quality work output. This implies that the association between job demands and procrastination behavior can be explained by work stress. Conversely, high job resources can lessen dysfunctional organizational behavior by raising worker's motivation. Thus, the relationship between high job resources and decreased employee procrastination may be mediated by work motivation. Work-related factors included job demands, job resources, and leadership resources. Work stress and work motivation were considered as mediating variables. Work stress was represented by cognitive stress, psychological stress, and burnout. Work motivation was represented by work performance, work satisfaction, and work engagement. The following hypotheses were formulated:

H.5.1. High job resources are indirectly associated with low weekly procrastination behavior at work through work motivation

H.5.2. High leadership resources are indirectly associated with low weekly procrastination at work through work motivation

H.5.3. High job demands are indirectly associated with high weekly procrastination at work through work stress

H.5.4. The interaction of job demands and job resources is indirectly associated with weekly procrastination at work through work motivation, such that the indirect effect of high job resources on weekly procrastination at work is stronger in high than low job demands conditions

H.5.5. The interaction of job demands and leadership resources is indirectly associated with weekly procrastination at work (through work motivation), the indirect effect of leadership resources on weekly procrastination at work is stronger in high than low job demands conditions

The pattern of assumed relationships is presented in Figure 3.15.

3.2.5.1 Participants and Procedure

Data collection was performed using the snowball method through the researcher's network. A total of 503 employees from various professions and industries participated in Study 5, comprising 285 women and 218 men. The participants' ages ranged from 19 to 76 years ($M = 37.9$; $SD = 10.1$), and their average tenure was 15.2 years ($SD = 10.9$). The analysis included 389 participants, consisting of 221 women and 168 men, with ages 19 to 75 years ($M = 38.5$; $SD = 10.3$) and an average job tenure of 16.3 years ($SD = 11.5$).

At the between-person level, job demands and resources, procrastination at work, work stress, and work motivation variables were measured. At the

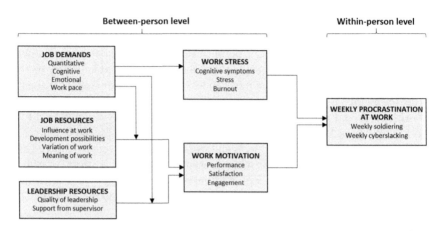

Figure 3.15 A conceptual model of the relationships between the variables tested in Study 5.

within-person level, weekly procrastination behaviors were assessed. Data collection was performed in five sessions with 1-week intervals, in which participants assessed their procrastination behaviors at work during the last week. The weekly data took a hierarchical form, with up to five weekly observations nested within each of the 389 participants. In the first session, job demands, job and leadership resources, work stress, and work motivation were assessed. In the second session, stress, job, and leadership resources were measured.

3.2.5.2 Weekly Level Measures

Weekly Procrastination Behavior at Work: To measure procrastination behavior at work, a questionnaire with 12 behavioral indicators referring to soldiering and cyberslacking in the workplace was developed. Soldiering subscale included six items representing behavior of task postponing at work (e.g. 'Last week, I put off meetings with my client or someone outside the company for no reason'.). Cyberslacking subscale consisted of six behaviors related to non-work-related online activities at work (e.g. 'Last week, I sent and received private e-mails on the job'.). All items were rated on a 7-point scale (1 – not at all, 7 – a few times a day). The internal consistency of both dimensions in this study was satisfactory (0.75–0.86).

3.2.5.3 Person-Level Measures

(1) *Job Demands*: In this study, the COPSOQ II (Pejtersen et al., 2010) was used to measure job demands including quantitative demands, cognitive demands, emotional demands, and work pace. The internal consistency of these subscales in this study was high (0.74–0.89).

(2) *Job resources*: To assess job resources, the influence at work, possibilities for development, variation, and meaning of work subscales from the COPSOQ II were used. The reliability of subscales was acceptable (0.77–0.86).
(3) *Leadership Resources*: Two subscales of social support from supervisors and quality of leadership were used to measure leadership resources. The internal consistency of these subscales in this study was high (0.74–0.89).

All subscales are described in detail in Section 3.2.4.2. Similar to previous studies, the confirmatory factor analysis confirmed the three second-order factor solution and achieved a good fit to the data (χ^2/df = 3.55; RMSEA = 0.074; SMSR = 0.046; CFI = 0.92; TLI = 0.96).

Work Stress: Stress at work was measured using three subscales of the COPSOQ II (Pejtersen et al., 2010): cognitive symptoms, stress, and burnout, which were described in Section 3.2.2.2. In this study, the internal consistency of the work stress subscale was very high (0.90–0.93).

Work Motivation: Work motivation was measured as work performance, work satisfaction, and work engagement in the same way as in Study 1 (see Section 3.2.1.2).

3.2.5.4 Results

To examine hypothesized relationships, the direct, indirect, and interactive effects of job demands, job resources, and leadership resources on weekly changes in procrastination behavior at work.

Within-Person-Level Analysis: First, this investigation considered whether the dependent variables differed from week to week using HLM. Within-subject correlations were calculated for weekly measures of procrastination dimensions and ranged from 0.46 to 0.65 for soldiering and from 0.36 to 0.72 for cyberslacking. The intraclass correlation for the week-level variable was calculated. The ICC for procrastination at work was 0.66 when taking into account the interaction between measurements. The ICC was 0.56 for soldiering and 0.63 for cyberslacking. This indicates a moderate consistency of procrastination behaviors at time points within a person.

Between-Subject Correlations: Procrastination behavior showed a low to moderate correlation between job resources (−0.12 to −0.22), work engagement (−0.15 to −0.27), work performance (−0.16 to −0.27), stress (0.09–0.17), cognitive stress symptoms (0.17–0.31) with soldiering, cyberslacking, and a total score of procrastination at work. Low or nonsignificant correlations were also observed between job demands (0.05 to −0.20), burnout (0.05–0.17), work satisfaction

(−0.01 to −0.13), and weekly measures of overall procrastination and its dimensions. The highest correlation was below 0.70 (0.66) and the variance inflation factor scores (VIF = 1.37) did not exceed 6, neither collinearity nor multicollinearity was a problem in the study (Tabachnick et al., 2019).

Test of Mixed Linear Model: To test the hypotheses, the nested moderated mediation model was estimated using structural equation analysis with the maximum likelihood estimation method in MPlus. In the first step, job demands, job resources, and leadership resources as predictors and weekly procrastination at work (outcome variable) were entered into the model. Work stress and work motivation were included as mediators. Work stress was operationalized as a latent variable consisting of cognitive stress, burnout, and tension, while work motivation was a latent variable consisting of work engagement, satisfaction, and performance. The outcome variable was operationalized as soldiering and cyberslacking measured at the within-subject level (correlated), while the remaining variables were measured at the between-subject level. In the second step, the interaction between job resources and job demands, as well as the interaction between leadership resources and job demands were added to the model, assuming that they could impact stress, motivation, and procrastination at work. In step 1, the model had acceptable fit indices (χ^2/df = 4.28, RMSEA = 0.039, CFI = 0.93, TLI = 0.88, SRMR for within part = 0.001, SRMR for between part = 0.053). The direct effects of job demands, job resources, and leadership resources on the weekly procrastination behaviors were statistically nonsignificant. However, job resources strongly, and leadership resources marginally significantly were related to work motivation (Table 3.15 and Figure 3.16). Work stress was predicted by high job demands and low job resources. Furthermore, work motivation was strongly related to weekly procrastination behaviors, while work stress was not related to procrastination behaviors, supporting hypothesis H.5.1.

In the tested model, a significant mediating effect of work motivation was observed in the relationships between job resources and weekly procrastination behaviors (effect = −0.26, *boot se* = 0.10, BC 95% CI [−0.46, −0.06]), supporting hypothesis H.5.1. Work motivation did not mediate the relationships between leadership and procrastination behaviors (hypothesis H.5.2 not supported). Additionally, work stress did not mediate any relationship between job demands and procrastination behaviors at work (hypothesis H.5.3. not supported). The results did not reveal the mediational effects of work stress in the associations between leadership and job resources with weekly procrastination behaviors. Additionally, no mediational effect of work motivation was observed for relationships between leadership resources, job demands, and procrastination behaviors. In Step 2, the interactions of 'job resources x job demands' and 'leadership resources x job demands' were added to the path model that was investigated in Step 1, assuming that they might impact the mediators (stress and motivation) as

Table 3.15 Direct effects in the mixed linear model tested in Study 5

Direct path		Mediation model β(se)	Moderated mediation model β(se)
Job demands	→ Weekly procrastination	−0.05(.11)	0.03(.10)
Job resources	→ Weekly procrastination	−0.06(0.11)	−0.08(0.11)
Leadership resources	→ Weekly procrastination	0.06(0.07)	0.07(0.06)
Work stress	→ Weekly procrastination	0.06(0.07)	0.06(0.07)
Work motivation	→ Weekly procrastination	−0.51(0.11)***	−0.51(0.10)***
Job demands x job resources	→ Weekly procrastination		0.13(0.06)*
Job demands x leadership resources	→ Weekly procrastination		−0.04(0.06)
Job demands	→ Work motivation	−0.01(0.07)	−0.01(0.06)
Job resources	→ Work motivation	0.60(0.07)***	0.60(0.06)***
Leadership resources	→ Work motivation	0.11(0.06)†	0.11(0.06)†
Job demands x job resources	→ Work motivation		−0.10(0.06)†
Job demands x leadership resources	→ Work motivation		0.01(0.06)
Job demands	→ Work stress	0.23(0.06)***	0.23(0.06)***
Job resources	→ Work stress	0.30(0.06)***	−0.29(0.06)***
Leadership resources	→ Work stress	−0.05(0.06)	−0.06(0.05)
Job demands x job resources	→ Work stress		0.04(0.05)
Job demands x leadership resources	→ Work stress		−0.06(0.06)

Note. †$p < 0.05$, *$p < 0.05$, **$p < 0.01$, ***$p < 0.001$.

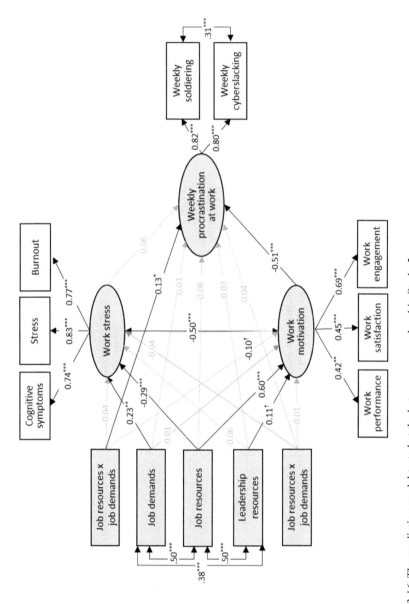

Figure 3.16 The mediation model tested at the between-person level in Study 5.

Note. $^{\dagger}p < 0.10$ $^{*}p < 0.05$, $^{**}p < 0.01$, $^{***}p < 0.001$. Path values are standardized regression coefficients β. Statistically nonsignificant paths are gray.

well as the outcome variable (weekly procrastination behavior). The fit for this model was acceptable in the light of most indices, $\chi^2/df = 3.65$, RMSEA $= 0.036$, CFI $= 0.92$, TLI $= 0.87$, SRMR for within part $= 0.001$, SRMR for between part $= 0.057$. In this step, a pattern of direct relationships was observed. The interaction effect between job demands and job resources significantly predicted weekly procrastination behaviors but did not predict procrastination behaviors indirectly by either work stress or work motivation (hypothesis H.5.4 not supported). The interaction of job demands and leadership resources effect on weekly procrastination behaviors was nonsignificant, and it was not mediated by work stress or work motivation (hypothesis H.5.5. not supported) (see Table 3.16 and Figure 3.16). Lastly, the decomposition of the marginally significant effect of the interaction of job demands x job resources on weekly procrastination behavior indicated that in high job demands conditions, job resources were significantly negatively related to weekly procrastination at work ($\beta = -0.15$, $t = 4.09$, $p < 0.001$), whereas in low job demands conditions, job resources were nonsignificantly associated with weekly procrastination behaviors ($\beta = -0.03$, $t = -1.32$, ns).

3.2.5.5 Summary of Study 5

The aim of Study 5 was to investigate the effects of work-related factors on employee procrastination behavior at the within-person level. Additionally, the study aimed to examine the mediating effects of work stress and work motivation on procrastination behaviors in the workplace at the between-person level. Soldiering and cyberslacking behavior measured during five consecutive working weeks was found to vary within a person over time. The results showed that employees exhibit relatively moderate fluctuations in their level of procrastination behaviors when measured weekly.

As predicted, job resources considered at the between-person level were positively associated with weekly soldiering and cyberslacking behaviors at work. In addition, work motivation mediated the relationship between job resources and procrastination behavior at work. This suggests that intra-individual changes in procrastination behavior are determined by job resources with high motivational potential. Providing employees with the necessary resources at work, such as autonomy, variation, meaning of work, and development opportunities, can foster a motivating work environment that does not create opportunities to procrastinate with its fluctuations at the person-level. A work environment offering employees a high level of possibilities for development, autonomy, variation, and meaning of work can foster motivation to work. Moreover, job demands, leadership resources, and work stress did not affect the weekly variation of procrastination behavior at work. Similar to studies 1, 3, and 4, the results of Study 5 revealed the mediational effect of work motivation between job resources and the weekly procrastination behavior of employees. Therefore, the motivational mechanism explaining procrastination at work proposed by the JD–R model (Bakker & Demerouti, 2014)

Table 3.16 Indirect effects in the empirical models tested in Study 5

Tested model	Effect	BC 95% CI
Mediation model		
Job demands→work stress→weekly procrastination	0.03(0.02)	[−0.02, 0.07]
Job demands→work motivation→weekly procrastination	0.01(0.03)	[−0.05, 0.06]
Job resources→work stress→weekly procrastination	−0.03(0.03)	[−0.09, 0.02]
Job resources→work motivation→weekly procrastination	−0.26(0.10)	[−0.46, −0.06]
Leadership resources→work stress→weekly procrastination	−0.01(0.01)	[−0.02, 0.01]
Leadership resources→work motivation→weekly procrastination	−0.05(0.03)	[−0.11, 0.01]
Moderated mediation model		
Job demands→work stress→weekly procrastination	0.01(0.02)	[0.03, 0.06]
Job demands→work motivation→weekly procrastination	0.01(0.03)	[0.06, 0.07]
Job resources→work stress→weekly procrastination	−0.02(0.03)	[−0.08, 0.04]
Job resources→work motivation→weekly procrastination	−0.30(0.11)	[−0.51, 0.09]
Leadership resources→work stress→weekly procrastination	−0.01(0.01)	[−0.02, 0.01]
Leadership resources→work motivation→weekly procrastination	−0.06(0.04)	[−0.13, 0.01]
Job resources x job demands→work stress→weekly procrastination	0.01(0.01)	[−0.01, 0.01]
Job resources x job demands→work motivation→weekly procrastination	−0.05(0.03)	[−0.12, 0.02]
Leadership resources x job demands→work stress→weekly procrastination	−0.01(0.01)	[−0.02, 0.01]
Leadership resources x job demands→work motivation→weekly procrastination	−0.01(0.03)	[−0.07, 0.05]

Note. BC 95% CI – Bias-corrected 95% confidence interval.

was supported. This suggests that motivational processes, initiated by high job resources, increased positive work-related outcomes (such as job performance and satisfaction), as well as a decrease in dysfunctional work behaviors (Schaufeli & Taris, 2013), including procrastination at work. Thus, work motivation is an important factor that may explain how a resourceful work environment contributes to a decrease in weekly procrastination behavior at work. Contrary to expectations, energetic processes did not contribute to the explanation of the effects of work-related factors on within-individual fluctuations of procrastination at work. This study found that the variance in procrastination at work is not only due to individual and work-related factors but also to individual variability in procrastination.

3.3 General Discussion

3.3.1 General Research Findings

Current research validated a general conceptual model that identifies antecedents and underlying mechanisms of workplace procrastination. The findings confirmed a two-dimensional concept of work procrastination and its measurement tool, as well as its relationships with other constructs. Five studies were conducted to investigate the impact of individual and work-related factors on procrastination at work. The studies modeled direct and indirect relationships, as well as the mediating role of work stress and motivation in explaining procrastination. The results revealed the systematic effects of these characteristics on workplace procrastination and shed light on its potential antecedents and explanatory mechanisms.

3.3.1.1 Procrastination as a Specific Construct in the Workplace

To gain a deeper understanding of procrastination in the workplace, the PAWS (Metin et al., 2016) was validated in the Polish professional context. The validation process demonstrated a high level of reliability analyzed at both the item and scale levels, including item discrimination, internal consistency, and temporal stability, thus establishing the measure as a reliable and valid instrument. As a result, procrastination at work emerged as a construct comprising two intertwined types of delay behavior: offline procrastination, referred to as 'soldiering', and online procrastination, referred to as 'cyberslacking'. Research findings also revealed that procrastination at work exhibited moderate short- and long-term stability. Furthermore, analysis of weekly measures indicated moderate fluctuations in work procrastination over time among individuals, suggesting potential situational sources of variability in this behavior.

Procrastination at work was moderately or highly associated with general procrastination, as measured by various questionnaires. Both constructs share common dispositional determinants but they represent slightly different phenomena. This is consistent with previous findings indicating moderate relationships between these constructs (Hen et al., 2021; Metin et al., 2016). Therefore, soldering and cyberslacking behavior may be considered specific manifestations of general procrastination (Klingsieck, 2013; van Eerde, 2016), justifying the investigation of procrastination within the workplace. Moreover, procrastination at work exhibits certain attributes of counterproductive work behavior. It is more like a passive behavior of withdrawal than active counterproductive behaviors such as theft, abuse, or sabotage. Employees can intentionally avoid aversive work tasks by delaying them, thereby conserving time and energy. Scholars suggest that this misuse of resources is counterproductive and stems from self-regulatory deficits, maladaptive stress-coping and resource-restoring strategies (Balducci et al., 2011). Thus, procrastination appears to be a strategy for avoiding aversive work tasks and unfavorable work conditions to protect against negative experiences (He et al., 2021) rather than to retaliate and cause harm to the organization (Koay et al., 2022).

In summary, the current findings support the theoretical validity of the procrastination at work, emphasizing its association with dispositional procrastination and counterproductive work behavior. Despite different approaches to procrastination, the research in this monograph supports the claim that procrastination at work is destructive and maladaptive.

3.3.1.2 Individual and Work-Related Factors in the Prediction of Procrastination at Work

Individual Characteristics: According to the current findings, procrastination at work is mainly determined by individual characteristics, such as the negative profile of personality traits, core self-evaluations, and dispositional procrastination (see Figure 3.17).

The study found a direct association between a specific negative profile of personality traits and higher levels of work procrastination, which supports the assumed hypotheses (see Table 3.17). Individuals with low emotional stability, conscientiousness, and high levels of narcissism, Machiavellianism, and psychopathy appear to be more susceptible to procrastination at work. Furthermore, the general disposition toward procrastination can serve as a source of fueling procrastination behaviors in the workplace. Trait procrastination impacted also indirectly on high employee procrastination through increased work stress, thereby fueling procrastination behaviors in the workplace. Additionally, low level of core self-evaluations encompassing self-esteem, self-efficacy, and external locus of control, contributed to increased procrastination at work. This effect is compounded by increased work stress and diminished work motivation, painting a complex picture of how individual characteristics intertwine to influence procrastination in the workplace. The parallel mediating effects of work stress and motivation processes were discussed in Section 3.3.1.3.

The current research supported the predictive role of individual characteristics, such as dispositional procrastination, core self-evaluations, positive and

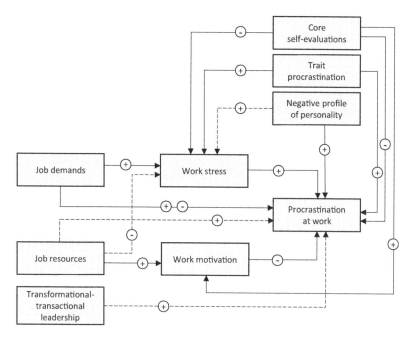

Figure 3.17 A synthetic pattern of the effects of individual and work-related factors in predicting procrastination at work revealed in studies 1–5.

Note. The +/– in a circle indicates the direction of the relationship. The dashed arrow reflects the weak effect.

dark personality traits, in predicting procrastination at work, thus contributing to a better understanding of procrastination at work by extending findings on the personal sources of this phenomenon. It is worth noting that the impact of personal traits was stronger than work-related factors.

Work-related Factors: Nevertheless, the present research has also revealed an important role for work-related factors in predicting procrastination at work. Based on the JD–R model (Bakker & Demerouti, 2014), five studies revealed the association of job demands, job resources, and leadership resources with procrastination at work, as well as the mediating role of work stress or work motivation in these relationships.

Job demands including quantitative, cognitive, and emotional demands, hiding emotions, work pace, job insecurity, role conflict, negative social relationships, unpleasant teasing, conflicts and quarrels, gossip, and slander were analyzed in various configurations across conducted studies. The results revealed inconsistent direct effects of these variables on procrastination behavior at work:

Table 3.17 Summary of research hypotheses in studies 1–5

Hypotheses	Support
Study 1	
H.1.1. Core self-evaluations are directly associated with low procrastination at work.	+
H.1.2. Core self-evaluations are indirectly associated with procrastination at work through work motivation.	+
H.1.3. High job resources are indirectly associated with low procrastination at work through work motivation.	+
H.1.4. Transformational–transactional leadership is indirectly associated with low procrastination at work through work motivation.	–
H.1.5. The interaction of job demands and job resources is indirectly associated with procrastination at work through work motivation, such that the indirect effect of job resources on procrastination at work via work motivation is stronger in high than in low job demands conditions.	–
H.1.6. The interaction of job demands with transformational–transformational leadership is indirectly related to procrastination at work through work motivation, such that the indirect effect of transformational–transformational leadership on procrastination at work via work motivation is stronger in high than in low job demands conditions.	–
Study 2	
H.2.1. Trait procrastination is directly related to high procrastination at work.	+
H.2.2. Trait procrastination is indirectly related to procrastination at work through work stress.	+
H.2.3. High job demands are indirectly associated with high procrastination at work through work stress.	+
H.2.4. High work-related resources are indirectly associated with low procrastination at work through work stress.	+
H.2.5. High organization-related resources are indirectly associated with low procrastination at work through work stress.	–
H.2.6. The interaction of job demands and work-related resources is indirectly related to procrastination at work through work stress, such that the indirect effect of work-related resources on procrastination at work via work stress is stronger in high than in low job demands conditions.	+
H.2.7. The interaction of job demands and organization-related resources is indirectly associated with procrastination at work through work stress, such that the indirect effect of organization-related resources on procrastination at work via work stress is stronger in high than in low job demands conditions.	–
Study 3	
H.3.1. The negative profile of personality traits is directly related to high procrastination at work.	+
H.3.2. The negative profile of personality traits is indirectly associated with high procrastination at work through work engagement.	–

(Continued)

Table 3.17 (Continued)

Hypotheses	Support
H.3.3. High job resources are indirectly associated with low procrastination at work through work engagement.	+
H.3.4. Destructive leadership is indirectly associated with high procrastination at work through work engagement.	−
H.3.5. The interaction of job demands and job resources is indirectly associated with procrastination at work through work engagement, such that the indirect effect of job resources on procrastination at work via work engagement is stronger in high than low job demands conditions.	−
H.3.6. The interaction of job demands and destructive leadership is indirectly associated with procrastination at work through work engagement such that the indirect effect of destructive leadership on procrastination at work via work engagement is stronger in high than low job demand conditions.	−
Study 4	
H.4.1. Core self-evaluations are directly related to low procrastination at work.	+
H.4.3. The negative profile of personality traits is directly related to high procrastination at work.	+
H.4.2. Core self-evaluations are indirectly associated with low procrastination at work parallelly via stress and work motivation.	+
H.4.4. The negative profile of personality traits is indirectly associated with low procrastination at work parallelly through work stress and work motivation.	+/−
H.4.5. High job demands are indirectly related to high procrastination at work through work stress.	+
H.4.6. High job resources are indirectly associated with low procrastination at work through work motivation.	+
H.4.7. High leadership resources are indirectly associated with low procrastination at work parallelly through work stress and work motivation.	−
H.4.8. The interaction of job demands and job resources is indirectly related to procrastination at work through work motivation, such that the indirect effect of job resources on procrastination at work via work motivation is stronger in high than low job demands conditions.	−
H.4.9. The interaction of job demands and leadership resources is indirectly related to procrastination at work through work motivation, such that the indirect effect of leadership resources on procrastination at work via work motivation is stronger in high than low job demands conditions.	+
Study 5	
H.5.1. High job resources are indirectly associated with low weekly procrastination behavior at work through work motivation.	+
H.5.2. High leadership resources are indirectly associated with low weekly procrastination at work through work motivation.	−
H.5.3. High job demands are indirectly associated with high weekly procrastination at work through work stress.	−

(*Continued*)

Table 3.17 (Continued)

Hypotheses	Support
H.5.4. The interaction of job demands and job resources is indirectly associated with weekly procrastination at work through work motivation, such that the indirect effect of high job resources on weekly procrastination at work is stronger in high- than low job demands conditions.	–
H.5.5. The interaction of job demands and leadership resources is indirectly associated with weekly procrastination at work (through work motivation), the indirect effect of leadership resources on weekly procrastination at work is stronger in high than low job demands conditions.	–

Note. + hypothesis supported, – hypothesis not supported.

a positive impact in two studies and a negligible or nonsignificant effect in three studies (see Figure 3.17). High job demands require significant effort to be put to carry on work tasks, potentially depleting personal resources. To recover resources, employees may engage in non-work-related activities both online and offline, such as chatting with colleagues, taking breaks (DeArmond et al., 2014; Metin et al., 2016), browsing the Internet, or attending to personal matters online (Henle & Blanchard, 2008; Varghese & Barber, 2017), and thereby procrastinate work tasks. These delay behaviors, known as soldiering or cyberslacking, may serve as a strategy for employees to cope with overwhelming work demands. More light on these effects sheds the mediational role of work stress, described in Section 3.3.1.3.

Job Resources: Five distinct studies provided more insight into the role of the role of various job resources in predicting procrastination phenomenon. Job resources were related to job content and work organization, encompassing influence at work, development opportunities, variation of work, meaning of work, control over work, role clarity, and positive changes in the workplace. The direct effects of job resources were very small or nonsignificant. Organization-related resources represented by social and organizational capital factors did not directly affect employee procrastination either. Taken together, a resourceful work environment does not directly foster procrastination at work. More insight into the procrastination phenomenon provides an analysis of the indirect effects of job resources on work procrastination through work motivation.

Leadership Resources: Unexpectedly, these results revealed statistically non-significant or very weak effects of leadership resources represented by trans-formational–transactional style, high quality of leadership, and managerial support, as well as low destructive leadership in predicting procrastination at work. These findings do not support previous research, which has shown the predictive role of transformational and inclusive leadership in decreasing procrastination (Göncü Köse & Metin, 2018; Lin, 2018), while abusive supervision was correlated with increased procrastination (He et al., 2021; Koay et al., 2022; Lim et al., 2021). Shaufeli (2015) posits that leadership plays a crucial role in shaping both job demands and resources, consequently impacting various work-related outcomes. It is conceivable that leadership exerts a similar influential pathway on workplace procrastination. Although hypotheses assuming the effects of leadership resources are mostly supported (Table 3.17), the observed very weak effects indicate the need for further empirical verification in future studies.

To summarize, leadership and job resources were not directly related to procrastination at work. Job demands were directly related to procrastination at work; however, it had a relatively weak impact. Interestingly, the research did not provide enough evidence to support a direct effect of job and leadership resources on procrastination at work. Further insight into these relationships was gained through mediation analysis.

3.3.1.3 *Mediating Effects of Work Stress and Work Motivation*

This research unveiled that work stress and work motivation serve as mediators between job demands, job resources, personal resources, and procrastination at work, supporting most of the hypotheses assuming mediating effects (see. Table 3.17). Job demands were found to increase procrastination through elevated work stress, while job resources decreased procrastination by enhancing employee motivation (see Figure 3.17).Similarly, personal resources impacted on procrastination at work indirectly through work stress and work motivation. These relationships emphasize two parallel regulatory mechanisms underlying employee procrastination, similar to the energetic and motivational processes proposed in the JD–R model (Bakker et al., 2023).

Work stress mediated the link between job demands and procrastination, aligning with the energetic process of the JD–R model, where demanding work triggers strain and exhaustion of resources, leading to adverse work outcomes. Excessive job demands can induce negative emotions, stress, and exhaustion, increasing susceptibility to procrastination. Among the examined job demands, those related to the work-specific, workload, role conflicts, job insecurity, offensive behavior, and interpersonal relations in the organization, may induce stress at work. Furthermore, work stress mediated the impact of personal characteristics on procrastination at work. Dispositional procrastination, negative personality profile, and low core self-evaluations were found to enhance employee stress and subsequently led to higher procrastination. Thus, individuals with a personality profile that includes a general tendency to procrastinate, low self-esteem, self-efficacy, elevated negative personality traits may be more prone to experiencing stress. As a result, job demands and specific personality traits induce stress that can lead to seeking relief in activities other than work, ultimately leading to procrastinating behavior at work. While job resources related to content and work organization affected low work stress and then low procrastination behavior. These effects correspond to the energy-driven process related to stress regulation (Bakker et al., 2023), which explains that high job demands can lead to exhaustion of psychological resources and even burnout and the manifestation of psychosomatic symptoms. Employees may look for different ways to achieve balance and to recover from fatigue and exhaustion. Therefore, procrastination at work may be a response to difficulties in dealing with work overload. Excessive job demands can lead to negative emotions, stress, and exhaustion (Hobfoll, 1989), which can increase employees' susceptibility to procrastination. This may prompt employees to engage in non-work-related activities to regenerate lost resources and reduce stress. It has also been found that job resources have a diminishing effect on procrastination through stress reduction. Hence, employees may use soldiering or cyberslacking at work as a coping mechanism to deal with stress and protect their resources. However, these behaviors may prove ineffective and lead to negative consequences, thereby driving the downward spiral of stress and further enhancing procrastination or other maladaptive behaviors.

Work Motivation: Furthermore, current research revealed a systematic impact of core self-evaluations and job resources on work procrastination, indirectly through intrinsic motivation processes (Figure 3.17). Both high core self-evaluations and job resources enhanced work motivation, leading to decreased procrastination at work. These findings align with the JD–R model assumptions (Bakker et al., 2023) and emphasize the essential role of motivational processes in explaining procrastination at work. Personal resources and job resources, having motivational potential, lead to higher intrinsic motivation to work, thereby increasing positive work outcomes and decreasing negative ones. In the same vein, job resources that are instrumental in achieving work goals, such as financial incentives, promotions, recognition or positive organizational climate, can serve as sources of employee extrinsic motivation to work and enhance intrinsic motivation. This is how high motivation can alleviate soldiering and cyberslacking behavior in the workplace. Therefore, motivational processes underlie an efficient strategy for reducing employee procrastination at work, which corresponds to one of the lines of well-established interventions for general and academic procrastination (e.g. van Eerde & Klingsieck, 2018). Contrary to expectations, indirect effects of leadership resources on employee procrastination through motivation or stress were generally nonsignificant or negligible. These relationships may become clearer when considering the interaction effect of leadership resources with job demands, which are presented in Section 3.3.1.4. In light of the previous findings on the significant impact of leadership on employee motivation and procrastination, these findings may suggest that the impact of leadership resources on work procrastination is more complex and needs further investigation.

Summarizing, both work stress and motivation mediated the impact of job demands and job and personal resources on procrastination at work, indicating the emotional and motivational mechanisms underlying the impact of individual and work-related characteristics on employee procrastination behavior. On the one hand, motivation was influenced by available resources and job demands, which ultimately alleviated employee procrastination. On the other hand, stress caused by unfavorable work conditions or insufficient job resources can increase employees' tendency to delay work tasks. These findings contribute to a comprehensive understanding of procrastination at work by revealing the parallel role of emotional and motivational processes in the regulation of procrastination behavior, as well as providing important cues to develop strategies to address procrastination at work. Research results may suggest that procrastination at work is behavior-oriented toward self-protection rather than active behavior harmful to the organization/employers.

3.3.1.4 Interaction effect between job demands and job resources

According to the JD–R model (Bakker et al., 2023), job resources can buffer the impact of job demands on the strain, while high job demands enhance the effect of job resources on motivation. In the current studies, the interaction effect of job demands and job resources implied different patterns of relationships between individual and work-related factors and procrastination at work, depending on the level of job demands (see Figure 3.18).

Specifically, the effects of work-related factors (e.g. job resources, leadership resources) on procrastination at work were moderated by the level of job demands. In *low job demands* conditions (Figure 3.18.A), job resources appeared to have a direct enhancement and/or decrease (albeit weak) impact on procrastination at work. These different effects may result from different configurations of job resources. Also, transformational-transactional leadership determined directly (but very weakly) high subordinates' procrastination. Also, transformational-transactional leadership determined directly (but very weakly) high subordinates' procrastination. In a low-demanding work environment, the negative profile of personality traits impacted procrastination at work directly and indirectly by increasing work stress. Moreover, the relationships of job resources with employee procrastination were mediated by work motivation. Job resources can enhance employees' motivation at work, reducing the likelihood of procrastination behavior, while organization-related resources may reduce work procrastination indirectly, through lowering stress. Employees are more likely to be willing and motivated to engage in their work while controlling their emotions when they have acceptable workloads, supportive leadership, and organizational resources accessible. This reduces the

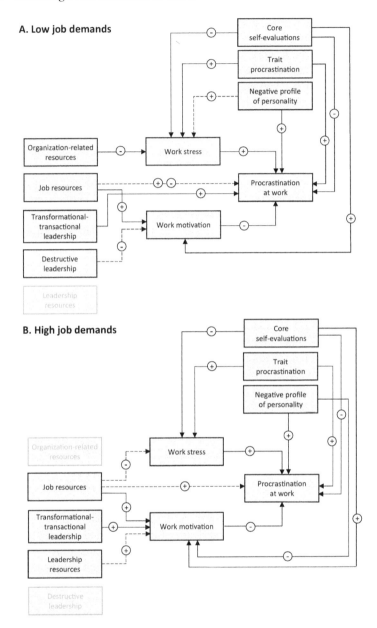

Figure 3.18 A synthetic pattern of the effects of individual and work-related factors in predicting procrastination at work in low (A) and high (B) job demands conditions revealed in studies 1–5.

Note. The gray variables did not achieve a significant effect. The dashed arrow reflects the weak effect.

need for individuals to engage in other activities or rebuild their emotional well-being through procrastinating behavior. Moreover, destructive leadership very weakly determines low work motivation, which subsequently leads to procrastination, although current studies do not provide robust evidence for this effect. In *high job demand* conditions (Figure 3.18.B), job resources predicted work procrastination directly (albeit very weakly) and indirectly twofold through increasing employees' motivation and reducing work stress. Thus, a highly demanding workplace, when coupled with high job resources, can reduce the detrimental behavior of procrastination at work. Furthermore, leadership resources and transformational-transactional leadership employees' tendency to delay work through enhanced motivation. To conclude, the impact of job and leadership resources on procrastination was dependent on the level of job demands.

In both *low* and *high job demands*, personal resources were found to determine procrastination at work, although with different intensities. High levels of general procrastination and negative personality traits directly impacted procrastination at work. Core self-evaluations indirectly reduced procrastination by decreasing work stress and increasing work motivation. Among individual characteristics, trait procrastination contributed to non-work-related behaviors through heightened stress levels only in low job demands, while negative personality traits increased procrastination through work motivation. To conclude, the impact of job and leadership resources on procrastination was dependent on the level of job demands.

Despite different patterns of relationships in low and high job demands conditions, most of the hypotheses about the moderation role of job demands were not supported (see Table 3.17). Moreover, some effects were surprising and contradictory to the hypotheses. This suggests that these relationships require further research, which will ultimately verify the assumptions about the boosting effect of high job demands proposed in the JD–R model.

3.3.1.5 Risk and Protective Factors

Taking into account the function of revealed predictors of procrastination at work, one may indicate risk or protective factors contributing to employees' procrastination tendencies. Negative personality traits and general procrastination are individual characteristics that increase the risk of procrastination, whereas core self-evaluations can protect individuals against procrastination. Among work-related factors, job demands can be both a risk and a protective factor depending on whether they are high or low, and whether they are perceived as hindrances or challenges. This may suggest a U-shaped relationship between job demands and procrastination; both low and high job demands determine high procrastination, while moderate levels of workload can reduce procrastination at work. Research indicated that job resources and leadership resources can increase or decrease the likelihood of procrastination at work, depending on the specific resources tested. Work-related resources reflecting job content and work organization were found to be protective factors against procrastination at work, consistently reducing employee procrastination both through the motivation and stress regulation mechanism, although the direct impact of job resources is not clear. Organization-related resources represented by social and organizational capital were a risk factor for procrastination only under low job demands conditions. Leadership resources can be considered as protective factors, but the research did not provide conclusive evidence that constructive and supportive leadership reduces the tendency to procrastinate. The relationship between leadership resources and employee procrastination is still unclear. In general, in low job demands conditions, destructive leadership may enhance employee procrastination by decreasing their motivation to work, while in high job demands, leadership resources represented by high-level leaders support and orientation toward employees, or transformational–transactional leadership can diminish employees' tendency to procrastinate through stimulating work motivation. In summary, the research results suggest a stronger effect of individual characteristics and a slightly weaker influence of work-related factors on procrastination at work.

3.3.2 Implications

3.3.2.1 Theoretical Implications

The monograph makes several potential contributions to the literature on workplace procrastination. First, it provides an extensive review of the theoretical perspectives and empirical findings concerning general procrastination. This serves as a foundation for understanding procrastination as a specific phenomenon in work settings. Additionally, it presents a comprehensive exploration of concepts and recent findings on procrastination at work, including an analysis of its various forms (offline vs. online), underlying causes, processes, and resulting consequences. The research findings presented lend empirical support to a two-dimensional conceptualization of procrastination at work, distinguishing between soldiering (offline procrastination) and cyberslacking (online procrastination). The excellent reliability and validity indices of the PAWS were estimated in a sample of Polish employees. This confirmed the usefulness of the PAWS in assessing procrastination in the workplace. In addition, the short-and long-term stability of the PAWS was supported by weekly measures of procrastination behavior (in a within-person analysis), suggesting that some of the variance in procrastination is explained by the individual dynamics of employees' tendency to procrastinate. The associations between general procrastination and work procrastination suggest a moderate convergence of these constructs. As described in Section 3.1.3, there is a significant relationship between work procrastination and withdrawal as a type of passive counterproductive work behavior. This suggests that there is a dysfunctional component to the construct of procrastination at work. These findings extend existing research and provide valuable insight into understanding the nature of workplace procrastination within the broader network of related constructs.

Based on an interactional approach to procrastination at work, a conceptual predictive model was proposed that integrates both individual and work-related sources of procrastination at work. In doing so, the monograph advances knowledge about antecedents and sheds light on the explanatory mechanisms underlying procrastination in the work context. This approach enhances our understanding of potential risk and protective factors for work procrastination. The JD-R framework (Bakker & Demerouti, 2014) been shown to well describe the predictors and mechanisms of procrastination. The results of five studies contributed to the knowledge of procrastination at work by providing findings on the predictive effects of (1) personal resources, (2) job demands, job resources, and their interaction, as well as (3) mediating role of the emotional and motivational processes that explain it. Thereby, these findings extended the research stream that integrates trait- and situation-based approaches to procrastination (Steel, 2007; van Eerde, 2016). Specifically, the results showed consistent support for personal resources represented by personality traits, core self-evaluations, and general procrastination in predicting procrastination at work. General procrastination and a negative profile of personality traits, including low emotional stability, low conscientiousness, high narcissism, high Machiavellianism, and high psychopathy, promoted high procrastination at work. Core self-evaluations represented by high self-esteem, high self-efficacy, and internal locus of control were negatively associated with procrastination at work. These results are consistent with previous research showing that personality traits explained more variance in work engagement, which is the behavior opposite to procrastination, than situational work-related factors (Mäkikangas et al., 2010). At the same time, job demands and job resources that include various job and organizational factors determined procrastination at work to a lesser extent than individual characteristics. Job demands contributing to increased procrastination at work can be explained by the mechanism of recovery from work (Sonnentag & Fritz, 2015). This concept refers to the actions aimed at reducing physical and psychological stress symptoms caused by work. In this context, individuals seek some recovery from the demands of their work. In consequence, they procrastinate to diminish the strain caused by high job demands. It seems that employees reduce or eliminate work-related stress by soldiering and cyberslacking at work. Job resources related to the content and organization of work had a diminishing effect on employee procrastination, i.e. they stimulate diligent work behavior rather than non-work-related activities. Surprisingly, the effect of leadership resources was minimal. The weak and unclear effects of leadership-related factors on work procrastination may indicate more complex relationships between these constructs and require more thorough investigation.

Thus, the research findings provided more insight into the mechanisms explaining procrastination in the workplace by establishing the mediating role of stress and motivation between job demands and resources, and procrastination behavior. It supported the propositions of the JD–R model (Bakker et al., 2023) that job demands and resources trigger two different underlying processes, i.e. energetic and motivational. Job demands may induce high strain, exhaustion, or burnout, whereas job resources may induce work engagement or motivation. The identified relationships support the dual mechanism that clarifies procrastination at work. The *energetic process* may serve as a plausible means for increasing work procrastination through work stress, while the *motivational process* may serve as a mechanism for decreasing work procrastination through work motivation. The mediating role of work stress and motivation in the effects of individual and work-related factors on procrastination at work can be explained through the lens of the conservation of resources theory (COR) (Hobfoll, 1989), which posits that loss or threat of loss of resources can lead to strain, exhaustion, and negative outcomes. Similarly, job resources can mitigate resource loss and protect against negative outcomes. Stress can be viewed as a response to the perceived threat of resource loss, while motivation can be viewed as a mechanism for acquiring or retaining resources. In general, the present findings can be aligned with COR theory by highlighting the role of job demands and resources in shaping individuals' stress reactions, motivation, and ultimately, their procrastination behavior in the workplace. Furthermore, empirically supported motivational pathways between job resources and procrastination at work are relevant to the role of intrinsic motivation, postulated by self-determination theory (Deci & Ryan, 2008). Consistent with these assumptions, job resources are a source of work motivation and engagement, because they satisfy basic psychological needs, such as the need for autonomy, relatedness, and competence, which can lead to high work-related outcomes (Halbesleben, 2010). Low work motivation may prompt employees to take breaks from work or substitute for non-work-related activities. Engaged employees, who are highly committed to their work, demonstrate greater perseverance in completing tasks and experience positive emotions during work, making it easier for them to resist the temptation to procrastinate.

Finally, the moderating effect of job demands implies the differential pattern relationships between individual and work-related factors and procrastination behavior. However, it should be noted that regardless of the level of job demands, procrastination at work was predicted by personal resources, such as trait procrastination, core self-evaluations, and negative profile of second-order personality traits. Furthermore, in low-demanding job conditions, work motivation acted as a mediating factor in the relationships of high job resources and low destructive leadership with procrastination at work. Employees seem to be more ready and energized to work and retain emotional stability when work is not overbearing or urgent, organizational tools are available, and leadership is not detrimental. As a result, workers do not feel the need to regain the resources to work on their tasks through engaging in non-work-related activities, like soldering or cyberslacking. These results provide empirical support for situational strength theory (Meyer et al., 2020), assuming that the expression of personality traits is greater in weak situations (here low job demands), which impacts subsequent behaviors. In high job demand conditions, work procrastination was predicted by job resources, leadership resources, and transformational–transactional leadership indirectly through work motivation. Job resources decreased procrastination by increasing employee work-related motivation and reducing stress. It seems that even in a tough work environment, the presence of ample resources for the job might reduce undesirable behaviors such as procrastination. Additionally, leadership resources and transformational-transactional leaders behavior increase employees' tendency to delay work by decreasing motivation. It may mean that in high demanding work supportive and person-oriented leaders behavior contributes to a increase employees' internal motivation to initiate or complete tasks independently. As a result, employees may decrease their likelihood of procrastinating in the workplace.

To summarize, individual factors, such as positive and negative personality traits, explain procrastination at work to a greater extent than work-related factors, which include job demands, job resources, and leadership resources. Although work-related factors are important, it seems they are not the primary cause of procrastination at work. It needs to be emphasized, however, that it is important to consider both, individual and work-related factors when developing strategies and solutions to prevent procrastination. The stronger impact of individual factors is likely due to the variability in the behavioral expression of personality resulting from individual psychological differences (Mischel & Shoda, 1995). It follows that individual characteristics promote employees tendency to engage or not engage in procrastination in situations that may activate processes such as emotional or behavioral self-regulation, restoration of resources, or response to motivational triggers. These findings can be explained through the lens of situational strength theory (Meyer et al., 2020), which suggests that the behavioral expression of personality depends on the strength of the situation. In strong situations, some strong expectations and constraints can override individual personality differences. When work-related factors create weak situations, they may not be sufficient to explain the impact of individual factors on procrastination behavior. It should be highlighted that current findings, like previous research results, do not fully explain the sources of procrastination at work; rather, they identify important antecedents of procrastination and provide possible implications as well as ideas for further research.

In summary, the monograph on procrastination at work integrated psychological and organizational perspectives by examining individual and contextual work-related sources, as well as emotional–motivational mechanisms of procrastination behavior in the workplace. By doing so, the monograph contributed

Table 3.18 Contribution of research results to management sciences

Theoretical area	
Management and organization theory	• Advancing theoretical knowledge by establishing procrastination behavior at work as a source of potential barriers or stimulators of effective management in the organization. • Providing a synthetic overview of concepts and empirical data on procrastination as a theoretical basis for the design of future research. • Extending up-to-date knowledge of the set of individual and contextual causes of procrastination at work
Methodology of management sciences	• Supporting the usability of applied research methods in the management field, such as the validation of measurement instruments and the modeling of the relationships between predictors and procrastination behavior at the within- and between-person levels. • Providing a methodological background and approach for further research on procrastination in the workplace.
Practical perspective	
Organizational behavior	• Creating the opportunity to diagnose procrastination behaviors in the organization and monitoring the scale and consequences of this organizational behavior. • Providing valuable insight into understanding the nature of procrastination and recognition of personal and work-related risk and protective factors of procrastination behavior and its underlying processes in professional settings. - • Gaining insight into when employees procrastinate, whether it has negative consequences, and how to motivate and guide them to change their behavior at work.
Supporting managerial decisions Human resources management	• Providing knowledge that help organizations create a work environment that promotes employee engagement, creativity, and performance and limits employee procrastination behavior. • Taking procrastination into account as a negative criterion in employee recruitment processes. • Enabling organizations to set the direction of maximizing the efficiency of human resource management. • Providing the framework for developing and implementing a strategy to manage employee procrastination.

to advancing knowledge in the field of management and organization theory, providing a synthetic review of conceptions and research-based findings as a theoretical background of procrastination phenomenon as a source of potential barriers or stimulators of effective management in the organization. Moreover, current research extended knowledge that allow for a more comprehensive recognition and understanding of procrastination in terms of individual and contextual causes.

Presented in the monograph empirical project may be supportive for the usability of applied research methods in the management science, such as the validation of measurement instruments and the modeling of the complex relationships between predictors and procrastination behavior at the within- and between-person levels. Thereby, it provides a methodological background and analytical approach for further research on procrastination in the workplace. Within organizations, the monograph can be used to identify the risk- and protective factors for procrastination in the workplace that can either inhibit or promote effective management. More specific contributions of current findings to different areas of management science are presented in Table 3.18.

3.3.2.2 Managerial and Organizational Implications

The prevalence of employee procrastination and its harmful effects on the employee and the organization are often underestimated by practitioners. Stress, decreased motivation, productivity, and employee morale are regularly attributed to causes other than procrastination. However, if procrastination becomes a chronic problem, it can lead to organizational inertia that hinders performance. The broad knowledge on the nature, sources, and consequences of procrastination behavior may be useful for the organizational practice, especially for recognition of organizational behavior, effective supporting managerial decisions, and more effective human resources management, as indicated in Table 3.18. A systematic overview of theoretical conceptions and empirical findings in the monograph extended the view of *organizational behavior* in many aspects. Organizations' management will better recognize, diagnose and address employee procrastination using growing scientific knowledge that provides many different tools on how to address this problem. Employee procrastination can be identified using self-reported and behavioral measures. The PAWS as a reliable and valid instrument may be useful in diagnosing soldiering and cyberslacking at work. The opportunity of assessment of employee procrastination may provide insight into the prevalence of this behavior in the organization as a starting point for initiating the intervention. The findings revealed in this research provide the organization with knowledge about potential individual and work-related antecedents and mechanisms explaining procrastination, which can facilitate recognizing its risk and protective factors to draw effective preventive actions. Moreover, it allows for a more comprehensive understanding the nature and recognition personal and work-related risk and protective factors of procrastination as the organizational behavior in professional settings and its underlying processes. Finally, this knowledge provides insight into when employees procrastinate, whether it has negative consequences, and premises to the development of strategies to motivate and guide employees to change their behavior at work. All contributions indicated above provide the *support for managerial decisions*. This knowledge may help managers make favorable work conditions to increase work motivation, engagement, creativity and performance, as well as alleviate procrastination behavior. Furthermore, the knowledge contained in the monograph may also increase the efficiency of human resources management in several ways. For example, it can enable organizations to set the direction for improving the efficiency of human resource management. Due to detrimental effect, procrastination behavior may be used in the recruitment processes as a negative criterion of selection. Also, better insight into the nature of employees procrastination may help to develop intervention practices to address procrastination at work and its detrimental effects. Following the JD–R assumptions (Bakker & Demerouti, 2014), interventions for procrastination at work should be oriented to optimize job demands, and job resources, and strengthen personal resources. In addition, these interventions should be considered from both individual and organizational perspectives, including top-down and bottom-up approaches. Individual-focused interventions are oriented toward changing employee perceptions, attitudes, or behaviors at work. Organization-focused intervention addresses organizational policies, procedures, and benefits, as well as aspects of organizational culture (Murphy & Sauter, 2004). The framework resulting from this research can serve as the foundation for developing strategies to address procrastination behavior.

Personal Resources-based Interventions: Organizations can address employee procrastination tendencies by implementing primary and secondary treatments after defining the specific risk factors that lead to procrastination. An effective plan to avoid procrastination in the workplace may begin at the individual level by implementing basic interventions that capitalize on individuals' strengths to reduce their tendency to delay tasks. Establishing work environments that maximize employees' capacity for self-regulation in the face of procrastination might also be beneficial.

- *Reducing Individual Risk Factors*: When hiring for jobs where procrastination is a factor, management should pay particular attention to negative personality characteristics, low core self-evaluation traits, and a high predisposition to general procrastination. Additionally, there is a need to raise management's knowledge about variations in time-wasting practices. Management can identify potential triggers of weekly variation in procrastination represented by soldiering (i.e. intentionally reducing work effort) and cyberslacking (i.e. excessive online activities during work hours) through ongoing monitoring and temporal changes in work procrastination behaviors.
- *Fostering :Individual Protective Factors*: People with low levels of negative qualities and high levels of positive traits, such as conscientiousness, emotional stability, high self-efficacy and self-esteem, and an internal locus of control, are believed to be less prone to delay work. Consequently, managers

should make an effort to establish work environments that stimulate these individual traits, which decrease the propensity to put things off.

- *Enhancing Self-awareness and Reducing Own Procrastination*: Employees with a higher tendency to procrastinate may avoid task delaying when they are aware of the detrimental consequences of procrastination behavior in the workplace. Enhancing employees' awareness may help them in inducing motivation to decrease their procrastination behavior at work. Organizations may also strengthen personal resources to address employee procrastination by implementing organizational programs that develop and train skills useful in preventing or reducing procrastination.
- *Time Management and Task Prioritization*: These are the most emphasized strategies for coping with procrastination. They involve goal setting, task planning, prioritizing, organizing, and monitoring time as a cognitive–motivational intervention (Claessens et al., 2007; van Eerde, 2015). Therefore, organizations should provide training or resources to help employees manage their time effectively, prioritize tasks, and allocate sufficient time for breaks and self-care. It is considered as one of the most effective intervention strategies.
- *Work Stress Management*: Stress at work appears to be a source of a strong tendency to soldiering and cyberslacking. Implementing employee stress reduction training and programs, including coping strategies, and resilience-building activities can help reduce procrastination and other counterproductive behaviors.
- *Mindfulness and Relaxation Techniques*: Encouragement of mindfulness practices, meditation, deep breathing exercises, or other relaxation techniques may be used to treat employee procrastination. These practices facilitate stress management and encourage a goal-oriented approach to work.
- *Acceptance and Commitment Therapy*: It is a combination of practices that aim to induce acceptance and mindfulness, along with commitment and behavior change. The main goal is to manage stress, improve well-being, and decrease inefficiency in the organization. However, one experimental study confirmed the usability of ACT in addressing work procrastination (Salehi, 2020).
- *Employee Assistance or Caching Programs*: Organizations shall provide access to employee assistance and coaching programs or counseling services that can offer support, guidance, and resources to cope with special needs such as overcoming procrastination tendencies. If employee procrastination has a detrimental effect on the organization, secondary interventions can be used to reduce delayed behavior by enhancing individuals' strengths and resources. This is supported by a meta-analysis conducted by van Eerde and Klingsieck (2018), which is based on self-regulation, cognitive behavioral therapy, and other therapeutic approaches.
- *Cognitive Behavioral Therapy Interventions*: These are the most effective in helping an individual reduce procrastination. For example, cognitive

therapy techniques are used to focus on changing rigid and dysfunctional thought patterns and pair them with behavioral techniques that facilitate reevaluating work methods and assumptions about one's ability to achieve certain goals.

• *Self-regulation Skills Training*: This is considered useful in building emotional strength and resilience in addressing procrastination (Eckert et al., 2016; van Eerde & Klingsieck, 2018). Emotion regulation skills refer to resilience and persistence, which enable individuals to tolerate and modify their aversive emotional states.

Additionally, various cognitive and behavioral strategies may be useful in reducing negative emotions and procrastination, such as providing social support to sustain desirable behavior self-regulation, cognitive appraisal of the situation, and considering potential threats before task completion, as well as the cognitive reappraisal of task performance in terms of self-efficacy and negative emotions experienced during task completion (Eckert et al., 2016; van Eerde & Klingsieck, 2018), as well as behavior reorientation from procrastination toward engagement and task completion (Rozental & Carlbring, 2013).

Job Demand- and Resource-based Interventions: Research has consistently shown that work-related factors play a significant albeit weaker than individual factors role in employee procrastination. To address this issue, job design should focus on redesigning the work environment that balances job demands and resources. Optimizing job demands and resources can reduce employee stress and counteract procrastination. Therefore, interventions aimed at reducing stress can be an effective strategy to combat procrastination. Procrastination is often caused by feeling overwhelmed or stressed due to an excessive workload.

• *Job Crafting*: At the individual level, a well-documented and successful intervention is the bottom-up strategy of job crafting (Demerouti et al., 2019). Job crafting involves the employee redefining their job characteristics to reduce stress or enhance motivation, which in turn can alleviate procrastination. When employees create their work environment, they experience less stress, are more motivated, satisfied, and productive at work, and are less likely to procrastinate on job-related tasks. At the organizational level, managers may also redesign the work environment or help employees find their optimal balance between demands and resources to alleviate employee procrastination. This can be achieved through:
• *Reducing Excessive Job Demands:* Managers should review workload distribution, work organization, and time management to reduce overwhelming job demands. Employees can acquire skills in time and work organization, which reduce stress at work to mitigate the impact of job demands on procrastination. Organizations should avoid allowing employees to perceive excessive

hindrance demands, which intensify stress or alleviate work motivation, hinder their work engagement, leading to passive behaviors, including procrastination. Additionally, managers should help employees operationalize large and complex tasks into smaller and more manageable ones. This can make tasks feel less daunting and increase motivation to get started, decreasing the escape to procrastination behavior.

- *Creating a Challenging Work Environment:* Managers can create a challenge for their employees by setting tasks that are slightly beyond their current abilities. This can stimulate employees and promote their growth and development.
- *Job Demands (Re)appraisals*: When employees perceive job demands as hindrances rather than challenges, they may avoid aversive work by procrastinating. Therefore, managers should monitor how employees perceive work conditions and provide clear instructions that foster a positive appraisal of tasks or induce a reappraisal into a challenge.
- *Creating Opportunities for Detachment:* Creating opportunities for detachment from work and recovery of exhausted personal resources should be encouraged. Work conditions should allow employees to take breaks from work to recover personal resources needed to highly perform their jobs. Managers should emphasize the importance of regular breaks during work and encourage employees to rest, recharge, and engage in self-care activities outside of work, such as exercise, spending time in nature, or pursuing hobbies.
- *Promotion of a Healthy Work Environment*: A positive work environment recognizes the importance of reducing stress, as well as the maintenance of work–life balance. When employees have the flexibility and support to manage their personal and professional lives, they are less likely to feel overwhelmed or stressed. Promoting work–life balance helps employees maintain a mental and physically healthy mindset and approach their work with focus and determination.
- *Providing Clear Goals and Expectations*: Employees are more prone to put off tasks when their goals are inflated. Offering advice on how to divide more ambitious objectives into smaller, more achievable tasks can boost motivation and clarity, managers can assist staff members in setting demanding but realistic goals that are also measurable and achievable. Employees are less likely to procrastinate if they know exactly what is expected of them and by when. Managers should set clear instructions and expectations for all tasks and projects, including real deadlines, and provide regular feedback to their employees, highlighting their strengths and areas for improvement. Encouraging a culture of constructive criticism where feedback is given in a respectful and supportive manner helps employees grow and develop professionally. Importantly, stress reduction interventions should be implemented holistically, taking into account both individual and organizational factors.

Creating a favorable work environment and promoting a healthy work–life balance can help employees effectively manage stress and reduce the likelihood of procrastination at work. Furthermore, coping with employee procrastination can probably be most effective by using strategies oriented toward enhancing intrinsic and extrinsic work motivation, which subsequently reduces the employee procrastination tendency. Some of the most promising interventions could include the following:

- *Job Enrichment:* Job resources can enhance motivational potential and help employees manage stress while balancing job demands. According to the JCM (Hackman & Oldham, 1980). Management can improve job resources or make them more widely available, creating a positive and challenging work environment that does not foster procrastination behavior. Other research indicates that resources related to job content and work organization can reduce soldiering and cyberslacking at work. However, the research presented in the monograph suggests that the development of interventions should include different effects of work- and organization-related resources on procrastination, as well as the conditional effects of job resources in low vs. high job demands. Redesigning the work environment in terms of job demands and resources should take into account the promotion of a positive work and organizational culture and the stimulation of intrinsic motivation to work. To enhance intrinsic motivation and decrease procrastination, organizations can provide opportunities for employees to engage in meaningful and challenging work, offer autonomy and decision-making authority, provide avenues for personal growth and development, and create a supportive and positive work environment that values and recognizes employees' efforts. Moreover, by nurturing intrinsic motivation, organizations can tap into employees' innate drive and passion, creating a work culture that minimizes procrastination and maximizes productivity and engagement.

- *Adequate Reward System*: The tendency toward procrastination can be limited by implementing an *adequate reward system*. When employees are acknowledged and rewarded for their efforts and progress at work, they are more motivated to continue working and avoid procrastination. Therefore, managers should implement a clear reward system that promotes progress and achievements at work. Managers should foster a positive work environment that provides a sense of accomplishment and motivation to continue working. Specifically, recognizing and rewarding timely work is crucial in decreasing the risk of work avoidance due to delays. These strategies aim to create a proactive and supportive work environment that addresses both individual characteristics and work-related factors contributing to procrastination at work.

To summarize, interventions aimed at addressing employee procrastination are based on research findings presented in the monograph. Successful implementation of these interventions requires consistent effort and commitment at both the individual and organizational levels. The selection of interventions should be based on the specific needs, goals, and context of the organization. Regular training, monitoring, and implementation of interventions can contribute to a healthier and more productive workplace. This, in turn, can help overcome procrastination at work.

3.3.3 Limitations and Future Research

Current studies have several weaknesses. Above all, they are cross-sectional in design. While cross-sectional studies are useful in generating hypotheses, identifying associations between variables, and assessing the prevalence of phenomena within a population, the relationships are primarily correlational. Hence, the empirical findings require further validation. Studies rely on the use of self-evaluations that represent employee behavior and perceptions of various external factors, which may not fully capture the complexity and nuances of actual behaviors. Overreliance on self-reported procrastination can weaken theory testing and lead to inaccurate or misleading conclusions about variable relationships. Studies may not fully capture the dynamic nature of employee behaviors, as they predominantly relied on static measurements through questionnaires. Behaviors, particularly in the workplace, are subject to change over time, and the research static approach may overlook important fluctuations and nuances in employees' actions. This research faces challenges in inferring causality due to the cross-sectional design of the studies and the prevalent reliance on questionnaires for perceptions and evaluations. As a result, it is difficult to establish causal relationships between variables, which limits our understanding of the temporal order of behaviors and their determining factors. Furthermore, employing multiple self-reported measures is often susceptible to common-method variance bias, which can lead to an overestimation of the relationships among study variables (Podsakoff et al., 2003). Although the CMV estimate indicated that the current results are free of this error, caution must still be taken when interpreting the results.

To address the limitations of relying solely on questionnaires and proxies, researchers can use various study methods to measure workplace procrastination. These methods include observational studies, where employee behaviors are directly observed, or video recordings are made to capture real-time procrastination behavior. Utilizing time-tracking software to objectively measure time spent on tasks could be a potential option, subject to the agreement of company management. Such tools would aid in analyzing patterns of task initiation and completion to identify procrastination tendencies. Another method that would provide a more objective and detailed account of procrastination behaviors is to keep records of the start and end times of tasks and assignments.

There are also project management tools, often powered by artificial intelligence, that provide a visual representation of task completion rates and delays. Gathering multiple perspectives in the form of feedback or evaluation from colleagues, peers, or supervisors can contribute to a more comprehensive understanding of procrastination in the workplace. Conducting case studies or gathering qualitative data from interviews can provide rich insights into the context and reasons behind procrastination. Finally, designing controlled experiments would allow researchers to observe the impact of specific interventions or environmental changes on procrastination behaviors. By combining multiple methods, researchers can enhance the reliability of the measurements, provide more comprehensive findings, and gain an enhanced understanding of workplace procrastination.

There is also a need to expand understanding of the individual and work-related causes of procrastination in the workplace. This can be achieved by investigating the interaction effects of individual and work-related factors, as postulated in the literature. Furthermore, it is important to explore other personal and work-related characteristics that have not yet been examined in predicting procrastination at work. Moreover, the current studies used various configurations of variables, which were aggregated into more general factors representing job demands, job resources, and leadership resources. It may be questionable to test the effects of different variables represented by latent variables, such as stress, work motivation, personality traits, and the main outcome variable of procrastination at work. Future research should examine specific predictors of procrastination instead of combining them into latent variables. Although these predictors of work procrastination are correlated, they may exhibit distinct patterns. Further research may focus on confirming the revealed effects; identifying relationships between each job demands, job resources, and each dimension of procrastination at work, as well as exploring alternative cognitive, emotional, and motivational mechanisms that explain the reduction and exacerbation of procrastination behavior in the workplace. For this reason, weak, inconsistent, or unclear effects of job demands, job resources, and leadership resources in predicting employee procrastination create a space for further research that can bring more insight into leadership-related antecedents of procrastination at work.

Research regarding the role of organizational and social resources in predicting employee procrastination is particularly intriguing. Studies on academic procrastination suggest that factors related to group work, such as social interdependence and the perceived indispensability of individual contributions to group performance can reduce procrastination among students (Koppenborg & Klingsieck, 2022). It seems that coworkers' attitudes and patterns of organizational behavior regarding work, performance, obligations towards the employer, and procrastination itself may reinforce employees' procrastination behaviors.

In addition, aspects of the organizational culture or values promoted within the organization may play a role in managing procrastination behavior. Despite the current studies indicating weak effects of leaders' and coworkers' attitudes or behaviors on employee procrastination, further exploration in this area is warranted.

Another weakness of current research appears to use different measures of the job characteristics, which could have increased the measurement error and reduced the reliability of the results. Determining whether the variations in results are due to true differences in measured variables or differences in measurement instruments can be challenging. However, it is important to interpret the results with nuance. To enhance the comparability and reliability of the results across studies, standardized questionnaires were used and the psychometric evaluation of new instruments was carried out with rigor. Studies focus primarily on organizational behavior within specific contexts, potentially limiting the generalizability of their findings in other settings. Variability in organizational structures, cultural contexts, and industry types may affect the applicability of the study's conclusions beyond the examined scenarios. Therefore, this research provided initial evidence on the sources of procrastination at work as inspiration for a deeper and more detailed investigation. The revealed findings require further verification in different sectors, industries, organizational formats, profiles, cultures, specific professions, and work settings. Moreover, an examination of the reverse effects of employee procrastination on the work environment and its appraisal seems to very interesting area of future exploration. According to postulates about the potential role of vicious and virtuous cycles and spirals in explaining procrastination at work (Sirois, 2023; Steel, 2007; Wäschle et al., 2014), the relationship between individual and contextual factors and procrastination behavior may be reciprocal.

Although procrastination seems to be a psychological phenomenon, it has wide-ranging consequences for organizations and is an important problem in light of the changing modern work environment. Traditionally, the workplace and working time provide a framework for identifying work performance and procrastination behavior. However, the contemporary realities of work are conducive to the devaluation/redefinition of where and when work. Work is increasingly characterized by a high degree of freedom in the implementation of work. Employees often work remotely, in various locations outside the company's headquarters, and with flexible working time. Hence, nowadays, it is more appropriate to define the work framework in terms of 'work conditions' than the time and place of work. This makes it extremely difficult for supervisors and employees to identify procrastination behavior. Therefore, the challenge for researchers and organizational practitioners is to recognize and address procrastination in mobile work and non-standard working hours. It seems that basic models for motivating, engaging, and sustaining work quality are no longer sufficient.

References

Agarwal, U. A., & Avey, J. B. (2020). Abusive supervisors and employees who cyberloaf. *Internet Research, 30*(3), 789–809. https://doi.org/10.1108/INTR-05-2019-0208

Ahmad, Z., Munir, N., & Hussain, M. (2021). Procrastination and job performance of employees working in public and private sector organizations. *Pakistan Social Sciences Review, 5*(2), 1166–1176. https://doi.org/10.35484/pssr.2021(5-II)89

Aronsson, G., Theorell, T., Grape, T., Hammarström, A., Hogstedt, C., Marteinsdottir, I., Skoog, I., Träskman-Bendz, L., & Hall, C. (2017). A systematic review including meta-analysis of work environment and burnout symptoms. *BMC Public Health, 17*(1), 264. https://doi.org/10.1186/s12889-017-4153-7

Arshad, M., Aftab, M., & Bukhari, H. (2016). The impact of job characteristics and role stressors on cyberloafing: The case of Pakistan. *International Journal of Scientific and Research Publications, 6*(12), 244–252.

Bajcar, B., & Babiak, J. (2020). Job characteristics and cyberloafing among Polish IT professionals: Mediating role of work stress. In K. S. Soliman (Ed.), *Proceedings of the 36th International Business Information Management Association Conference* (pp. 6565–6578). The IBIMA Conference, 4-5 November, Granada, Spain.

Bajcar, B., & Babiak, J. (2022). Transformational and transactional leadership in the Polish organizational context: Validation of the full and short forms of the Multifactor Leadership Questionnaire. *Frontiers in Psychology, 13*, 908594. https://doi.org/10.3389/fpsyg.2022.908594

Baka, Ł., Derbis, R., & Walczak, R. (2015). Psychometryczne właściwości Kwestionariusza Zachowań Kontrproduktywnych CWB-C [Psychometric properties of the Polish version of Counterproductive Work Behavior – Checklist (CWB-C)]. *Czasopismo Psychologiczne [Psychological Journal], 21*(2), 163–174. https://doi.org/10.14691/CPPJ.21.2.163

Bakker, A. B., & Demerouti, E. (2007). The job demands-resources model: State of the art. *Journal of Managerial Psychology, 22*(3), 309–328. https://doi.org/10.1108/02683940710733115

Bakker, A. B., & Demerouti, E. (2014). Job demands–resources theory. In P. Y. Chen & C. L. Cooper (Eds.), *Wellbeing: A complete reference guide* (pp. 1–28). John Wiley & Sons Inc. https://doi.org/10.1002/9781118539415.wbwell019

Bakker, A. B., Demerouti, E., & Sanz-Vergel, A. (2023). Job demands–resources theory: Ten years later. *Annual Review of Organizational Psychology and Organizational Behavior, 10*(1), 25–53. https://doi.org/10.1146/annurev-orgpsych-120920-053933

Bakker, A. B., Hakanen, J. J., Demerouti, E., & Xanthopoulou, D. (2007). Job resources boost work engagement, particularly when job demands are high. *Journal of Educational Psychology, 99*(2), 274–284. https://doi.org/10.1037/0022-0663.99.2.274

Balducci, C., Schaufeli, W. B., & Fraccaroli, F. (2011). The job demands–resources model and counterproductive work behaviour: The role of job-related affect. *European Journal of Work and Organizational Psychology, 20*(4), 467–496. https://doi.org/10.1080/13594321003669061

Barabanshchikova, V. V., Ivanova, S. A., & Klimova, O. A. (2018). The impact of organizational and personal factors on procrastination in employees of a modern Russian industrial enterprise. *Psychology in Russia: State of the Art, 11*(3), 69–85. https://doi.org/10.11621/pir.2018.0305

Bass, B. M., & Avolio, B. J. (1994). Transformational leadership and organizational culture. *International Journal of Public Administration, 17*(3-4), 541–554. https://doi.org/10.1080/01900699408524907

Beaton, D. E., Bombardier, C., Guillemin, F., & Ferraz, M. B. (2000). Guidelines for the process of cross-cultural adaptation of self-report measures. *Spine, 25*(24), 3186–3191. https://doi.org/10.1097/00007632-200012150-00014

Berthelsen, H., Hakanen, J. J., & Westerlund, H. (2018). Copenhagen Psychosocial Questionnaire - A validation study using the job demand-resources model. *PLoS One, 13*(4), e0196450. https://doi.org/10.1371/journal.pone.0196450

Black, E., Light, J., Black, N. P., & Thomson, L. (2013). Online social network use by health care providers in a high traffic patient care environment. *Journal of Medical Internet Research, 15*(5), e94. https://doi.org/10.2196/jmir.2421

Blanchard, A. L., & Henle, C. A. (2008). Correlates of different forms of cyberloafing: The role of norms and external locus of control. *Computers in Human Behavior, 24*(3), 1067–1084. https://doi.org/10.1016/j.chb.2007.03.008

Byrne, B. M. (2016). *Structural equation modeling with AMOS: Basic concepts, applications, and programming* (3rd ed.). Routledge. https://doi.org/10.4324/9781315757421

Cadena, X., Schoar, A., Cristea, A., & Delgado-Medrano, H. (2011). *Fighting procrastination in the workplace: An experiment.* https://doi.org/10.3386/w16944

Chen, J. V., Ross, W. H., & Yang, H.-H. (2011). Personality and motivational factors predicting Internet abuse at work. *Cyberpsychology: Journal of Psychosocial Research on Cyberspace, 5*(1), Article 5.

Chevrenidi, A., & Bolotova, A. (2018). Relationships between time perspectives and procrastination of employees with different job titles. *Psychology. Journal of the Higher School Economics, 15*(3), 573–589. https://doi.org/10.17323/1813-8918-2018-3-573-589

Choi, J. N., & Moran, S. V. (2009). Why not procrastinate? Development and validation of a new active procrastination scale. *The Journal of Social Psychology, 149*(2), 195–211. https://doi.org/10.3200/SOCP.149.2.195-212

Claessens, B. J., van Eerde, W., Rutte, C. G., & Roe, R. A. (2007). A review of the time management literature. *Personnel Review, 36*(2), 255–276. https://doi.org/10.1108/00483480710726136

Cohen, J. (1992). A power primer. *Psychological Bulletin, 112*(1), 155–159. https://doi.org/10.1037/0033-2909.112.1.155

Cronbach, L. J. (1951). Coefficient alpha and the internal structure of tests. *Psychometrika, 16*(3), 297–334. https://doi.org/10.1007/BF02310555

DeArmond, S., Matthews, R. A., & Bunk, J. (2014). Workload and procrastination: The roles of psychological detachment and fatigue. *International Journal of Stress Management, 21*(2), 137–161. https://doi.org/10.1037/a0034893

Deci, E. L., & Ryan, R. M. (2008). Self-determination theory: A macrotheory of human motivation, development, and health. *Canadian Psychology / Psychologie Canadienne, 49*(3), 182–185. https://doi.org/10.1037/a0012801

Demerouti, E., Peeters, M. C. W., & van den Heuvel, M. (2019). Job crafting interventions: Do they work and why? In L. E. van Zyl & S. Rothmann (Eds.), *Positive psychological intervention design and protocols for multi-cultural contexts* (1st ed. 2019, pp. 103–125). Springer International Publishing. https://doi.org/10.1007/978-3-030-20020-6_5

Eckert, M., Ebert, D. D., Lehr, D., Sieland, B., & Berking, M. (2016). Overcome procrastination: Enhancing emotion regulation skills reduce procrastination. *Learning and Individual Differences*, *52*, 10–18. https://doi.org/10.1016/j.lindif.2016.10.001

Edwards, J. A., Webster, S., van Laar, D., & Easton, S. (2008). Psychometric analysis of the UK Health and Safety Executive's Management Standards work-related stress indicator tool. *Work & Stress*, *22*(2), 96–107. https://doi.org/10.1080/02678370802166599

Ellen, B. P., Alexander, K. C., Mackey, J. D., McAllister, C. P., & Carson, J. E. (2021). Portrait of a workplace deviant: A clearer picture of the big five and Dark Triad as predictors of workplace deviance. *The Journal of Applied Psychology*, *106*(12), 1950–1961. https://doi.org/10.1037/apl0000880

Elpidorou, A. (2018). The bored mind is a guiding mind: Toward a regulatory theory of boredom. *Phenomenology and the Cognitive Sciences*, *17*(3), 455–484. https://doi.org/10.1007/s11097-017-9515-1

Elrehail, H., Rehman, S. U., Chaudhry, N. I., & Alzghoul, A. (2021). Nexus among cyberloafing behavior, job demands and job resources: A mediated-moderated model. *Education and Information Technologies*, *26*(4), 4731–4749. https://doi.org/10.1007/s10639-021-10496-1

Fernie, B. A., Bharucha, Z., Nikčević, A. V., & Spada, M. M. (2017). The Unintentional Procrastination Scale. *Journal of Rational-Emotive and Cognitive-Behavior Therapy: RET*, *35*(2), 136–149. https://doi.org/10.1007/s10942-016-0247-x

Fernie, B. A., Spada, M. M., Nikčević, A. V., Georgiou, G. A., & Moneta, G. B. (2009). Metacognitive beliefs about procrastination: Development and concurrent validity of a self-report questionnaire. *Journal of Cognitive Psychotherapy*, *23*(4), 283–293. https://doi.org/10.1891/0889-8391.23.4.283

Ferrari, J. R. (1992a). Procrastination in the workplace: Attributions for failure among individuals with similar behavioral tendencies. *Personality and Individual Differences*, *13*(3), 315–319. https://doi.org/10.1016/0191-8869(92)90108-2

Ferrari, J. R. (1992b). Psychometric validation of two procrastination inventories for adults: Arousal and avoidance measures. *Journal of Psychopathology and Behavioral Assessment*, *14*(2), 97–110. https://doi.org/10.1007/BF00965170

Ferrari, J. R., Díaz-Morales, J. F., O'Callaghan, J., Díaz, K., & Argumedo, D. (2007). Frequent behavioral delay tendencies by adults. *Journal of Cross-Cultural Psychology*, *38*(4), 458–464. https://doi.org/10.1177/0022022107302314

Ferrari, J. R., Doroszko, E., & Joseph, N. (2005). Exploring procrastination in corporate settings: Sex, status, and settings for arousal and avoidance types. *Individual Differences Research*, *3*(2), 140–149.

Ferrari, J. R., & Patel, T. (2004). Social comparisons by procrastinators: Rating peers with similar or dissimilar delay tendencies. Personality and Individual Differences, 37(7), 1493–1501. https://doi.org/10.1016/j.paid.2004.02.006

Ferris, D. L., Rosen, C. R., Johnson, R. E., Brown, D. J., Risavy, S. D., & Heller, D. (2011). Approach or avoidance (or both?): Integrating core self-evaluations within an approach/avoidance framework. *Personnel Psychology*, *64*(1), 137–161. https://doi.org/10.1111/j.1744-6570.2010.01204.x

Flett, G. L., Blankstein, K. R., & Martin, T. R. (1995). Procrastination, negative self-evaluation, and stress in depression and anxiety. In J. R. Ferrari, J. L. Johnson, & W. G. McCown (Eds.), *Procrastination and task avoidance* (pp. 137–167). Springer US. https://doi.org/10.1007/978-1-4899-0227-6_7

Fox, S., & Spector, P. E. (Eds.). (2005). *Counterproductive work behavior: Investigations of actors and targets* (1st ed.). American Psychological Association. https://doi.org /10.1037/10893-000

Garrett, R. K., & Danziger, J. N. (2008). On cyberslacking: Workplace status and personal Internet use at work. *CyberPsychology & Behavior, 11*(3), 287–292. https:// doi.org/10.1089/cpb.2007.0146

Göncü Köse, A., & Metin, U. B. (2018). Linking leadership style and workplace procrastination: The role of organizational citizenship behavior and turnover intention. *Journal of Prevention & Intervention in the Community, 46*(3), 245–262. https://doi .org/10.1080/10852352.2018.1470369

Gosling, S. D., Rentfrow, P. J., & Swann, W. B. (2003). A very brief measure of the big-five personality domains. *Journal of Research in Personality, 37*(6), 504–528. https:// doi.org/10.1016/S0092-6566(03)00046-1

Gruys, M. L., & Sackett, P. R. (2003). Investigating the dimensionality of counterproductive work behavior. *International Journal of Selection and Assessment, 11*(1), 30–42. https://doi.org/10.1111/1468-2389.00224

Gupta, R., Hershey, D. A., & Gaur, J. (2012). Time perspective and procrastination in the workplace: An empirical investigation. *Current Psychology, 31*(2), 195–211. https:// doi.org/10.1007/s12144-012-9136-3

Hackman, J. R., & Oldham, G. R. (1980). *Work redesign.* Addison-Wesley.

Haesevoets, T., de Cremer, D., Hirst, G., de Schutter, L., Stouten, J., van Dijke, M., & van Hiel, A. (2022). The effect of decisional leader procrastination on employee innovation: Investigating the moderating role of employees' resistance to change. *Journal of Leadership & Organizational Studies, 29*(1), 131–146. https://doi.org/10 .1177/15480518211044166

Hair, J. F., Howard, M. C., & Nitzl, C. (2020). Assessing measurement model quality in PLS-SEM using confirmatory composite analysis. *Journal of Business Research, 109,* 101–110. https://doi.org/10.1016/j.jbusres.2019.11.069

Hajloo, N. (2014). Relationships between self-efficacy, self-esteem and procrastination in undergraduate psychology students. *Iranian Journal of Psychiatry and Behavioral Sciences, 8*(3), 42–49. https://pubmed.ncbi.nlm.nih.gov/25780374/

Hakanen, J. J., Schaufeli, W. B., & Ahola, K. (2008). The job demands-resources model: A three-year cross-lagged study of burnout, depression, commitment, and work engagement. *Work & Stress, 22*(3), 224–241. https://doi.org/10.1080 /02678370802379432

Halbesleben, J. R. B. (2010). A meta-analysis of work engagement: Relationships with burnout, demands, resources, and consequences. In A. B. Bakker & M. P. Leiter (Eds.), *Work engagement: A handbook of essential theory and research* (pp. 102–117). Psychology Press.

Hammer, C. A., & Ferrari, J. R. (2002). Differential incidence of procrastination between blue and white-collar workers. *Current Psychology, 21*(4), 333–338. https://doi.org /10.1007/s12144-002-1022-y

Hayes, A. F. (2022). *Introduction to mediation, moderation, and conditional process analysis: A regression-based approach* (3rd ed.). The Guilford Press.

He, Q., Wu, M., Wu, W., & Fu, J. (2021). The effect of abusive supervision on employees' work procrastination behavior. *Frontiers in Psychology, 12,* 596704. https://doi.org /10.3389/fpsyg.2021.596704

Hen, M., & Goroshit, M. (2018). General and life-domain procrastination in highly educated adults in Israel. *Frontiers in Psychology*, *9*, 1173. https://doi.org/10.3389/fpsyg.2018.01173

Hen, M., Goroshit, M., & Viengarten, S. (2021). How decisional and general procrastination relate to procrastination at work: An investigation of office and non-office workers. *Personality and Individual Differences*, *172*, 110581. https://doi.org/10.1016/j.paid.2020.110581

Henle, C. A., & Blanchard, A. L. (2008). The interaction of work stressors and organizational sanctions on cyberloafing. *Journal of Managerial Issues*, *20*(3), 383–400. https://www.jstor.org/stable/40604617

Hobfoll, S. E. (1989). Conservation of resources. A new attempt at conceptualizing stress. *American Psychologist*, *44*(3), 513–524. https://doi.org/10.1037/0003-066x.44.3.513

Howell, A. J., Watson, D. C., Powell, R. A., & Buro, K. (2006). Academic procrastination: The pattern and correlates of behavioural postponement. *Personality and Individual Differences*, *40*(8), 1519–1530. https://doi.org/10.1016/j.paid.2005.11.023

Hu, L. T., & Bentler, P. M. (1999). Cutoff criteria for fit indexes in covariance structure analysis: Conventional criteria versus new alternatives. *Structural Equation Modeling: A Multidisciplinary Journal*, *6*, 1–55. http://dx.doi.org/10.1080/10705519909540118

Huang, Q., Zhang, K., Huang, Y., Bodla, A. A., & Zou, X. (2023). The interactive effect of stressor appraisals and personal traits on employees' procrastination behavior: The conservation of resources perspective. *Psychology Research and Behavior Management*, *16*, 781–800. https://doi.org/10.2147/PRBM.S399406

Hutmanová, N., Hajduová, Z., Dorčák, P., & Laskovský, V. (2022). Prevention of procrastination at work through motivation enhancement in small and medium enterprises in Slovakia. *Entrepreneurship and Sustainability Issues*, *10*(2), 418–428. https://doi.org/10.9770/jesi.2022.10.2(26)

Jiang, H., Siponen, M., & Tsohou, A. (2021). Personal use of technology at work: A literature review and a theoretical model for understanding how it affects employee job performance. *European Journal of Information Systems*, 1–15. https://doi.org/10.1080/0960085X.2021.1963193

Jonason, P. K., & Webster, G. D. (2010). The dirty dozen: A concise measure of the dark triad. *Psychological Assessment*, *22*(2), 420–432. https://doi.org/10.1037/a0019265

Judge, T. A., Erez, A., Bono, J. E., & Thoresen, C. J. (2002). Are measures of self-esteem, neuroticism, locus of control, and generalized self-efficacy indicators of a common core construct? *Journal of Personality and Social Psychology*, *83*(3), 693–710. https://doi.org/10.1037//0022-3514.83.3.693

Judge, T. A., Ilies, R., & Zhang, Z. (2012). Genetic influences on core self-evaluations, job satisfaction, and work stress: A behavioral genetics mediated model. *Organizational Behavior and Human Decision Processes*, *117*(1), 208–220. https://doi.org/10.1016/j.obhdp.2011.08.005

Khoshouei, M. S. (2017). Prediction of procrastination considering job characteristics and locus of control in nurses. *Journal of Holistic Nursing and Midwifery*, *27*(2), 27–35. https://doi.org/10.18869/acadpub.hnmj.27.2.27

Kircaburun, K., & Griffiths, M. D. (2018). The dark side of Internet: Preliminary evidence for the associations of dark personality traits with specific online activities and problematic Internet use. *Journal of Behavioral Addictions*, *7*(4), 993–1003. https://doi.org/10.1556/2006.7.2018.109

Klassen, R. M., Krawchuk, L. L., & Rajani, S. (2008). Academic procrastination of undergraduates: Low self-efficacy to self-regulate predicts higher levels of procrastination. *Contemporary Educational Psychology*, *33*(4), 915–931. https://doi.org/10.1016/j.cedpsych.2007.07.001

Klingsieck, K. B. (2013). Procrastination in different life-domains: Is procrastination domain specific? *Current Psychology*, *32*(2), 175–185. https://doi.org/10.1007/s12144-013-9171-8

Koay, K. Y., Lim, V. K., Soh, P. C.-H., Ong, D. L. T., Ho, J. S. Y., & Lim, P. K. (2022). Abusive supervision and cyberloafing: A moderated moderation model of moral disengagement and negative reciprocity beliefs. *Information & Management*, *59*(2), 103600. https://doi.org/10.1016/j.im.2022.103600

Koay, K. Y., Soh, P. C.-H., & Chew, K. W. (2017). Do employees' private demands lead to cyberloafing? The mediating role of job stress. *Management Research Review*, *40*(9), 1025–1038. https://doi.org/10.1108/MRR-11-2016-0252

Koppenborg, M., & Klingsieck, K. B. (2022). Social factors of procrastination: Group work can reduce procrastination among students. *Social Psychology of Education*, 25, 249–274. https://doi.org/10.1007/s11218-021-09682-3

Kühnel, J., Bledow, R., & Feuerhahn, N. (2016). When do you procrastinate? Sleep quality and social sleep lag jointly predict self-regulatory failure at work. *Journal of Organizational Behavior*, *37*(7), 983–1002. https://doi.org/10.1002/job.2084

Kühnel, J., Sonnentag, S., Bledow, R., & Melchers, K. G. (2018). The relevance of sleep and circadian misalignment for procrastination among shift workers. *Journal of Occupational and Organizational Psychology*, *91*(1), 110–133. https://doi.org/10.1111/joop.12191

Lavoie, J. A. A., & Pychyl, T. A. (2001). Cyberslacking and the procrastination superhighway. *Social Science Computer Review*, *19*(4), 431–444. https://doi.org/10.1177/089443930101900403

Lay, C. H. (1986). At last, my research article on procrastination. *Journal of Research in Personality*, *20*(4), 474–495. https://doi.org/10.1016/0092-6566(86)90127-3

Lay, C. H. (1997). Explaining lower-order traits through higher-order factors: the case of trait procrastination, conscientiousness, and the specificity dilemma. *European Journal of Personality*, *11*(4), 267–278. https://doi.org/10.1002/(SICI)1099-0984(199711)11:4<267::AID-PER281>3.0.CO;2-P

Laybourn, S., Frenzel, A. C., & Fenzl, T. (2019). Teacher procrastination, emotions, and stress: A qualitative study. *Frontiers in Psychology*, *10*, 2325. https://doi.org/10.3389/fpsyg.2019.02325

Legood, A., Lee, A., Schwarz, G., & Newman, A. (2018). From self-defeating to other defeating: Examining the effects of leader procrastination on follower work outcomes. *Journal of Occupational and Organizational Psychology*, *91*(2), 430–439. https://doi.org/10.1111/joop.12205

Liberman, B., Seidman, G., McKenna, K. Y., & Buffardi, L. E. (2011). Employee job attitudes and organizational characteristics as predictors of cyberloafing. *Computers in Human Behavior*, *27*(6), 2192–2199. https://doi.org/10.1016/j.chb.2011.06.015

Lim, P. K., Koay, K. Y., & Chong, W. Y. (2021). The effects of abusive supervision, emotional exhaustion and organizational commitment on cyberloafing: A moderated-mediation examination. *Internet Research*, *31*(2), 497–518. https://doi.org/10.1108/INTR-03-2020-0165

Lim, V. K. G., & Chen, D. J. Q. (2012). Cyberloafing at the workplace: Gain or drain on work? *Behaviour & Information Technology, 31*(4), 343–353. https://doi.org/10.1080/01449290903353054

Lim, V. K. G., & Teo, T. S. H. (2024). Cyberloafing: A review and research agenda. *Applied Psychology, 73*(1), 441–484. https://doi.org/10.1111/apps.12452

Lin, H. (2018). The effect of inclusive leadership on employees' procrastination. *Psychology, 9*(4), 714–727. https://doi.org/10.4236/psych.2018.94045

Lonergan, J. M., & Maher, K. J. (2000). The relationship between job characteristics and workplace procrastination as moderated by locus of control. *Journal of Social Behavior & Personality, 15*(5), 213–224.

Lowe-Calverley, E., & Grieve, R. (2017). Web of deceit: Relationships between the dark triad, perceived ability to deceive and cyberloafing. *Cyberpsychology: Journal of Psychosocial Research on Cyberspace, 11*(2). https://doi.org/10.5817/CP2017-2-5

Lyons, M., & Rice, H. (2014). Thieves of time? Procrastination and the Dark Triad of personality. *Personality and Individual Differences, 61–62,* 34–37. https://doi.org/10.1016/j.paid.2014.01.002

Ma, H., Zou, J.-M., Zhong, Y., & He, J.-Q. (2021). The influence of mobile phone addiction and work procrastination on burnout among newly graduated Chinese nurses. *Perspectives in Psychiatric Care, 57*(4), 1798–1805. https://doi.org/10.1111/ppc.12752

Mäkikangas, A., Bakker, A. B., Aunola, K., & Demerouti, E. (2010). Job resources and flow at work: Modelling the relationship via latent growth curve and mixture model methodology. *Journal of Occupational and Organizational Psychology, 83*(3), 795–814. https://doi.org/10.1348/096317909X476333

Mann, L., Burnett, P., Radford, M., & Ford, S. (1997). The Melbourne Decision Making Questionnaire: An instrument for measuring patterns for coping with decisional conflict. *Journal of Behavioral Decision Making, 10*(1), 1–19. https://doi.org/10.1002/(SICI)1099-0771(199703)10:1<1::AID-BDM242>3.0.CO;2-X

Mariani, M. G., & Ferrari, J. R. (2012). Adult Inventory of Procrastination scale (AIP): A comparison of models with an Italian sample. *TPM - Testing, Psychometrics, Methodology in Applied Psychology, 1,* 3–14. https://doi.org/10.4473/TPM19.1.1

Markiewicz, K., & Dziewulska, P. (2018). Procrastination predictors and moderating effect of personality traits. *Polish Psychological Forum, 23*(3), 593–603. https://doi.org/10.14656/PFP20180308

McCown, W., Johnson, J., & Petzel, T. (1989). Procrastination, a principal components analysis. *Personality and Individual Differences, 10*(2), 197–202. https://doi.org/10.1016/0191-8869(89)90204-3

McCrae, R. R., & Costa, P. T. (2003). *Personality in adulthood: A five-factor theory perspective* (2nd ed.). Guilford Press. https://doi.org/10.4324/9780203428412

Meng, X., Pan, Y., & Li, C. (2024). Portraits of procrastinators: A meta-analysis of personality and procrastination. *Personality and Individual Differences, 218,* 112490. https://doi.org/10.1016/j.paid.2023.112490

Mercado, B. K., Dilchert, S., Giordano, C., & Ones, D. S. (2017). Counterproductive work behaviors. In D. S. Ones, N. Anderson, C. Viswesvaran, & H. K. Sinangil (Eds.), *The SAGE Handbook of Industrial, Work and Organizational Psychology: Personnel Psychology and Employee Performance* (pp. 109–210). SAGE Publications Ltd. https://doi.org/10.4135/9781473914940.n7

Mercado, B. K., Giordano, C., & Dilchert, S. (2017). A meta-analytic investigation of cyberloafing. *Career Development International*, *22*(5), 546–564. https://doi.org/10.1108/CDI-08-2017-0142

Metin, U. B., Peeters, M. C. W., & Taris, T. W. (2018). Correlates of procrastination and performance at work: The role of having "good fit". *Journal of Prevention & Intervention in the Community*, *46*(3), 228–244. https://doi.org/10.1080/10852352.2018.1470187

Metin, U. B., Taris, T. W., & Peeters, M. C. (2016). Measuring procrastination at work and its associated workplace aspects. *Personality and Individual Differences*, *101*, 254–263. https://doi.org/10.1016/j.paid.2016.06.006

Metin, U. B., Taris, T. W., Peeters, M. C. W., Korpinen, M., Smrke, U., Razum, J., Kolářová, M., Baykova, R., & Gaioshko, D. (2020). Validation of the Procrastination at Work Scale. *European Journal of Psychological Assessment*, *36*(5), 767–776. https://doi.org/10.1027/1015-5759/a000554

Meyer, R. D., Kelly, E. D., & Bowling, N. A. (2020). Situational strength theory. In D. C. Funder, J. F. Rauthmann, & R. Sherman (Eds.), *Oxford library of psychology. The Oxford handbook of psychological situations* (pp. 78–95). Oxford University Press. https://doi.org/10.1093/oxfordhb/9780190263348.013.7

Mischel, W., & Shoda, Y. (1995). A cognitive-affective system theory of personality: Reconceptualizing situations, dispositions, dynamics, and invariance in personality structure. *Psychological Review*, *102*(2), 246–268. https://doi.org/10.1037//0033-295x.102.2.246

Mohsin, F. Z., & Ayub, N. (2014). The relationship between procrastination, delay of gratification, and job satisfaction among high school teachers. *Japanese Psychological Research*, *56*(3), 224–234. https://doi.org/10.1111/jpr.12046

Moon, S. M., & Illingworth, A. J. (2005). Exploring the dynamic nature of procrastination: A latent growth curve analysis of academic procrastination. *Personality and Individual Differences*, *38*(2), 297–309. https://doi.org/10.1016/j.paid.2004.04.009

Moor, L., & Anderson, J. R. (2019). A systematic literature review of the relationship between dark personality traits and antisocial online behaviours. *Personality and Individual Differences*, *144*, 40–55. https://doi.org/10.1016/j.paid.2019.02.027

Mosquera, P., Soares, M. E., Dordio, P., & Melo, L. A. E. (2022). The thief of time and social sustainability: Analysis of a procrastination at work model. *Revista De Administração De Empresas*, *62*(5), Article e2021-0313. https://doi.org/10.1590/s0034-759020220510

Munjal, S., & Mishra, R. (2019). Associative impact of personality orientation and levels of stress on procrastination in middle-level managers. *Indian Journal of Public Administration*, *65*(1), 53–70. https://doi.org/10.1177/0019556118820456

Murphy, L. R., & Sauter, S. L. (2004). Work organization interventions: State of knowledge and future directions. *Sozial- Und Praventivmedizin*, *49*(2), 79–86. https://doi.org/10.1007/s00038-004-3085-z

Muthén, B. O., Muthén, L. K., & Asparouhov, T. (2017). *Regression and mediation analysis using Mplus*. Muthén & Muthén.

Paulhus, D. L., & Williams, K. M. (2002). The Dark Triad of personality: Narcissism, Machiavellianism, and psychopathy. *Journal of Research in Personality*, *36*(6), 556–563. https://doi.org/10.1016/S0092-6566(02)00505-6

Pearlman-Avnion, S., & Zibenberg, A. (2018). Prediction and job-related outcomes of procrastination in the workplace. *Journal of Prevention & Intervention in the Community*, *46*(3), 263–278. https://doi.org/10.1080/10852352.2018.1470418

Pejtersen, J. H., Kristensen, T. S., Borg, V., & Bjorner, J. B. (2010). The second version of the Copenhagen Psychosocial Questionnaire. *Scandinavian Journal of Public Health*, *38*(3 Suppl), 8–24. https://doi.org/10.1177/1403494809349858

Peterson, R. A. (1994). A meta-analysis of Cronbach's coefficient alpha. *Journal of Consumer Research*, *21*(2), 381. https://doi.org/10.1086/209405

Pindek, S., Krajcevska, A., & Spector, P. E. (2018). Cyberloafing as a coping mechanism: Dealing with workplace boredom. *Computers in Human Behavior*, *86*, 147–152. https://doi.org/10.1016/j.chb.2018.04.040

Pletzer, J. L., Breevaart, K., & Bakker, A. B. (2024). Constructive and destructive leadership in job demands-resources theory: A meta-analytic test of the motivational and health-impairment pathways. *Organizational Psychology Review*, *14*(1), 131–165. https://doi.org/10.1177/20413866231197519

Podsakoff, P. M., MacKenzie, S. B., Lee, J.-Y., & Podsakoff, N. P. (2003). Common method biases in behavioral research: A critical review of the literature and recommended remedies. *Journal of Applied Psychology*, *88*(5), 879–903. https://doi.org/10.1037/0021-9010.88.5.879

Polit, D. F. (2014). Getting serious about test-retest reliability: A critique of retest research and some recommendations. *Quality of Life Research*, *23*(6), 1713–1720. https://doi.org/10.1007/s11136-014-0632-9

Prem, R., Scheel, T. E., Weigelt, O., Hoffmann, K., & Korunka, C. (2018). Procrastination in daily working life: A diary study on within-person processes that link work characteristics to workplace procrastination. *Frontiers in Psychology*, *9*, 1087. https://doi.org/10.3389/fpsyg.2018.01087

Rehman, S., Qamar-ul-islam, & Ali, Z.Z. A. (2019). Predictive relationship between procrastination, pork stress and mental well-being among bank employees of Gujranwala. *International Journal of Scientific Research in Multidisciplinary Studies*, *5*(12), 79–85.

Reijseger, G., Schaufeli, W. B., Peeters, M. C. W., Taris, T. W., van Beek, I., & Ouweneel, E. (2013). Watching the paint dry at work: Psychometric examination of the Dutch Boredom Scale. *Anxiety, Stress & Coping*, *26*(5), 508–525. https://doi.org/10.1080/10615806.2012.720676

Rosenberg, M. (1965). *Rosenberg Self-Esteem Scale (RSES)*. APA PsycTests. https://doi.org/10.1037/t01038-000

Roster, C. A., & Ferrari, J. R. (2020). Time is on my side-or Is It? Assessing how perceived control of time and procrastination influence emotional exhaustion on the job. *Behavioral Sciences*, *10*(6), 98. https://doi.org/10.3390/bs10060098

Rozental, A., & Carlbring, P. (2013). Internet-based cognitive behavior therapy for procrastination: Study protocol for a randomized controlled trial. *JMIR Research Protocols*, *2*(2), e46. https://doi.org/10.2196/resprot.2801

Rucker, D. D., Preacher, K. J., Tormala, Z. L., & Petty, R. E. (2011). Mediation analysis in social psychology: Current practices and new recommendations. *Social and Personality Psychology Compass*, *5*(6), 359–371. doi:10.1111/j.1751-9004.2011.00355.x

Salehi, R. (2020). Effect of ACT on work procrastination and work performance. *Journal of Preventive Counselling*, *1*(1), 33–46. https://jpc.uma.ac.ir/article_976.html

Saman, A., & Wirawan, H. (2021). Examining the impact of psychological capital on academic achievement and work performance: The roles of procrastination and conscientiousness. *Cogent Psychology*, *8*(1), Article 1938853. https://doi.org/10.1080/23311908.2021.1938853

Sanecka, E. (2022). Psychopathy and procrastination: Triarchic conceptualization of psychopathy and its relations to active and passive procrastination. *Current Psychology*, *41*(2), 863–876. https://doi.org/10.1007/s12144-020-00604-8

Sarwat, N., Ali, R., & Khan, T. I. (2021). Cognitive job demands, presenteeism and procrastination: The moderating role of psychological capital. *Sir Syed Journal of Education & Social Research*, *4*(1), 193–203. https://doi.org/10.36902/sjesr-vol4-iss1 -2021(193-203)

Schaufeli, W. B. (2015). Engaging leadership in the job demands-resources model. *Career Development International*, *20*(5), 446–463. https://doi.org/10.1108/cdi-02 -2015-0025

Schaufeli, W. B., Bakker, A. B., & Salanova, M. (2006). The measurement of work engagement with a short questionnaire. *Educational and Psychological Measurement*, *66*(4), 701–716. https://doi.org/10.1177/0013164405282471

Schaufeli, W. B., Leiter, M. P., & Maslach, C. (2009). Burnout: 35 years of research and practice. *Career Development International*, *14*(3), 204–220. https://doi.org/10.1108 /13620430910966406

Schaufeli, W. B., & Taris, T. W. (2013). A critical review of the job demands-resources model: Implications for improving work and health. In G. F. Bauer (Ed.), *Bridging occupational* (pp. 43–68). Springer. https://doi.org/10.1007/978-94-007-5640-3_4

Schwarzer, R., & Jerusalem, M. (1995). *PsycTESTS dataset*. https://doi.org/10.1037/ t00393-000

Senécal, C., Lavoie, K., & Koestner, R. (1997). Trait and situational factors in procrastination: An interactional model. *Journal of Social Behavior & Personality*, *12*(4), 889–903.

Shin, J., & Grant, A. M. (2021). When putting work off pays off: The curvilinear relationship between procrastination and creativity. *Academy of Management Journal*, *64*(3), 772–798. https://doi.org/10.5465/amj.2018.1471

Singh, S., & Bala, R. (2020). Mediating role of self-efficacy on the relationship between conscientiousness and procrastination. *International Journal of Work Organisation and Emotion*, *11*(1), Article 109422, 41. https://doi.org/10.1504/IJWOE.2020.109422

Singh, S., & Singh, D. R. (2015). Procrastination patterns of transactional and transformational leaders. *Pacific Business Review International*, *8*(1), 33–40. http:// www.pbr.co.in/2015/2015_month/july/5.pdf

Sirois, F. M. (2023). Procrastination and stress: A conceptual review of why context matters. *International Journal of Environmental Research and Public Health*, *20*(6), 5031. https://doi.org/10.3390/ijerph20065031

Sirois, F. M., Yang, S., & van Eerde, W. (2019). Development and validation of the General Procrastination Scale (GPS-9): A short and reliable measure of trait procrastination. *Personality and Individual Differences*, *146*, 26–33. https://doi.org /10.1016/j.paid.2019.03.039

Sonnentag, S., & Fritz, C. (2015). Recovery from job stress: The stressor-detachment model as an integrative framework. *Journal of Organizational Behavior*, *36*(S1), S72–S103. https://doi.org/10.1002/job.1924

Steel, P. (2007). The nature of procrastination: A meta-analytic and theoretical review of quintessential self-regulatory failure. *Psychological Bulletin*, *133*(1), 65–94.

Steel, P. (2010). Arousal, avoidant and decisional procrastinators: Do they exist? *Personality and Individual Differences*, *48*(8), 926–934.

Steel, P., Brothen, T., & Wambach, C. (2001). Procrastination and personality, performance, and mood. *Personality and Individual Differences*, *30*(1), 95–106. https://doi.org/10.1016/S0191-8869(00)00013-1

Sümer, C., & Büttner, O. B. (2022). I'll do it - after one more scroll: The effects of boredom proneness, self-control, and impulsivity on online procrastination. *Frontiers in Psychology*, *13*, 918306. https://doi.org/10.3389/fpsyg.2022.918306

Svartdal, F., Granmo, S., & Færevaag, F. S. (2018). On the behavioral side of procrastination: Exploring behavioral delay in real-life settings. *Frontiers in Psychology*, *9*, 746. https://doi.org/10.3389/fpsyg.2018.00746

Svartdal, F., & Steel, P. (2017). Irrational delay revisited: Examining five procrastination scales in a global sample. *Frontiers in Psychology*, *8*, 1927. https://doi.org/10.3389/fpsyg.2017.01927

Tabachnick, B. G., Fidell, L. S., & Ullman, J. B. (2019). *Using multivariate statistics* (7th ed.). Pearson.

Tandon, A., Kaur, P., Ruparel, N., Islam, J. U., & Dhir, A. (2022). Cyberloafing and cyberslacking in the workplace: Systematic literature review of past achievements and future promises. *Internet Research*, *32*(1), 55–89. https://doi.org/10.1108/INTR-06-2020-0332

Tepper, B. J. (2000). Consequences of abusive supervision. *Academy of Management Journal*, *43*(2), 178–190. https://doi.org/10.5465/1556375

Tice, D. M., & Baumeister, R. F. (2018). Longitudinal study of procrastination, performance, stress, and health: The costs and benefits of dawdling. In R. F. Baumeister (Ed.), *Self-regulation and self-control* (pp. 299–309). Routledge. https://doi.org/10.4324/9781315175775-9

Tuckman, B. W. (1991). The development and concurrent validity of the procrastination scale. *Educational and Psychological Measurement*, *51*(2), 473–480. https://doi.org/10.1177/0013164491512022

Tudose, C.-M., & Pavalache-Ilie, M. (2021). Procrastination and work satisfaction. *Social Science and Law*, *14(63)*(1), 37–46. https://doi.org/10.31926/but.ssl.2021.14.63.1.4

Uysal, H. T., & Yilmaz, F. (2020). Procrastination in the workplace: The role of hierarchical career plateau. *Upravlenets*, *11*(3), 82–101.

van den Berg, J., & Roosen, S. (2018). Two faces of employee inactivity: Procrastination and recovery. *Journal of Prevention & Intervention in the Community*, *46*(3), 295–307. https://doi.org/10.1080/10852352.2018.1470423

van Eerde, W. (2003). A meta-analytically derived nomological network of procrastination. *Personality and Individual Differences*, *35*(6), 1401–1418. https://doi.org/10.1016/S0191-8869(02)00358-6

van Eerde, W. (2004). Procrastination in academic settings and the Big Five model of personality: A meta-analysis. In H. C. Schouwenburg, C. H. Lay, T. A. Pychyl, & J. R. Ferrari (Eds.), *Counseling the procrastinator in academic settings* (pp. 29–40). American Psychological Association. https://doi.org/10.1037/10808-003

van Eerde, W. (2015). Time management and procrastination. In M. D. Mumford & M. Frese (Eds.), *The psychology of planning in organizations: Research and applications* (pp. 312–333). Routledge/Taylor & Francis Group.

van Eerde, W. (2016). Procrastination and well-being at work. In F. M. Sirois & T. A. Pychyl (Eds.), *Procrastination, health, and well-being* (pp. 233–253). Academic Press. https://doi.org/10.1016/B978-0-12-802862-9.00011-6

van Eerde, W., & Klingsieck, K. B. (2018). Overcoming procrastination? A meta-analysis of intervention studies. *Educational Research Review, 25*, 73–85. https://doi.org/10.1016/j.edurev.2018.09.002

van Eerde, W., & Venus, M. (2018). A daily diary study on sleep quality and procrastination at work: The moderating role of trait self-control. *Frontiers in Psychology, 9*, 2029. https://doi.org/10.3389/fpsyg.2018.02029

Vandenberg, R. J., & Lance, C. E. (2000). A review and synthesis of the measurement invariance literature: Suggestions, practices, and recommendations for organizational research. *Organizational Research Methods, 3*(1), 4–70. https://doi.org/10.1177/109442810031002

Vangsness, L., Voss, N. M., Maddox, N., Devereaux, V., & Martin, E. (2022). Self-report measures of procrastination exhibit inconsistent concurrent validity, predictive validity, and psychometric properties. *Frontiers in Psychology 13*, 784471. https://doi.org/10.3389/fpsyg.2022.784471

Varghese, L., & Barber, L. K. (2017). A preliminary study exploring moderating effects of role stressors on the relationship between Big Five personality traits and workplace cyberloafing. *Cyberpsychology: Journal of Psychosocial Research on Cyberspace, 11*(4). https://doi.org/10.5817/CP2017-4-4

Wäschle, K., Allgaier, A., Lachner, A., Fink, S., & Nückles, M. (2014). Procrastination and self-efficacy: Tracing vicious and virtuous circles in self-regulated learning. *Learning and Instruction, 29*, 103–114. https://doi.org/10.1016/j.learninstruc.2013.09.005

Wan, H. C., Downey, L. A., & Stough, C. (2014). Understanding non-work presenteeism: Relationships between emotional intelligence, boredom, procrastination and job stress. *Personality and Individual Differences, 65*, 86–90. https://doi.org/10.1016/j.paid.2014.01.018

Wang, J., Li, C., Meng, X., & Liu, D. (2021). Validation of the Chinese version of the Procrastination at Work Wcale. *Frontiers in Psychology, 12*, 726595. https://doi.org/10.3389/fpsyg.2021.726595

Weymann, E. C. (1988). Procrastination in the workplace: Dispositional and situational determinants of delay behavior at work. *Academy of Management Proceedings, 1988*(1), 226–230. https://doi.org/10.5465/ambpp.1988.4980589

Wu, J., Mei, W., Liu, L., & Ugrin, J. C. (2020). The bright and dark sides of social cyberloafing: Effects on employee mental health in China. *Journal of Business Research, 112*, 56–64. https://doi.org/10.1016/j.jbusres.2020.02.043

Yao, S., Lu, J., Wang, H., Montgomery, J. J. W., Gorny, T., & Ogbonnaya, C. (2023). Excessive technology use in the post-pandemic context: How work connectivity behavior increases procrastination at work. *Information Technology & People* (ahead-of-print). https://doi.org/10.1108/ITP-08-2022-0573

Zhou, B., Li, Y., Hai, M., Wang, W., & Niu, B. (2023). Challenge-hindrance stressors and cyberloafing: A perspective of resource conservation versus resource acquisition. *Current Psychology, 42*, 1172–1181. https://doi.org/10.1007/s12144-021-01505-0

Zhu, J., Wei, H., Li, H., & Osburn, H. (2021). The paradoxical effect of responsible leadership on employee cyberloafing: A moderated mediation model. *Human Resource Development Quarterly, 32*(4), 597–624. https://doi.org/10.1002/hrdq.21432

Zoghbi-Manrique-de-Lara, P., Viera-Armas, M., & de Blasio García, G. (2020). Does supervisors' mindfulness keep employees from engaging in cyberloafing out of compassion at work? *Personnel Review, 49*(2), 670–687. https://doi.org/10.1108/PR-12-2017-0384

Conclusions

Procrastination at work has gained increasing attention in contemporary social sciences research. This emphasizes the significance of understanding this phenomenon from both individual and organizational perspectives. Generally perceived as a common tendency to irrationally delay tasks, procrastination at work is influenced by a range of personal and situational factors. Consequently, it emerges as a prevalent and complex organizational behavior, evident in forms such as soldiering (offline procrastination) and cyberslacking (online procrastination). Theoretical frameworks and empirical findings considered procrastination at work as a specific manifestation of the general tendency to procrastinate. This tendency probably has dispositional roots for work-delaying behavior, enhanced by job-related characteristics or organizational environments. Procrastination at work as a type of organizational behavior yields mainly detrimental consequences for employees and the organization as a whole. It can act as a hindrance to success and impact employee mood and well-being by increasing levels of anxiety and depression, as well as lowering self-esteem, consequently affecting health. In the workplace, procrastination may lead to poorer job performance, slower career advancements, and decreased organizational efficiency. However, it is worth noting that procrastination at work may also have potential benefits for individuals and organizations. Particularly, its restorative function seems worthy of exploration and acknowledgment.

By integrating individual and contextual perspectives, the current research has validated a conceptual framework of individual and work-related sources and underlying mechanisms of procrastination at work, embedded in the JD–R theory (Bakker et al., 2023). As a result, procrastination at work is primarily determined by personal characteristics, while also being shaped by work-related factors such as job demands and job resources. Among individual traits, the negative profile of personality traits, core self-evaluations, and trait procrastination were directly associated with work procrastination, as well as indirectly through increased work stress or work motivation. While job demands and job resources also influence employee procrastination, however, their effects are comparatively weaker than personal features. Nonetheless, their predictive role in procrastination is well established. The impact of job demands, job resources, and personal resources on procrastination behaviors was mediated by work

DOI: 10.4324/9781003422860-5

stress and motivation, emphasizing the emotional and motivational processes in explaining this phenomenon. These parallel processes delineate potential pathways for managing and regulating procrastination behaviors. Additionally, job demands proved to have a moderating effect on the relationship between personal and job resources and procrastination at work, determining different patterns of relationships under conditions of low and high job demands.

The prevailing understanding of procrastination at work, drawn from past research and supported by current findings, depicts it as a form of maladaptive behavior among employees oriented toward self-protection and conservation of their resources rather than a purposeful strategy aimed at harming the organization. Therefore, the organization and employer should cultivate a conducive work environment where employees have no reason or incentives to postpone work. Empirical evidence holds promise for the effective management of human resources by creating work conditions that mitigate soldiering and cyberslacking behavior. Additionally, developing various personal and organization-based intervention practices can help address employee procrastination. However, a lack of consistency in theoretical positions and empirical findings suggests the complexity and dynamism inherent in procrastination behavior. Therefore, there is a pressing need for continuous exploration into the nature of procrastination at work, its sources, and its consequences across diverse organizational, professional, social, and cultural contexts. Moreover, the contemporary changing work reality provides an additional enhancement for inducing procrastination behaviors due to the ongoing influx of new requirements, goals, or forms of work. In addition, access to new technologies and work tools such as artificial intelligence serves as an unlimited source of distractions and temptations for engaging in non-work-related activities, thus exacerbating work procrastination. Consequently, employee procrastination emerges as both a problem and a challenge for management practices. In particular, cyberslacking as a modern manifestation of procrastination poses significant challenges for employees and employers alike. Addressing these challenges necessitates a multifaceted approach that combines organizational support, targeted interventions, and an understanding of the underlying dynamics driving procrastination behaviors in the contemporary workplace.

Index